CONGRESSIONAL CONSERVATISM
AND THE NEW DEAL

CONGRESSIONAL CONSERVATISM AND THE NEW DEAL

The Growth of the Conservative
Coalition in Congress, 1933-1939

by

JAMES T. PATTERSON

For the Organization of American Historians
UNIVERSITY OF KENTUCKY PRESS, 1967

COPYRIGHT © 1967
by the University of Kentucky Press, Lexington
Manufactured in the United States of America
Library of Congress Catalog Card No. 67-17845

To my wife, Nancy

PREFACE

As MANY observers have pointed out, the formation of a conservative coalition in Congress by 1939 was one of the most significant developments of recent American political history.[1] But there has been no serious effort to look at the conservatives themselves in order to answer such questions as: who were they; what characteristics did they share; when and why did they form a coalition; to what extent were they consciously organized; and finally, was the coalition, such as it was, inevitable? This book attempts to provide tentative answers to these questions.

My use of the word "conservative" may bother some readers. Certainly no two conservatives voted alike on all major issues. Some of these men might better be termed reactionaries, others moderates. Many spoke the language of Social Darwinism; others were Burkean conservatives. Some were agrarian conservatives; others were spokesmen for urban business interests. But the unifying factor, as Clinton Rossiter has pointed out, was opposition to most of the domestic program of the New Deal.[2] By and large the congressional conservatives by 1939 agreed in opposing the spread of federal power and bureaucracy, in denouncing deficit spending, in criticizing industrial labor unions, and in excoriating most welfare programs. They sought to "conserve" an America which they believed to have existed before 1933.

This book concentrates upon domestic issues, mainly because questions of foreign policy before 1939 were not very important in helping to develop a conservative coalition. When foreign policy programs finally became central congressional issues in 1939, the coalition had already formed, and the alignments on subsequent foreign policy problems were different from those which had already served to stymie the domestic New Deal. Indeed, the fact of these differing alignments was but one more illustration of the lack of conservative unity on many important occasions.

Many people have helped me with this book. I am grateful to the staffs of the various libraries and historical societies who facilitated my search for materials. I also thank the Graduate School of Indiana University for providing me with financial assistance. I received very helpful suggestions and comments from Professors Chase Mooney and Walter Nugent of Indiana University, Peter Filene of Lincoln University, Professor James M. Burns of Williams College, and Professor John Thomas of Brown University, all of whom read earlier drafts of the manuscript. I also want to thank my friends at Indiana University, Robert Marcus, G. Cullom Davis, and Irene Neu, and Ronald Schaffer of San Fernando Valley State College for excellent suggestions regarding Chapters Nine and Ten. Professors William E. Leuchtenburg of Columbia University, Frederick Rudolph of Williams College, and John E. Wiltz of Indiana

[1] Samuel Lubell, *The Future of American Politics* (2nd rev. ed.; New York, 1956), esp. chap. 10; James M. Burns, *Deadlock of Democracy: Four-Party Politics in America* (Englewood Cliffs, N.J., 1963).

[2] Clinton Rossiter, *Conservatism in America: The Thankless Persuasion* (2nd rev. ed.; New York, 1962), esp. chap. 6.

were especially helpful; each spent many hours of his time and provided me with reams of critical comments. I owe a special debt to Professor Frank Freidel of Harvard, whose aid and encouragement throughout this project and on many other matters has been essential.

J. T. P.

CONTENTS

ILLUSTRATIONS

1

A TRACTABLE CONGRESS

THE NEW Congress," observed Walter Lippmann in January 1933, "will be an excitable and impetuous body, and it will respect only a President who knows his own mind and will not hesitate to employ the whole authority of his position." Congressmen, he advised, should grant President-elect Franklin D. Roosevelt "the widest and fullest powers possible under the most liberal interpretation of the Constitution."[1] Key Pittman of Nevada, a senator since 1913, also expected congressional difficulties. In a letter to Roosevelt a month later he warned, "your leadership . . . is going to be exceedingly difficult for a while. Democrats have grown out of the habit of being led. During the long Republican regime they have grown individualistic, they have lost the habit of cooperation, they have grown unaccustomed to discipline."[2]

Such predictions of an unruly Congress in a time of social

and economic crisis were commonplace in the months prior to Roosevelt's inauguration on March 4, 1933. To some extent these apprehensions reflected low opinions of the President-elect. Lippmann had earlier referred to Roosevelt as a nice young man who would very much like to become President, and many of the President-elect's most enthusiastic admirers fretted over Roosevelt's apparent lack of policy and blithe gaiety in the face of the worst depression the nation had ever experienced.

As Lippmann and Pittman revealed, however, Congress, not Roosevelt, was the primary reason for concern. Its record from the League of Nations debate in 1919 through the Depression years had incensed many liberal commentators.[3] Reacting against Woodrow Wilson's strong leadership, the Congresses of the 1920's had insisted upon their independence. Happily for congressional rebels, Presidents Harding, Coolidge, and Hoover were either unwilling or unable to exert significant pressure upon recalcitrant legislators. Congress, rebellious enough under large party majorities, became an angry, turbulent, and ineffective body during the evenly divided lame-duck session of 1932-1933. Such an atmosphere led Alfred M. Landon, who was to be the 1936 Republican presidential nominee, to say at the time: "Even the iron hand of a national dictator is in preference to a paralytic stroke. . . . I now enlist for the duration of the war."[4] Arthur H. Vandenberg, a Republican senator from Michigan, agreed. "I think we need a 'dictator,' " he wrote. "But a dictator is of no use unless he *dictates*."[5]

[1] *Interpretations, 1933-1935*, ed. Allan Nevins (New York, 1936), Jan. 17, 1933 column.

[2] Feb. 11, 1933, Pittman MSS, Box 14. Locations of manuscript collections mentioned in footnotes are given in the bibliography.

[3] Wilfred E. Binkley, *President and Congress* (3rd rev. ed.; New York, 1962), pp. 265-88.

[4] Quoted in Arthur M. Schlesinger, Jr., *The Coming of the New Deal* (Boston, 1959), p. 3.

[5] To Ernest Kanzler, March 7, 1933, Vandenberg MSS, 1937 Folder.

Neither a national dictator nor a rebellious Congress appeared. The record of the 1933 congressional session was not only voluminous and productive but psychologically encouraging, especially in contrast to what many had expected. To stimulate business recovery and guarantee minimal rights of labor, Congress passed the National Industrial Recovery Act. To bolster farm prices, it approved the Agricultural Adjustment Act incorporating domestic crop allotment and benefit payments. To provide for emergency relief, it appropriated $500 million for direct aid. It also enacted the Emergency Banking Act to relieve the national banking crisis, the Economy Act authorizing the President to make sweeping economies in government, the Thomas Amendment to the Agricultural Adjustment Act granting the President wide powers to devalue the dollar, and the Tennessee Valley Authority (TVA).

Significantly, Roosevelt received not only almost everything he wanted from a willing Congress, but he received it easily. The passage of eleven key bills in the House consumed only forty hours of debate.[6] "Legislation," said one experienced Democratic congressman, "was coming in and being passed like grist from a mill, most of the time, with very little debate. . . ."[7] Most spectacularly, the emergency banking bill passed in the House after forty minutes' debate, before printed copies had reached the hands of the representatives, and with a din of voices shouting, "Vote, Vote, Vote."[8] In the more deliberate Senate the legislative process was more careful, but even there no serious delays occurred.

Congress was not only quick, it was unprecedentedly generous in its grants of power to the President and to executive agencies. Roosevelt, in his inaugural address, said

[6] E. Pendleton Herring, "First Session of the 73rd Congress," *American Political Science Review*, XXVII (Feb. 1934), 65-83.

[7] Joseph A. Gavagan, Oral History Project, Columbia University, p. 37.

[8] James M. Burns, *Roosevelt: The Lion and the Fox* (New York, 1956), p. 167.

he might ask for "broad executive power to wage a war against the emergency as great as the power that would be given if we were in fact invaded by a foreign foe."[9] During the ensuing "100 Days," he did on occasion ask for wide discretionary powers—the economy and banking bills were cases in point. Congress not only granted such requests but usually did so eagerly. By delegating authority, Congress also delegated responsibility, leaving to executive departments the resolution of troublesome policy matters. Congressional delegation of power was so generous that one veteran newsman sighed, "all my adjectives are exhausted in expressing my admiration, awe, wonder, and terror at the vast grants of power which Roosevelt demands, one after the other, from Congress."[10]

Congressional readiness to surrender cherished prerogatives underscored a significant aspect of the 1933 session: in many areas it was considerably less orthodox than Roosevelt. Far from favoring conservative business interests in the manner of the Congresses of the 1920's, it approved an income-tax amendment requiring incomes to be publicized, and it passed the TVA with remarkable ease. Far from ignoring labor, it enacted the labor provisions of the National Industrial Recovery Act, while the Senate passed the Black thirty-hour work-week bill in spite of Roosevelt's lack of enthusiasm. And far from wedding itself to orthodox monetary theory, Congress passed the Thomas Amendment, pushing Roosevelt in the direction of devaluation or inflation.[11] Congressmen witnessed the end of the gold standard with scarcely a protest. Many conservative congressmen who were later to attack Roosevelt's policies were posing no objections to his proposals in 1933.

[9] Samuel Rosenman (ed.), *The Public Papers and Addresses of Franklin D. Roosevelt,* II (New York, 1938), 11-15.

[10] Henry Hyde Diary, May 18, 1933, Hyde MSS, p. 39.

[11] New York *Times,* April 18, 1933, p. 1.

Above all, congressmen were eager to spend. Under great pressure from constituents to relieve economic distress, they realized that a simple and tangible solution was to appropriate, appropriate, appropriate, while leaving taxes alone. Budget balancing, an almost sacred conservative panacea, fell by the wayside. The 1933 session, like those throughout the New Deal, was often a more liberal spender than the administration, particularly when strong pressure groups such as farmers or veterans threatened the hapless congressman with electoral extinction. As one contemporary observer commented, Roosevelt's chief difficulties with Congress in 1933 emanated from such pressure groups. The President, he said, could "do little more than keep order in the bread line that reached into the Treasury."[12]

Aside from such pressure, Roosevelt's first congressional session was remarkably cooperative. He later said of the Seventy-third Congress that it "displayed a greater freedom from mere partisanship than any other peacetime Congress since the Administration of President Washington himself."[13] Roosevelt's most obvious congressional asset was strictly numerical. The election of 1932 had given the Democrats large majorities: 311-116 in the House and 60-35 in the Senate. These were the largest majorities Democrats had ever enjoyed and the largest for any party since 1910. In the House many Democrats had to sit on the Republican side, leaving only a narrow "Polish Corridor" for Republicans. As a Democratic colleague remarked to Republican House Leader Bertrand Snell of New York, "A few years ago you had to use the whole house for your caucus—now you can hold it in a phone booth."[14]

Moreover, of the 311 House Democrats, 131 were fresh-

[12] E. Pendleton Herring, "Second Session of the 73rd Congress," *American Political Science Review*, XXVIII (Oct. 1934), 865.

[13] Rosenman, *Public Papers of FDR*, II, 372.

[14] Raymond Clapper Diary, Feb. 9, 1934, Clapper MSS.

men, many from normally Republican districts who would and did follow Democratic House leadership during the baffling 100 Days. And the leadership was loyal to the President. As Speaker Henry T. Rainey of Illinois announced, "The determination of policies will come from the party. We will put over Mr. Roosevelt's programs."[15] Rainey and Majority Leader Joseph T. Byrns of Tennessee were generally acquiescent leaders during this session. Similarly, in the Senate a skilled and powerful quartet of southern Democratic veterans ably navigated the Roosevelt program. They were Vice President John N. Garner of Texas, Majority Leader Joseph T. Robinson of Arkansas, Finance Committee Chairman Byron ("Pat") Harrison of Mississippi, and James F. Byrnes of South Carolina. Roosevelt enjoyed reliable leaders and a host of lesser figures anxious to attract presidential favor in 1933-1934.

To add to Roosevelt's good fortune, Republicans split badly. Unhappy, disorganized, and acutely aware of Roosevelt's tremendous popularity, many of them did not dare defy the administration.[16] In general, columnist Arthur Krock remarked, "Republicans qualified their attitude by saying that Mr. Roosevelt's guidance must be 'sound.' But their present mood is to try hard to find anything 'sound.'"[17] As

[15] Herring, "Second Session," p. 869.

[16] The following chart indicates the tractability of the 1933-1934 Congress. It is based on the following major roll-call votes: Senate—Black 30-hour bill, AAA, TVA, Relief, NRA, Economy, and Gold Payments Suspension. For the House, they were the same except for the Black bill (no vote) and TVA (conference vote).

	Pro-FDR Votes	Anti-FDR Votes	Anti-FDR GOP	Anti-FDR % of GOP	Anti-FDR Dem	Anti-FDR % of Dem	Avg. Total Anti-FDR
Senate	596	221	175	50	43	7	22
House	2,741	800	599	53	201	8	89

[17] New York *Times*, March 3, 1933, p. 2. A useful study is Harry W. Morris, "The Republicans in a Minority Role, 1933-1938" (unpublished Ph.D. dissertation, State University of Iowa, 1960).

a House Democrat later recalled, "the Republican side . . . looked pitiful—mostly empty seats as they had been well thinned out in the previous election. The few remaining members were afraid to squawk."[18] This Republican caution helped to destroy chances for effective congressional opposition to the New Deal in 1933-1934. With loyal leaders, docile Democratic followers, and divided Republicans, the early New Deal program could nearly always rely upon overwhelming numerical backing in Congress.[19]

Party majorities alone do not guarantee executive-congressional harmony, as future New Deal Congresses were to demonstrate. Indeed, Roosevelt's majority was so comfortable that party responsibility might well have been lax. The President himself deserved a great deal of credit for his success.

Perhaps no American President was so complex or so difficult to fathom as Franklin Roosevelt. Born to an old and wealthy New York family and educated at Groton and Harvard, he nonetheless came to excite unparalleled hatred from those of similar upbringing. Essentially undoctrinaire and practical, he had a stubborn bent which exasperated congressional politicians. Though not an intellectual, he attracted so many professors, authors, and bright young men to his administration that party regulars criticized him for bypassing the party faithful. A charming, gay extrovert, he had few intimate friends; few men, in fact, claimed to understand him.

One characteristic, however, even his enemies did not deny: his charm was infectious. Senate Republican Leader Charles L. McNary of Oregon never fully escaped the

---

[18] Wilburn Cartwright (Okla.), "Sixteen Years in Congress" (unpublished MS, 1942, Cartwright MSS), Pt. I, p. 84.

[19] For discussions of Republican strategy, see Turner Catledge, New York *Times*, Oct. 15, 1933, IV, 1; Frank Kent, *Without Gloves* (New York, 1934), April 24, 1933, pp. 8-9.

Roosevelt personality. The President, he wrote home early in 1933, "is very affable and I think much on the square and I am sure it will be a pleasure to work with him."[20] Two months later, at the height of the hectic 100 Days, he added, "I have just had a call from the White House to come down to see the President. . . . I like him very much."[21] Author Frederick Lewis Allen, writing in 1933, expressed well the reaction of so many congressmen on first meeting the new President: "The President was of course cordial, easy, attractive as advertised: an extremely likeable person: nor does one have any sense of his being *too charming*—of being exposed to a deliberate lure. I think it is a fact that he is too charming—I mean that he too completely adjusts himself to people and to circumstances as to give his policies a rubbery aspect; but one does not feel it when with him. There is no feeling of being seduced, so to speak; he is simply a thoroughly attractive and engaging man."[22] As Senator Huey Long of Louisiana was to phrase it, Hoover was a hoot owl, Roosevelt a scrootch owl. A hoot owl, Long said, knocks the hen off the roost and seizes her as she topples to the ground. "But a scrootch owl slips into the roost and scrootches up to the hen and talks softly to her. And the hen falls in love with him, and the first thing you know, *there ain't no hen*."[23]

Charm alone, like numerical majorities, was also to prove insufficient in later years. Perhaps more important in 1933 was Roosevelt's undeniable and all but unprecedented popularity with the people. Roosevelt had led his ticket in the 1932 election, outpolling congressional candidates in four-fifths of the states and receiving 10 percent more votes

[20] To John H. McNary, Jan. 1, 1933, McNary MSS.
[21] To John H. McNary, March 20, 1933, *ibid.*
[22] To Hildegarde, Oct. 28, 1934, Allen MSS. Italics his.
[23] Quoted in Arthur M. Schlesinger, Jr., *The Politics of Upheaval* (Boston, 1960), p. 56.

nationwide.[24] Although his percentage of the total vote (57.4) was not so high as Harding's in 1920 or Hoover's in 1928, it was still extremely impressive: few congressmen questioned his popular mandate. "There can be no doubt," one wise Republican senator wrote, "that at the moment the President has an extraordinary support throughout the country and is able to do with the Congress as he wills. I suppose prudence dictates that one should not attempt to swim against the tide."[25]

To these assets Roosevelt added an unexpected tactical finesse in congressional relations. Recognizing congressional distaste for his economy bill, he requested it immediately after disposing of the banking crisis, knowing that this tactic presented congressmen with the choice of passing it quickly or delaying other urgent legislation. To make the bill more palatable, he dangled the tempting bait of the popular bill to legalize beer next on the calendar. Successful with these bills, Roosevelt followed with messages proposing a Civilian Conservation Corps (CCC) and other relatively noncontroversial pieces of legislation before seeking final passage of such complicated measures as the National Industrial Recovery Act and Agricultural Adjustment Act. These enacted, he allowed Congress to adjourn before it could embarrass him with a spending spree.

Likewise, the President seemed to have an instinctive sense of when to compromise and thus avoid the appearance of defeat. Often his popular leadership made compromise unnecessary, but in April 1933 a growing inflationist bloc led by Senator Elmer Thomas of Oklahoma refused to be

[24] Harold Gosnell, *Champion Campaigner: Franklin D. Roosevelt* (New York, 1952), p. 133; also Cortez A. M. Ewing, *Congressional Elections, 1896-1944* (Norman, Okla., 1947), p. 19; and Edgar E. Robinson, *The Roosevelt Leadership, 1933-1945* (Philadelphia, 1955), pp. 72-73.

[25] Wallace White to Wingate F. Cram, March 20, 1933, Wallace White MSS, Box 1.

ignored. When the bloc appeared to have enough strength to pass inflationary measures, Roosevelt realized that the time had arrived to give in gracefully. Calling Thomas to the White House and flattering him assiduously, Roosevelt told him to present as his own an amendment which would permit but not compel the President to devalue the dollar, remonetize silver, or print more money. Thomas did so, and the amendment passed. Roosevelt thus avoided a mandatory inflationist amendment, temporarily pacified Thomas and his allies, received additional discretionary powers for himself, and in general enhanced his prestige.[26]

Roosevelt not only charmed and flattered congressmen but he also worked carefully with them. In later years, conservatives complained that intellectuals and bureaucrats devised utopian proposals, handed them to Congress, and demanded their immediate approval. In 1933, however, executive drafting was not an important issue: clearly it was the quickest way in an emergency. Furthermore, the President consulted his leaders as often as time would allow and did his best not to place them in embarrassing positions with their followers. Considering the rapid pace of the 100 Days, most of the legislation of the period was clear, well drafted, and acceptable to leaders as well as rank and file.[27]

When tactical finesse failed, the President had one more effective weapon: patronage. For the Democratic party it had been a lean twelve years, and office seekers descended anxiously upon congressmen. The horde, large enough at the start of any administration, multiplied alarmingly in 1933 owing to widespread unemployment and the many thousands of openings available with the proliferation of New Deal alphabetical agencies. "They advance," grumbled a

[26] See James F. Byrnes, *All in One Lifetime* (New York, 1958), p. 77.

[27] For a summary of the reasons for Roosevelt's success with Congress in 1933, see Schlesinger, *Coming of the New Deal*, pp. 554-55. See also Roland Young, *This Is Congress* (New York, 1943), pp. 55-56, for a discussion of New Deal draftsmanship.

disgusted Senator Joseph Robinson, "single file, in double columns, in platoons, brigades, regiments, corps, and divisions. They sing and play; they laugh and shout; they whine and curse. . . . It is simply impossible to make a showing of efficiency."[28]

Roosevelt dealt with this problem serenely, effectively, and a little ruthlessly. "We haven't got to patronage yet," he told anxious congressmen.[29] As Pittman ruefully explained to a job seeker: "The President will not interfere with any of the Departments until after his program has been successfully put into effect. . . . I think we have got to grin and bear it at least until after the next Congress."[30] Roosevelt kept the carrot on the stick, out of reach of hungry congressmen. The result, as one expert put it, was that "his relations to Congress were to the very end of the session tinged with a shade of expectancy which is the best part of young love."[31]

All these assets combined—Roosevelt's numerical majorities in Congress, his popularity, charm, tactical ability, and handling of patronage—profoundly affected congressmen. Yet these advantages were secondary compared to the influence of the Depression. In 1937, for example, Roosevelt had larger congressional majorities, no less charm, a great deal more experience, and even greater popularity with the people, yet Congress gave him next to nothing in a long and bitter session. Similarly, Presidents Eisenhower and Kennedy had liberal endowments of charm, ability, and popularity, yet they too experienced frustrating and often unsuccessful relations with Congress. Twentieth-century American political history has so far amply demonstrated that congressional powers can be more than adequate to frustrate the most

[28] To Bernard Baruch, June 26, 1935, quoted in Nevin E. Neal, "A Biography of Joseph T. Robinson," (unpublished Ph.D. dissertation, University of Oklahoma, 1957), p. 434.

[29] Binkley, *President and Congress*, p. 302.

[30] To William McKnight, Aug. 17, 1933, Pittman MSS, Box 13.

[31] Herring, "First Session of the 73rd Congress," p. 82.

skillful and popular of Presidents unless extraordinary external circumstances such as a depression or a war lend the executive a helping hand.

The year 1933 was such an extraordinary period. Statistics show that at the time of Roosevelt's inauguration nearly fourteen million people were jobless, and that business bankruptcies were mounting alarmingly. Statistics cannot recreate, however, the powerful demand for government action to alleviate distress. Landon and Vandenberg talked of suffering a dictator if necessary; many Americans, ordinarily quite conservative, were of like mind. The people wanted action; they demanded leadership. Congressmen, reminded of this groundswell by their constituents, were no exception.[32] Said the New York *Times* on the passage of the banking bill, "Congress hardly knew what it passed today. . . . They were glad to place the responsibility in the hands of one man, happy that a man had offered to assume the burden."[33] Such extravagant reliance upon the President was common to both sides of the aisle, to conservatives and avid New Dealers alike. Even Senator Josiah W. Bailey of North Carolina, none too happy with the New Deal from the start, wrote as late as 1934, "I still think the element of faith in the President is the most valuable asset in the country, and we ought to pursue a course tending to maintain this faith."[34]

[32] Pittman wrote: "The President had a tough Congress to deal with if it ever got loose, but he held such a strong hold upon the people of the country without regard to party that the Congress did not dare to oppose him to the extent they would have had it not been for the sentiment at home." To J. B. Clinedinst, June 6, 1934, Pittman MSS, Box 11.

[33] March 10, 1933, p. 1.

[34] To James A. Farley, July 19, 1934, Bailey MSS, Political File. Others also agreed in late 1933 and 1934. Senator Elbert Thomas, a Democrat from Utah, was rhapsodic about his chief. "Roosevelt," he said, "to me hits pretty closely the fundamental striving of a great mind for an attunement with the world's universal striving. He seems to really have caught the spirit of what one of the Hebrew prophets called the desire of the nations. If he were in India today, they would probably decide that he had become

Bailey, like so many other congressional conservatives in 1933-1934, temporarily set aside some of his scruples while the emergency lasted. It was the Great Depression which above all helped make the Congresses of 1933 and 1934 the most cooperative in recent American history.[35]

From the very beginning of the New Deal, however, a cluster of congressmen regarded the New Deal, in the words of Virginia's peppery Senator Carter Glass, as "an utterly dangerous effort of the federal government to transplant Hitlerism to every corner of the nation."[36] Opposed to heavy government spending, fearful of the spread of federal bureaucracy, loud in defense of states' rights and individual liberty, these men composed the earliest conservative force in Congress under Roosevelt's administrations.[37] They were unable to work together at that time; they seldom managed more than 35 votes in the Senate or 100 in the House; and more often than not they were wary of denouncing the New

---

Mahatma—that is, one in tune with the infinite." Elmer Thomas to Col. E. Leroy Bourne, Jan. 6, 1934, Elmer Thomas MSS, Box 23. For another example of congressional faith in Roosevelt, see Hiram Johnson to FDR, Nov. 16, 1933: "I'm eager to do my small part," Johnson wrote. "I return to Washington with my faith in my President strengthened, my pride in his achievements increased, and with wholehearted devotion to his great purposes." Roosevelt MSS, PPF 1134. As Rep. Samuel Pettengill, a conservative Indiana Democrat, wrote at the time, "I think our people are so darn tired of the depression and so anxious to get out of it that they would welcome strong party discipline. . . ." To Marvin McIntyre, Feb. 24, 1934, Roosevelt MSS, OF 299.

[35] This is not to say that it was a "rubber stamp." Raymond Moley, in *After Seven Years* (New York, 1939), p. 192, remarked that there was a "good deal more give and take between Roosevelt and Congress even during the 100 Days than was generally realized." For the way in which Congress forced Roosevelt to accept the Federal Deposit Insurance Corporation, see Byrnes, *All in One Lifetime*, p. 88. See also John L. Shover, "Populism in the 1930's: The Battle for the AAA," *Agricultural History*, XXXIX (Jan. 1965), 17-24, for evidence of congressional reluctance to pass the AAA.

[36] To Walter Lippmann, Aug. 10, 1933, Glass MSS, Box 4.

[37] The word "conservative" will be used to refer to congressmen who opposed Roosevelt and the New Deal on most key issues. See Preface.

Deal in public. Yet some of them, especially the conservative Democrats, were to remain in Congress and were to plague the President in later years.

Though the thinking of these men varied considerably, a few repeated themes stood out. Some simply resented Roosevelt's tardy distribution of patronage, and though they held their tongues and their adverse votes until the pork rolled into their districts, they remained embittered. Others, chiefly rural Republicans, had nothing to gain in the way of patronage and felt secure enough in their home districts to attack Roosevelt for partisan or factional reasons. And a handful of others, closely allied to reactionary financial interests, came to oppose the New Deal because they feared for their pocketbooks or their jobs.

A more important source of irritation resulted from Roosevelt's very success with Congress: the more adeptly he handled congressmen, the angrier some of them became. Though this Congress was not simply a rubber stamp, it was so much more tractable than any previous Congress within memory that a spate of magazine and newspaper articles began referring to congressmen as Roosevelt "lackeys," "errand boys," or "rubber stamps."[38] When senators meet nowadays, observed columnist Frank Kent acidly, they simply have an "exchange of baffled exclamations." When reporters ask them where the New Deal is going, they laugh, "That's what I want to ask you."[39] Representative Franklin W. Hancock, Jr., of North Carolina, normally a reliable Democrat throughout the early New Deal, was so exasperated that he exploded, "I am getting sick and tired, as a working member of this House, being led, so to speak, with a ring in my nose. . . . I am even willing to bury

[38] A few examples are A. Shaw, "Evils of our Congressional System," *Review of Reviews*, LXXXIX (April 1934), 42-44; and "What's Wrong with Congress," *Colliers*, XCI (March 25, 1933), 50.

[39] Kent, *Without Gloves*, May 2, 1933, p. 10.

temporarily definite convictions of long standing and submit gracefully to being called a rubber stamp, but my God, are we to embalm our bodies and chloroform our minds?"[40]

Related to this frustration was distrust of the bureaucrat, the man who in the minds of some congressmen held his job by flattering the President, who had never won and never could win a popular election, and whose preconceived ideas were ill fitted for the subtleties of congressional politics. This distrust, natural enough in congressmen of all eras, grew enormously during the early New Deal because the number of bureaucrats grew so rapidly and because bureaucrats served as useful scapegoats for congressmen who did not dare attack Roosevelt directly. Above all, since some of the bureaucrats were liberal intellectuals, they made ideal targets for conservatives. As Carter Glass complained, "The sooner Washington is rid of impatient academicians whose threatening manifestos and decrees keep business and banks alike in suspense, if not in consternation, the sooner and more certain will we have a complete restoration of confidence and resumption of business in every line of endeavor. *Terram coelo miscent;* or, as Cicero has it, *"Damnant quod non intellegunt."*[41]

A similar aspect of conservative congressional thinking was a fondness for what many called legislative integrity. As Glass phrased it to his Virginia colleague, Senator Harry F. Byrd, "I derive some satisfaction from the thought that if Virginia wants two rubber stamps in the Senate it would be better not to select us. I would rather be remembered, if at all, for intellectual integrity than for party subservience. . . ."[42] "A Senator," Bailey added, "should be guided by

[40] *Congressional Record,* 73rd Cong., 1st Sess., 2502.

[41] To C. S. Hamlin, Dec. 18, 1934, Glass MSS, Box 4. A rough translation is, "They [the academicians] are all mixed up. They condemn what they can't understand."

[42] July 2, 1934, *ibid.,* Box 320.

certain great principles. He should have a theory of government and hold to his theory."[43] To some degree, these sentiments merely reflected the need of Republicans or defecting
Democrats to justify their independent ways. More often,
they could be accepted at face value: the conservatives,
most of them, were for one reason or another temperamentally inflexible. Unwilling to accept the New Deal, they
clung to the Burkean ideal of the independent legislator
who keeps no counsel but his own. As Senator Millard E.
Tydings of Maryland was later to explain (not without some
exaggeration), "If I can't vote my convictions here, to hell
with this job."[44]

In retrospect, it is difficult to distinguish conservative
rhetoric from conviction, particularly since in years to come
these men violated their principles in practice more than
once; no congressman opposed all administration proposals.
Nevertheless, it is fair to say that most of these earliest
congressional opponents were essentially Jeffersonian Democrats, to the degree that politics permitted. They had been
reared in, and then represented, rural areas so conservative
that even Roosevelt's great electoral strength was not enough
to displace them. They sought to recreate Jefferson's vision
of America: a rural nation of independent yeomen, a small
government which left people alone. Whether this form of
society had existed in the twentieth century, or even in their
lifetimes, did not matter: these men thought that it had.[45]
Glum about the New Deal world they confronted, they were
nonetheless the great optimists of the era, for they sought
to live in an irretrievable, idyllic land and believed it could
be created simply by leaving things alone.

[43] Josiah Bailey to Prof. R. S. Rankin, Bailey MSS, Political File.

[44] *Time*, Sept. 19, 1938, p. 27.

[45] For a discussion of this "agrarian myth," see Richard Hofstadter, *The Age of Reform* (New York, 1955), chap. 1; and Henry Nash Smith, *Virgin Land* (New York, 1950), *passim*.

As a group, the conservative congressmen of 1933-1934 were as varied as the arguments they used. The largest conservative bloc in both houses was Republican. Although some 10 of the 35 GOP senators were veteran progressives who would support much of New Deal domestic policy from 1933 through 1936, the remaining 25 were in varying degrees conservative as well as partisan. Similarly, in the House, some 100 of the 116 Republicans were regulars whose views more closely approached those of Hoover than of the New Dealers. Their role prior to 1937, however, was minimal. For one thing, they were disorganized, demoralized, and ineffectual. For another, their opposition was at least partly partisan, and it is difficult to learn much about conservative reactions to various New Deal programs through their eyes.[46] Finally, many of these conservative Republicans were to fall before the Democratic landslides of 1934 and 1936, and few remained to play parts in the efforts to form a conservative coalition in subsequent congressional sessions.

For these reasons the early conservative Democrats were more important in the long run. Like the conservative Republicans, they acted as individuals in 1933-1934 and made no serious efforts to arrange coalitions against the New Deal. Similarly, they were numerically insignificant: only five Senate Democrats consistently opposed the President in 1933-1934, a group more than offset by the progressive Republicans. But these five acted out of conviction; partisanship had little to do with their viewpoints. Moreover, with one exception, they remained in the Senate through World War II as central figures in the loose conservative bloc which had begun to form by 1936. These five men well

[46] For an excellent study of roll-call votes stressing the great importance of party pressures on congressional voting, see Julius Turner, *Party and Constituency: Pressures on Congress* (Baltimore, 1951), pp. 33, 74. See also Donald R. Matthews, *United States Senators and Their World* (Chapel Hill, N.C., 1960), *passim*.

illustrate the forces which created the earliest—and consistently most vehement—conservative Democrats in Congress.[47]

Easily the most outspoken Democratic conservative of
the first Roosevelt Congress was the venerable Carter Glass
of Virginia. Born in Lynchburg in 1858, he learned to hate
Yankees as a child and played an important role in Virginia's
disfranchisement of Negroes in 1901. He was, as Roosevelt
called him, the "Unreconstructed Rebel." As a boy, Glass
became a printer's devil on the Lynchburg News and by
1933 had long been its editor. His career, significantly, was
self-made; he never attended college.[48] By 1933 he could
also point to a successful political career in which he had
served as United States representative for sixteen years,
Wilson's secretary of the treasury, and senator since 1920.

In appearance, Glass was a cartoonist's delight. No more
than 100 pounds, he was but five feet, four inches tall. His
white hair stood stiffly and wildly like a porcupine roach; his
nose was beaked and crooked. His narrow mouth grimly
dropped down at one corner and twisted up at the other.[49]
His words slid raspingly from his mouth in such a way that
Woodrow Wilson (Glass's great idol) once said, "Carter
Glass is the only man I ever saw who can whisper in his
own ear."[50]

In the shifting game of politics, it is never easy to pick
the precise moment when a man changes sides; thus so with

[47] The five men are chosen because they were by far the most anti-New
Deal Democratic senators. Between them, they accounted for 19 of the 36
adverse Democratic Senate votes cast on the seven major measures of the
1933 session. (The remaining sixty Democrats cast but 17 adverse votes.)

[48] Rixey Smith and Norman Beasley, Carter Glass: A Biography (New
York, 1939), chaps. 1-5.

[49] "Too Many Democrats," Colliers, XCIV (Nov. 3, 1934), 50. See also
James E. Palmer, Jr., Carter Glass: Unreconstructed Rebel (Roanoke, Va.,
1938), p. 171.

[50] Allan A. Michie and Frank Rhylick, Dixie Demagogues (New York,
1939), p. 171.

Glass. To label conservative a man who had once been Woodrow Wilson's staunch ally in the House of Representatives and who had helped to father the Federal Reserve Act is misleading. Besides, Glass, in spite of his opposition to many New Deal policies, maintained grudging personal affection for his charming Chief Executive, a feeling which Roosevelt generally reciprocated.[51] He also occasionally supported what others called "radical" legislation—the TVA being the best early example. On the eve of the 1932 election, Glass climbed from his sickbed at Roosevelt's request and delivered in his behalf a resounding radio address.

But his support of the New Deal was short-lived. Suspecting Roosevelt's willingness to compromise halfway with the inflationists, he declined Roosevelt's offer of the post of secretary of the treasury. When the President, as the first act of his new administration, declared a bank holiday, Glass, though outwardly loyal to his chief, was shocked. "I think the President of the United States had no more valid authority to close or open a bank in the United States," he wrote, "than had my stable boy. . . . It looks to me as if Hoover carried the country to the edge of the precipice and this administration is shoving it over as fast as it can. I predict the righteous failure of every damned project that these arbitrary little bureaucrats are vainly endeavoring to put into effect."[52]

Other early New Deal measures also upset Glass, who from party loyalty kept quiet in public. The controversy over the National Recovery Administration (NRA), however, exposed the depth of his disaffection, and he announced that he would go to jail before permitting the Blue Eagle, symbol of the NRA, to hang outside his newspaper office. Characteristically, he wrote NRA administrator Hugh S. Johnson:

[51] See the exchange of raillery between the two in Glass MSS, Box 268, 1940-1941.

[52] To Russell C. Leffingwell, July 12, 1933, *ibid.*, Box 4.

"I just want to tell you, General, that your blue buzzard will not fly from the mastheads of my two newspapers."[53] The NRA, he wrote a friend, was "unconstitutional, and tyrannical and literally brutal."[54] Glass viewed it as harmful to individual initiative and he believed the provisions of the National Industrial Recovery Act for minimum wages and maximum hours were unjust to infant southern industry.

From 1933 on, Glass openly opposed most of the New Deal, often whether it helped Virginia or not.[55] In 1935 he wrote, in a letter as violent as any of the decade: "Now is about as good a time as anybody could find to die, when the country is being taken to hell as fast as a lot of miseducated fools can get it there. Nevertheless, it would be interesting to live long enough to see the thing tumble so that nobody could long doubt the infinite folly of what has been done for the past three years."[56]

To understand Glass's opposition to the New Deal, it is also necessary to understand Virginia's political configuration. On one hand, it would seem to have been foolhardy for Glass to challenge Roosevelt in such a heavily Democratic state. As one commentator put it, "Roosevelt can't possibly lose Virginia. Every section of the state has been so well watered with federal benefits and federal money that potential votes lie out there in bunches."[57]

Roosevelt was indeed enormously popular in Virginia, and Glass knew it. He was sensible enough not to stray into the Republican camp. Yet such was the nature of Virginia

[53] Quoted in Smith and Beasley, *Glass*, pp. 362-63.

[54] To Oscar Callaway, Nov. 11, 1933, Glass MSS, Box 312.

[55] Of the ten major issues of 1933-1934, Glass voted against six and failed to record himself on a seventh. His record of opposition to the New Deal, based on a study of thirty-one bills on which he voted, 1933-1939, was 81 percent opposed—easily the highest of all Democratic senators of the period. See Appendix B.

[56] To Lewis Douglas, Nov. 26, 1935, Glass MSS, Box 341.

[57] Turner Catledge, New York *Times*, Dec. 4, 1935.

politics that Glass could be reelected in 1936 by a large margin, while Roosevelt also swept the state. In short, Glass and his friend Harry Byrd ran the most powerful state machine in the nation. Their organization, perpetuated by considerable financial support, generally able leadership, and an extremely low percentage of voter participation, was invincible. Consequently, Glass, unlike most other instinctively conservative Democrats, was able to demonstrate openly his dislike of the New Deal.[58]

Glass's opposition to the New Deal was not the result only of specific measures or of his home political situation. Perhaps as important in the long run—not only to him but to many other congressional conservatives—was his mental makeup. He was by all accounts incredibly inflexible. His old friend, Vice-President Garner, expressed it saying, "No one can help but like that old rooster, but once Glass gets a notion in his head, neither hell nor Woodrow Wilson could change him."[59] Pittman agreed. Glass, he said, "is too indissolubly wedded to his own opinions and accomplishments of the past to tolerate any changes that might be considered, even as natural evolutions."[60] Glass really enjoyed being irascible. After living in one hotel in Washington for twenty-five years, he moved out, enraged, because it remodeled its lobby.[61] For such a man, stubborn and jealous of his independence, refusal to "go along" with the New

[58] For an excellent study of Virginia (and other southern state) politics, see V. O. Key, Jr., *Southern Politics in State and Nation* (New York, 1949), pp. 19-35. Because of the conservative nature of the machine, Virginia's senators and representatives were easily the most conservative Democratic state delegation during the 1933-1939 period. Besides Glass and Byrd, seven of the thirty-five most anti-New Deal Democratic representatives were Virginians (based on a study of thirty-one House roll-call votes). See Appendix A.

[59] Bascom N. Timmons, *Garner of Texas* (New York, 1948), p. 182.

[60] To Roosevelt, Feb. 11, 1933, Pittman MSS, Box 14.

[61] Marquis James, "The Gentleman from Virginia," *Saturday Evening Post*, CCX (Aug. 28, 1937), 16.

Deal was not surprising. For to Glass, old and steeped in his memories of the days of Woodrow Wilson, the New Deal was not progressive; it was radical. "I am," he admitted in 1938, "a relic of constitutional government. . . . I entertain what may be the misguided notion that the Constitution of the United States, as it existed in the time of Grover Cleveland is the same Constitution that exists today."[62] In 1938 he summed up his problem. "I have lived too long," he said.[63]

Second only to Glass among vocally anti-New Deal Democrats in the Senate was Thomas P. Gore of Oklahoma, a tall, distinguished-looking man who had been totally blind since the age of eleven. Like Glass, he was no longer a young man by the time Roosevelt took office; he was sixty-three in 1933. Born and reared in the South, he too had experienced a less conservative political past; indeed, he had run unsuccessfully as a Populist candidate for Congress from Texas in 1898.[64] Moving to Oklahoma at the turn of the century, he built up a successful record in law and politics and was chosen senator when Oklahoma became a state in 1907. Bitterly opposing American entrance into World War I, he failed to gain renomination in 1920. Ten years later he became senator again. Though neither so influential nor so senior as Glass, and severely handicapped in his job by blindness, he was a knowledgeable veteran of the political wars of the previous generation.

To Gore the New Deal was as obnoxious as it was to Glass. Opposing large-scale government expenditures for relief in 1933 (though drought-plagued Oklahoma citizens needed it perhaps more than any), he said, "As I see it credit is to a nation what chastity is to a woman. Without

[62] Quoted in Smith and Beasley, *Glass,* p. 381.

[63] *Current Biography,* 1941, p. 321.

[64] For his early voting record, see Howard W. Allen, "Geography and Politics: Voting on Reform Issues in the United States Senate, 1911-1916," *Journal of Southern History,* XXVII (May 1961), 216-28.

it, nothing counts."[65] Widely read (thanks to the aid of his wife), he spoke the language of Social Darwinism. In a letter to Senator Bailey in 1936 he explained his stand against the New Deal. To begin with, he had constitutional scruples, but aside from these, he was "under one restraint which goes to the very root of things. I think that the struggle for existence accounts for practically all the progress that the race has made in the past and will likewise account pretty much for the progress the race will make in the future."[66] Perhaps because of his success in overcoming a physical handicap, Gore was a true believer in rugged individualism.

Accordingly, he opposed Roosevelt's policies almost from the start. A self-styled expert on farming, he viewed crop-reduction schemes of the Agricultural Adjustment Administration (AAA) as foolish and unnatural. Remembering distastefully the planning agencies of the Wilson war administration, he denounced the NRA. Once the enemy of powerful oil interests in his home state, he was by 1933 one of their spokesmen. Above all, Gore was as staunch a fiscal conservative as Glass. Ever concerned with the self-reliance of the individual, Gore believed that recipients of relief were loafers. "The dole spoils the soul," he insisted.[67] Like Glass, Gore looked to a bygone era and was temperamentally too inflexible to accept the changing present. No Democratic senator was more firmly opposed to the early New Deal.[68]

In one fatal respect he was unlike Glass; he did not control Oklahoma's political organization. Indeed, his blindness extended to the realm of political reality. Drought and depression hit Oklahomans particularly hard; they had no use for talk of rugged individualism or survival of the fittest.

[65] *Congressional Record*, 73rd Cong., 1st Sess., 4397.

[66] Nov. 25, 1936, Bailey MSS, Political File.

[67] Monroe L. Billington, "Thomas P. Gore: Oklahoma's Blind Senator" (unpublished Ph.D. dissertation, University of Kentucky, 1955), p. 357.

[68] Like Glass, Gore opposed six of the ten key measures of the 1933-1934 session. For the years 1933-1936 he was second only to Glass in his percentage of opposition (57.8) to the New Deal. See Appendix B.

So whereas Glass was able to win with ease in Virginia in 1936, Gore, in the same year, failed even to receive the Democratic nomination. He lost his seat to the youthful inflationist, Joshua Byran Lee, finishing last in a four-way Democratic primary in which only he spoke out against the New Deal. Like other conservatives who put principle before expediency, Gore was a political relic long before he was defeated.[69]

No other Democratic senator was so outspoken as Glass or so rash as Gore in 1933-1934. In fact, no other Senate Democrat saw fit to oppose a majority of the major pieces of legislation. There were nonetheless three others whose conservative sentiments were a matter of record before the 1934 election, who voted against a number of major New Deal measures, and who undoubtedly would have been even more outspoken had they enjoyed Glass's political immunity.

Perhaps the most uncompromising of the three, and certainly the most cordially disliked by New Dealers, was Millard E. Tydings of Maryland. He was also proof of the dangers of generalizing about Roosevelt's conservative Democratic opposition in Congress. For whereas Glass and Gore were older men and products of the rural South, Tydings was at forty-three in 1933 among the younger men in the Senate. The son of a poor marine engineer, he was raised in predominantly white sections of Maryland and did not follow his southern colleagues on racial issues. Influential friends of his family helped him attain a college education and law degree, and throughout his life his tastes and interests were sophisticated. He was fond of opera, John Galsworthy, and Maxwell Anderson; a painter, author, and pianist, he cherished the idea of becoming a playwright.[70]

[69] See Glass to Stephen Early, Dec. 29, 1936, Roosevelt MSS, PPF 687, for evidence of Gore's problems after his defeat.

[70] Holmes Alexander, "Millard E. Tydings," in J. T. Salter (ed.), The American Politician (Chapel Hill, 1938), pp. 124-38; Current Biography, 1945, pp. 634-35.

For a man of such youth and cosmopolitan tastes Tydings was remarkably consistent in his political beliefs over the years. His first act as a senator in 1927 had been to stage a one-man filibuster against government development of Muscle Shoals. He was also one of the nation's more prominent "wets," taking his stand on the conservative grounds that the Prohibition Amendment was a violation of individual liberty. Though not at first a very vocal opponent of the New Deal, he clung to his conservatism, even though the New Deal funneled huge amounts of patronage through him in the first year of its existence.[71] He voted against the creation of the AAA, TVA, and NRA during the 100 Days[72] and by the end of 1933 was congratulating Glass on "taking the lead if a disintegration of our institutions is to be stopped."[73]

Social and business connections reinforced his beliefs. His Maryland law firm had so many wealthy clients that one unfriendly critic called him the "outstanding spokesman for corporate wealth in Congress."[74] Tall, lean, erect, with well-chiseled features and an immaculate appearance, he was a model of sartorial elegance and an avid participant in the most prominent Washington social circles. After his marriage in 1936 to a breakfast-cereal heiress, some hostile observers in a play on his first name referred to him as "Mi-Lord."[75] Indeed, his cool and self-contained personality caused many New Dealers to dislike him intensely. He was the only Senate Democrat whom Democratic National Chairman James A. Farley agreed to try to purge in 1938. And Roosevelt, according to Secretary of the Interior Harold L.

[71] Alexander, "Tydings," pp. 124-38.

[72] Next to Glass, Tydings was the most conservative Democratic senator on the basis of roll-call votes, 1933-1939. He opposed the administration 77 percent of the time on them. In 1933-1934, he opposed the New Deal on four of ten key votes. See Appendix B.

[73] Oct. 27, 1933, Glass MSS, Box 312.

[74] Michie and Rhylick, *Dixie Demagogues,* p. 166.

[75] *Ibid.*

Ickes (who loathed Tydings), was once so annoyed at "Mi-Lord" that he advised Ickes to "take Tydings' hide off and rub salt in."[76]

It is a mistake to see only his cold side. Friends and enemies alike conceded his quick intelligence, his ability to perceive the heart of a complex issue, his effectiveness as a debater and behind-the-scenes manipulator. Furthermore, like so many other conservative Democrats, he prided himself upon his independence.[77] Intelligent, experienced, vigorous, few Democrats in the Congresses of the 1930's were more consistent opponents of New Deal domestic policy.

A fourth anti-New Deal Democrat in 1933-1934 was perhaps more complex than Tydings, and no less influential. Josiah W. Bailey of North Carolina was sixty years old in 1933, or roughly the average age of senators at the time. The son and grandson of Baptist preachers, he attended Wake Forest College and upon graduation became editor of a North Carolina Baptist publication. After fourteen years at this task, he passed the state bar examination in 1908. Gradually devoting more time to politics, he received from Wilson a collectorship of internal revenue, a post he held until 1921.[78]

During the later 1920's Bailey joined a group of younger men who began to challenge the powerful state machine of Furnifold M. Simmons, senator since 1900. The rebels, forming largely for factional reasons, gained strength when Simmons made the fatal mistake for a southern Democrat of opposing Alfred E. Smith in 1928. Capitalizing on this

[76] Harold Ickes, *The Secret Diary of Harold Ickes* (3 vols.; New York, 1954), I, 390, July 12, 1935.

[77] Tydings did not face reelection until 1938, and he had five years of grace in 1933 in which to oppose the New Deal. His opposition to the New Deal in 1937-1938 (or soon before his reelection attempt), was considerably less vocal than it had been. For Maryland politics, see John H. Fenton, *Politics in the Border States: A Study of the Patterns of Political Organization and Political Change* (New Orleans, 1957), pp. 182-89, 201-202.

[78] *Current Biography*, 1945, p. 30.

issue, Bailey won a sweeping primary victory over Simmons in 1930, and by 1934 he was almost as powerful as Simmons had been.[79] Though opposed in 1936 by a candidate who made the most of Bailey's anti-New Deal attitudes, Bailey won with ease. He, too, could oppose the New Deal and not suffer political extinction.

When Roosevelt assumed office, few predicted that Bailey would eventually emerge as an implacable opponent. Indeed, one liberal publication had said in 1931 that "his record indicated [he'll] be found casting his ballot more frequently with the liberal (not radical) than the conservative blocs."[80] A strong party man, Bailey worked for Roosevelt in 1932. During the 100 Days, however, he began to bridle at large-scale federal expenditures and at grants of power to the executive.[81] Soon he was opposing many administration proposals.

Bailey, a man of intense convictions, was nonetheless wise enough to realize that outright opposition of the Glass-Gore variety was foolish if he expected to keep receiving the benefits of New Deal bounty. Thus, he tried to appear sympathetic to the New Deal: the objectives, he would say, were admirable, but the means dangerous. "I am supporting the Roosevelt administration," he wrote home in 1935. "It is the Administration of my Party, and if I did not support it, I certainly would have no other to support."[82] Elsewhere, he

[79] For this story, see Elmer L. Puryear, *Democratic Party Dissension in North Carolina, 1928-1936* (Chapel Hill, N.C., 1962), *passim*. For North Carolina politics in general, see Key, *Southern Politics*, pp. 205-28. An excellent study is Richard L. Watson, Jr., "A Southern Democratic Primary: Simmons vs. Bailey in 1930," *North Carolina Historical Review*, XLII (Winter 1965), 21-46.

[80] *Nation*, CXXXII (Jan. 7, 1931), 12.

[81] Of the ten major measures in 1933-1934, Bailey opposed three and failed to record himself on a fourth. From 1933-1939 he opposed 58 percent of the thirty-one New Deal measures he voted on. This record made him the seventh most conservative Democrat in the Senate. See Appendix B.

[82] To Dr. J. B. Cranfill, May 22, 1935, Bailey MSS, Political File.

added, "I feel that we should stand by the Administration and not attack it. At worst it is much better than any Republican administration and is also much safer than any radical administration would be. . . . I have disagreed with him [Roosevelt] on matters but never have I thought of going back on him as the head of our Government and the head of our Party."[83] It was for Bailey an unhappy time; cherishing the ideal of the upright legislator of principle, he was aware of political expediency. Until his successful 1936 campaign was over, it was often hard to tell from his public utterances where he stood.[84]

To close allies, however, Bailey's hostility to the administration was unconcealed, and from his voluminous letters, it is perhaps safe to suggest why. He was, said one unfriendly critic, "superethical, superconstitutional, and supercilious."[85] Lantern-jawed, with piercing eyes, a long sharp nose, and a lean angular face, Bailey was also a humorless man; "my friends," he admitted, "sometimes think I am unduly solemn. I think it all goes back to the little prayer meetings. . . ."[86] Above all, he was fond of seeing issues in terms of great moral and legal principles. Perhaps it was the "little prayer meetings," perhaps not; but no man better exemplified the conservative tendency to approach problems in abstract terms. To such a man, there was a wrong side and a side of the angels: "We must make the choice between the policy of liberty and the policy of control. I have made my choice [it was 1935] and it is based upon religious as well as politi-

[83] To Stacy Brewer, May 11, 1935, *ibid.*

[84] Josephus Daniels, the progressive North Carolinian then serving as American ambassador to Mexico, commented upon Bailey's fence-sitting during the struggle over public utility regulation in 1935. "Bailey," he wrote, "trying to carry water on both shoulders, voted to cut out the heart and thereby please the power trust, and then voted for the measure to please those who believe the holding companies are rackets." Daniels to FDR, July 5, 1935, Roosevelt MSS, PPF 86.

[85] Michie and Rhylick, *Dixie Demagogues*, pp. 159-65.

[86] To R. F. Beasley, Dec. 11, 1936, Bailey MSS, Political File.

cal convictions. Being a Baptist, I am liberal, and believe in liberty. Being a Democrat, I am a liberal and believe in liberty. Once we abandon the voluntary principles, we run squarely into Communism. . . . There can be no half-way control."[87]

Bailey was not an especially popular senator, but he was politically astute, intelligent, and persistent. When the time came in 1937, after his reelection and after Roosevelt's prestige began to fade, Josiah Bailey was most prominent in efforts for a conservative coalition in the Senate.

A fifth anti-New Deal Democratic senator of the 1933-1934 period was Harry Flood Byrd, Glass's Virginia colleague. At forty-six in 1933, he had already enjoyed wide political experience. The nephew of "Hal" Flood, Virginia's political boss in the Wilson era, he left school to run the family newspapers, nurtured very prosperous apple orchards in the Shenandoah Valley, and entered politics at an early age. By 1933 he had been a state senator, chairman of the state Democratic committee, and governor. As Glass's protégé and inheritor of his uncle's political machine, he became a senator early in 1933 when Roosevelt named Claude A. Swanson, Glass's former colleague, as navy secretary. Although he and fellow Governor Roosevelt had been friendly before 1933 (Byrd's brother, Admiral Richard Byrd, was then and later a warm friend of Roosevelt), Byrd quickly left the Roosevelt bandwagon. The NRA and AAA became special bones of contention.[88] As an apple producer he objected to the wage codes of the NRA and the licensing policies of the AAA; as an apple processor he disliked the AAA processing tax. "I know what's the matter with Harry Byrd," Roosevelt told Assistant Secretary of Agriculture Rexford G. Tugwell. "He's afraid you'll force him to pay

---

[87] To Thurman Kitchin, Oct. 28, 1935, *ibid.*, General File.

[88] Forrest Davis, "The Fourth Term's Hair Shirt," *Saturday Evening Post*, CCXVI (April 8, 1944), Pt. I and (April 15, 1944), Pt. II, is a study of Byrd.

more than ten cents an hour for his apple pickers."[89] By late 1934, Byrd was already a frequent critic of the New Deal.[90]

Byrd's chief objections were indeed economic. There was no more determined exponent of fiscal orthodoxy. Affable, soft-spoken, even-tempered, even a little cherubic-looking with his pink complexion and moon-face, he had on the subject of deficit spending the "peculiar, angry, dry pertinacity more typical of New England than the easy-going South."[91] As governor, he had cut corporation taxes, spent comparatively little on state services, and made a wide reputation as an economizer. Indeed, he considered such efficiency "progressive."[92] Safe from electoral defeat, Byrd was by 1934 the fifth conservative Senate Democrat to leave the New Deal fold.

Besides these five there were other Democratic senators in the first session whose reliability was questionable. Robert J. Bulkley of Ohio voted against the Agricultural Adjustment Act and the suspension of gold payments in private contracts. Marcus A. Coolidge of Massachusetts opposed TVA and the gold payments resolution. Patrick A. McCarran of Nevada and Bennett Champ Clark of Missouri, liberals in some respects, also demonstrated their independence on occasion. But none of these men expressed open hostility to the New

[89] Rexford G. Tugwell, *The Democratic Roosevelt* (Garden City, N.Y., 1957), p. 444.

[90] Perhaps because of his impending election in 1934, Byrd was not a consistent New Deal opponent on key votes until 1935. But in 1933-1934 he voted against the NRA and did not vote on the FERA. He was the fifth most conservative Senate Democrat over the 1933-1939 period, voting against 65 percent of key New Deal measures. Charles Michelson, in *The Ghost Talks* (New York, 1941), p. 140, suggested that Byrd's opposition stemmed from disappointment at not being named vice-president. While this may have been a factor, it by no means accounted for Byrd's insistent stand on economy.

[91] Joseph Alsop and Robert Kintner, Washington *Star*, July 31, 1939, A-11.

[92] See George B. Tindall, "Business Progressivism: Southern Politics in the Twenties," *South Atlantic Quarterly*, LXII (Winter 1963), 92-106.

Deal at this time. Of the 43 adverse Democratic votes in the Senate on ten key issues of the 1933-1934 sessions, 22 came from the five hard-core conservatives. The remaining sixty Democrats cast only 21 adverse votes.[93]

These five men, warm friends, were the Democratic irreconcilables of the Senate. To them the New Deal was not only new; it was revolutionary. In the 1933-1934 Congress their impact upon legislation was negligible, and coalition with conservative Republicans was far from their thoughts. But in later years these men, not conservative Republicans, became the leading spokesmen for a conservative coalition in the Senate. Even in this most tractable of Congresses the conservative stalwarts of the future were rather forlornly voicing their complaints against the New Deal. Later, they were to find a more receptive audience.

[93] See Appendix B.

2

A LONG HOT SUMMER

HUMORIST Will Rogers surveyed the political scene soon after the astonishing New Deal victory in the 1934 election. "The Republicans," he said, "have had a saying . . . 'The Roosevelt honeymoon is over.' They were mighty poor judges of a lovesick couple. Why, he and the people have got a real love match and it looks like it would run for another six years." President Roosevelt, added William Allen White, "has been all but crowned by the people."[1]

By any form of analysis, this election was a remarkable victory for the Democratic party and for the President.[2] For only the second time in American history, an administration increased its strength in an off-year congressional election. Democrats gained nine Senate seats, losing no incumbents, and nine House seats. The new Senate included 69 Democrats and 25 Republicans, plus Farmer-Laborite Henrik Shipstead of Minnesota and Robert M. La Follette, Jr., of Wisconsin, who called himself a Progressive.[3] The new House had 319 Democrats and 103 Republicans, with 3 Minnesota Farmer-Laborites, 7 Wisconsin Progressives, and 3 vacancies rounding out the total.

The new Congress promised to be even more progressive than its partisan makeup suggested. In the Senate some 10 of the 25 Republicans were western progressives who had already demonstrated that their sympathies lay with Roosevelt on domestic policy. These men even ignored the few meetings that Republicans bothered to hold; even McNary voted with the progressives most of the time. As the session opened, 70 senators were sympathetic to most of New Deal domestic policy as it had thus far unfolded. In the House, although 10 to 20 returning Democratic representatives had been unreliable during the 1933-1934 session, some 13 progressive Republicans and the 10 third-party members easily compensated for them. In the lower house Roosevelt could apparently rely upon approximately 325 representatives. The potential for a conservative coalition was most unpromising. No congressional session in American history had augured so well for its Chief Executive.

Some circumstances appeared to make Roosevelt's task more difficult than it had been in 1933. For one, patronage would obviously not be so important: by 1935 the multiplication of alphabetical agencies had helped to subdue though by no means to satisfy the hunger of congressmen. It would no longer be so easy for Roosevelt to entice wavering

[1] *Time*, Nov. 12, 1934, p. 11.

[2] For analyses, see E. Francis Brown, "The Moral of the Elections," *Current History*, XLI (Dec. 1934), 279-83; Harry W. Morris, "The Republicans in a Minority Role, 1933-1938" (unpublished Ph.D. dissertation, State University of Iowa, 1960), pp. 89-93; and John Harding, "The 1942 Congressional Elections," *American Political Science Review*, XXXVIII (Feb. 1944), 41-57 (this contains many interesting contrasts to previous congressional elections).

[3] See E. Francis Brown, "The Progressives Make a New Bid," *Current History*, XLI (Nov. 1934), 149-54.

Democrats with a handful of plums. In addition, many congressmen had not forgotten some of the grievances which they had expressed hesitantly, if at all, in 1933-1934. Pittman, for instance, although remaining loyal to Roosevelt, complained to a constituent about bureaucracy: "It is apparent from your letter that even you do not understand the situation here in Washington. This government is run by bureaus, pure and simple. The influence of Senators and congressmen is purely persuasive."[4] Percy Lee Gassaway, an Oklahoma Democrat, was more pungent: "The only difference between a damned congressman and a street car conductor in Washington is that the conductor knows where he is going, and if six or eight fellows would drop dead up here at the same time they would have to get a janitor to open and close Congress for them."[5] The natural desire of congressmen for independence, frustrated by Roosevelt's strong leadership, was to become more powerful as the session wore on.

Finally, a few observers were afraid the huge Democratic majorities would dissolve in factionalism. In the makeup of this Congress there existed the nascent coalition of strong interest groups—Negroes, unions, relief workers, farm organizations—that had already pressed for more spending in 1933-1934 and that was eventually to prove unmanageable. House leaders, recognizing the potential power of these groups, quickly forced through a rules change to require 218 votes instead of the previous 145 for a discharge petition.[6] As Pittman noted in an observation fraught with future significance: "We will have a great majority in the Senate but I am afraid that many of them will not realize that they have been elected by reason of the great popularity of President

[4] Key Pittman to R. L. Douglass, July 1, 1935, Pittman MSS, Box 12.

[5] To Dale Crawford, Feb. 15, 1935, Correspondence 1935, Gassaway MSS.

[6] E. Pendleton Herring, "First Session of the 74th Congress," *American Political Science Review*, XXIX (Dec. 1935), 985-1005.

Roosevelt. I am afraid that many of them, not realizing this, will divide off into factions on many issues and thus split us apart."[7]

On balance, however, these seemed to be merely minor irritations and difficulties. Clearly, the election had demonstrated that Roosevelt's magic was as strong as ever. "The attitude of Congress towards Roosevelt," said one veteran newsman at the time, "is abject and cowardly. Most of the members of both parties rode into Congress on Roosevelt's shirt tail. They feel—quite correctly—that the popularity of Roosevelt with the great mass of people was never greater."[8] Many congressmen were fearful of more innovation, but pressure from their home districts was often too strong and they did not dare to oppose the chief.[9] The winning combination of Roosevelt's popularity and economic emergency promised to be easily sufficient to beat down congressional rebellion.

When the session finally ended in September, the record fulfilled all but the fondest New Deal expectations. For several months, however, the administration had seemed to falter. In January, the Senate defiantly had defeated the President's plan to make the United States a participant in the World Court. And from January through March, controversy over the administration's $4.8-billion relief bill had ensnared the Senate. Conservatives, secure at least until 1936, had been generally more vocal, more willing to ob-

[7] To Sen. Henry F. Ashurst (Ariz.), Nov. 13, 1934, Pittman MSS, Box 15.

[8] Henry Hyde Diary, Jan. 27, 1935, Hyde MSS. For a similar view, see Frank Kent, *Without Grease: Political Behavior, 1934-1936* (New York, 1936), pp. 56-57.

[9] George W. Norris, for instance, wrote in late 1934, "I have been all over the state of Nebraska during this campaign, and I have found the sentiment among the Democrats and the Republicans alike that Roosevelt was sincere —that he was doing the best he could, and that, while he did not always know just how he was coming out, he was always willing to try. The people have great respect for this kind of a policy." Norris to Ray Tucker, Nov. 10, 1934, Norris MSS, Tray 2, Box 2.

struct than before. As Roosevelt himself had noted as early as February, "the rest of this session will be more or less a madhouse—every senator a law unto himself and everyone seeking the spotlight."[10]

To his congressional supporters, the President had appeared vacillating, irritable, careless. "New senators," Pittman told Ickes, "hadn't been able to get in to see him, with resultant loss of dignity and hard feelings."[11] Even McNary, still very fond of the Chief Executive, wrote: "The President has lost considerable of his influence with his party and has developed a rather childish peevishness which should not be a part of the big fellow. . . ."[12] No conservative coalition had formed, but factionalism promised as late as May to delay if not to destroy the dreams of New Dealers.

In the last weeks of May, however, Roosevelt's love of action returned. On May 22 he went in person to the House to read a veto of a veterans' bonus bill; the next day the Senate upheld him. Then, on May 27, came "Black Monday." The Supreme Court delivered a series of decisions against the New Deal, including a unanimous verdict against the NRA. The President countered with a reasoned but sharp attack on the court, including a widely quoted remark that the Supreme Court was pushing the Constitution back to the "horse and buggy days." He then proceeded to galvanize

[10] Elliott Roosevelt (ed.), *The Roosevelt Letters* (3 vols.; London, 1952), III, 141 (Roosevelt to Col. House, Feb., 16, 1935).

[11] Harold Ickes, *The Secret Diary of Harold Ickes* (3 vols.; New York, 1954), I, 302, Feb. 20, 1935. Pittman, pessimistic as usual, worried about the state of affairs. Writing FDR, he complained: "We are faced with an unscrupulous, regular Republican representation; a progressive Republican membership determined upon going further to the left than you will go; a Democratic representation who have [*sic*] more sympathy for the Republican progressive position than they have [*sic*] for yours. And in the midst of this disloyalty you have a regular Democratic representation that conscientiously believe they [*sic*] are saving you by destroying you. . . . There is no Democratic Party in the Senate." Feb. 19, 1935, Roosevelt MSS, PPF 745.

[12] Charles L. McNary to John H. McNary, Feb. 26, 1935, McNary MSS.

Congress into action with the old determination he had shown in the 100 Days. The result was the so-called second New Deal of June–August 1935.

Historians have not agreed whether the "first" or "second" New Deal was more "radical."[13] They have, however, usually agreed that about the time of the "second" there was at least a shift in emphasis. The "first" New Deal, they say, relied essentially upon the AAA and NRA, experiments in government-business and government-agriculture cooperation that were not unduly concerned whether big business or big farms dominated the joint planning. Under the NRA, in fact, antitrust laws were suspended, and under the AAA many small farmers and tenants found themselves squeezed off their lands. By contrast, the "second" New Deal (so the argument goes) placed less emphasis upon government planning, more upon restoring free competition among smaller economic units. Under the "second" New Deal, there was therefore a somewhat greater animus against bigness, against large concentrations of wealth, against monopoly.

There are exceptions to this generalization about the distinction between legislation before and after May 1935, as its exponents realize. No serious effort was made in 1935-1936 to save the small farmer. The ideology behind the utility holding-company bill of 1935 long antedated this period. The Social Security and National Labor Relations acts, passed in the summer of 1935, were structural reforms with little or no relation to any "war" against monopoly. And it is certainly arguable that Roosevelt's entire first term, in its undiminished sympathy for the underprivileged and lack of sympathy for certain of the privileged, was considerably more consistent than some historians have cared to stress.

[13] For an excellent survey of this controversy, see Otis Graham, Jr., "Historians and the New Deals, 1944-1960," *Social Studies*, LIV (April 1963), 133-40.

Yet it is true that the two most bitter issues of the post-May period were the utility holding-company bill and the "wealth tax," and that both sought to reduce the power of large-scale corporate enterprise. Furthermore, these measures, whether regressive or radical by later standards, disturbed conservatives more than had any previous proposals. These two issues opened a division in Democratic party ranks which would later assume lasting and significant proportions. They also witnessed the formation of loose but nonetheless potentially dangerous conservative coalitions in both houses.

The public utility holding-company bill drew its inspiration from several sources, most notably from the widespread publicity given to abuses of the holding-company system under such utility magnates as the recently exposed Samuel Insull of Chicago. As the bill finally reached Congress, however, it was essentially the product of Roosevelt's determination and the expert draftsmanship of Thomas C. (Tommy the Cork) Corcoran, an ebullient Irishman, and Benjamin V. Cohen, a shy and brilliant Jew. These two men, young bachelor lawyers, were roommates in Georgetown and served as Roosevelt's draftsmen on several occasions.

Introduced by Commerce Committee Chairman Burton K. Wheeler of Montana in the Senate and by Sam Rayburn of Texas in the House, the utility bill had two main titles. Title II provided for federal coordination and integration of operating companies along efficient lines, but the controversial section was Title I, especially the famous "death sentence" provision. This clause authorized the Securities and Exchange Commission (SEC) to take steps to simplify the complex system of holding companies in the electric power field. So far as possible, this simplification was to be voluntary; but if the companies refused to cooperate, the bill empowered the SEC to compel the dissolution as of

January 1, 1940, of all such holding companies that could not demonstrate sound economic reasons for their existence. This "death sentence" sought not only to reform abuses but to expel many holding-company operators from the national scene.

Utility interests immediately organized a powerful campaign against the bill. "Millions of letters are being carted into Washington," reported Montana's Democratic Senator James Murray.[14] Many of them, as subsequent investigations were to reveal, came from professional lobbyists who copied names from phone books. Holding-company spokesmen, led by Wendell L. Willkie, president of the Commonwealth and Southern Utility Company, also waged a strong battle in congressional hearings and in the press. Such pressure encouraged conservative senators, already angry at the sternness of the bill, to obstruct and delay. More important, conservatives used a standard anti-administration weapon: crippling amendments. Democratic Senator William H. Dieterich of Illinois, under strong utilities pressure, led the effort for the key amendment substituting regulation for dissolution. It would have removed the heart of the "death sentence."

The bill began moving through the hail of amendments early in June. But for the first time moderate as well as irreconcilable Senate Democrats worked against an important New Deal measure. Not only Dieterich but other Democratic regulars such as Augustine Lonergan of Connecticut and Matthew M. Neely of West Virginia joined in the attack on the measure. Other New Deal Democrats such as James F. Byrnes of South Carolina, then and later a Roosevelt aide, William F. Ashurst of Arizona, the genial Judiciary Committee chairman, and freshman Senator George L. Radcliffe of Maryland, a former business associate of the

14 Quoted in William Leuchtenburg, *Franklin D. Roosevelt and the New Deal* (New York, 1963), p. 155.

President who owed his election in 1934 partly to Roosevelt's influence, also left the New Deal fold.[15] Still others, such as Alva B. Adams of Colorado and William G. McAdoo of California were undecided. As the day for the vote on the Dieterich amendment approached, observers predicted a close result.

At this point, Wheeler and Roosevelt moved to the attack. Hurrying to the White House for presidential aid, Wheeler emerged with a scribbled message insisting that any amendment against the "death sentence" "would strike at the bill itself and is wholly contrary to the recommendations of my message."[16] When Wheeler read the message to the Senate, it was clear to fence-sitting Democrats that the "death sentence" clause was a test of party loyalty.

The administration also sent its own lobbyists into action. National Chairman Farley and a host of aides were daily visitors to the Hill. Corcoran lobbied so tirelessly that a Republican representative later accused him of threatening to withhold federal funds from a local project. Democrats complained to Vice-President Garner of this unseemly presidential pressure. "Now look here," Garner reminded them. "It doesn't matter what kind of a fool you think he is; he's your fool just as long as he's President and the leader of your party."[17]

When the time to vote arrived, the administration won a narrow victory: Dieterich's amendment lost, 44-45.[18] Adams

[15] In a letter to FDR Radcliffe wrote, "There has been strong and growing opposition in Maryland to many administration measures." He added: "I am disturbed about certain features of pending bills—or policies." June 21, 1935, Roosevelt MSS, PPF 410.

[16] Arthur Schlesinger, Jr., *The Politics of Upheaval* (Boston, 1960), p. 313.

[17] Joseph Alsop and Turner Catledge, *The 168 Days* (Garden City, N.Y., 1938), p. 130.

[18] See Washington *Post*, June 12, 1935, p. 1, and New York *Times*, June 12, 1935, p. 2, for analyses of the vote. It is recorded in *Congressional Record*, 74th Cong., 1st Sess., 9053.

and McAdoo remained loyal to the administration, but twenty-nine other Democrats did not. The opposing Democrats included not only the five Democratic irreconcilables and former unreliables Clark, Coolidge, and Bulkley but some twenty more who had until then steadfastly supported the New Deal. Only the loyalty of eight progressive Republicans (Peter Norbeck of South Dakota was a key last-minute convert) saved the "death sentence." The final bill then passed with comparative ease 56-32, as eleven Democrats realized the futility of further opposition. The vote on this bill was one of the most significant of the New Deal years, for it revealed major Democratic defections from the administration. Having left the New Deal on one key issue, these Democrats were to find it easier to do so again and again. The public utilities holding-company bill thus marked an important milestone in the shift of essentially conservative Democratic senators from unhappy loyalty to open opposition.

The nature of the opposition to the bill was revealing. First, though western support was widespread, the bill was not a sectional issue. Of the twenty-nine Democratic supporters of the Dieterich amendment, six were easterners (of eleven eastern Democrats in all), eight were southerners (of twenty-two), four were border Democrats (of eight), four were midwesterners (of nine), and seven were westerners (of twenty). On certain labor and relief questions southerners would be more conservative than Democrats from other sections, but on the utilities issue, they divided much as did their colleagues throughout the country.[19]

Of the key twenty-nine, some twelve were to remain

---

[19] Throughout, the following sectional definitions will hold: East: New England, plus N.Y., N.J., Del., Pa.; South: the eleven states of the Confederacy; Border: Md., W. Va., Ky., Mo.; Midwest: Old Northwest, plus Iowa and Minn.; West: Plains, Rocky Mts., and Pacific Coast. See Appendix A.

generally dependable on later New Deal measures. Dieterich himself was one of these, Neely another, Radcliffe a third. To most of these men political pressures in their home states suggested that they were safer voting against the measure than for it; four of them, for instance, faced potentially difficult reelection contests in 1936. Five more of the twenty-nine were the irreconcilables whose open opposition to the New Deal was long a matter of record, and three, Clark, Bulkley, and Coolidge, had also already proved unreliable on several occasions.

Thus the shifts of the remaining nine Democrats of the twenty-nine opponents were most significant. Representing all sections of the country, of all ages (including the most veteran and the most junior), these men were to become by 1938 as unreliable and almost as irreconcilable as the original Democratic quintet. All of them were unhappy with the New Deal for one reason or another by the time the utilities bill matured; for all of them the "death sentence" provision proved to be the expressed beginning of sustained opposition to the New Deal. In later years they would seek a conservative coalition.

The most veteran of these nine Democrats—and by far the most colorful—was Ellison D. Smith of South Carolina. "Cotton Ed" had first entered the Senate in 1908 and was seventy-one in 1935.[20] He was the joy of caricaturists. One critic described him as "bulky, ponderous, grumpy, grizzled, baggy-faced, and crusty."[21] He had a square face, a bulldog look, pouchy eyes, and so many chins that they quivered as he talked. He was fond of contorting his extremely flabby face like Popeye to accommodate delighted photographers.

[20] Allan Michie and Frank Rhylick, *Dixie Demagogues* (New York, 1939), pp. 265-86, contains a devastating commentary on Smith.

[21] Leonard Niel Plummer describes Smith in J. T. Salter (ed.), *Public Men In and Out of Office* (Chapel Hill, N.C., 1946), pp. 344-54. Quote is on p. 345.

As a politician "Cotton Ed" was a South Carolina institution; he won six straight senatorial elections over the years. A wild campaigner, he was an authentic demagogue. When a Negro minister began a prayer in the 1936 Democratic national convention, Smith loudly left the scene. "By God," Cotton Ed shouted, "he's as black as melted midnight."[22] His Negrophobia was so extreme that southern leaders during most of the 1930's were reluctant to let him speak during filibusters against race legislation. In a state rampant with party factionalism, Smith's appeals to racial prejudice, class consciousness, and sectional pride were useful political assets.[23]

Racism and demagoguery do not explain his view of the New Deal. A fellow southern demagogue, Theodore G. Bilbo of Mississippi, for instance, was among the most loyal of New Deal senators. Perhaps the best way to understand Smith is to realize that more than any other senator of his time, he lived in the past. He was, one observer remarked, the "last of the spittoon senators."[24] Like Glass, Smith was a veteran of Wilson's political wars and temperamentally unable to adjust himself to the rapidly changing circumstances of the New Deal.[25] "Senator Smith," commented a New Deal agricultural official who knew him well, "was getting quite old. . . . He reached the stage that he didn't fully comprehend what we were trying to do."[26]

Unlike the irreconcilables, Smith did not consistently oppose the New Deal until 1935; his vote on the Dieterich

[22] *Ibid.*

[23] V. O. Key, Jr., *Southern Politics in State and Nation* (New York, 1949), pp. 130-55, discusses South Carolina politics.

[24] Plummer, "Smith," p. 345.

[25] See Howard W. Allen, "Geography and Politics: Voting on Reform Issues in the United States Senate, 1911-1916," *Journal of Southern History*, XXVII (May 1961), 216-28.

[26] John Hutson, Oral History Project, Columbia University, pp. 128-29. See also Wesley McCune, *The Farm Bloc* (Garden City, N.Y., 1943), pp. 37-38.

amendment was his first major defection on New Deal domestic policies. In part he delayed because of Roosevelt's great popularity in South Carolina, in part because he was chairman of the Senate Agriculture Committee; like other Democrats in responsible positions, he found it somewhat more difficult to make a final break.

He irritated New Dealers almost from the start. A large cotton farmer who fancied himself the leading Senate authority on agriculture, he had been a touchy committee chairman during the 1933 fight for the Agricultural Adjustment Act. "If turning over to the Secretary of Agriculture an overlordship over every farm and the power to tax every producer is the only hope," he had shouted, "I despair of the future."[27] He also grumbled that Roosevelt and his intellectual advisers underrated his knowledge and influence; he disliked Agriculture Undersecretary Tugwell because he was not a "dirt farmer." Not a useful, and certainly not a happy backer of the New Deal before 1935, Smith considered the "death sentence" provision extreme and vindictive. His vote on the Dieterich amendment signified the beginning of open, sustained opposition to the New Deal.

Walter F. George of Georgia was a southern conservative of a different stripe. George, a journalist wrote, was "of medium height, rather slender of stature, with fast-greying hair and well-chiselled features. He looks the part of a southern statesman who never thought to let his hair grow long or to sprout a goatee."[28] Fifty-seven years old in 1935, George was of a younger generation than Smith or Glass, and he was to be a vigorous and alert senator for two more decades. Perhaps George's most commonly noticed trait was his reserved, somewhat pompous manner. Unlike many conservative senators of the 1930's, he was not an eager, vibrant orator. A former judge, he was so formal that even

[27] *Time*, April 3, 1933, p. 12.
[28] New York *Times*, Aug. 8, 1938, p. 5.

to his wife he was "Mr. George."[29] He had no colorful
stories to tell and little sense of humor. Typically, he sat
quietly in his Senate seat, leaned back with eyes closed, and
gravely pondered the points of debate.[30]

His political advancement had been rapid. The son of a
tenant farmer, he often professed pride in his humble
beginnings, but he had been able to get a college education,
and at thirty-nine he became a state supreme court judge.
When Tom Watson died in 1922, George replaced him as
senator. In 1926 and 1932 he won full terms, and by 1935
he had earned a solid place in the hearts of Georgia voters.[31]
Generally a loyal party man, he had opposed few major
New Deal domestic measures when the 1935 session began.

But George did not claim to be fond of innovation; his
judicial mind sought precedents, not departures. When the
"second" New Deal began to emerge, he became more and
more perturbed. For George was not an old-school Jeffersonian Democrat whose America was rooted to the soil; he
was frankly closer to business elements. Among his close
friends were officials of the Coca Cola Company of Atlanta
and the Georgia Power Company. Criticized because the
power company openly backed him, he admitted willingly,
"so do most business interests in Georgia."[32] Thus, the
utilities "death sentence" clause was in itself distressing to
George; the wealth tax which followed was even more so.
By the end of the 1935 session, George was unenthusiastic
about the New Deal. He would support it when his careful
mind allowed him to do so, but no longer would he do so
out of sympathy or party loyalty.

[29] *Current Biography,* 1943, pp. 232-33.

[30] Michie and Rhylick, *Dixie Demagogues,* pp. 187-201, sketch George.

[31] Key, *Southern Politics,* has a clear discussion of Georgia politics, pp.
106-29.

[32] For a survey of his voting record, see press release by *Editorial Research
Reports,* Aug. 26, 1938, in Clapper MSS, Box 118. This publication, also
issued in annual volumes, contains detailed roll-call vote tabulations.

In 1933-1934 what little Democratic congressional opposition there had been had come largely from south of the
Mason-Dixon Line. But of the remaining seven Democrats
who began to break with the New Deal in 1935 none was a
southerner. Two of the more conservative of the seven will
suffice to show the nature and impulse behind much of this
nonsouthern conservatism.

The more senior of the two was Royal S. Copeland of
New York. Few American politicians have had such a
strange political apprenticeship. Born in Michigan in 1868,
he became a doctor, Republican mayor of Ann Arbor, and
a widely syndicated Hearst columnist on medicine.[33] Moving to New York City in 1908, he switched his party
allegiance, joined Tammany Hall, and eventually became
city health commissioner. When Alfred E. Smith, running
for governor, refused to accept William Randolph Hearst
as his Senate running mate in 1922, Copeland got the
chance and proved an able campaigner. Originally a Republican, Copeland always ran very well in conservative upstate
New York; his appeal to conservatives, combined with his
strong showing in New York City, made him a formidable
opponent. In 1928 he carried New York by 51,000 votes
while Roosevelt won the gubernatorial race by a mere 25,000
and Smith lost his presidential contest in New York by
100,000.

Like George and Smith, Copeland was generally dependable in the 1933-1934 session, though he absented himself
on a number of occasions. By no means a liberal, however,
he frankly identified himself with the mild pre-Depression
progressivism of Al Smith, and gradually developed a strong
antipathy to Roosevelt. A supporter of Smith for the 1932
Democratic nomination, he was never close to Roosevelt,

---

[33] See "Tammany's Last Stand," *Nation*, CXLV (Sept. 11, 1937), 255-57,
for a study of Copeland. See also lengthy obituary in New York *Times*,
June 18, 1938, pp. 1, 3.

and the President, owing him nothing, was even stingier in giving Copeland patronage than he was to the others.[34] A somewhat querulous man whose perpetual red carnation affected a cheery disposition, Copeland was also regarded by some Democratic leaders as a headline-seeker.[35] They tended to ignore him in planning strategy, and this neglect understandably offended him. Worst of all, Roosevelt had not been eager to support Copeland for reelection in 1934 and might have tried to discard him had not others decided that shelving him would create more problems than it would solve.[36]

From this election until his death in 1938, Copeland was a vocal opponent of the New Deal. The utility issue provided but the first important occasion for his many subsequent anti-New Deal votes, and by 1936 he refused even to attend the Democratic national convention. "They have plenty of New Dealers," he said sourly. "They don't need me."[37] Copeland's reaction to the New Deal, like Cotton Ed Smith's, illustrates the pitfalls involved in referring too carelessly to a "conservative-liberal" lineup in the New Deal. Factional splits and personal feelings could and did contribute considerably to ideological differences as a cause of anti-New Deal sentiments.

Personal feeling helped influence a second nonsouthern dissenter, Edward R. Burke of Nebraska. A thin-haired, conservatively dressed Omaha lawyer, Burke's biggest political asset was his friendship with Arthur Mullen, former Nebras-

[34] Binghamton (N.Y.) *Press,* April 20, 1933. In Copeland Scrapbook, Copeland MSS.

[35] Interview, Burton K. Wheeler, June, 1963. See also portrait by Joseph Alsop and Robert Kintner, Washington *Star,* April 9, 1938, A-9.

[36] New York *Times,* June 18, 1938, p. 1. Edward J. Flynn, in *You're the Boss* (New York, 1947), pp. 147-48, said that Roosevelt tried to name Copeland ambassador to Germany in 1933, with Flynn to succeed him in the Senate.

[37] New York *Times,* June 16, 1936, p. 1.

ka Democratic national committeeman and Roosevelt's floor leader at the 1932 national convention.[38] Mullen, gruff and undiplomatic, was powerful, and his support helped Burke, who was then an obscure first-term representative, gain the 1934 senatorial nomination.[39] Burke won the election with ease and was a fifty-five-year-old freshman senator when the 1935 session opened.

As a representative, Burke had loyally supported the New Deal. But even before he took his Senate seat his Nebraska political associates had begun to complain about Roosevelt. Mullen, by this time a lobbyist for Nebraska power interests, was becoming increasingly angry at Secretary of the Interior Ickes, a former Bull Moose Progressive. He claimed that Ickes was turning over Nebraska Public Works Administration (PWA) funds to power districts controlled by George W. Norris, Nebraska's progressive Republican senator.[40] Many regular Nebraska Democrats also complained that Roosevelt was favoring Norris at the expense of the state Democratic organization: indeed, in 1936 Roosevelt was to give vigorous support to Norris.

Burke's attitude toward organized labor added to these political differences. Wholly in sympathy with large Nebraska business and manufacturing interests in their developing struggles with unions, he had been the only Democratic senator outside the old irreconcilables to oppose the Wagner Labor Relations Act on the final vote in May. In later years he was to become a leading Democratic critic of the new Committee for Industrial Organization (CIO) and of the National Labor Relations Board (NLRB). Denied

[38] *Current Biography*, 1940, pp. 125-26.

[39] See Norris MSS, Tray 7, Box 5, for letters indicating the nature of Democratic factionalism in Nebraska. Norris, for one, considered Burke a puppet of Mullen. See New York *Times*, Aug. 14, 1934, IV, 7, for Mullen's role.

[40] See *New Republic*, XCI (May 26, 1937), 72-73, for a discussion of Burke, Roosevelt, and Nebraska politics.

renomination by his party in 1940, he openly supported
Republican presidential nominee Wendell Willkie.

By the time the utilities bill entered its final stages Burke
already nourished political and economic grievances against
the New Deal. With Mullen an avid lobbyist against the
bill, it was not surprising that Burke opposed it. As was the
case with Copeland, a combination of conservative economic
views and political differences helped to make Burke as
hostile to the New Deal as any Democrat in the Senate.

Burke's case also illustrated a significant phenomenon
of the era, and of American politics in general: conservative
Democrats could be, and were, elected to Congress even
at the high tide of the New Deal. Burke was not the only
such conservative to take office in 1934; of the thirteen freshmen Democratic senators that year, five backed the Dieterich
amendment and eight were to become conservative or unreliable Democrats within three years. As later events were to
prove, not only veterans such as Glass and Smith opposed
the New Deal; many new "coattail" Democrats were to
join them in 1935 and thereafter.

This apparent anomaly of conservative Democrats chosen
in a progressive era is not difficult to understand, nor was it
unusual in American political history. There were as many
Democratic parties in the United States as there were states,
and as Roosevelt's later unsuccessful purge was to demonstrate, the determination of senatorial nominees was largely
a state matter over which the national administration had
limited control. If future conservatives such as Burke were
the nominees of state Democratic organizations, there was
little Roosevelt could do.

Once in office, these men were free to oppose the New
Deal, and for six years the most liberal electorates could not
touch them. Thus it was not surprising that of the twenty
Democratic senators who were to leave the party fold on
many key occasions by 1936, only four had to face reelection

that year. One, Coolidge, did not want to be reelected and was not. One, Glass, had an impregnable state machine behind him. The third, Bailey, combined strong organization backing with his own off-again, on-again backing of the President as the election drew near. Only Gore dared oppose Roosevelt without machine backing, and he was not even renominated. The remaining sixteen opposed New Deal policies knowing they would have at least two more years of grace.

The careers of Smith, George, Copeland, and Burke suggest the variety of reasons—personal, political, and philo-sophical—that led some Democrats to oppose the New Deal by 1935. They were not the only Democrats to do so. Others who began to combat New Deal policies at this time were: Peter G. Gerry of Rhode Island, a wealthy Harvard graduate, lawyer-businessman, and veteran Democratic politico who came to believe that AAA processing taxes were ruining Rhode Island textile mills; Augustine Lonergan of Con-necticut, a freshman of 1932 who began to veer away during the utilities fight; the veteran William H. King of Utah, a seventy-two-year-old former Mormon missionary whose de-fenses of states' rights approached those of Glass and Gore; and newcomer Arthur H. Moore, Boss Frank Hague's former governor of New Jersey. Others, such as former Governor A. Victor ("Honest Vic") Donahey of Ohio, a self-made man and an advocate of economy who first reached the Senate in 1934, Alva B. Adams of Colorado, a mild-mannered, shrewd banker who combined a belief in balanced budgets with a fondness for government silver purchasing, and Bennett Champ Clark of Missouri also proved unreliable on occasion in this session and were to become more so later.[41] Still others, such as outspoken Patrick A. McCarran of Nevada and veteran David I. Walsh of Massachusetts, combined

[41] For Donahey, see Clapper MSS, Box 118; also New York *Times* (obituary), April 9, 1946, p. 27.

complaints over patronage with philosophical objections to many administration policies.[42] And last, Rush D. Holt of West Virginia, a thirty-year-old freshman whose youth prevented his seating until June 1935, was within a short time to parlay patronage disputes into vehement opposition to the New Deal and all its works. Before long, New Dealers would find even Tydings pleasant company by contrast.

The utility bill stimulated sizable Democratic dissent in the Senate, but it precipitated near chaos in the House, turning a previously docile group of men into fervent partisans of congressional independence. And when the bill finally slipped through a last roll call in late August, the lower chamber was no longer the tractable house it had been; it was an aroused, assertive legislative body.[43]

The minute the "death sentence" bill passed the Senate, conservatives, far from discouraged, girded for renewed effort. "The bill is going to be moderated to some extent in the House and I have assurances to this effect from very high sources," Bailey wrote to a constituent. "An amendment will be drawn along the lines of the Dieterich amendment for which I voted. I have this from Jimmie Byrnes, Jack Garner and Senator Wheeler."[44] Only a few days later the House Interstate Commerce Committee, despite Chairman Rayburn's pleas, reported its own more moderate version.[45]

Included among the committee's amendments was one that tempered the death sentence. It is important in light of later developments, however, to emphasize that this House committee version differed little from the Senate

[42] For Walsh, see Dorothy G. Wayman, *David I. Walsh: Citizen-Patriot* (Milwaukee, 1952), a laudatory and uncritical work. For his early career, see William J. Grattan, "David I. Walsh and His Associates: A Study in Political Theory" (unpublished Ph.D. dissertation, Harvard University, 1957).

[43] Arthur Krock, New York *Times*, July 5, 1935, p. 12, argued persuasively that House leaders resented Roosevelt's catering to the Senate.

[44] Josiah Bailey to Mrs. Bailey, June 13, 1935, Bailey MSS, Personal File.

[45] New York *Times*, June 23, 1935, p. 25.

bill.[46] In effect, the Senate bill placed the burden of proof on holding companies; the House version said that holding companies might not be dissolved if the SEC were unable to prove that dissolution was in the public interest. There was irony here, for this more "conservative" House bill gave the SEC, a New Deal creation, the very type of discretionary authority that conservatives ordinarily protested so bitterly.

Such fine distinctions went relatively unnoticed at the time. The important reality was that though the two versions were not far apart, both Roosevelt and his House opponents acted as if they were. Both sides quickly insisted upon their respective versions; neither found it possible to back down gracefully. Hence the ensuing struggle, carried on as if a clear-cut substantive issue were involved, was largely a struggle for prestige. In retrospect the issue has the appearance of a contest which might have been prevented; nonetheless, it was an important symbolic test of strength. It was just this sort of test of prestige which was to form the basis of many future New Deal legislative controversies.

Administration forces, beaten in committee, assumed that rebellious representatives would not dare record themselves against a popular administration measure when it reached the floor, and they quickly took steps to insure a roll-call vote. Under normal House procedure, however, such a record vote required a special rule. Pressed by Roosevelt, Rayburn went before the Rules Committee to plead for a special rule allowing a record vote on an amendment restoring the "death sentence."

In 1933-1934 the Rules Committee under William B. Bankhead of Alabama had been a strong right arm of the administration, approving so many favorable rules that Re-

[46] New York *Times,* June 26, 1935, p. 1, makes this clear. See also Clapper, Washington *Post,* July 1, 1935, p. 2; Lippmann, New York *Herald Tribune,* July 4, 1935, p. 15; and Mario Einaudi, *The Roosevelt Revolution* (New York, 1959), pp. 189-96.

publicans constantly fumed about "gag rules." But the death of Speaker Henry Rainey before the 1935 session created a change in Democratic House leadership. Joseph T. Byrns of Tennessee, previously majority leader, became speaker in a deal that made Bankhead majority leader. John J. O'Conner of New York, the senior Democrat, vaulted to the head of the Rules Committee.

His chairmanship was a perfect example of the way in which the congressional seniority system elevated men whom administration leaders found intolerable. O'Connor, a red-headed, aggressive Tammany Democrat, was "one of the most unpopular members of a supposedly popular House."[47] A representative since 1923, he had quickly landed on the powerful Rules Committee; through defeats, retirements, and advancements of other senior Rules Committee Democrats, he gained his chairmanship in the rather short time of twelve years.

Before June 1935 O'Connor had generally aided the administration. But he was neither on good terms with the President nor in favor of the "death sentence," and he and many fellow Rules Committee members balked at granting a special rule of this kind.[48] They were afraid of retaliation on other issues by the many Democrats who feared going on record against the measure. O'Connor helped persuade his committee to refuse Rayburn's request: no record vote on the "death sentence" alone was allowed. For the first time the House Rules Committee emerged on the scene to play a role it would later perform with abandon: the "villain" in an otherwise pro-New Deal drama.

The bill accordingly had to run the gauntlet of an unruly

[47] *Time*, Jan. 14, 1935, p. 13.

[48] His brother Basil O'Connor, Roosevelt's former law partner, had in Nov. 1934 represented the Associated Gas and Electric Company, one of the more notorious of the holding companies. See O'Connor to Lowell Mellett, Aug. 16, 1935, Utility Holding Co. Bill File, O'Connor MSS.

House, and the events of the week ending July 4 revealed a remarkable display of congressional assertiveness. Opening the onslaught, Republicans encountered, as in the past, gibes from Democratic leaders. This time, however, cries of "Sit down," "Shut up," and "Let 'em talk" greeted Democratic interruptions. Sustained applause greeted a description of the Senate bill as "the most vicious, un-American proposition ever presented to Congress." Cheers gratified another member who referred to the modified committee version as one "born of obsession and nurtured on the milk of destruction."[49]

The next day Roosevelt passed the word, as he had done successfully in the Senate, that he might veto the more moderate House version. At this point George Huddleston of Alabama delivered one of those extraordinary congressional speeches which actually aroused those who heard it. Huddleston, a small, sixty-five-year-old veteran who had been a representative since 1915, had attracted little attention until this time. In committee he and Samuel B. Pettengill of Indiana, another anti-administration Democrat, had led the successful fight for the House version. Then came his big moment.

Proclaiming himself a believer in the "old fashioned Southern Democracy of Thomas Jefferson," Huddleston began by attacking the bureaucrats who drew up the bill. Corcoran and Cohen, he shouted, were "a couple of bright young men brought down from New York to teach Congress how to shoot." So confused was the bill that "a Philadelphia lawyer would get down on his knees and pray God to be delivered from the task of interpretation." He concluded with an eloquent appeal for representatives to follow him in casting off their shackles. "Whether it be the threat of the demagogues and the agitators, or whether it be to oppose

[49] *Congressional Record*, 74th Cong., 1st Sess. (Speeches by Cooper of Ohio and Wilson of Pa.), 10327, 10331-32.

the chief executive of this nation, I will do what I think right and all hell cannot stop me from it."[50]

When he finished, House members "jumped up and applauded for several minutes."[51] For the first time a Democrat had stood up in the House, excoriated a major administration proposal, and been cheered for his efforts. In forceful, emotional terms he had unleashed the frustrations that had mounted in many congressmen since the New Deal began.

The voting three days later indicated the depth of House feeling. Denied a record vote, administration forces called for a teller vote on the Senate "death sentence" version. By this procedure representatives simply filed to the well of the House, signifying their stands by going past one of two tellers, or counters, stationed at the ends of the aisles. The result would not record the stands of individual congressmen, but it would give a fair indication of sentiment. On this vote the rebels held their ranks, and the press reported a 224-152 vote against the "death sentence."[52] It was Roosevelt's first major defeat in the House. Encouraged, the rebels remained firm the next day. New Dealers, seeking to substitute the entire Senate bill (which included not only the "death sentence" but several other provisions to which even Rayburn objected), went down to defeat on a record vote, 258-147. The House Committee version then passed with ease, 323-81, with prolonged cheering again greeting the result.[53] The key 258-147 vote revealed the existence—for the first time since the New Deal began—of a conservative coalition in the House.

The most striking aspect of the vote was the number of deserting Democrats. Of the 319 House Democrats, 166, or

[50] *Ibid.*, pp. 10353-55.
[51] New York *Times*, June 29, 1935, p. 2.
[52] The tellers counted the vote as 216-146. Neither side claimed absolute accuracy in the confusion.
[53] New York *Times*, July 3, 1935, p. 2.

slightly more than half, bolted the administration, and 23 more failed to record themselves. Only 130 remained loyal. Since the 92 Republicans who joined the 166 could be counted upon to oppose any major New Deal measure, the 166 were a formidable number if they coalesced against future legislation.[54] Moreover, many of these Democrats were to become fairly consistent opponents of the New Deal.[55] More than in the Senate, the "death sentence" controversy was the breaking point for many unhappy Democrats. Annoyed at what they considered Roosevelt's undue hostility to private enterprise, frustrated for so long by his relentless leadership, and encouraged by the lobbying campaign against the "death sentence," House members saw a chance to oppose the President and get away with it. Having done so once, many did so again and again. This vote, coming the day before July 4, was indeed a congressional declaration of independence.

The epilogue was anticlimactic. To gain support for the Senate version, a Senate Lobby Committee under the zealous chairmanship of Senator Hugo L. Black of Alabama made

[54] As in the Senate, opposition to the "death sentence" was not sectional in nature, though congressmen from Pacific northwestern states were the most loyal to the administration. Among Democrats, opponents of the administration included 39 (of 70) easterners, 18 (of 32) border Democrats, 55 (of 99) southerners, and 19 (of 52) westerners. See n. 19 above for a definition of these sections.

There was also little correlation between length of service in the House and the voting on this bill. Of the 145 veteran Democrats (pre-1933), 80 opposed the administration; of 174 newcomers, 86 opposed. These were percentages of opposition, respectively, of 55 and 49. For Pettengill's reasons see Pettengill to FDR, Aug. 17, 1935, Roosevelt MSS, OF 293.

[55] Of the nearly 150 Democratic anti-"death sentence" representatives still in the House in 1937, 74 opposed the fair labor standards bill in Dec. 1937 (of 136 opposing Democrats in all); and 66 opposed the reorganization bill in 1938 (of 108 Democrats in all). In 1939, 31 of the 48 Democrats who opposed the spend-lend program of that year had also opposed the "death sentence," as had 45 of the 105 Democrats who voted to investigate the NLRB.

one sensational exposé of utility lobbyists after another. House rebels, however, composed a majority of the House conferees (Huddleston was one), and, remembering the slim Senate margin for the "death sentence," they refused to surrender. They even barred (and received House approval of their stand) author Cohen from the conferences.[56] On August 1 the House again held firm, voting down the "death sentence," this time 210-155, and for two more weeks Wheeler, chairman of the Senate conferees, let the conferences bog down completely.

Finally, the Senate yielded—slightly. Roosevelt authorized the Senate to accept a third version. It directed the SEC to permit holding companies to control more than one integrated utility system if such a system could not stand alone or if its operation did not harm localized management, efficient operation, or effective regulation. Otherwise, holding companies must limit themselves to one operating company and one subsidiary.[57] With relief the House, eager to escape a long hot Washington summer, authorized its conferees to accept the compromise by a vote of 219-142. This time 203 House Democrats voted for the compromise; 59, including Pettengill and Huddleston, remained opposed to the end. Backed by both houses, the conferees quickly agreed to the new version. On August 25 it finally passed both houses.

Who won? In terms of what had happened to previous efforts at regulation of public utilities, the final bill was an astonishing piece of reform legislation. Certainly, utility

[56] Joseph Alsop and Robert Kintner, in *Men Around the President* (New York, 1939), p. 182, told a revealing story about congressional opinions of men such as Cohen. Garner, meeting Byrnes during the fight, mentioned, "Whatever you think of these fellows [such as Cohen], you've got to admit they're smart." Byrnes answered, "You better look out or you'll find they're too damned smart."

[57] New York *Times*, Aug. 23, 1935, p. 1, and Aug. 24, p. 3, described the compromise version.

companies thought so; they immediately set out to negate it through the courts. And Roosevelt on signing it called it his greatest legislative victory.[58] He had received most of what he wanted even though he had faced an open rebellion in the House.

It was a costly triumph. Roosevelt's insistence upon the original version strained relations with many moderate congressmen in his own party. Eventually these men permitted compromise, but only grudgingly. As a conservative representative put it: "All the sensible Democrats in the Congress are sorely disturbed. . . . There are too many sheep being driven in the opposite direction." Democrats, he added, "have determined in their desperation to hang together, else they might hang separately."[59] Hang together they did in the hot summer of 1935, but only after Roosevelt had used some of his political ammunition.

Compared to the tax fight which simmered simultaneously in both houses, the utilities issue was but a momentary rebellion. Though the "death sentence" gained the support, however unenthusiastic, of Roosevelt's powerful congressional leaders, his tax plan did not. No issue prior to the court-packing controversy two years later did so much to undermine Roosevelt's Democratic congressional strength. It was over this controversy, Raymond Moley said later, "that the split in the Democratic Party began."[60]

Treasury Department officials presented a tax plan to Roosevelt in December 1934 aimed at taxing large concentrations of capital and stopping revenue leaks.[61] The President was not interested; in his annual message he declared he wanted no major changes in the tax structure, and as

[58] New York *Herald Tribune*, Aug. 27, 1935, p. 1.

[59] James Wadsworth to Edward R. Bolton, July 25, 1935, Wadsworth MSS, Box 28.

[60] *After Seven Years* (New York, 1939), p. 312.

[61] John M. Blum, *From the Morgenthau Diaries: Years of Crisis, 1928-1938* (Boston, 1959), pp. 298-305.

late as June 7 he told reporters, "I haven't thought of taxes or looked at taxes for a month."[62] Early in 1935, however, what the historian Charles A. Beard called "thunder on the left" awakened Roosevelt's political sensibilities. Senator Huey P. Long of Louisiana, crude and clownish but powerfully appealing, was converting thousands—perhaps millions—of depression-ridden Americans to his "Share the Wealth" plan, a demagogic scheme to "make every man a King" by redistributing income. In addition, a few key New Deal advisers, echoing the antimonopolism of Supreme Court Justice Louis D. Brandeis, were urging the President to press for a tax program that would destroy large concentrations of capital. Anxious to forestall the thunder on the left and angered by the hostility of wealthy conservatives, Roosevelt determined to act. In a message to Congress on June 19, he called for sweeping tax revisions, including a steep inheritance tax, an intercorporate dividend tax, a graduated corporation tax designed to increase rates on large corporations, an increased surtax rate on large personal incomes, and a gift tax on fortunes.[63] The proposal reflected an animus against great wealth and bigness. It was the most representative plan of the "second" New Deal.

Moderates as well as conservatives were appalled. One prominent national Republican figure wrote: "In the old days we were opposed by a party whose slogan was 'a tariff for revenue only.' Now the fact is, whatever the slogan may be, that it is a party which favors a tax not only for revenue, but for revenge."[64] Raymond Clapper, ordinarily a friendly journalist, criticized the political motive behind the message and then ridiculed its economic philosophy: "It looks to some

[62] Roosevelt Press Conference, June 7, 1935, 353 (Microfilm Transcript, Harvard University Archives).

[63] Samuel Rosenman (ed.), *The Public Papers and Addresses of Franklin D. Roosevelt*, IV (New York, 1938), 270-74.

[64] Charles D. Hilles to James Wadsworth, June 24, 1935, Wadsworth MSS, Box 28.

like an effort to drive business back to the horse and buggy stage by penalizing large units. . . ."[65]

Congressional critics joined in the assault. If anything, they wanted less, not more taxation. Robert L. ("Muley") Doughton of North Carolina, veteran chairman of the House Ways and Means Committee which was to start the bill through Congress, wrote, "I feel it would have been better to have delayed the matter, or perhaps better not to have brought it up at all. . . . I shall use my best efforts to keep it within a reasonable and conservative balance."[66]

Congressmen had other grievances. For one thing, conservatives noticed that the plan promised to harvest little additional revenue and that it would do little to balance the budget. For another, they resented the way in which Roosevelt had sprung it as a surprise, apparently gleeful at the discomfort he was creating. Ordinarily, American Congresses prior to 1935 had adjourned before the hot, muggy Washington weather inflamed tempers. In 1935, congressmen had planned to leave the city in mid-July. Then Roosevelt introduced this proposal at a time when Congress still had to deal with the utilities bill, a social security plan tied up in conference, and a coal bill which was to excite almost as much antagonism in the House as the "death sentence." The mood of Congress, wrote Turner Catledge in the New York *Times,* was "something like that of a small schoolboy who was being detained after hours to get his lessons, including a lesson which had not been given to him until the time for the three o'clock bell was in sight and his mind was on a baseball game in the neighborhood sandlot."[67]

[65] Washington *Post,* June 21, 1935, p. 2.

[66] To Thurmond Chatham, July 19, 1935, Doughton MSS, Folder 497. See also letters to Chatham, July 3, 1935, Folder 496, and June 27, 1935, Folder 494. For a description of Doughton see Robert S. Rankin sketch in Salter, *Public Men,* pp. 167-80.

[67] July 7, 1935, IV, 3.

An Oklahoma representative added, "it is disgusting to have to stay here and wrangle and the President keeps shooting new and more argumentative legislation to us. The Lord only knows when we will adjourn."[68]

Congressmen also complained that Roosevelt had left to them the nasty and unpopular details, giving them very little guidance. This was so. Roosevelt's message was a broad statement of policy objectives, not a carefully drawn piece of legislation, and Treasury Secretary Henry Morgenthau, Jr., was soon to throw the burden of decision upon confused congressmen: "The Treasury has not," he said, "and as long as I am secretary, is not going to have any views on an income tax bill."[69] The administration did not seem to be able to find a middle ground in gratifying congressional wishes on the procedure for introducing legislation: with the utilities bill congressmen resented presentation of a *fait accompli;* with the tax bill they resented the casual, ill-prepared way in which it was dropped in their laps.

Most of all, the plan appeared vindictive because it singled out a particular class of men for "punishment." This aspect of the plan accounted for its political appeal, but it also spawned the vehement and violent protests which emanated from conservatives. Encouraged by this outcry, many congressmen used the tax issue as another avenue away from the New Deal. As Moley phrased it later, the plan "stunned the Congressional leaders": "Those like Pat Harrison, who felt that *party loyalty* compelled them to support it, bled inwardly. Many, cut to the quick by the peremptory tone of the message, said bitterly 'they'd go down the line' this time, but that they'd be damned if they ever would under like circumstances. Others announced in the cloakrooms that, party loyalty or no party loyalty, they

[68] Wilburn Cartwright (Dem.) to "Shirley and Clifford," June 29, 1935, Cartwright MSS, Personal Correspondence 1934-1936.

[69] Quoted in Schlesinger, *Politics of Upheaval*, p. 332.

were going to turn the scheme inside out and show of what it was made."[70]

The events in the next few days transformed sullen resentment into outright hostility. Within a week Roosevelt faced the potential opposition not only of Republicans and irreconcilable Democrats but of his staunchest leaders as well. For this turn of events he was partly to blame.

When Roosevelt initiated the plan on June 19, the Senate Finance Committee was about to report a bill extending for two years various nuisance taxes which were to expire June 30. The next day it did so. At this point La Follette announced he would attempt to add to these taxes a rider incorporating not only Roosevelt's wealth tax but his own plan to raise revenue by reducing tax exemptions of middle-income groups.[71] On June 21 he succeeded in getting twenty-one other progressive senators to sign a round robin proclaiming they would keep the Senate in session until Roosevelt's measure was passed.[72]

Three days later Roosevelt held a strategy conference with congressional leaders at the White House. Present were Majority Leader Robinson, Finance Committee Chairman Harrison, Vice-President Garner, Speaker Byrns, and Doughton. After the meeting newsmen questioned the leaders on the White House steps. What, they asked, would the administration do to implement the tax message? Robinson replied that the Senate would proceed to add the tax plan to the nuisance-tax extension.[73] Pat Harrison obliged the next day by presenting a series of rates which, though bowing to congressional demands for more revenue, essentially reflected Roosevelt's desires.

The ensuing outcry forced New Dealers to reconsider. It did not require much intelligence to realize that this pro-

[70] *After Seven Years*, p. 312.
[71] New York *Times*, June 21, 1935, p. 1.
[72] *Ibid.*, June 22, 1935, p. 1.
[73] *Ibid.*, June 25, 1935, p. 1.

cedure was astonishingly hasty. What Roosevelt proposed was to enact a complex and already controversial tax program by tacking it casually on another minor measure, all in the space of six days. As the pro-New Deal New York *Daily News* wryly noted: "It took six days to make the world."[74]

As if this were not enough, Roosevelt then proceeded to make matters worse at a press conference the next day. Although he had said nothing following the previous day's strategy meeting, reporters naturally assumed that he had authorized Robinson's statement and Harrison's plans. Pressing Roosevelt closely, a newsman then asked if the nuisance taxes would be void if not passed by June 30, a Saturday. The following exchange ensued:

Roosevelt: What made you assume that there was any possibility of passing a complete new tax measure for these three recommendations by Saturday?

Reporter: That is what Harrison indicated, that it is costing you a million and a half a day if it is not passed.

Roosevelt: Did he say it would be passed on Saturday?

Reporter: He hoped so.

Reporter: I heard him say it, Mr. President.

Reporter: It is quoted in the record.

President: I did not know he said it. . . . I have never said anything to that effect and you can go back and look at the record.

He added, "I am not Congress. I am just a person down here to make recommendations. I feel I must make this clear in fairness to myself."[75]

Roosevelt was too clever. Suspecting that public opinion was disturbed at the unseemly haste, he sought to absolve himself of blame. Nothing he said was untrue: he had not "said anything to that effect." But every newsman present knew—and many said so in print—that Roosevelt had

[74] Quoted in Schlesinger, *Politics of Upheaval*, p. 331.
[75] See Press Conference, V, 385-88, microfilm transcript, Harvard University Archives.

implied that his congressional stalwarts were liars. Had
Robinson and Harrison been enthusiastic New Dealers,
Roosevelt's circumlocution might not have disturbed them.
But both senators already had reservations about the New
Deal. Their viewpoints represented a brand of moderate
conservatism that was to become increasingly trying to the
administration, especially after 1936.

Robinson, sometimes described as "bullish," "vile-tem-
pered," and "brutal," was not the easy-going genial leader
one might have expected.[76] But he was enormously powerful. A senator since 1912, he had been Democratic leader
since the early 1920's. Most of the senior Democratic senators
in the 1930's owed him countless favors for the support he
had given them over the years.

He was also inherently conservative. During the 1920's
he had consistently opposed government development of
Muscle Shoals, and under the New Deal he had been less
than happy as early as 1933.[77] To begin with, he feared the
effect of NRA labor codes upon southern industry. Moreover, he and Roosevelt—the one blunt and forceful, the other
cheery and indirect—failed to develop warm personal relations. Above all, Robinson disliked deficit spending. If
continued, he wrote in 1935, it would "bankrupt the country
and tend to centralize all power in the national government."[78]

Fortunately for the administration, Robinson had remained loyal. Party faith was one reason: like many other
southerners who had suffered in the Republican Congresses
of the 1920's, Robinson was anxious that the Democratic

[76] For studies of Robinson see Drew Pearson and Robert S. Allen, *More
Merry-Go-Round* (New York, 1932), pp. 340-44; Alsop and Catledge, *The
168 Days,* pp. 219-22; and Nevin E. Neal, "A Biography of Joseph T.
Robinson" (unpublished Ph.D. dissertation, University of Oklahoma, 1957).
Also "The Senator from Arkansas," *Fortune,* XV (Jan. 1937), 88.

[77] Neal, "Robinson," pp. 217-18.

[78] To Henry G. Riegler, June 7, 1935. Cited in *ibid.,* p. 413.

party hold together in the 1930's. Patronage was another. "You can't imagine the hell I have to go through," he once complained to his friend Carter Glass. "In your case, Joe," snapped Glass, "the road seems to be lined with post offices."[79] Also, the New Deal left sensitive southern problems alone. As one observer put it crudely, Robinson's loyalty was understandable: "so long as they [New Dealers] fought the money power and the big industries—so long as they were pro-farmer and did not stir up the niggers—he was with them."[80] Finally, Robinson enjoyed his prestigious post. Facing a reelection struggle in 1936 and realizing that neither he nor the party would benefit from an open break, Robinson had wisely stayed with the New Deal.[81]

Harrison was Robinson's complement in the Senate leadership. Where Robinson was blunt and ferocious, Harrison, nicknamed the "Grey Fox of the Delta," was smooth and conciliatory.[82] Though he had been a congressman since 1910 and a senator since 1918, he was perhaps best known to the public for his humorous sallies against Republicans in the 1920's and early 1930's.[83] Few senators of his time were so adept at remaining friendly with all factions.

Like his friend Robinson, Harrison was basically conservative. His depression remedy of 1933 had been to end prohibition, balance the budget, ease farm credits, lower income-tax exemptions to obtain more revenue, stabilize

[79] Joseph Alsop and Robert Kintner, "Joe Robinson, The New Deal's Old Reliable," *Saturday Evening Post*, CCIX (Sept. 26, 1936), 5.

[80] For an assessment emphasizing Robinson's loyalty, see Travis M. Adams, "The Arkansas Congressional Delegation During the New Deal, 1933-1936" (unpublished M.A. thesis, Vanderbilt University, 1962), esp. pp. 248-49.

[81] "The Senator from Arkansas," p. 102.

[82] "The United States Senate," *Fortune*, XI (Feb. 1935), 134. See also Joseph and Stewart Alsop, *The Reporter's Trade* (New York, 1958), p. 20.

[83] Paul Mallon, "Swordsman of the Senate," *Today*, III (Dec. 8, 1934), 5. In his best-known speech along these lines he had belittled Agriculture Department pamphlets entitled "The Love Life of a Bullfrog," and "How to Dress for a Sun Bath."

foreign exchanges, and pass a reciprocal trade law.[84] An idolizer of Woodrow Wilson, he approved of measures to curb the "money power," to improve world trade, and to give limited aid to distressed sectors of the economy; for more fundamental measures he had—and continued to have —little use. He especially feared inflationary measures. "Your lifetime and mine," he said in 1933, "depend for their fullness upon the credit of the government."[85]

Despite these reservations, Harrison also remained loyal, and his services to the administration were very important. As chairman of the Finance Committee he reported out the NRA, social security, and reciprocal trade bills.[86] His smooth handling of these and other measures was admired and appreciated by the administration.

The reasons for his support were similar to Robinson's. First of all, Harrison was personally friendly with Roosevelt and had been since their days in the Wilson administration.[87] Second, patronage and pork helped him in Mississippi.[88] Finally, he liked his nearness to power. Facing reelection in 1936, he did not relish a break. Before the introduction of the wealth tax, Harrison's reasons for remaining loyal to the New Deal considerably outweighed his reservations.

Neither senator aired publicly his fury at Roosevelt's tax strategy. Robinson was at first so angry that he threatened to publicize a written Roosevelt memo on the tax

[84] New York *Times*, Feb. 4, 1933, p. 2.

[85] Cited in C. O'Neal Gregory, "Pat Harrison and the New Deal" (unpublished M.A. thesis, University of Mississippi, 1960), p. 39.

[86] Robinson, valuing his friend's talents, sent as much potentially controversial legislation as possible to Harrison's Finance Committee.

[87] Gregory, "Harrison," pp. 17-25.

[88] Note, for instance, this example of Harrison's campaign methods in 1936. "Pat Harrison has secured more money per capita for needy Mississippians than any other state has received. Pat Harrison has obtained for state schools millions of dollars. Pat Harrison has supported and fought for New Deal legislation that has brought hundreds of millions of dollars into Mississippi, a state which pays only a few million dollars in Federal taxes." *Ibid.*, pp. 75-76.

strategy devised at the conference; it took the entire Roosevelt high command to pacify him.[89] But when reporters reached him for comment, he "retreated into an attitude of humor on the whole proceeding and simply laughed at the suggestion that the course of events was curious."[90]

For Harrison the ordeal was equally harrowing. A fiscal conservative, he had not favored the wealth tax from the start, especially since it came as a complete surprise. His initial reaction to the plan had been not far from Roosevelt's glib prediction to Moley: "Pat Harrison's going to have kittens on the spot."[91] Yet he had swallowed his doubts and was weakly defending the new strategy to fellow senators when Roosevelt's press statement reached him. Always quick on his feet, Harrison met newsmen shortly afterward. "Whatever erroneous impression may have gone out to the country," he said, "do not blame it on the President. I take it on my shoulders. So let's close this page and not talk any more about it."[92]

Thanks to the silence of his leaders, the page did remain closed; a serious intraparty brawl failed to erupt. But this incident, minor though it may seem, revealed Roosevelt's occasional carelessness with congressional leaders; it continued to rankle these two men, who felt that Roosevelt did not appreciate their devotion. Primarily because they were leaders, they held their tongues. But henceforth they were watchful and suspicious, and Harrison was later to defect on a number of occasions. The incident also annoyed their friends in the Senate, and over the years they had enjoyed a good many, to the point that even Republicans arose the next day to defend Harrison's integrity. Finally, it meant the end of the strategy to rush the bill. Roosevelt's

[89] Alsop and Kintner, "Joe Robinson, The New Deal's Old Reliable," p. 5.
[90] New York *Times*, June 27, 1935, p. 2.
[91] Moley, *After Seven Years*, p. 310.
[92] Washington *Post*, June 28, 1935, p. 1. For more on Harrison's reactions see *Literary Digest*, July 6, 1935, p. 4.

actions on the tax issue had helped to make its passage difficult almost from the start.

The bill then foundered while Doughton's committee heard six weeks of generally conservative testimony, emerging on the House floor on July 30. Though similar in many respects to the original version, it was essentially the committee's creation. It removed the intercorporate dividend tax, reduced Roosevelt's proposed progressive corporate rates, and substituted an excess-profits tax to raise revenue.[93] Tempered to meet House objections, it passed on August 5. The final vote of 282-96 included only 18 Democratic opponents, 5 of whom were Virginians.[94]

The Senate by this time was thoroughly anxious to escape a hot Washington summer that had taken an unusually heavy toll. Some fifty congressmen were sick, and Dr. Copeland had already remarked unhappily, "I don't think I've ever seen Congress in such bad shape."[95] The usual pressures of the closing weeks of a session were all the more intense, with cotton-bloc congressmen fighting for higher crop loans, the utilities bill still deadlocked in conference committee, neutrality legislation to be considered, and veterans' bonus advocates again pressing for action.

Eager to escape before these lobbies succeeded, Harrison worked for compromise. After two weeks of frantic maneuvering during which La Follette's plans almost succeeded, his committee reported a somewhat softened tax bill.[96] It

[93] New York *Times*, July 30, 1935, p. 1; July 31, 1935, p. 16.

[94] *Congressional Record*, 74th Cong., 1st Sess., 12499.

[95] New York *Times*, July 14, 1935, IV, 1.

[96] Conservatives split on the La Follette amendment to lower exemptions on middle-income tax brackets. For it were such Finance Committee conservatives as King, George, Byrd, and Gerry. Against it, however, were Bailey, Lonergan, and Metcalf (a conservative Republican from Rhode Island). Those in favor thought of bringing in more revenue; those conservatives against it feared that La Follette and others would urge additional spending. This conservative division over taxation persisted throughout the decade and was evidence that conservatism was not—and is not—easy to define.

removed the inheritance tax, increased the estate tax, restored the tax on intercorporate dividends, and deleted the House excess-profits tax.[97] Adeptly handled by Harrison on the floor, it escaped additional amendments and passed on August 15, 57-22.[98] As in the House, smooth leadership work had prevented protracted debate on the floor, and only ten Senate Democrats remained dissatisfied enough to oppose it on the final vote.[99] A conference committee quickly reconciled the two versions, and Roosevelt signed the measure on August 31. Shortly afterward, Congress finally adjourned.

Once again Roosevelt could fairly claim a victory. The law raised top surtax rates on individual incomes from 59 to 75 percent. It also included graduated corporate taxes and dividend taxes. Though it is perhaps a little strong to call it, as one expert has, a "landmark in the history of American taxation," it was a definite step away from Republican tax policies of the 1920's.[100] Even with better tactics, it is doubtful that any President could have received much more, and it is certain that few important tax bills had ever passed so quickly.

It was a Pyrrhic victory. Moderate congressional Democrats who had begun to lose enthusiasm during the struggle for the "death sentence" hardened in their opposition. Roosevelt's handling of the tax plan aroused the suspicions not only of conservatives but of his previously loyal leaders as well. The tax bill was the most divisive issue in Congress of all controversies of his first term.

The 1935 Congress was a glorious triumph for the New Deal and for Roosevelt's personal popularity. "More legisla-

[97] Blum, *Morgenthau Diaries,* pp. 304-305.

[98] *Congressional Record,* 74th Cong., 1st Sess., 13254.

[99] They were Byrd, Glass, and Tydings of the old irreconcilables, and Adams (Colorado), Burke, Copeland, Gerry, Lonergan, Moore, and McCarran. Bailey continued to tread carefully and voted for it; Gore did not record himself.

[100] Blum, *Morgenthau Diaries,* p. 305. See Randolph E. Paul, *Taxation in the United States* (Boston, 1954), pp. 183-88.

tion of far-reaching social and economic consequence was enacted last year," wrote one disgruntled but awe-struck Republican, "than in any previous session—and yet every one of the extraordinary new laws was passed by a Congress which operated for the most part in a complete fog and without any understanding of the ultimate meaning of its own actions. The chief distinction of the Congress was the docility with which it played the rubber stamp to F.D.R., a performance never equalled in the history of legislatures since those rump Parliaments which, under the Stuarts, so seriously jeopardized English liberty in the seventeenth century."[101] Even discounting the partisanship and exaggeration of this statement, this was the ultimate tribute to Roosevelt's strong and successful leadership.

In retrospect, however, it is possible to see some trouble spots which went relatively unnoticed at the time. Roosevelt had entered the session consistently opposed in the Senate by only five irreconcilable Democrats and sixteen Republican conservatives. Three or four more Democratic senators had occasionally proven unreliable. When the session closed, some nineteen of the seventy Democratic senators had voted against at least two of the seven key New Deal measures enacted.[102] Average Democratic opposition on these seven key roll calls was fourteen, or 20 percent, as opposed to 7 percent on the major measures of the 1933-

[101] Lester J. Dickinson, "What's the Matter with Congress?" *American Mercury*, XXXVII (Feb. 1936), 129. Dickinson was then a Republican senator from Iowa.

[102] The nineteen (with number of adverse votes cast) were: Byrd (6), Glass (6), Tydings (5), Gore (4), Burke (4), Gerry (4), Copeland (3), Bailey (3), Moore (3), Smith (3), Walsh (3), Coolidge (2), Clark (2), Lonergan (2), Dieterich (2), King (2), George (2), Donahey (2), and Bulkley (2). Holt was a twentieth but did not sit in time to vote on many issues. The bills considered were: World Court, WPA, Dieterich Amendment, Wagner National Labor Relations Act, Social Security, Wealth Tax, and Guffey Coal Bill. The figures would be slightly higher had key amendments been included.

1934 session. Furthermore, these Democrats were to vote reluctantly, if at all, for the New Deal in future years. Among them the nineteen conservative Democrats accounted for 60 of the 100 adverse Democratic votes on these roll calls. With the help of sixteen Republican conservatives, this group of nineteen formed a loose coalition large enough to create annoying delay. A shift of some ten to fifteen Democratic moderates such as Harrison or Byrnes would be enough in the future to smash carelessly introduced or overly "radical" administration proposals.

A similar situation existed in the House. There, Roosevelt entered the 1935 session with an extremely dependable body. In the 1933-1934 Congress an average of only 25, or 8 percent, of the 311 House Democrats had voted against the nine key measures of the Congress. In 1935 the average was 61, or 19 percent. Together with 90 conservative Republicans, this group totalled some 150 on many controversial issues and needed only some 70 more moderates to constitute a majority. On the utilities bill 166 Democrats had deserted; on a coal bill applying minimum standards to the coal industry, 100 Democrats defected, and it barely passed 194-168.

The percentage of conservatively inclined Democrats more than doubled during this session, despite the apparently liberal mandate of the 1934 election. In both houses, a loose and unpremeditated voting coalition of Republicans and conservative Democrats could muster nearly 40 percent of the votes on some, though by no means all, key issues. Easily another 30 percent was still doggedly loyal but by no means enthusiastic. At the end of the session Roosevelt was in control, and the conservatives were by no means united, but he had to watch his step: his magic had diminished.

The reasons for this conservative growth were varied, yet certainly the changing nature of the New Deal was one.

It was not by accident that such fundamental reforms as the Wagner Act and social security passed Congress with less controversy than the utilities and wealth-tax plans. The first two were structural reforms involving a certain amount of federal government planning and responsibility for the public welfare. The latter were efforts, at least in part, to strike down large business combinations. To many congressmen they appeared vindictive, absurd, and even a little unrealistic. Furthermore, these bills encountered intense business opposition of which many congressmen were extremely conscious. "As you notice by the papers," wrote one key Democratic congressman, "we are having a very hectic time, and, of course, confidentially, I feel that the trend of the country is running pretty strongly against the President's policies, and our actions are getting many vehement criticisms. . . . The boys are all getting letters from their Democratic county chairmen and committeemen just repudiating our whole business. . . . That is the situation. All the Democrats are feeling the effects of it, especially us people from doubtful districts who are bound to be confronted with a fusillade of criticism."[103] The "second" New Deal, such as it may be defined, may in retrospect appear to have been more conservative than the first, but to many congressmen at the time it was considerably more explosive politically.

Raymond Moley has suggested other reasons for the increased congressional opposition of the 1935 session. Writing three years later as a disenchanted New Dealer, Moley felt that the 1935 session was the beginning of Roosevelt's congressional problems. "There were two clear reasons," he said, "why F.D.R.'s wishes carried less weight with the 74th Congress than with the 73rd: most of the patronage had

---

[103] Edward T. Taylor to William Bankhead, July 3, 1935. Cited in Walter J. Heacock, "William Brockman Bankhead: A Biography" (unpublished Ph.D. dissertation, University of Wisconsin, 1952), p. 204. Taylor, a Democrat from Colorado, was acting majority leader in the absence of Bankhead, who was ill the entire session.

been given out, and the administration itself, rather than Congress alone, had to face an election in 1936."[104] As a result, Moley explained, Roosevelt tended to view each issue in terms of the 1936 election and became unnecessarily demanding and stubborn in his dealings with Congress.

Unquestionably, Roosevelt's congressional tactics were not above reproach. He tended to be breezy and jaunty to visiting congressmen;[105] some he offended over patronage matters; others he did not have time to see at all.[106] As one critic has pointed out, he did not work very hard at cultivating strong party relations with loyal rank-and-file members, tending instead to rely heavily upon his leaders.[107] These do not, however, seem to have been fatal faults. No President could possibly hope to please all his congressmen, and Roosevelt's charm certainly captivated many more than it offended. As for his reputed failure to work with his rank and file, there are limits to a President's time, and working with his leaders was generally successful. These adverse criticisms miss the heart of Roosevelt's chief weaknesses as revealed in the tax and utilities fights.

In both struggles his main fault was in carelessly insisting upon his own way even though it was not always substantively important. His demand for the "death sentence," in the face of a House revolt and despite the insignificant difference between the House and the Senate versions, was not worth the price. Yet it was understandable, for Wheeler might have deserted him in disgust had Roosevelt not been so uncompromising. His handling of the tax bill, however, revealed him to be, admitted an admirer, "a poor general

[104] *After Seven Years,* p. 302.

[105] Jerry Voorhis, *Confessions of a Congressman* (New York, 1948), pp. 175-76, commented upon Roosevelt's casual manner with visiting congressmen.

[106] See Glass's fury in this context in Ickes, *Secret Diary,* I, 318, March 14, 1935.

[107] James M. Burns, *Roosevelt: The Lion and the Fox* (New York, 1956), pp. 347-49, emphasized this point.

and a happy warrior."[108] To throw it at Congress without consulting his legislative leaders, at a time when most of them were eager to go home, was careless procedure. To try to push it through in one week was unrealistic. And to conclude by denying that he had tried to do so was a slap in the faces of his chief aides. Only his continued great popularity with the people and the loyalty of his leaders saved him from a rebuff.

The 1935 tax bill was also an apt example of what would later be revealed as Roosevelt's chief weakness in congressional relations: his love of surprising, dramatic presidential action. In the crisis days of 1933 such dramatics had seemed to work; certainly they had been psychologically valuable in reviving a despairing people. But in 1935 they failed to move many suspicious congressmen. Such men were not very impressed by verbal fireworks. The tax bill, with its political appeal of taxing a few while leaving the masses alone, scraped through in a form reasonably close to Roosevelt's original demands. Later, with less appealing measures, Roosevelt would not be so fortunate.

Roosevelt also underestimated congressional caution. Congressional Democrats, safely embedded in their seats under a popular administration, tried to keep things that way. As early as March, Rayburn, Byrnes, Pittman and others had agreed that when the session was over (and they had not expected a tax bill) Roosevelt should "ask for no further legislation and no further appropriations for relief."[109] McNary, a full year earlier, had felt the same way. "I find here," he said, "the same unrest and feeling of uncertainty that I feel obtained in the past. I wish the

[108] Drew Pearson and Robert Allen, Aug. 24, 1935 (syndicated column). They also stressed that Roosevelt had poor leadership in the House, and that Roosevelt's chief weakness was lack of planning, especially on the tax and banking bills.

[109] Pittman to Adm. Cary T. Grayson, March 30, 1935, Pittman MSS, Box 12.

President would make a statement concerning his program so that business could adjust itself thereto. I think he could say, 'This is my program and only a great emergency will cause me to add a chapter.' "[110] These men, well before the summer of 1935 was over, had become uneasy at Roosevelt's constant motion, his fondness for introducing sweeping new plans at any time. Roosevelt, so brilliant at exciting public support, sometimes failed to appreciate the degree to which congressmen, dependent upon powerful interests in their constituencies, preferred a moderate course.

In the last analysis the fundamental reason for the growth of congressional conservatism in 1935 was not presidential failure but the instinctive feeling among basically conservative congressmen that the New Deal had gone far enough —or too far. These men had not become more conservative; from the start they had supported the New Deal partly because it had seemed a conservative way to deal with a revolutionary impasse. But once the emergency seemed to be diminishing, they began to express their thoughts openly. These men reflected the feelings of many Americans who were beginning to think in terms of security rather than innovation. Said Lippmann, himself becoming estranged from the New Deal:

As the forces of recovery grow stronger, the people will be more eager for a government which promises to let them consolidate their gains and begin to enjoy what they regard as their normal standard in life. They will be conservative. They will be inter-

110 To Senator James Couzens, Aug. 14, 1934, McNary MSS. Another urging caution was Secretary of Commerce Daniel Roper. See Roper to McIntyre, March 6, 1935, Roosevelt MSS, OF 3. See especially O'Connor MSS, Election Results File, 1935, in which many Democratic congressmen wrote O'Connor in the fall of 1935 to give their impressions of the New Deal and its future course. Several of these urged caution. Many agreed with Rep. Percy Gassaway (Dem.-Okla.), who wrote, "I sincerely wish the President would let us go home and let the people of this country carefully study some of the newly proposed legislation. . . ." Letter to Rev. C. C. Morris, July 6, 1935, Gassaway MSS, 1935 Correspondence.

ested in quiet government, in solid and steadfast leaders, in the deflation of public activity. Whether Mr. Roosevelt, given his temperament, his social ideals, his political affiliations, can transform himself into the kind of President the American people like when they are normally prosperous—this is the great question for him and his party. It will be one of the most difficult personal adjustments that a political leader ever made, and I am not sure Mr. Roosevelt would even wish to make it if he could.[111]

Roosevelt was still strong enough in 1935 to succeed with Congress, but many moderates and conservatives were ready for a rest. As publisher Roy Howard phrased it to Roosevelt when the session was over, it was time for a "breathing spell . . . and a recess from further experimentation." The President answered agreeably, "the breathing spell of which you speak is here—very decidedly so."[112] Upon the interpretation of this "breathing spell" would depend his future relations with congressional conservatives.

[111] *Yale Review*, Sept. 1935, pp. 6-8. See also Clapper, Washington *Post*, July 13, 1935, p. 2. For evidence of this more conservative temper, see Robert and Helen Lynd, *Middletown in Transition* (New York, 1937).

[112] Moley, *After Seven Years*, pp. 317-18. Howard's letter is widely quoted.

3

SENATE REALIGNMENTS: THE
COURT CONTROVERSY

COMPARED to the hot summer of 1935, the next year and
a half was relatively peaceful. During this interlude
few congressmen changed their opinions of Roosevelt and
the New Deal, and the 1936 session was generally free of
serious controversy, mainly because Roosevelt and Congress
alike were anxious to avoid altercations in an election year.[1]
Congress again passed a veterans' bonus bill, but because
Roosevelt knew it was fruitless to pose serious opposition,
no bitterness developed. Congress failed to pass a new coal
act, a housing act, and a food and drug act, but Roosevelt,
hurrying to adjourn Congress, did not insist upon passage.[2]

Taxes were again the most divisive issue of the session.
Needing new revenue to pay veterans' bonuses and to com-
pensate for funds lost when the Supreme Court invalidated
AAA processing taxes, Roosevelt called for a graduated tax

on undistributed corporate profits. He hoped to raise additional revenue to strike against economic bigness and to increase purchasing power by forcing corporations to distribute these profits in the form of dividends.[3]

The plan caused the same kind of hostility among conservatives as had the 1935 bill, but Harrison and Doughton again helped to find a compromise after a long and at times acrimonious struggle.[4] Thus although the issue left no major scars, Roosevelt in introducing it revealed that "breathing spell" did not mean retreat, and conservatives in fighting it despaired more than ever of coming to terms with the New Deal.[5] Eighteen Senate Democrats (plus two paired against) remained opposed on the final 42-29 vote. When the session closed in June, many Democrats continued to back the New Deal out of caution rather than sympathy. As Glass wrote, "I have heard many Senators in the cloakroom denounce in unmeasured terms so-called New Deal experiments and then go through the swinging doors when the roll was called and vote for them."[6]

[1] O. R. Altman, "Second Session of the 74th Congress," *American Political Science Review*, XXX (Dec. 1936), 1086-1107.

[2] See Raymond Clapper, "Can Congress Come Back?" *Review of Reviews*, XCIII (Feb. 1936), 29-31, for the main issues of the session.

[3] John M. Blum, *From the Morgenthau Diaries: Years of Crisis, 1928-1938* (Boston, 1959), pp. 305-19. See also Randolph E. Paul, *Taxation in the United States* (Boston, 1954), pp. 188-99.

[4] Concerning this tax Doughton sneered, "we have had too many theories in key places under this administration." To Alex Howard, June 27, 1936, Doughton MSS, Folder 561.

[5] The Democrats opposed were Adams (Colo.), Bailey, Bilbo (Miss.), Bulkley, Burke, Byrd, Clark, Copeland, Gerry, Glass, Holt, Lonergan, Moore, Murphy (Iowa), Pittman, Russell, Tydings, and Walsh. Coolidge and McCarran were paired against it. George, Gore, and Smith were not recorded. Except for Bilbo, Murphy, and Russell, these were votes from men already known for anti-New Deal sentiments.

For an irate GOP reaction, see James W. Wadsworth to Mrs. Ernest Adee, April 25, 1936, Wadsworth MSS, Box 24.

[6] To Dr. R. E. Blackwell, July 25, 1936, Glass MSS, Box 345.

If particular measures such as the tax bill perturbed certain congressmen, federal bureaucracy agitated them still more. Some veterans such as Pittman had privately grumbled about New Deal administrative agencies well before 1935. Accustomed to deference from the executive branch, these men considered Hopkins, Ickes, Wallace, and their subordinates hostile or at best indifferent to the claims and complaints emanating from Capitol Hill. And newcomers such as Burke of Nebraska and Holt of West Virginia had come to oppose the New Deal at least partly because they found executive officials unresponsive to their political demands.

This feeling was not limited to the Senate. In November 1935 John O'Connor wrote Democratic congressmen asking for their comments regarding the administration. Responses were generally favorable, but a recurring complaint was that executive agencies failed to appreciate the needs of congressmen. "I am frank to say," one Democrat wrote O'Connor, "that the Personnel situation with regard to these alphabetical organizations has certainly not helped the Democratic Party in this section. . . ." Another thought "it would be helpful if Federal agencies and departments would be more cooperative with individual members of Congress. . . . WPA is so muddled that you do not know from one day's end until the next whether a project is going to go forward or eventually be rejected."[7]

It is difficult to say how many moderate Democrats came to feel this way by 1937, and it is impossible to state categorically that these moderates opposed specific programs in

[7] These sentiments were expressed, respectively, by Graham A. Barden (N. C.) and Dow W. Harter (Ohio), on Nov. 21, 1935 and Nov. 11, 1935, O'Connor MSS, Comments on Election Results File, 1935. Barden became known as one of the most anti-union members of the House. His first term began in 1935. Harter, a freshman in 1933, was ordinarily a New Deal supporter.

the ensuing two or three years because of such sentiments.[8] But there is no doubt that congressmen were especially sensitive on the subject of these agencies. By 1937 this sensitivity was sufficiently strong to be one of the many ingredients composing congressional obstructiveness.

The election of 1936 was a final factor influencing congressional opinion. Roosevelt, running serenely on his past record and his personality, scarcely mentioned his opponent. As Pittman wrote the President, "this is one campaign in which there is but one issue and one speaker, and that is you."[9] The result was an astonishing personal victory. Receiving 60.4 percent of the popular vote, the President carried every state except Maine and Vermont. His margin of eleven million was unsurpassed until 1964.[10] But his most remarkable achievement was awakening the political consciousness of many millions of previously indifferent men and women. Most of these were from the "forgotten" elements of society: the "one third of ill-housed, ill-clad, and ill-nourished," the Negroes, union men, farmers, immigrants, and relief workers. It was a significantly new voting coalition, and one which in months to come would provide insistent and all but irresistible pressure for its own particular interests.[11]

[8] Samuel Hays, in "New Possibilities for American Political History: The Social Analysis of Political Life" (paper delivered before American Historical Association, Washington, D. C., Dec. 1964) emphasizes these factors. See esp. p. 8.

[9] To FDR, Oct. 17, 1936, Pittman MSS, Box 14. For another good discussion of Roosevelt's air of nonpartisanship, see James M. Burns, *Roosevelt: The Lion and the Fox* (New York, 1956), p. 276.

[10] Malcolm Moos, *The Republicans: A History of Their Party* (New York, 1956), p. 392; Cortez A. M. Ewing, *Congressional Elections, 1896-1944* (Norman, Okla., 1947), *passim;* and Harry W. Morris, "The Republicans in a Minority Role, 1933-1938" (unpublished Ph.D. dissertation, State University of Iowa, 1960), pp. 170-80.

[11] See Arthur N. Holcombe, *The Middle Classes in American Politics* (Cambridge, Mass., 1940), for one of many sources commenting on this coalition. See also Samuel Lubell, *The Future of American Politics* (2nd rev.

Congressional results were also favorable. Democrats gained six seats in the Senate for a record total of seventy-six. Sixteen Republicans, Farmer-Laborite Shipstead, Progressive La Follette, Norris (who called himself an Independent), and Ernest Lundeen, a new Farmer-Laborite from Minnesota, composed the rest. In the House Democrats gained 12 seats for a record high of 331, while Republicans dropped to a modern low of 89. Completing the total were 13 Farmer-Laborites and Progressives. In both houses Democrats crowded the tiny Republican bands into small huddles, and in the Senate there were so many new Democrats that veterans were asked to share congressional patronage with them.[12]

Conservative prospects had never looked so bleak. In the Senate four of the five original irreconcilable Democrats returned, as did fourteen other Democrats whose prior records had stamped them as generally unreliable. The number of conservative or unenthusiastic Senate Democrats remaining in 1937 was eighteen: the election had left them relatively unharmed. But since conservative Republicans numbered only ten, total conservative strength was only twenty-eight, or some eight to ten less than at the end of the 1935 session. One more fact was also clear: conservative Democrats outnumbered all Republicans. If a conservative renaissance was to develop, it would have to begin as a split within the New Deal coalition.

---

ed., New York, 1956), pp. 1-60; Walter Johnson, *1600 Pennsylvania Avenue* (Boston, 1960), pp. 76-82; and Samuel J. Eldersfeld, "The Influence of Metropolitan Party Pluralities in Presidential Elections Since 1920," *American Political Science Review*, XLIII (Dec. 1949), 1189-1206.

[12] For statistical studies of the new Congress, see O. R. Altman, "First Session of the 75th Congress," *American Political Science Review*, XXXI (Dec. 1937), 1071-94. Also see Raymond Clapper, "Leadership in Congress," *Review of Reviews*, XCV (Jan. 1937), 47-51. Some interesting statistics: the average ages were fifty-nine in the Senate and fifty-two in the House (roughly the same as 1933); 70 of the 96 senators were lawyers; and 269 of the representatives started their service during the New Deal era.

A similar situation existed in the House. Here, too, the election did no serious damage to the anti-New Deal Democrats, for most of them represented safe conservative districts. Roughly 30 Democrats who had already openly criticized many aspects of the New Deal returned. Together with some 80 conservative Republicans, they formed a conservative voting bloc of roughly 110, again slightly less than in 1935. One Republican congressman moaned, "the overwhelming Democratic majority is inclined to put through whatever the President wants and equally inclined to prevent the passage of any legislation which he does not want."[13]

As the 1937 session opened, conservatives, even if they were all voting and able to agree, could rely upon no more than 28 senators and 110 of the 435 representatives. If they were to stop Roosevelt's programs in the future, they would need some 20 more senators and 110 representatives. The 1935 session had shown that such numbers were by no means impossible, for there were more than enough moderates whose loyalty had already been extended. But conservative prospects were distinctly unencouraging; if Roosevelt acted moderately, his congressional opponents appeared doomed to a series of defeats.

Many conservatives, notably the old irreconcilable Democrats, remained stubbornly optimistic. Their letters indicate that even in these darkest days they were conferring with one another, seeking to stop further advances of the New Deal. Glass had run for reelection mainly to be able to continue his opposition. "I think it vastly more important," he wrote Tydings just before the election, "to have men of our type in Congress than to elect a President."[14] Bailey was convinced that his election was a mandate for con-

[13] Carl Mapes (Mich.) to Abbott L. Norris, Jan. 30, 1937, Norris Family Papers.
[14] Oct. 9, 1936, Glass MSS, Box 380.

servatism. "I am going back as a conservative," he wrote, "and I am a conservative by nature."[15] "My course in the Senate," he told Dieterich, "did not adversely affect my standing before our people. The election did not change my views and will not change my course. I think it quite salutary that the conservative leadership has been transferred by the election from the Republican side to the Democratic side. It will be more effectual from our side. We can manage to go along with the President and at the same time sustain moderately constructive policies."[16]

These men, forlorn though their hopes seemed at the time, intended to stop Roosevelt and the New Deal. Senator Peter G. Gerry of Rhode Island, a staunch Democratic conservative, wrote his friend Bailey, "eventually there are bound to be splits in Washington, and I agree with you that if we will stick to fundamental principles and fight for the constitution we are going to have much more to say in the future than the people now think."[17] And Bailey, safe for six years from Roosevelt's electoral magic, was actively urging the formation of a conservative bloc. "I intend," he said, "to maintain the conservative course and to cut through regardless in 1940 towards the conservative objectives. This implies a new line-up in America, but I believe the conservatives will be able to win the battle." He pointed out that a 10 percent shift—this was a little optimistic—could swing Congress to the conservative side: "This shift can be brought about but I question whether it can be brought about by the Republican leadership. In this view, it is fortunate that the conservative leadership may now pass to the Democratic side. There are conservatives in the Senate —Glass, George, Adams, Burke, Moore, King, Gerry, perhaps Smith, and surely myself, and some others of whom I have

15 To George G. Battle, Nov. 10, 1936, Bailey MSS, Political File.
16 Nov. 18, 1936, *ibid.*, General File.
17 Dec. 15, 1936, *ibid.*, Political File.

hopes, who can put forward the conservative policies and create the background for the contest of 1940."[18]

Conservative determination was present even among a few Republicans. Congressman Clifford R. Hope of Kansas, a moderate veteran, far from despairing the 1936 election, turned his thoughts to party realignment as a means of reviving his party. "Roosevelt," he wrote, "has put himself in a position where he and his group have become the party of the great cities and the industrial labor groups of this country. I, personally, cannot see where Agriculture stands to mean anything by tying up with that alignment so that it seems to me a logical division would be that of the South and West against the cities and industrial centers of the East."[19] And Joseph W. Martin, Jr., of Massachusetts, a GOP House leader, wrote enthusiastically at the start of the session: "There is an excellent spirit among the few Republicans and hope is not entirely vanished. Tides ebb and flow."[20] Though few Republicans shared the optimism of Hope and Martin, they were ready to obstruct the New Deal.

Most of this conservative talk remained buried in private correspondence, and observers discounted conservative chances. Experts expected minor skirmishes, but they also agreed that "we may expect to see a Congress performing in the true tradition of party wheelhorses and party drudges, obediently turning out only those statutes the White House requests or smiles upon and using brute force of the majority to crush and stifle minority opinion."[21] As McNary wrote cheerfully, "I'm awaiting the opening of the Congress on Tuesday. Things will then start to buzz and the days

[18] To J. E. S. Thorpe, Nov. 13, 1936, *ibid.*
[19] To R. J. Laubengayer, Nov. 13, 1936, Hope MSS, General Correspondence 1936-37, I-Misc.
[20] To Alf Landon, Jan. 11, 1937, Landon MSS, Political File 1937, M-O.
[21] Paul W. Ward, "Nothing But Red Tape," *Nation*, CXLIV (Jan. 2, 1937), 8-9.

will slip by and before we know it spring will be here and you and the Colonel will be here and all will be fine."[22]

Roosevelt, however, had a surprise for them that would do more to bring about an effective conservative coalition in Congress than anything he ever did. Far from creating a breathing spell, the surprise left the Senate fatigued and angry, the House suspicious and unpredictable, and conservatives first aghast, then aggressive. It was the famous court reorganization message.

Ever since "Black Monday" of 1935, Roosevelt's hostility toward the Supreme Court had mounted. Besides striking down the NRA, the court in 1936 had invalidated the AAA and the Guffey Coal Act of 1935. In the spring of 1936, it added the New York minimum-wage law to its victims in a 5-4 decision that disturbed even Republican conservatives such as Hoover. It appeared that the court would continue to destroy New Deal legislation passed by large congressional majorities.

To find a means of restraining the court was difficult. At first Roosevelt considered limiting its jurisdiction by constitutional amendment.[23] But as he mulled over this possibility, he concluded it would take too long to secure the necessary ratification of three-fourths of the states. Previously the alternative of "packing" the court by adding liberal judges had seemed a "distasteful idea."[24] But since new justices could be added by simple legislation, he gradually changed his mind. Such a method suited his predilection for a quick, simple solution. The journalist George Creel, interviewing him in December 1936, reported that the President, "his face like a fist," excitedly told him, "Congress can *enlarge* the Supreme Court."[25] A month later

[22] To Mrs. W. T. Stolz, Jan. 2, 1937, McNary MSS.
[23] Harold Ickes, *The Secret Diary of Harold Ickes* (3 vols.; New York, 1954), I, 467, Nov. 13, 1935.
[24] *Ibid.*, p. 496, Dec. 27, 1935.
[25] *Rebel at Large* (New York, 1947), p. 293. Italics his.

another journalist noted in his diary, "Roosevelt is in an audacious mood and is even thinking of proposing to pack [the] Supreme Court by enlarging it. . . . Roosevelt is determined to curb the court and put it in its place, and will go ahead even if many people think it is unwise."[26]

To all but a few insiders Roosevelt's court plan on February 5, 1937 came as a complete surprise. The problem, he said in his message to Congress, was that the federal courts were too slow, too overworked. Pointing to the number of petitions for hearing on appeal which the court had denied, he suggested this raised "the question of aged or infirm judges—a subject of delicacy and yet one which requires frank discussion. . . ."[27] Accordingly, he asked Congress to authorize him to appoint a new judge whenever a federal judge with ten or more years of service failed to retire within six months after his seventieth birthday. He requested a maximum of six such new "coadjutors" on the Supreme Court (there were then six judges over seventy) and two each on the other twenty-two federal courts.[28]

Perhaps no presidential message has excited such an immediate and enraged outcry. Many remembered Roosevelt's Madison Square Garden speech in the closing days of the 1936 campaign in which the President had proclaimed, "I should like to have it said of my first administration that in it the forces of selfishness and lust for power met their match. I should like to have it said of my second administration that in it these forces met their *master*."[29] To some

[26] Clapper Diary, Jan. 20, 1937, Clapper MSS. His informant was Donald Richberg.

[27] Samuel Rosenman (ed.), *The Public Papers and Addresses of Franklin D. Roosevelt*, VI (New York, 1938), 51-66.

[28] The plan is summarized in Joseph Alsop and Turner Catledge, *The 168 Days* (Garden City, N.Y., 1938), pp. 54-55. This book, written within a few months of the end of the court battle in the summer of 1937, is an excellent study of the controversy.

[29] Rosenman, *Public Papers of FDR*, V (New York, 1938), 568-69. Italics mine.

fearful conservatives, this court plan appeared to be Roosevelt's preliminary move for dictatorial power; it suggested the dawn of Hitlerism in America. One citizen wrote, "Mr. Roosevelt and the Congress, and the Senate (with a few exceptions) seem to have become intoxicated with the DEMOCRATIC FEVER which brought them into power and there is no influence which can stop their headlong rush into the CHASM where STALIN, MUSSOLINI, and HITLER have led their countries."[30] Columnist Dorothy Thompson added, "This is the beginning of pure personal government. Do you want it? Do you like it? Look around the world—there are plenty of examples—and make up your mind."[31]

Perhaps a more widespread popular view reflected a reverence for the Supreme Court as an institution. Despite overwhelming national support for the New Deal and despite general disapproval of some of the court's decisions, many Americans were suspicious of tampering with the court. To these people court and Constitution were almost synonymous. "Only a Supreme Court, independent and unawed," Senator Burke said, "stands guard to protect the rights and liberties of the people."[32] If the plan succeeds, prophesied Henry L. Mencken, "the court will become as ductile as a gob of chewing gum, changing shape from day to day and even from hour to hour as this or that wizard edges his way to the President's ear."[33]

Within a few weeks of the message such opposition, emanating largely from people already unfriendly to Roosevelt, had developed into a crusade. Letters deluged senators; newspapers denounced the plan; and many organizations,

---

[30] Franklin O. Elliott to William E. Borah, March 4, 1937, Borah MSS, Box 621. This was but one of literally hundreds of such letters in the Borah papers.

[31] New York *Herald Tribune*, Feb. 11, 1937, p. 23.

[32] In preface to Merlo J. Pusey, *The Supreme Court Crisis* (New York, 1937).

[33] Baltimore *Sun*, Feb. 7, 1937.

notably publisher Frank E. Gannett's well-financed National Committee to Uphold Constitutional Government, developed expert letter-writing campaigns against it.[34] As one amazed senator wrote, "the protests reaching Washington from all sections have been overwhelming. We have seen nothing like it in years."[35] Ickes summed up the furor: "To listen to the clamor, one would think that Moses from Mt. Sinai had declared that God himself had decreed that if and when there should be a Supreme Court of the United States, the number Nine was to be sacred. All that is left to do now is to declare that it is infallible; that it is the spiritual descendent of Moses and that the number Nine is three times three, and three stands for the Trinity."[36]

Although the intensity of conservative outcries was unexpectedly high, the nature of the opposition was even more surprising. Critics came to include not only conservatives but liberals as well. For this development, Roosevelt was partly at fault. In the first place the plan was "clever, too damned clever."[37] Instead of stating honestly that the court needed liberal judges who would look favorably upon New Deal legislation, the President based his appeal upon court inefficiency and old age. Since Justice Brandeis, a leading court liberal, was then eighty-one, Roosevelt's arguments not only offended the many liberal admirers of Brandeis but they were also clearly inadequate. The charge of inefficiency also seemed contrived, and it was easy for opponents to show that Attorney General Homer S. Cum-

[34] An excellent discussion of the arguments of letters regarding the plan is in E. Kimbark MacColl, "The Supreme Court and Public Opinion: A Study of the Court Fight of 1937" (unpublished Ph.D. dissertation, University of California, Los Angeles, 1953), pp. 223-25. He estimated senators averaged 10,000 letters each in the first two weeks.

[35] Arthur Capper to William Allen White, Feb. 25, 1937, W. A. White MSS, Box 186.

[36] To William Allen White, Feb. 25, 1937, *ibid.*, Box 186.

[37] Quoted in Burns, *Roosevelt*, p. 297.

mings, an architect of the plan, had said in his most recent annual report that the court was fully abreast of its work.[38] Roosevelt's reasoning seemed both absurd and disingenuous. "Such an issue," a liberal representative wrote later, "can never be met rightly by oblique proposals which conceal their real objectives."[39]

More important, the plan itself was unsatisfactory to liberals. For years progressives had urged "fundamental" court reform, such as constitutional amendments making immune to judicial review certain kinds of social and economic legislation or requiring a two-thirds or three-fourths Supreme Court majority to invalidate congressional statutes. A third liberal plan, popularized by Senator Wheeler, would have permitted Congress to veto court decisions invalidating congressional acts, provided the congressional veto was at least three-fourths of both houses and followed an intervening congressional election. Roosevelt's plan, however, left the court's jurisdiction untouched and pragmatically concerned itself only with the immediate situation. As Norris complained, "I do not like the President's proposal, not because it is unconstitutional, but because I doubt the wisdom of proceeding in that way and because it is not, in my judgment, fundamental, and will only be a temporary remedy."[40]

Finally, some congressmen objected to the proposal because they believed that it threatened civil liberties. As a Democratic representative put it: "The weapon which the President has chosen to achieve his end is a two edged

[38] *Annual Report of the Attorney General*, 1936, p. 9.

[39] Jerry Voorhis, *Confessions of a Congressman* (New York, 1948), p. 78.

[40] George W. Norris to Jerome F. Heyn, April 3, 1937, Norris MSS, Tray 27, Box 1. Roosevelt recognized the almost insuperable problems involved in getting conservative state legislatures to approve such amendments. It should also be emphasized that Norris eventually accepted the plan, though reluctantly.

sword. It may serve the cause of liberty today but tomorrow it could prove just as effective in the hands of a despotic reactionary."[41] Disturbed at the deviousness of the plan, fearful of some of its consequences, and disgusted with its short-run character, many American liberals either failed to respond with enthusiasm or became outright opponents of a plan whose immediate purpose they warmly welcomed.

Roosevelt's manner of introducing the plan was also offensive. No congressmen knew of it until a few minutes before he announced the scheme to the press. Henry F. Ashurst, the easy-going Arizonan who headed the Senate committee that would have to introduce the bill, had recently denounced as "the prelude to tyranny" suggestions that such a plan would be attempted.[42] Bankhead, then House speaker, and Senate Majority Leader Robinson had recently spoken in favor of a constitutional amendment to handle the court problem.[43] And Representative Hatton W. Sumners of Texas, chairman of the House Judiciary Committee, had already revived his bill to entice the retirement of federal judges by granting justices liberal pensions.[44] Roosevelt knew that his new plan would place congressional leaders in awkward positions, yet he failed to consult them. Such secretiveness not only isolated him, probably deliberately, from honest warnings; it infuriated congressional leaders. "Lindsay," wrote Bankhead to Representative Lindsay C. Warren of North Carolina, "wouldn't you have thought that the President would have told his own party leaders what he was going to do? He didn't because he

[41] D. Worth Clark to Borah, Feb. 23, 1937, Borah MSS.

[42] *Congressional Record*, 75th Cong., 1st Sess., 562.

[43] Raymond Clapper, "Along the Potomac," *Review of Reviews*, XCV (March 1937), 29-31.

[44] Alsop and Catledge, *The 168 Days*, p. 41. Josephus Daniels described Sumners as "an able lawyer of the type that Wilson was wont to call 'legalistic,' meaning by that term that 'black letter' learning influenced him more than the making of law an instrument of humanity and justice." Daniels to FDR, April 5, 1937, Roosevelt MSS, PPF 87.

knew that hell would break loose."[45] Flushed with his over-whelming triumph, convinced that "the people are with me," and ever fond of the surprising, dramatic pronouncement, Roosevelt had delightedly kept his own counsel.[46] As Senator Alben Barkley of Kentucky later admitted, he was a "poor quarterback. He didn't give us the signals in advance of the play."[47] This secrecy, almost as much as the artful plan itself, was one of his many mistakes in the whole mismanaged affair.[48]

The first congressmen to hear of the plan were the Democratic leaders. On the afternoon of February 4 Roosevelt sent word he wanted to see them on an important matter, and the next morning they assembled at the White House. Present were Ashurst, Sumners, Robinson, Bankhead, Rayburn, and Garner. The President then told them, quietly and without asking for comment, what he told the press only a few minutes later.

It was a revealing conference. Silently, Robinson "flushed mahogany and stared down at the table top."[49] Bankhead sat with a "pokerish expression." Garner, Rayburn, and Sumners were silent, and Ashurst managed only to mumble that the plan sounded all right.[50] Without a word the

[45] Quoted in William Leuchtenburg, *Franklin D. Roosevelt and the New Deal* (New York, 1963), p. 234.

[46] Creel, *Rebel*, p. 294, said he asked Roosevelt before the court plan was introduced if he would consult Congress. Roosevelt, according to Creel, "shrugged off the question as if it dealt with an unimportance."

[47] Alben Barkley, *That Reminds Me* (Garden City, N.Y., 1954), p. 153.

[48] Rep. Edward H. Rees, a freshman Republican congressman from Kansas, wrote William Allen White to say, "Honestly, this beats me. He [FDR] was not fair to his party . . . and not decent to the people when he did not disclose this kind of a plan . . . as far as I can find out, hardly a Congressman knew that he expected to propose such a plan. There isn't even an excuse of an 'emergency' for it. As a matter of fact he told us on the first day of the session that 'the emergency is practically over.'" Feb. 16, 1937, W. A. White MSS.

[49] Alsop and Catledge, *The 168 Days*, p. 66.

[50] Harold Ickes, "My Twelve Years with FDR," *Saturday Evening Post*, CCXXI (July 3, 1948), 30.

assemblage departed, climbed into Garner's car and drove back to the Capitol. On the way Sumners broke the silence. "Boys," he said, "here's where I cash in."[51] Otherwise, recalled Garner, "we were all so stunned we hardly spoke."[52]

Remarkably, of these men only Sumners was to denounce the plan openly. The others not only suppressed their misgivings but in varying degrees lent support to it. The cynical, silver-tongued, and gloriously senatorial Ashurst, a shrewd Democratic Senate regular since 1913, hesitated for a day, then frankly reversed his prior position.[53] Fond of carrying in his pocket tracts on the virtues of political inconsistency, he replied to a woman who wrote to congratulate him on his stand on the plan, "which stand?" Never enthusiastic, fond of the spotlight, he was to be only a lukewarm supporter of the plan. He was, nonetheless, a supporter.[54]

Garner was displeased. When the bill was read in the Senate, he strode from the rostrum holding his nose, making the thumbs down gesture of the Roman arena.[55] Later, he left Washington in the midst of the battle to go fishing at home in Texas. But he, too, was outwardly loyal. He disliked the plan, but for him it was not the stuff of which party splits are made.

Rayburn, a shrewd, self-contained bachelor from Texas, and a warm friend of Garner, also had misgivings about the "reform." But he was more sympathetic to the New Deal than many of his fellow leaders, and he also believed that party loyalty was both desirable in itself and the best way to advance in the House. "The way to get along," he

---

[51] Sumners to Thomas B. Love, Oct. 23, 1937, Roosevelt MSS, PPF 4925.

[52] Bascom N. Timmons, *Garner of Texas* (New York, 1948), p. 23.

[53] Alva Johnston, "The Dean of Inconsistency," *Saturday Evening Post*, CCX (Dec. 25, 1937), 23.

[54] See Ashurst's diary, *A Many Colored Toga: The Diary of Henry Fountain Ashurst* (Tucson, 1962), especially Feb. 19, 1937, p. 370, for his own humorous realization of his inconsistency.

[55] Alsop and Catledge, *The 168 Days*, p. 69.

liked to say, "is to go along."[56] He kept his doubts to himself. Together with Bankhead, he quickly persuaded Roosevelt that the plan must begin in the Senate. It was unfair, he insisted, to force House members to vote on such a plan with elections impending for all of them in two years. Besides, he said, Sumners' opposition made it extremely unlikely that the House Judiciary Committee would ever report the bill to the floor. Rayburn was primarily interested in avoiding the issue. In this, he succeeded.[57]

Speaker Bankhead agreed with Rayburn. A well-educated, urbane Alabaman from an old political family, he was generally sympathetic to most New Deal measures. Similarly, "party loyalty was an article of faith" with him.[58] "There come times," he wrote a friend, "when as leader of my party I am compelled to assume some duties that are not always entirely to my liking. This latter expression is, of course, entirely personal."[59] He too was loyal still—very still.

Thanks to Sumners' opposition and the entreaties of Rayburn and Bankhead, it was clear that the measure would have to begin in the Senate, where Majority Leader Robinson remained in command. Remembering Roosevelt's actions during the wealth-tax controversy, Robinson was again annoyed by the President's procedure. Roosevelt, he complained privately, "would have done well to have advised more frankly with his friends before precipitating this issue."[60] But once again Robinson decided to remain loyal

[56] Raymond Moley, *Twenty-Seven Masters of Politics in a Personal Perspective* (New York, 1949), p. 242.

[57] Alsop and Catledge, *The 168 Days*, p. 201.

[58] Quoted in Walter J. Heacock, "William B. Bankhead and the New Deal," *Journal of Southern History*, XXI (Aug. 1955), 348.

[59] *Ibid.*, pp. 355-56. For Heacock's more extended study, see "William Brockman Bankhead: A Biography" (unpublished Ph.D. dissertation, University of Wisconsin, 1952).

[60] Cited in Nevin E. Neal, "A Biography of Joseph T. Robinson" (unpublished Ph.D. dissertation, University of Oklahoma, 1957), p. 445. Robinson letter, March 2, 1937.

to the administration. Party faith was one main reason; another was his expectation that he would harvest a life ambition intimated by Roosevelt two years earlier: a Supreme Court justiceship himself.[61] As New Deal publicity man Charles Michelson commented later, Robinson "plunged into the fray with all the vigor of his virile soul."[62]

For the first few days it looked as if Roosevelt, as always, would eventually have his way. "All we have to do," the President told Farley when opposition arose, "is to let the flood of mail settle on Congress. You just see. All I have to do is devise a better speech, and the opposition will be beating a path to the White House door."[63] In the last resort, Roosevelt also planned to hold up bills dear to individual legislators until they followed his wishes. For the next three months the President remained serenely confident, refusing even to discuss the possibility of compromise.

Within two weeks, however, it became apparent that the court proposal would spark one of the hottest controversies in American history. *Time* magazine at first had reflected the general belief in Roosevelt's omnipotence and had reported on February 15 the results of a poll of newsmen which indicated "the bill would be passed without serious difficulty." A week later, it had changed its tune, prophesying a "battle . . . more uncertain than that of any which the New Deal had fought."[64] In their determination

[61] For Robinson's hopes for a judgeship, see Thomas T. Connally, *My Name Is Tom Connally* (New York, 1954), p. 166; and Alsop and Catledge, *The 168 Days*, p. 220.

[62] *The Ghost Talks* (New York, 1941), p. 66. See also Joseph Alsop and Robert Kintner, "Joe Robinson, the New Deal's Old Reliable," *Saturday Evening Post*, CCIX (Sept. 26, 1936), 5.

[63] *Jim Farley's Story* (New York, 1948), p. 70. FDR gleefully wrote Daniels saying: "I wish you were here to see the way the conservatives are running around tearing their hair and using language about me which surpasses even that of the campaign." Feb. 8, 1937, Roosevelt MSS, PPF 87.

[64] *Time*, Feb. 15, 1937, p. 19, and Feb. 22, 1937, p. 11. For the most optimistic view, see Paul W. Ward, "Roosevelt Will Win," *Nation*, CXLIV (Feb. 20, 1937), 202.

to stop the plan, hostile senators were obviously prepared to filibuster. Ashurst delayed the bill while opinions formed, and during the crucial weeks from February 5 until the Judiciary Committee finally released the bill unfavorably in June senatorial blocs arose which formed the basis of deep divisions lasting long beyond the life of the court fight. Despite the loyalty of the leaders, senators from both sides of the aisle at first opposed the plan as individuals; within a few weeks they had organized a well-disciplined interparty group against it; and by late spring they had formed a conservative bloc strong enough to deal Roosevelt his first serious setback in four years. The bloc was composed of the irreconcilable Democrats, Republicans, and, most important, previously loyal moderate Democrats.

The most vociferous of these three groups was the old band of anti-New Deal Democrats that had already broken with the President two or four years before. To Glass the plan was unspeakably vile. "Of course I shall oppose it," he said. "I shall oppose it with all the strength which runs to me, but I don't imagine for a minute that it'll do any good. Why, if the President asked Congress to commit suicide tomorrow, they'd do it."[65] To Harry Byrd he later added, "it is vindictiveness run mad."[66] Soon after the plan became public, Glass sat down to compose a speech against it and after twenty days of preparation he shook off his various ailments, left his sickbed, and went on the air. "I am speaking," he said with no exaggeration, "from the depths of a soul filled with bitterness against a proposition which appears to me utterly destitute of a moral sensibility and without parallel since the foundation of the Republic." Continuing, he branded the plan as an attempt to "rape the Supreme Court." A quotation from Rudyard Kipling completed his long oration:

[65] Alsop and Catledge, *The 168 Days*, p. 71.
[66] May 17, 1937, Glass MSS, Box 345.

He shall break his judges, if they cross his word;
He shall rule above the law, calling on the Lord.
Strangers of his counsel, hirelings of his pay,
These shall deal out justice; sell, deny, delay.
We shall take our station, dirt beneath our feet,
While his hired captains jeer us in the street.[67]

Bailey's sentiments were similar. Soon after the election, he had suspected Roosevelt of plans to change the court. To George he had written, "I am not inclined to tolerate anything like tampering with the Supreme Court, its membership or its jurisdiction and I question whether I can get the consent of my mind to vote for such a constitutional amendment as may be proposed."[68] Two months later he had not changed his mind. On the day it was announced, he wrote, "I am very much distressed by the President's message, but I am not unready for the battle. I have known for months that it was coming. I have hoped and prayed against it. Now it is here, and it is unnecessary for me to try to predicate what it means with respect to the future of our country and our Party and men like you and myself. I shall move slowly and considerately, but I shall not run away from the battle."[69]

To Bailey and other irreconcilable Democrats the court issue was also cause for a crucial struggle within the Democratic party. In their eyes, Congress had been simply "a mob of legislative spendthrifts, completely under the thumb of the White House."[70] The Supreme Court had thus served conservatives as the only means of curbing the New Deal. Roosevelt had long since captured Congress; if he could

[67] *Ibid.*, Box 314. Also *Congressional Record*, 75th Cong., 1st Sess., 661.
[68] Nov. 18, 1936, Bailey MSS, Political File. George answered and agreed. See also Bailey to Jouett Shouse, Nov. 10, 1936: "I should bitterly oppose any tampering with the Supreme Court, and I shall not be inclined to submit an amendment to extend the Commerce Clause or the police power." *Ibid.*, General File.
[69] To Ernest M. Green, Feb. 5, 1937, *ibid.*, General File.
[70] Glass to Jeannette C. Mix, July 2, 1937, Glass MSS, Box 340.

pack the court as well, it would be the end of the "old" conservative Democratic party. As Bailey put it: "What we have going on in this country is a political revolution. . . . The President controls Congress and the people help him do it. He is now seeking to control the Court. . . . Give the President control over Congress and the Court and you will have a one man government. It may not be a dictatorship. A rose by any other name would smell as sweet."[71]

The southern Democratic opposition, joined by George, Byrd, and Smith (though not by most other southern Democratic senators), also suspected Roosevelt of trying to revolutionize race relations. Prior to the 1936 election few southern politicians had anticipated this possibility. Happy to receive large amounts of federal money and patronage, southerners had found the New Deal generally congenial. Indeed, they were so content that they let New Dealers abolish their cherished two-thirds rule in national conventions, the rule by which southerners had previously been able to prevent the nomination of candidates hostile to their views on racial questions.[72]

[71] Bailey to Thurmond Chatham, April 13, 1937, Bailey MSS, General File. A study entitled "The Republican-Southern Democratic Coalition, 1937-1959," by a Democratic Study Group, Staff Memo, Dec. 1959, stresses the idea that a conservative coalition arose in the Senate mainly because senators now realized that the court would no longer be a reliable line of defense. This letter by Bailey is evidence of this kind of thinking.

Rexford G. Tugwell, in *The Democratic Roosevelt* (Garden City, N.Y., 1957), p. 418, commented that "the Supreme Court fight, beginning almost at once, [after the 1936 election] would not be one for defense of the Constitution nearly so much as one for the return of the party to their [professional politicians] control."

[72] Tugwell, *Democratic Roosevelt*, 419-20, discusses southern feelings on this issue. The abolition is also recounted in New York *Herald Tribune*, June 25, 1936. For another discussion of the South and the New Deal, see William B. Hesseltine and David L. Smiley, *The South in American History* (2nd ed.; Englewood Cliffs, N.J., 1960), pp. 528-37. See also Donald Davidson, "The Politics of Agrarianism," *Review of Politics*, I (April 1939), 114-26. A survey is Marian D. Irish, "The Southern One-Party System and National Politics," *Journal of Politics*, IV (Feb. 1942), 80-94.

Roosevelt, for his part, had assiduously avoided ruffling southern feelings on race problems. Though sympathetic to the plight of the Negro, he had not pressed for civil rights legislation and had tried to keep race issues out of Congress. When Pennsylvania Senator Joseph F. Guffey, for instance, tried to secure a post for Robert L. Vann, a powerful ally in collecting Negro votes for Roosevelt, the President started to speak. Guffey interrupted, "'Before you say anything about Bob Vann, I ought to tell you he's colored.'

"'Will I have to get him confirmed by the Senate?' Roosevelt asked.

"'No,' said Joe grinning.

"'The job's yours, Joe.'"[73]

The elections of 1934 and 1936 led many southern politicians to think again, for it was then that Negroes in northern urban areas first began in large numbers to desert the party of Lincoln for the party of the New Deal. Roosevelt may have kept thorny race issues out of Congress, but his relief policies had been more than enough to convince Negroes that here, at last, was a man who cared about them. When the court proposal appeared, these same southerners perceived in it a Roosevelt plot to cement this growing Negro allegiance by appointing judges who would upset southern racial patterns. Glass, angry at New Deal catering to the northern Negro vote during the campaign, complained that Roosevelt was more intent upon helping the Negro "than any President except Lincoln. . . . This has incensed me beyond expression, and but for the very peculiar political situation [the campaign] at this time I would bitterly denounce it in a public statement."[74] Bailey likewise saw sinister motives in the court plan. The President, he said, "is determined to get the Negro vote and I do not have to

[73] Joseph Alsop and Robert Kintner, "The Guffey: Biography of a Boss, New Style," *Saturday Evening Post*, CCX (March 26, 1938), 6.

[74] To Clifton Woodrum, Sept. 29, 1936, Glass MSS, Box 380.

Senator Carter Glass (D–Va.)
(Courtesy National Archives, Washington, D.C.)

Senator Harry F. Byrd (D–Va.)
(Courtesy National Archives, Washington, D.C.)

Senator Ellison D. ("Cotton Ed") Smith (D–S.C.)
(Copyright by Cowles Communications, Inc.)

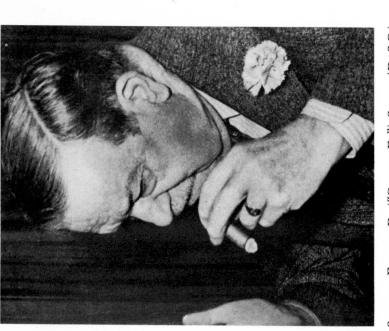

Senator Royal S. Copeland (D–N.Y.)
(Courtesy National Archives, Washington, D.C.)

tell you what *this* means."[75] To southern irreconcilables such as Bailey and Glass the court plan sought not only to destroy the last bulwark against the New Deal but it was also the first step toward the destruction of white supremacy.

The southern Democratic irreconcilables were not alone in denouncing the plan. Within a few days after its announcement most of the Democratic senators who had opposed the utilities and tax plans of 1935 joined them. Burke and Gerry needed no prodding to denounce the plan. George, facing a campaign in 1938, waited a week and then added his voice to the chorus. Copeland followed soon afterward. Tydings, though taking part in plans then underway to organize the opposition, remained quiet a little longer: even more than George, he feared for his political life in 1938. But by April he too openly entered the conservative legions.[76] Within two months following introduction of the plan, every Democratic senator (fourteen in all) whose dissatisfaction with the New Deal had already been apparent in late 1935 was also an open opponent of the court plan. Powerless alone, they looked across the aisle for help in forming a bipartisan coalition.

Before the court issue Senate Republicans had been badly divided. By and large, conservatives had captured the eastern and midwestern wings of the Republican party by the 1920's. But the Depression destroyed their strength in southern New England, the mid-Atlantic states, and the broad midwestern band from Ohio through Iowa and including Michigan. Narrowly partisan and unable to adjust to

[75] To Julian Miller, May 18, 1937, Bailey MSS, Political File. Italics his. Ickes, *Secret Diary,* II, April 9, 1937, noted southern fears on the race issue.

[76] According to *Public Opinion Quarterly,* IV (June 1940), 229, only four of thirty-two senators who answered a poll said they based their views on public opinion. But MacColl, "Supreme Court," shows conclusively, pp. 347-49, that there was a striking parallel between home state sentiment and the stand of senators on the court issue. In those states where opinion was divided, so too were senators.

their sudden minority status, these frustrated conservatives too often sounded like the economic royalists whom Roosevelt was able to denounce so effectively. And though they voted with conservative Democrats on many occasions in 1935-1936, they refused to coalesce with them. By 1937 they were a negligible band of ten. One reporter even suggested—and not entirely in jest—that these Republicans could "make the Era of Good Feelings unanimous by doing what the Federalists did a hundred years ago—they can disappear."[77]

In the West (including Wisconsin), however, the party had an important progressive element. During the 1930's, this wing included such veteran senators as William E. Borah of Idaho, Norris of Nebraska, La Follette of Wisconsin, and Hiram W. Johnson of California. Their progressivism had an antimonopoly, isolationist tone which did not harmonize very well with the more urban liberalism of the New Deal.[78] But it harmonized even less with Old Guard Republicanism; progressive Republicans, normally about ten strong in the Senate before 1937, had been a generally reliable left arm of the New Deal.

But by 1937 even this wing was beginning to succumb to the Democratic renaissance. Such former Republicans as Norris and La Follette, disgusted with their eastern brethren, had renounced their Republican labels and turned Independent and Progressive respectively. Another, James Couzens of Michigan, failed to be renominated in 1936.[79] Another, Peter Norbeck of South Dakota, died in that year, as had Bronson M. Cutting of New Mexico in 1935.[80] When

[77] Fortune, XV (Feb. 1937), 188.

[78] See Russell Nye, Midwestern Progressive Politics: A Historical Study of Its Origins and Development, 1870-1958 (Lansing, Mich., 1959), passim.

[79] Harry Barnard, Independent Man: The Life of Senator James Couzens (New York, 1958), is a well-written study. See especially pp. 304-13 for his unhappy last days; his dilemma was typical of Republican progressives.

[80] A good study of Norbeck is Gilbert Fite, Peter Norbeck: Prairie Statesman (University of Missouri Studies, XXII, No. 2 [Columbia, 1948]).

the 1937 session opened, the only remaining progressive Republicans in the Senate were the venerable Borah and Johnson, the mild progressive veterans Arthur Capper of Kansas and Charles McNary of Oregon, and North Dakota's isolationist progressives Lynn J. Frazier and Gerald P. Nye.

It was a feeble and divided group of Republicans to whom the conservative Democrats looked for aid. Deeply demoralized by the 1936 election, they were quiet and impotent, expecting to be defeated themselves when their terms of office expired. One Republican said: "The emotional tide is now and has been *with* the Democrats. . . . A Republican Senator attempting by speech to stem this tide cuts about as sorry a figure as a man who attempts to stem a cyclone with an open umbrella. It is better judgment to seek a cellar until the storm passes."[81]

The court proposal, however, did what no Republican strategem could have done; it united Senate Republicans for the first time in some three decades. As William Allen White correctly predicted at the time, "I don't see where we can get enough cohesion to stand for another victory unless the President hands us the issue. He might do it on the Supreme Court . . . but nothing that we can do to him is going to help much."[82] Besides Roosevelt, three Republicans shared much of the credit for this Republican reunification. They were Arthur H. Vandenberg of Michigan, Charles L. McNary of Oregon, and William E. Borah of Idaho. That three men so different could finally work harmoniously indicates the intense feeling that the court scheme was able to engender.

The most conservative of the three was Vandenberg. The son of a Grand Rapids, Michigan, harness maker, Vandenberg did not have an easy childhood. His father's business collapsed in the depression of 1893, and the family

---

[81] George W. Maxey to Sen. James Davis, Jan. 9, 1937, Davis MSS, Box 24. Italics his.

[82] To Gifford Pinchot, March 23, 1937, White MSS, Box 187.

moved to a side street where his mother ran a boarding house.[83] Supporting himself with odd jobs, he finished high school, briefly attended the University of Michigan Law School, and in 1906, at age twenty-one, began work on the Grand Rapids *Herald.* Proud of his self-reliant background, he was later to eulogize Alexander Hamilton, his boyhood idol, in a series of books. By 1928 he had reached the Senate.

Since the beginning of the New Deal, Vandenberg's public posture had been rather aggressive. Like most Republicans, he tended to believe that large doses of unfriendly oratory would drop the New Deal to its knees. "The sense of the oratorical," said one observer, "is never or rarely absent from him."[84] To some critics his fondness for florid speaking made him appear vain and pompous.[85] "He can strut sitting down," said one detractor.[86] Another remarked that he addressed people in conversation as if he were in a public hall.[87] Withal, no senator was more adept at acquiring extensive press coverage, and he was unquestionably the leading conservative Republican in Congress during the New Deal. Wise enough to deprecate efforts to make him run as a presidential or vice-presidential nominee in 1936, he remained in the Senate in 1937.

Despite his oratory, it was difficult for contemporary observers to know where he stood. As a member of the Nye Committee investigating American entrance into World War I, he established himself as a leading isolationist.[88] On domestic policy, however, he was variously described as a

[83] Paul M. Cuncannon, "Arthur H. Vandenberg," pp. 47-61, in J. T. Salter (ed.), *The American Politician* (Chapel Hill, N.C., 1938).

[84] *Ibid.,* p. 48.

[85] Joseph Alsop and Stewart Alsop, *The Reporter's Trade* (New York, 1958), p. 34.

[86] *Current Biography,* 1940, p. 823.

[87] Cuncannon, "Vandenberg," p. 49.

[88] C. David Tompkins, "Senator Arthur Hendrick Vandenberg: Middle Western Isolationist," *Michigan History,* XLIV (March 1960), 39-58.

"trimmer," a "liberal conservative," and a "conservative at heart who takes on a progressive coloring."[89] According to an unfriendly critic, he was "something like an onion. You peel off layer after layer, looking for the core. And when you've peeled him all away—by golly, there isn't any core."[90] Essentially·suspicious of innovation and experimentation, he had a sense of what he called "social responsibility."[91] Sympathetic to some New Deal objectives, he was at the same time a partisan by nature who tried to find happy ground for his party to stand on. His vagueness, though easy to ridicule, was a political asset. Unlike many other Republicans, he marked himself neither as an implacable opponent of Roosevelt nor as a tool of big business interests. In his 1934 campaign for reelection, he was the only Republican nonprogressive west of New England to be returned to the Senate. By 1937 he was a veteran of nine years in the Senate, a leading orator, and a proven vote-getter. His reaction to suggestions of coalition would be important in the weeks to come.

Borah of Idaho was perhaps the most progressive of the three leading Republicans of the court fight. Then the senior senator, Borah had entered the upper house in 1907, and was seventy-two in 1937. Perhaps no senator presented such an odd combination of personal traits. His clothes, excepting a fondness for fancy shoes, were plain, even shabby; his head was shaggy. Son of a devout Presbyterian, he was a teetotaler and lifelong prohibitionist. Married but childless, he seldom left his home while in Washington and played no part in Capital society. Until 1930 he did not

[89] Quoted in Frank Kent, *Without Grease: Political Behavior, 1934-1936* (New York, 1936), Nov. 18, 1935 column, p. 274.

[90] Milton S. Mayer, "Men Who Would Be President: Try to Find Vandenberg," *Nation*, CL (May 11, 1940), 587.

[91] See revealing letter to Couzens, cited in Barnard, *Couzens*, p. 318. Letter written Sept. 16, 1936.

even own a car. The quiet, even the isolation, of his private life contrasted sharply with the controversial public role in which he constantly found himself.

Unlike Vandenberg, Borah seldom left much doubt where he stood on an issue—but only on that particular issue. Once he made up his mind, Borah was inflexible; his position was clear, forceful, and phrased in terms of right and wrong. Biographer Marian McKenna, noting Borah's tendency to transform issues into moral causes, called him a "western copy of the Wilsonian model. . . . He seemed to think that a declaration of justice was equal to the realization."[92] It was not always easy to predict in which direction Borah's righteousness would take him. Safe from electoral defeat in Idaho, he kept his own counsel, ignored party platforms when it suited him, and acted as his own interpreter of the Constitution.

During the New Deal years Borah generally joined the other progressive Republicans in supporting most of the New Deal. He was also personally fond of Roosevelt. But unlike Norris or La Follette, he never seriously considered leaving his party. "I do not propose," he said in 1934, "to accept the line of least resistance and go into the Democratic Party. I propose to accept the line of most resistance and help make the Republican Party what it ought to be."[93] Indeed, he called himself a candidate for the 1936 Republican presidential nomination.

When the court plan was proposed, Borah's opposition should have surprised no one. For, as McKenna has noted, he was "an individualist who opposed all concentrations of power, political or economic."[94] His previous opposition to the New Deal—other progressives like Nye joined him here

[92] Marian Cecilia McKenna, *Borah* (Ann Arbor, 1961), pp. 282-86, discusses his moral tone.

[93] "Reorganization of the Republican Party," *Vital Speeches*, I (Dec. 31, 1934), 199-202; quote on p. 201.

[94] McKenna, *Borah*, p. 321.

—had been to the NRA on the grounds that it permitted concentration of economic power. His objection to the court plan exposed similar thinking: he thought it would centralize political power in the hands of one man. This stand approximated the thinking of many other western, essentially agrarian progressives of both parties and was to make Borah a central figure in the net of personal relationships which composed the liberal and progressive senatorial opposition to the plan.

Neither Vandenberg nor Borah was so important a figure during the court fight as McNary, Republican leader since 1933. Whereas the first two were imposing speakers whose names often graced the headlines, McNary was a shrewd, able, and personable parliamentarian whose influence in the Senate easily outranked that of his two zealous colleagues. One writer, a few years earlier, described him as "everybody's friend. They all like him. He doesn't bother much about making speeches, but can make a good one if he wants to, and spends his time moving about. . . . He is just under sixty, a ruddy faced, confident sort of a fellow, who can wander over to the Democratic side and get anything he wants within reason from his opponents, and sometimes without reason."[95]

A senator since 1917, McNary possessed the fortunate habit of usually finding a happy middle ground. He had been a mild reservationist in the League of Nations fight yet at the same time an intimate of the irreconcilable Hiram Johnson. A leader of the insurgent Republican farm bloc during the twenties, he had found it easy to vote with conservative Republicans on many other issues.[96] By 1930, he was firmly established in the hearts of Oregon voters

[95] Sam G. Blythe, "A Hunt for the Elephant," *Saturday Evening Post,* CCVI (Dec. 30, 1933), 85.

[96] For his early life, see Walter K. Roberts, "The Political Career of Senator Charles L. McNary, 1924-1944" (unpublished Ph.D. dissertation, University of North Carolina, 1954), pp. 1-120.

and was an important Republican figure in the Senate. After the New Deal sweep in 1932, he replaced James ("Sunny Jim") Watson of Indiana as Senate Republican leader. More often than not, he backed Roosevelt on major issues. During Roosevelt's first term, he supported the AAA, NRA, TVA, and the National Labor Relations Act. His only major speech during the entire 1935-1936 session was a fifteen-minute colloquy in favor of the social security bill.[97]

McNary's support of the New Deal was not popular with Vandenberg and the eastern conservative wing. But they liked McNary; he gave them free rein to speak; and he satisfied the progressive wing as well. He continued as leader. In 1937 he was in a good position to bring Republicans together against a plan which even he considered worth fighting. Like Borah, he disliked its centralizing tendency and its apparent lack of respect for the judiciary.

As soon as he heard of the court scheme, McNary convened his cohorts. Not surprisingly, he found Vandenberg and his nine conservative Republican colleagues ready to launch a partisan onslaught. "I have very deep convictions on this score," Vandenberg wrote, "and it would be impossible for me to surrender them even at the price of retiring from public service."[98] More surprisingly, McNary found not only Borah but Republican progressives such as Hiram Johnson and Arthur Capper also opposed. As Capper wrote to William Allen White, "I am quite certain the other progressive Republicans will oppose the President's program. Some of them want to modify the Roosevelt program. Others prefer to solve the problem through the constitutional route."[99] Johnson, tired and unwell at seventy-one, viewed

[97] *Current Biography,* 1940, pp. 542-44.
[98] To George M. Harrison, March 4, 1937, Vandenberg MSS, 1937 folder.
[99] Feb. 26, 1937, W. A. White MSS, Box 186. For a sketchy chapter on Capper and the New Deal, see Homer E. Socolofsky, *Arthur Capper: Publisher, Politician, and Philanthropist* (Lawrence, Kan., 1962), pp. 166-86.

the scheme with distaste.[100] The two remaining progressive Republicans, Nye and Frazier of North Dakota, were unhappy with the plan from the start.

Assured of Republican solidarity, McNary conferred with Borah and Vandenberg and persuaded these stalwart orators to do what he had done since 1933: keep quiet. "Let the boys across the aisle do the talking," he said. "We'll do the voting."[101] Similar directions went out not only to the other thirteen Senate Republicans but to GOP national leaders as well. House Leader Bertrand H. Snell hurried to New York to persuade Landon to discard a prepared Lincoln Day assault on the plan. Hoover also agreed to keep quiet, though only after repeated exhortations by Vandenberg and others. As Vandenberg explained in notes the day after the plan was announced,

Borah, McNary, and I had a conference in Borah's office at 11 o'clock. Borah is prepared to lead this fight; but he insisted that there is no hope if it is trademarked in advance as a 'Hoover fight' or a 'Republican fight.' McNary emphatically agreed. As a matter of fact, this was already my attitude. . . . What a bitterly unfair contemplation! That an ex-President must efface himself! Yet the need is realistically true. For example, I walked to lunch this noon with Senator Hatch. . . . He said: "I am inclined to vote NO; but you Republicans and particularly Mr. Hoover must not make it too hard for me." So the general agree-

---

See also Capper to Landon, Feb. 10, 1937, Landon MSS, Political File 1937, B-C.

100 See Ickes, *Secret Diary*, II, 139, May 12, 1937. Ickes, an old friend of Johnson, noted ". . . he has become an old man. All the resonance and timbre in his voice—and he had a wonderful speaking voice—are gone. He told me he couldn't stand much any more. He retires from the Senate chamber for prolonged rests."

101 Joseph Alsop and Robert Kintner, "Let Them Do the Talking," *Saturday Evening Post*, CCXIII (Sept. 28, 1940), 18. Also Karl Lamb, "The Opposition Party as Secret Agent: Republicans and the Court Fight," *Papers of the Michigan Academy of Arts and Letters*, XLVI (1961), 539-50.

ment is that Republicans shall stay in the background for a week or ten days and let the revolting Democrats make their own record.[102]

Started as a tactic to gain time and involve the Democrats, this Republican plan soon became established policy. Vandenberg, aching to speak out against the plan, reemphasized the wisdom of the strategy two weeks later. "It is the hardest job of self control I ever undertook," he wrote, "because this assault upon an independent court utterly burns me up. But the time will come: And the main thing is to *win*."[103] Three months later Capper added, "I think we are making some headway on the Supreme Court proposition. We are letting . . . Burke and the other Democratic Senators do most of the fighting."[104] Shrewdly, these men managed to resist the urge to speak out against the plan; until the court plan was defeated in July, most prominent Republican senators maintained a discreet—and to Democrats—infuriating silence.

This strategy of silence marked a momentous change in Republican thinking. Since 1933 quiet Republicans such as McNary had been rare. Convinced that the New Deal was not only iniquitous but politically doomed, many Republicans continued to think through 1936 that the way to defeat Roosevelt was to denounce the New Deal as loudly and as often as possible. But this strategy had failed to win voters, for as one Republican representative wrote bluntly, "the public thinks the Republicans simply knock."[105] Republican aggressiveness also prevented moderate Democrats from leaving the New Deal fold. Rather than participate in an unholy coalition with Republicans, such Democrats had

[102] Vandenberg Notes, Feb. 6, 1937, in Scrapbook 1937, Vandenberg MSS. Carl Hatch was a Democrat from New Mexico.

[103] *Ibid.*, Feb. 18, 1937. Italics his.

[104] To Landon, May 1, 1937, Landon MSS, Political File 1937, B-C.

[105] Rep. Francis Case to Rep. James Wadsworth, Feb. 3, 1937, Wadsworth MSS, Box 28.

preferred to identify themselves, however reluctantly, with the New Deal.

The election of 1936 at last convinced many of these vocal Republicans that the New Deal was not going to wither under their oratorical blasts. On the contrary, it looked to some as if the Grand Old Party would disappear unless it conserved its strength for more auspicious days. "Now we must be opportunists," William Allen White advised. "We must take counsel of expedience. We must turn, and duck, and dodge to survive as an opposition."[106] So when the court struggle began, Republicans found silence more palatable than they might have had Roosevelt sprung the plan before the election. As one Republican representative put it: "We are in a big, big battle on Roosevelt's proposal to pack the Supreme Court. If we are to win it we must do it with Democratic votes in the House and in the Senate. A group of bitterly earnest Democrats is already at work on the problem. They have urged that we Republicans refrain from taking a united party action for the time being, lest by putting a partisan tinge on the issue we drive reluctant Democrats back into Roosevelt's arms."[107]

Although Republicans wrote angry speeches against the court plan, they were wise enough not to deliver them. They let conservative Democrats carry the vocal attack, contenting themselves with the important task of delivering their adverse votes. Within a few weeks some Republicans were attending bipartisan conservative meetings and devising

106 Cited in Joseph Boskin, "Politics of an Opposition Party: The Republican Party in the New Deal Period, 1936-1940" (unpublished Ph.D. dissertation, University of Minnesota, 1960), p. 128. Letter, Dec. 17, 1936.

107 James W. Wadsworth to Thomas E. Broderick, Feb. 11, 1937, Wadsworth MSS, Box 28. See also Clifford R. Hope to Mr. and Mrs. C. A. Wells, March 16, 1937, Hope MSS, Legislative File, 1936-1937, "S": "the only way it [the court plan] can possibly be defeated is by a coalition between the Republicans and Democrats who oppose the proposal. Any attempt to make a purely partisan political issue . . . means that the President will win hands down."

strategy with Glass, Gerry, Burke, and others. As Vandenberg put it after the plan had been recommitted, there was a "bipartisan high command . . . only a coalition could succeed—a preponderantly Democratic coalition. This was frankly realized. There was no secret about it. . . . Republicans voluntarily subordinated themselves and withdrew to the reserve lines."[108] In this way Roosevelt's court plan ironically did more to infuse new vigor into Senate Republicans than anything they could have done themselves; and they became more useful allies of their Democratic comrades than they had been in earlier years with twice the numerical strength. Republicans were at last contributing to the formation of a successful conservative coalition in the Senate.

Besides the fourteen expected Democratic opponents and their fourteen Republican allies, there were sixty-eight other senators whose previous support of the New Deal, though not spotless, had been fairly regular. They became the men whom the subdued Republicans and vocal Democrats hoped to add to their coalition. Of this group, however, some thirty-five were unshakable allies of the President. Five of these were leaders, including Robinson, Pittman, Harrison, Ashurst, and Byrnes. Unenthusiastic about the court plan, they believed that their positions as leaders required loyalty. As Ickes described Harrison, he said he "would have to vote for it but he wouldn't say anything in its behalf."[109]

Some fifteen more of these thirty-five loyalists were neither disturbed nor enthusiastic about the plan and therefore saw no reason to bolt the party over it. Senator William

[108] "The Biography of an Undelivered Speech," *Saturday Evening Post,* CCX (Oct. 9, 1937), 25.

[109] Ickes, *Secret Diary,* II, 164. Pittman said he would back the plan but "you should be apprised of the sentiments I hear expressed by senators. Several of them who are very strong supporters of the President have deplored the fact that the President's procedure with regard to the Supreme Court is subject to the construction that it is actuated by a desire to punish the Court. . . ." Pittman to Homer Cummings, Feb. 8, 1937, Pittman MSS, Box 11.

G. McAdoo of California said: "I cannot understand all this hysteria and excitement about this matter but you might as well undertake to punch a hole through a piece of concrete with a hairpin as to try to convince any man or woman who is opposed to any increase in the membership of the court just because they feel that way. In other words, their emotions, prejudices, and politics forbid any dispassionate study of the question."[110]

Another eight loyalists were Democratic newcomers who recognized that their political futures depended in large part upon their positions on this first major test. And finally, there was a small band of six to eight aggressive liberals who wholeheartedly backed the plan. This group included La Follette and two future Supreme Court justices, Sherman Minton of Indiana and Hugo L. Black of Alabama. Most of these men were younger senators.

Denied support from the thirty-five loyalists, the coalitionists turned to the thirty-three remaining Democratic moderates, three of whom, in turning against the President, revealed how this plan made a shambles of Roosevelt's senatorial majority. Perhaps no member of this group reacted so quickly or so violently as sixty-year-old Thomas T. Connally of Texas. Before 1937 he had been as well known for his senatorial appearance as anything else. Inflated with grandeur, he wore a stand-up collar, a black string tie, and a broad-brimmed black hat. Big, blue-eyed, and gray-haired, he let his wavy locks grow long and curly over the back of his collar.[111] Bailey described him well as "the only man in the United States Senate who could wear a Roman toga and not look like a fat man in a nightgown."[112]

---

[110] Cited in Boskin, "Politics," p. 115, April 12, 1937.

[111] Gerald Movins and Jack Beall, "Plush-Covered Cactus," *Saturday Evening Post*, CCXIV (April 4, 1942), 27. This is a deft sketch of Connally. See also *Current Biography*, 1949, p. 122.

[112] Otis Miller and Anita F. Alpern, in J. T. Salter (ed.), *Public Men In and Out of Office* (Chapel Hill, N.C., 1946), pp. 311-21, describe Connally. Quote is on p. 311.

Before the court issue Connally had been a usually reliable supporter of the administration. Elected to the Senate in 1928 after twelve years in the House, he had been one of the many men whose counsel helped persuade Garner to swing his support to Roosevelt in the 1932 convention.[113] In turn, the New Deal was generous in its favors to Texas, and Roosevelt aided Connally in his struggle for reelection by publicly inviting him aboard his yacht. Except for adverse votes on the NRA and the Guffey Coal Act of 1935, Connally had backed most important New Deal measures through 1936.

But Connally's liberalism was limited. Responsive to large oil and financial interests, he had been somewhat uneasy, though still loyal, about such issues as the wealth tax in 1935. Above all, he had an almost reverential faith in the Democratic party and its traditional beliefs. "To me," he said in his autobiography, "most of what Roosevelt advocated was consistent with our party's past. One of my fears was that by referring to this progressive legislation as the 'New Deal' we might be building a separate group which would eventually branch off into a new political party."[114] Connally, like many other Democratic veterans of the Wilson era, was receptive to some New Deal recovery and reform measures but not to a radical change in party philosophy.

The court plan appeared to him just such a change. Suspicious of Roosevelt's intentions in abolishing the two-thirds rule in 1936, Connally felt his fears justified in the court plan. It looked to him like the opening gambit in an effort to transform Democratic philosophy. Moreover, as a lawyer he revered the judiciary. Four days after the plan was announced, Connally openly opposed it, and in the ensuing months his position as a member of the Senate Judiciary

[113] See Frank Freidel, *Franklin D. Roosevelt: The Triumph* (Boston, 1956), p. 308. For Tom Connally's own account see his autobiography, written with Alfred Steinburg, *My Name Is Tom Connally*, pp. 138–46.
[114] *Ibid.*, p. 154.

Committee enabled him to use all the wit and incisiveness which his genial exterior concealed. It was a major break: he and Roosevelt hardly spoke to each other again for the next two years.

A second key member of the crucial moderate group was Bennett Champ Clark of Missouri.[115] Only forty-seven years old in 1937, Clark had been on Capitol Hill literally since he was a boy. His father, Champ Clark, had been Democratic leader and speaker of the House, and the son had been his secretary and later House parliamentarian. Though a younger man, he cherished warm friendships with such former representatives of the Wilson era as Garner, Glass, Harrison, Byrnes, and many others who had since become senators. By 1937 he was one of the most powerful figures in Missouri politics and could afford to record his independent views if he chose.[116]

Well before the court battle he had chosen to differ with Roosevelt on several issues, including the NRA, AAA, the "death sentence," and 1936 tax bill. His voting record brought him close to the irreconcilables. His opposition, however, emanated less from a clear conservative philosophy than from an independent, almost maverick posture. A few liberal observers even thought him somewhat progressive. Paul Y. Anderson of the *Nation* said as late as 1938, "Let me urge liberals not to judge Senator Clark too hastily by his supporters. Some of us have felt that the TVA and the Labor Relations Act constitute the simplest test of progressivism. Clark voted for both. No flaming liberal, he is nevertheless intelligent, honest, humane and belligerently independent of corporate influence. . . ."[117]

But Clark, like Borah, was unable to accept the growing

[115] His real name was Joel Bennett Clark, but he changed it in honor of his father, Champ Clark.

[116] Jack Alexander, "Missouri's Dark Mule," *Saturday Evening Post*, CCXI (Oct. 8, 1938), 5.

[117] "What the Election Means," *Nation*, CXLVII (Nov. 19, 1938), 527-28.

complexity of modern life which was resulting in the mush-
rooming of federal and presidential power. In part this
feeling stemmed from passionate opposition to an interven-
tionist foreign policy: already, he was becoming suspicious
of Roosevelt's intentions in foreign affairs. Clark quickly
joined Connally in denouncing the court plan and became
one of the chief orators and organizers of the conservative
coalition.

The addition of these two influential men to the coalition
was symbolic of the many elements composing the new
opposition to the New Deal. But their positions were insignificant in comparison to the effect of a third convert to the
cause: Burton K. Wheeler of Montana. Whereas Connally
and Clark had been considered moderates, Wheeler was a
tried and true progressive veteran of many political battles.

Wheeler was a colorful figure. Tall, broad-shouldered,
and bony, he was jovial, not at all pompous, and frankly
outspoken. With his perpetual cigar, shambling gait,
rumpled suit, and battered Stetson, he looked the part he
played of the rugged, fearless statesman from the West.[118]
Only the rimless octagonal spectacles perched on his high
aquiline nose disturbed the picture.

He was proud of his self-made background. A native
of Massachusetts, he left the East to attend Michigan law
school and eventually landed in Montana at the age of
twenty-three when cardsharps on a westbound train fleeced
him near Butte. Settling there, he entered politics and
became a tormentor of the Anaconda Copper Company, the
dominant power in Montana politics. A United States attorney in Montana during World War I, he was courageous
in his defense of civil liberties. In 1922 he was elected to

[118] Joseph Alsop and Robert Kintner, Washington *Star*, June 6, 1938, A-8.
For another analysis of Wheeler, see Marquis W. Childs, *I Write from Washington* (New York, 1942), pp. 38-40, 189. Another physical description is
in Wheeler's autobiography done with Paul F. Healy, *Yankee from the
West* (Garden City, N.Y., 1962), pp. vii-ix.

Senator Millard E. Tydings (D—Md.)
(Courtesy National Archives, Washington, D.C.)

SENATE MAJORITY LEADER JOSEPH T. ROBINSON OF ARKAN-
SAS *(right)* AT THE INAUGURATION OF FRANKLIN D. ROOSE-
VELT IN 1933
(Courtesy Franklin D. Roosevelt Library, Hyde Park, N.Y.)

SENATORS *(from left)* CHARLES L. MCNARY (R–Ore.),
WARREN R. AUSTIN (R–Vt.), KEY PITTMAN (D–Nev.),
AND WILLIAM E. BORAH (R–Idaho)
(Courtesy National Archives, Washington, D.C.)

the Senate, where his aggressive attacks concerning Teapot Dome quickly made him a favorite of progressives.[119] In 1924 he was Robert M. La Follette, Sr.'s vice-presidential running mate, campaigning on a Progressive platform which demanded not only public ownership of railroads and utilities but a constitutional amendment to reduce the power of the Supreme Court.

Like Connally, Wheeler could lay claim to having had a small hand in Roosevelt's nomination; indeed, he was the first prominent Democrat publicly to announce his support. And during Roosevelt's first administration the only major New Deal measure he opposed was the World Court proposal of 1935. A rabid isolationist, he was not only loyal on domestic legislation but, as the utilities fight had indicated, insistent in his determination to diminish the power of large corporate interests.

Nevertheless, Wheeler was not happy with the New Deal. For one thing, he was extremely proud. Viewing himself as the true defender of liberalism in the party, he resented the adulation heaped upon Roosevelt. "Who does Roosevelt think he is?" he complained. "He used to be just one of the barons. I was the baron of the northwest, Huey Long was baron of the south."[120] He felt slighted, complaining that Roosevelt never saw him.[121] He also resented Roosevelt's recognition of Bruce Kremer, a New Deal insider close to the Anaconda interests. Proud and suspicious, Wheeler by 1937 had personal grievances to settle.

Wheeler's eventual antagonism to the court plan was not simply the result of personal bitterness; much of it must be laid at the door of the plan itself. After the 1936 election, he had written Norris of his desire for a constitutional

[119] See Robert Bendiner, "Men Who Would Be President: Burton K. Wheeler," *Nation*, CL (April 27, 1940), 532-36.

[120] Cited in Burns, *Roosevelt*, p. 341. See also Robert S. Allen, "Wheeler and the Liberals," *Current History*, LI (March 1940), 25-27.

[121] Ickes, *Secret Diary*, I, 363-64, May 15, 1935.

amendment to curb the court: "I would not want to go as far as some people do with reference to the fixing of prices and the curtailment of production. I do not believe that the people would back us in going that far at this time. It may be necessary in the future. I am willing and I think perhaps the people would go as far as to amend the Constitution to permit Congress to fix the hours of labor and minimum wages and let competition proceed from that point."[122] Wheeler, like Norris and many other progressives, was sincere in wishing to reduce the court's jurisdiction. But he wanted the change to be by amendment, not packing. "I am against the President's proposal," he wrote, "because it is a sham and a fake liberal proposal. It doesn't accomplish one of the things that the liberals of America have been fighting for. It merely places upon the Supreme Court six political hacks."[123]

In the last analysis it was a little surprising that Wheeler had not openly disagreed with the New Deal before he did. Aside from his proud nature, Wheeler's progressivism was essentially poles apart from that of the New Deal. Like Borah and other western progressives, he represented an older hostility to centralized power, be it corporate or governmental. In his defense of civil liberties, his insistence upon the holding company "death sentence," and his struggles against the Anaconda Company, he at all times revealed his concern that big government or finance would envelop the individual. But the New Deal, even during the utilities and tax struggles, was hardly antimonopolistic. And far from fearing a strong executive, most New Dealers welcomed it. When the court plan revealed the full extent of Roosevelt's willingness to advance executive power, Wheeler finally rebelled.

Within a few days of the announcement of the proposal,

[122] Nov. 25, 1936, Norris MSS, Tray 27, Box 3.

[123] Alva Johnston, "President Tamer," *Saturday Evening Post*, CCX (Nov. 13, 1937), 51 (a sketch of Wheeler).

"Burt" Wheeler had found a new cause. While insisting he still favored a constitutional amendment, he became an indefatigable agitator against the plan. His departure from the New Deal fold was the hardest blow of all to the administration, for Wheeler was an experienced and fearless fighter. Most of all, he was known as a liberal; from this point on the administration could not brand opponents of the plan as economic royalists or selfish partisans. As William Allen White expressed it: "The President need have no fear of opposition from the right, but opposition on the left he cannot overcome so easily. In the first place, he doesn't know the tactics, and in the second place, that group loves martyrdom and thrives on it, and the more he lambasts it, the bigger it gets."[124]

With Wheeler's conversion in the first few days, all the future elements of the opposition coalition were together: irreconcilable Democrats such as Glass, conservative Democrats such as Copeland and Burke, Republican conservatives such as Vandenberg, moderate Democrats such as Clark and Connally, and western progressives opposed to centralization of power such as Wheeler and Borah. The next step was to determine the leadership of the nascent coalition. This was easy to do. Immediately after the court plan appeared, conservatives began holding regular dinner meetings, usually at the homes of Gerry or Tydings. Diners on these occasions also included Byrd, Burke, George, Vandenberg, Bailey, Clark, Connally, and Walsh.[125] When Wheeler announced his opposition, he too attended one of these, at Tydings' home. It was an odd gathering. Wheeler, knowing he must join these men to stop Roosevelt, was uneasy with his new associates. He peered suspiciously at them, emphasizing this was a marriage of convenience. The old conservatives, for their part, distrusted Wheeler. But they immediately

[124] To Robert Appleton, March 8, 1937, W. A. White MSS.
[125] Joseph Alsop and Robert Kintner, Washington *Star*, June 6, 1938, A-9. See also Alsop and Catledge, *The 168 Days*, p. 104; Wheeler, *Yankee*, p. 323.

recognized his great value to the cause and named him official spokesman for the group. "Wheeler," Vandenberg commented privately, "is absolutely *essential* to us in this fight. He has taken a courageous stand against the President and is entitled to any co-operation we can give him."[126]

Wheeler started to work at a rapid pace. First, he installed himself as head of a steering committee; Gerry became whip. This committee coordinated strategy with Frank Gannett's National Committee to Uphold Constitutional Government and other voluntary church, women's, and business organizations.[127] It also dispatched prominent Democratic orators about the country: Walsh, Copeland, and Burke, for instance, conducted a mass meeting at Carnegie Hall in New York. Warning ultraconservatives and "economic royalists" to stay in the background, Wheeler sought to give his group the air of unselfish crusaders waging a holy war against totalitarianism. By March his coalition was already functioning smoothly, liberally financed, and generously covered by the press.

Perhaps the most interesting aspect of Wheeler's strategy was his effort in the direction of bipartisanship. Here he capitalized upon his friendship with Borah; indeed, Borah called his friend every night during the struggle to ask after his health. Wheeler also found support from the Republican National Committee. Under the leadership of National Chairman John D. M. Hamilton, a conservative Kansan, the committee pumped funds into the fight, especially in payment of travel of hostile witnesses to the Capitol. Finally, Burke had contacts among prominent Republicans and worked closely with Hamilton in these ventures.[128] The

[126] Vandenberg Notes, March 2, 1937, Vandenberg MSS, Scrapbook 1937. Italics his.

[127] See Samuel T. Williamson, *Imprint of a Publisher: The Story of Frank Gannett and His Independent Newspapers* (New York, 1940), pp. 241-52.

[128] Morris, "Republicans," p. 229. For Burke and Hamilton, see also George Wolfskill, *The Revolt of the Conservatives: A History of the American Liberty League, 1934-1936* (Boston, 1962), p. 252.

Wheeler-Gerry Democratic faction carried the brunt of the attack against the plan, and the chief Republican contribution was the strategy of silence. Yet given the natural hostility generated by the two-party system, these nascent moves marked a significant advance in the formation of a bipartisan senatorial coalition.[129]

Finally, Wheeler used his contacts on the court. Through his daughter's friendship with Mrs. Brandeis, he discovered that the venerable judge was upset at Roosevelt's proposal. Telephoning him, Wheeler found Brandeis willing to arrange a meeting with Chief Justice Charles Evans Hughes. Cautiously, Hughes assented to compose a letter about Roosevelt's plan, and Wheeler triumphantly brandished it in front of the Senate Judiciary Committee on March 22. The letter artfully demolished Roosevelt's spurious arguments concerning old age and inefficiency: it was one of the sharpest blows to the administration.[130]

The court itself then came to the aid of the coalition against the plan. In a series of decisions Justice Owen J. Roberts, formerly a swing man, joined the four formerly "liberal" judges to uphold New Deal legislation. On March 29 in a 5-4 decision the court validated a Washington state minimum-wage law, reversing its position of 1936. And on April 12 it sustained the Wagner Labor Relations Act, also by a 5-4 decision. For all practical purposes, these decisions marked the end of the original plan, for the court no longer

[129] Relations within the coalition were by no means always harmonious. In March the publicity director of the GOP National Committee complained: "The Democrats still seem to think that we Republicans should play dead. . . . Their thought seemed to be that not only should we ourselves keep silent but also that we should not endeavor to get others to be vocal. I asked Senator Wheeler last night just when he would restore our rights of citizenship to us. He declined to commit himself. Will you laugh or throw a fit?" William Hard to Landon, March 23, 1937, Landon MSS, Political File, 1937, H-K.

[130] For this story, see Wheeler, *Yankee*, pp. 327-32. MacColl, "Supreme Court," pp. 298-99, using notes by Hughes, tells substantially the same story.

needed reforming. "Why run for a train," remarked Byrnes, "after you've caught it." Even Roosevelt's staunchest political pressure groups—labor unions, farm organizations, and city machines—exerted only superficial pressure. Since the court endangered none of their favorite projects, they reasoned, why not dispense with court reform and push the bills they wanted?[131] The court's decisions in 1937 served to divide Roosevelt's liberal coalition at the same time a conservative coalition was forming.

The defection of men such as Connally, Clark, and Wheeler, Hughes's letter, and the court's "switch in time that saved nine" had the desired effect upon most of the moderate Democrats. By late May, Wheeler's aides were sure of the support of nearly fifty senators, and most of these had declared their opposition openly. Among them were usually dependable Democrats such as Frederick Van Nuys,[132] a bespectacled and mild-mannered Indianan whose forthright opposition approached that of Connally and Clark; Carl A. Hatch, a scholarly and respected moderate from New Mexico;[133] Patrick A. McCarran of Nevada, who had already posed difficulties for Roosevelt on earlier occasions;[134] and Joseph C. O'Mahoney of Wyoming, a political friend of Farley and a renowned foe of monopoly.[135] Other previously reliable Democrats who came to look unfavorably upon the plan included Alva Adams of Colorado; Guy M. Gillette of Iowa, a newcomer who had been a loyal representative

---

[131] For failure of elements of the New Deal coalition to lobby effectively, see Alsop and Catledge, *The 168 Days,* pp. 116, 198-99.

[132] Pronounced "Van-Neece."

[133] Alva Johnston, "I'll Write a Letter to Hatch," *Saturday Evening Post,* CCXIII (Oct. 13, 1940), 31.

[134] See Biographical Sketch, Pittman MSS, Box 150; also Max Stern, "Senator McCarran: Wrench Thrower," *Today,* III (May 4, 1935), 11.

[135] See New York *Herald Tribune,* June 3, 1937, p. 23; O'Mahoney, Oral History Project, Columbia, for early life; New York *Times,* June 17, 1937, p. 16 (speech against plan); Julia Snow (study of O'Mahoney) in J. T. Salter, *Public Men,* pp. 109-26.

before 1937; and Francis Maloney of Connecticut, a moderate who had entered the Senate in 1935.

Many incidents helped produce these defections. McCarran and O'Mahoney strongly resented Farley's remark (intended to be off-the-record) that they would support the plan when they realized their dependence upon the administration for favors.[136] Maloney discovered that sentiment in Connecticut reinforced his own initial reservations. O'Mahoney, like Wheeler, Borah, and other westerners, feared the potential strengthening of executive power. McCarran, besides resenting Farley's remark, already disliked Roosevelt's habit of funneling Nevada patronage through Pittman. Hatch was willing to compromise but eventually voted against the plan when Roosevelt refused to unbend.

Although many of these men had reasons to even a score with Roosevelt or his advisers, their opposition to the court plan was not born of petty grudges. Van Nuys and Gillette had little cause for complaint at past treatment but simply distrusted the plan and the motives behind it. Later, they would support most New Deal legislation. Fundamentally, the anti-Roosevelt coalition considered the plan dangerous and unwise, and the Judiciary Committee, after months of stalling, finally said so in June. Seven Democrats and three Republicans attacked the plan as follows:

We recommend the rejection of this bill as a needless, futile, and utterly dangerous abandonment of constitutional principle.

It was presented to the Congress in a most intricate form and for reasons that obscured its real purpose.

It would not banish age from the bench nor abolish divided decisions.

It would not affect the power of any court to hold laws unconstitutional nor withdraw from any judge the authority to issue injunctions.

[136] This incident is best told in Alsop and Catledge, *The 168 Days*, p. 192; see also Robert S. Allen, "Hughes Checkmates the President," *Nation*, CXLIV (May 29, 1937), 610-11.

It would not reduce the expense of litigation nor speed the decision of cases.

It is a proposal without precedent and without justification. . . .

It is a measure which should be so emphatically rejected that its parallel will never again be presented to the free representatives of the free people of America.[137]

Roosevelt, in the meantime, had been sternly rejecting suggestions of compromise; "the people are with me," he repeated endlessly. Through city and state machines he also applied the utmost pressure upon wavering senators. But with the Judiciary Committee's adverse decision on the bill May 18 (the report was not issued until a month later), he began to realize that his legislative lieutenants were right. That same day Justice Willis Van Devanter announced his intention to retire. Since Van Devanter had been one of the anti-New Deal judges, his departure offered still one more argument against a court reorganization scheme. And on May 24, the Supreme Court upheld the Social Security Act. At last, Roosevelt decided it was time to relent; in early June he told Robinson to seek a compromise to salvage administration prestige. It was too late. Had he shown moderation from the beginning, he might have succeeded in obtaining some sort of moderate reform; as it was, his tenacity cost him many supporters and destroyed his chances for any reform at all.

The rest, though thrilling and dramatic, was largely anti-climactic; the fundamental shift had already occurred. The court had seemed to say it would no longer strike down the New Deal, and the Senate had evinced its determination to replace the court as a bulwark of anti-administration strength. Robinson, piqued that Roosevelt did not offer him Van Devanter's place, angrily awaited instructions for two

[137] Reprinted in New York *Herald Tribune*, June 15, 1937, p. 1. Interestingly, of the seven Democratic signers of the report (King, McCarran, Burke, Connally, Hatch, Van Nuys, and O'Mahoney), five were westerners.

crucial weeks while Wheeler's lieutenants corralled enough senators to destroy even a compromise version offered by Hatch.[138] When debate on the compromise version finally started on July 6, it was unprecedentedly bitter.[139] Three days later Wheeler's forces opened up on the plan, led by an eloquent Bailey. To give a final act to the drama, Robinson collapsed and died in his apartment on July 14. With his death went innumerable votes for the compromise secured out of personal affection. It was the end, not only of the original plan, but the compromise version as well.

The last act was macabre. Robinson's death inflamed the heated atmosphere which had already seared Senate friendships and turned the nation's most famous club into a grim and deadly battleground. To pay their last respects senators postponed the debate and sweltered on a train that chugged slowly to Arkansas for the funeral. But they continued, two implacably hostile groups, to devise strategy all the way out and all the way back.

At this point Garner, who had packed his bags and gone disgustedly to Texas in June, returned with the funeral train and, on instructions from Roosevelt, sought to deal with Wheeler. Eager above all to bring to an end the issue that

[138] The Hatch compromise would have permitted the President to name a coadjutor for any Supreme Court justice who had passed the age of seventy-five (instead of seventy) yet who refused to retire. But it would have limited such appointments to one per year.

[139] A measure of the temper of senators at this point was a letter by McNary, ordinarily good-tempered and genial. "The last week has been terrible here," he wrote, "hot day and night. . . . I don't know when we will get home. . . . They can take the darn Senate and my job and send them below. I've been a slave to my constituency too long and I'm sure that only a few appreciate my services." McNary to Mrs. T. W. Stolz, July 12, 1937. Two days later he wrote Col. Stolz, "He [Robinson] died a martyr to the cause of the court plan which never should have been presented to a civilized legislative organization." McNary MSS.

Bailey wrote J. E. S. Thorpe, July 6, 1937 (Bailey MSS, File 139) "The remarks on the floor indicate that there is to be a great deal of spirit and fire as the fight develops. . . . My own opinion is that the debates will become bitter quickly."

was splitting the Democratic party, Garner did not haggle over terms. He told Wheeler to name his own ticket but "For God's sake and the sake of our party, be reasonable."[140] Since Wheeler had the votes, the result was recommittal, 70-20, of the compromise plan; a week later, an innocuous version which permitted no changes in federal court membership and provided only for minor ways to speed up the judicial process emerged from the committee. Garner quickly gaveled it through.[141] "The Supreme Court is out?" asked Hiram Johnson at the end of the struggle. "The Supreme Court is out," came the reply. "Glory be to God," said Johnson.[142] The battle was over.

Practically every appraisal of the court controversy agrees that the most important reason for Roosevelt's defeat was the plan itself and Roosevelt's handling of it. In both respects echoes of the 1935 tax fight were audible. As a former Roosevelt admirer put it bluntly but without too much exaggeration,

I think Roosevelt realizes now that he went at the court proposal with bad strategy. . . . Had Roosevelt been less cocky, proceeded with more circumspection in getting the advance advice and backing of his congressional leaders, he would have got a lot

[140] Alsop and Catledge, *The 168 Days,* p. 285. See Roosevelt's pleading letter to Garner, Elliott Roosevelt (ed.), *The Roosevelt Letters* (3 vols.; London, 1952), III, 211-13, July 7, 1937.

[141] The vote was not very meaningful. Many regular Democrats, including not only the leaders but many sincere New Dealers, voted to recommit because they knew Garner had planned this with Wheeler. It is perhaps interesting, however, to note that most of the veteran senators left the New Deal fold for the first time on this vote. Of the twenty supporters, only five—Caraway (Ark.), Black (Ala.), Neely (W. Va.), McKellar (Tenn.), and La Follette—had been senators before 1933. Seven were newcomers in 1936. This division of new senators and pre-Depression senators would occasionally recur in later years.

[142] *Congressional Record,* 75th Cong., 1st Sess., 7381. Roosevelt remained unbowed. "Judicial reform is coming just as sure as God made little apples," he wrote. Roosevelt to Sen. Theodore Green (R.I.), July 23, 1937, Green MSS, Box 1123.

further and faster. He was too fast and cocky on the trigger. As you say, his original argument was screwy. It didn't sound well. . . . Looking back over his record that is a very common fault of his. He is constantly going off half cocked on basically very excellent ideas and objectives. The reason why he has got away with so many bills of this kind is that his opposition is so incorrigibly and stupidly reactionary.[143]

This blanket indictment of Roosevelt was unfair: he did not "constantly" go off "half cocked." In reference to the court plan alone, however, it was true enough. The plan itself, his failure to consult his leaders, and his refusal to compromise marked the worst congressional bungling of his career.

It is arguable that Roosevelt had no choice, that a constitutional amendment could never have succeeded, and that a pragmatic, short-run plan such as this was his only hope. But if he had made court reform an election issue, if he had been forthright in his reasoning, he might have been more persuasive. And if he had consulted party leaders, he could have been spared the effort of trying. It is hard to conceive of a more politically impossible plan being handled in a more clumsy fashion.

It is said that the President lost the battle but won the war—that his plan scared the court into submission. That the court (or rather Justice Roberts) shifted was obvious. But Roosevelt's plan was not the reason. The court had privately decided the minimum-wage case before the court plan was broached to the public. If any external factors caused Roberts to shift, it was probably Roosevelt's sweeping election victory and not the plan.[144]

Above all, did he win the war? Even assuming that the

[143] Robert Allen to William Allen White, Aug. 6, 1937, W. A. White MSS, Box 191.
[144] It is arguable that Roberts did not shift—in the sense of reversing himself entirely.

court plan hastened the cluster of Supreme Court resignations in the next few years and helped create a Roosevelt court by 1939, it appears in retrospect that it was not worth it. Consider the statistics. In January, he could rely upon at least sixty tried-and-true veteran senators, plus some ten newcomers chosen on New Deal platforms. Yet during the court fight only thirty-five of these potential seventy were dependable, and only twenty ended up supporting a shadow of the original plan. And as other issues of the session were to demonstrate, at least ten of these new defectors would continue to a consistent degree their opposition to the New Deal. It is true that some of the opponents might have shifted anyway, believing with Clark and Connally that the New Deal had already gone far enough. It is true that some of these same moderates used the court plan as an excuse or an occasion to proclaim suspicions they had harbored since the long hot summer of 1935. For them "breathing spell" meant general acceptance of the status quo. And it is probably true that the growing complexity of twentieth-century American life would sooner or later have left western antimonopolists such as Wheeler and Borah in the wake.

The fact is, however, that the court plan gave these moderates a perfect occasion to bolt at a time when other important New Deal measures remained to be enacted. It also pushed other liberals, such as O'Mahoney, temporarily out of the New Deal camp. Not all these men deserted the President forever: even Wheeler's subsequent voting record was more liberal than his critics have claimed. But for many it was a major turning point; having left the New Deal fold once, they were marked men who would find it easier to do so again. The court plan undermined Roosevelt's powerful senatorial coalition; it alienated many western progressives and moderate Democrats; it helped to unite Republicans and to transform their strategy; and it led conservatives of both parties to begin to work together in bipartisan fashion.

From this point on the Senate retained many of the divisions of this fight, and the bipartisan conservative bloc, though neither permanent nor cohesive, recurred later using similar leaders and strategy. The President had gained a court but had begun to lose part of his Congress.

Above all, the court issue seriously damaged what had amounted to a myth of Rooseveltian invincibility. He had fought hard for a dear project and for the first time he had lost badly. One magazine commented after the battle: "There has been some change of sentiment toward Roosevelt since last fall. His following may be as great but it is less enthusiastic. . . . He commands support, but not the old awe, reverence, and idolatry."[145]

Peter Gerry, triumphant and happy, described the new situation as well as anyone. He wrote Bailey: "The court fight has proved that the Senate can say 'no' and I think it has taught Senators that they can disagree with the President on important legislation and yet not lose the support of the voters at home, even though these voters are largely in favor of the administration. . . . If my surmise is correct as to this, more and more Senators will take heart, especially those who lacked it last winter."[146]

As the rest of the session would prove, Gerry was right.

[145] Alva Johnson, "President Tamer," p. 9. See also Pittman to Ed. W. Clark, Pittman MSS, Aug. 2, 1937, Box 11. "It's a good thing the fight's over. Both sides were unreasonably bitter. I constantly attempted to act as an intermediary and a peacemaker. I don't know how far I succeeded."

[146] To Bailey, Oct. 19, 1937, Bailey MSS, Political File.

4

THE SENATE: SECTIONAL AND ECONOMIC DIVISIONS

Although the court plan was by far the most damaging single blow to Roosevelt's senatorial coalition, it was not the only issue of the 1937 session. Moreover, the plan had little effect upon a congressional development of lasting consequence: a menacing growth in sectional and economic antagonisms. The controversies in 1937 over such issues as relief spending, labor unions, and urban welfare programs indicate that Roosevelt would have encountered considerable conservative opposition in the 1937 session, court plan or not.

In understanding the development of these sectional-economic divisions in the Senate, few men are so revealing as the Democratic chieftains who had been so useful in countless congressional battles since 1933. Perhaps the most powerful of these leaders were Robinson and Harrison, but two others, James F. Byrnes of South Carolina and Vice-President John N. Garner, were also influential figures. Their reactions to much socio-economic legislation of the 1937 session clearly showed the impulses that led many congressmen to turn against the New Deal at this time.

Byrnes, cautious and self-contained, was as neat as Harrison was untidy. Small, wiry, compact, he had an angular face, sharp eyes, and a generally genial, quizzical expression. No orator, he was often to be found leaning gracefully behind the last row of seats, listening quietly to a colleague or gently persuading him to see his point of view.[1] Fifty-seven in 1937, he had served from 1911 to 1925 in the House, where he had become friendly with Harrison, Robinson, Glass, and other veterans of the Wilsonian period. In 1931 he advanced to the Senate, where his talents and friendships served him well. By 1937 he was already a power in the Senate.[2]

Generally, but not always, he had used this power on behalf of the New Deal.[3] In fact Byrnes was more national in outlook than his fellow Senate leaders, and his support of the New Deal was usually sincere. Yet even before his reelection in 1936, Byrnes had established himself as rather independent. Since he held no official leadership post, he had felt free to vote his convictions whenever they could not be reconciled with party loyalty. He had opposed the "death sentence" provision when Robinson and Harrison dared not. Roosevelt wisely tolerated Byrnes's infrequent but forceful departures. This quality of successful inde-

[1] Marquis W. Childs, "The President's Best Friend," *Saturday Evening Post*, CCXIII (April 26, 1941), 29.

[2] *Current Biography*, 1941, p. 127. For a study emphasizing Byrnes' early life as that of a "Bourbon Horatio Alger," see Jefferson Frazier, "The Southerner as American: A Political Biography of James Francis Byrnes" (Honors thesis, Harvard University, 1964), p. 16.

[3] Raymond Moley, *Twenty-Seven Masters of Politics in a Personal Perspective* (New York, 1949), p. 253.

pendence was partly responsible for his popularity with fellow senators.[4]

After his renomination in 1936 Byrnes, safe for six years, began to show still more independence. Long a foe of large government expenditures, he began to demand ways to reduce and systematize funds appropriated for relief. Open opposition would come later, but Byrnes's campaign already revealed ambivalent feelings on the New Deal. On the front of the "Byrnes Record," his newspaper to the voters, ran a headline in large type: "A Vote for Byrnes Is a Vote for FDR." But inside, prominently displayed on page three, was a picture of Byrnes and an old friend. The caption read, "Carter Glass Meets His Friend, Jimmie Byrnes."[5]

Of the four leaders Garner was easily the most colorful. Already sixty-nine in 1937, Garner was as firm and vigorous as many younger men. With his white shock of hair, clear blue eyes, bushy white eyebrows, and sharp beak of a nose, he looked like the blunt vinegary politician he was.[6] Plain in his tastes, he affected the common touch, avoided Washington society as much as possible, and liked nothing better than to visit the zoo while in Washington. As often as possible he went fishing in Uvalde, his home in southwest Texas.[7]

Long before the New Deal Garner was a well-known Washington figure. First a representative in 1903, he was the apostle of party regularity. "I have always done what I thought best for my country," he supposedly said, "never varying unless I was advised that two-thirds of the Demo-

[4] Joseph Alsop and Robert Kintner, "The Real Leader of the Senate, Jimmie Byrnes," *Saturday Evening Post*, CCXIII (July 20, 1940), 18.

[5] Allan A. Michie and Frank Rhylick, *Dixie Demagogues* (New York, 1939), p. 72.

[6] Bascom N. Timmons, *Garner of Texas* (New York, 1948), p. 260.

[7] Marquis W. Childs, *I Write from Washington* (New York, 1942), pp. 89-90.

crats were for a bill and then I voted for it."[8] Entirely safe
in his home district, he was reelected easily until he became
minority leader of the House in 1929 and speaker in 1931.[9]
After swinging his support to Roosevelt in 1932, he reluctantly became his running mate. His old congressional
friendships made him a valuable administration man in both
houses.

But Garner was also a true representative of the "new"
Southwest. Born in a mudchinked log cabin on the Texas
prairie, he received little education, attended college only
briefly, and advanced through the law and politics. By the
1930's he owned two banks, considerable valuable pecan
land, and mortgages on more than half the houses in Uvalde.
He was also as tight-fisted with his money as any man in
public life. He lived in inexpensive hotels or boarding
houses while in the Capitol, employed his wife as his
secretary, and even forswore his old poker games.[10] His
economic philosophy, noted one observer, was "spend less
than you make, whatever it is; never go into debt; learn to
invest your money or have someone do it for you."[11] He had
a deep respect for private property, an instinctive horror
of labor violence or class struggle. A practical man, he had
no use for "intellectuals" or "bureaucrats." Though he had
generally stayed with Roosevelt before 1937, party loyalty
was his main reason. Like his friends, he was becoming
increasingly upset by the trend of the New Deal, especially
its relief and labor policies.

[8] Michie and Rhylick, *Dixie Demagogues*, p. 35.

[9] Timmons, *Garner*, pp. 181-82. See Jordan S. Schwarz, "John N. Garner
and the Sales Tax Rebellion of 1932," *Journal of Southern History*, XXX
(May 1964), 162-80.

[10] Timmons, *Garner*, p. 181.

[11] Marquis James, "Poker-Playing, Whiskey-Drinking, Evil Old Man,"
Saturday Evening Post, CCXII (Sept. 9, 1939), 68. For Garner's personal
relations with FDR and his love of economy, see his letters in Roosevelt
MSS, PPF 1416.

Byrnes and Garner, together with Robinson and Harrison, were similar in many ways—all of which would lessen their sympathy with the New Deal. To begin with, they were close to conservative financial and business interests. Robinson, Harrison, and Byrnes were so friendly with Bernard Baruch, the erstwhile Wall Street speculator and occasional governmental adviser, that critics referred to the trio as Baruch's collection of "Old Masters." All three often hunted with Baruch and other financial titans on his sprawling South Carolina plantation, and Harrison probably received Baruch's financial support after becoming insolvent in 1932.[12] Baruch, for his part, was an old Wilsonian who approved of the 100 Days but very little of the New Deal thereafter. Among Garner's strongest political backers were large Texas financial interests. Though first of all practical politicians and loyal party men, these Senate leaders were also sympathetic with conservative business viewpoints on spending and labor policies.

These men also shared a common southern origin. Too much can be made of this fact, because many other southern congressmen did not react as they did on various issues. Yet their prominence indicated the overwhelmingly southern cast of the Senate leadership. So long as the New Deal did not disturb southern agricultural, industrial, or racial patterns, these leaders would support it, sometimes with enthusiasm. But if and when the northern wing of the party began to dominate (as it did after the 1936 election), a certain degree of friction was almost inevitable.

Moreover, after the 1936 election these leaders were "safe." Byrnes, Harrison, and Robinson were all reelected that year. Like Glass and Bailey, they were untouchable for six years, by which time it was expected Roosevelt would

[12] New York *Times* (obituary), June 23, 1941, pp. 16-17; Harold Ickes, *The Secret Diary of Harold Ickes* (3 vols.; New York, 1954), II, 164, July 16, 1937; Margaret L. Coit, *Mr. Baruch* (Boston, 1957), pp. 321, 389.

have returned to Hyde Park.[13] Garner opposed a third term
on principle, and expected in 1940 either to replace Roosevelt in the White House or to depart for his favorite fishing
spots in Texas. If a break had to come, these four men
realized that they had little to lose.

Finally, these leaders were essentially progressives of the
New Freędom vintage. They continued to believe that
their party stood for Wilsonian ideals: regulated competition, states' rights, and individual freedom where it did not
impinge upon the liberty of others.[14] They conceived of
themselves as the true progressives and as the bulwarks of
a party which they felt would have collapsed without them
in the 1920's.

A fundamental assumption of New Freedom thought,
however, was the existence of a healthy economy: in such
circumstances, government needed only to regulate excess
bigness or corruption. But the Depression of the 1930's
suggested that the economy needed stimulation, not regulation, and New Dealers came to think of a welfare state, not
the Wilsonian state which had contented itself with a few
deft regulatory efforts. More often than not, the New Deal
required vastly increased bureaucracy, huge increases in
federal spending, and unprecedented governmental intervention into the daily lives of the people. Though it may
not have been a "revolutionary response to a revolutionary
situation,"[15] it was truly a "New" Deal.

Roosevelt's rule also stimulated the formation of a new

[13] Ickes was of this opinion. "Byrnes," he said, "simply went along
because he was to be up for re-election last year. Now, with a term
extending beyond that of the President, he has jumped over the traces and
gone conservative." *Secret Diary*, II, 63, Jan. 30, 1937.

[14] For evidence of the progressivism of southern congressmen, 1906-1913,
see Anne Firor Scott, "A Progressive Wind from the South," *Journal of
Southern History*, XXIX (Feb. 1963), 53-70. She, too, emphasizes the
absence of a "Solid South."

[15] This assessment is by Carl N. Degler, *Out of Our Past* (New York,
1959), p. 416.

Democratic party. By 1937 the New Deal had begun to
create a revolution in expectations. Many people who had
long accepted low economic and social position began to
hope. Union men, Negroes, farmers, underprivileged ethnic
groups—all viewed the New Deal as their friend. They had
been the heart of Roosevelt's increased popular support in
1936 and had shifted the majority strength of the Democratic
party from its old southern enclave in the 1920's to a northern
urban base by 1937. From this point on they became
increasingly insistent, and they clamored for more federal
aid at the same time the old party wheelhorses were
demanding that it be curtailed.

"I consider myself a Democrat," Garner said, "without
any explanatory prefix [such as New Deal Democrat]. I
think I am a progressive and I hope a sound progressive.
There is a vast difference between progressivism and makeshift."[16] He thus expressed the dilemma that self-styled
progressives such as Byrnes, Harrison, and himself began to
face as the New Deal, transformed by the new forces in its
coalition, gradually became the party of northern liberalism.
These old Democrats either had to accept the revolutionary
"makeshift" of the New Deal or force it to return to the
"progressivism" of the New Freedom. The chasm was becoming too wide to accommodate both.

Until April 1937 these leaders made no vocal complaints.
Even the court plan failed to bring them into open opposition, for whatever its faults, they did not view it as a threat
to southern institutions. Despite the strain on party loyalty,
they still sided with the administration.

Even before announcement of the court plan, however,
labor-management problems had resulted in a new labor
tactic: the sitdown strike. Unionists of the fledgling CIO,
seeking both recognition and economic gains, sat in factories
threatening and in some cases using force to repulse manage-

[16] Timmons, *Garner,* p. 231.

ment attacks to regain their plants. By April 1937 this tactic had succeeded in defeating the biggest titans of them all: General Motors and United States Steel. It appeared then as if the sitdowns would succeed everywhere, for it was difficult to dislodge strikers without serious damage to plant and equipment—a possibility which most employers were not willing to chance. And Democratic Governor Frank Murphy of Michigan, center of the disturbances, refused to evict the strikers. Conservatives, frightened at what they regarded as seizure of private property, envisioned revolution unless the federal government intervened quickly on behalf of embattled employers. Roosevelt, however, refrained from taking sides, regarding the strikes as disputes for the antagonists to settle themselves.

The problem naturally attracted senatorial attention. In March Hiram Johnson, already incensed at the court plan, revealed his general disaffection with a denunciation of government authorities who permitted such activity. "Down that road lurks dictatorship," he insisted.[17] Senator King of Utah echoed his sentiments, and Senator Allen J. Ellender of Louisiana (later one of the twenty senators to back Roosevelt's compromise court plan) continued the attack. If CIO leader John L. Lewis was responsible for the strikes, Ellender proclaimed, he was "a traitor to American ideals and a menace to the peace and prosperity of the Nation."[18] In the House Martin Dies, Jr., of Texas urged a congressional investigation. Desultory senatorial discussion of the sitdowns broke out from time to time through the end of March.

Labor unrest had particularly infuriated both Garner and Byrnes. Sitdowns, said the Vice-President, were "mass lawlessness, which, to me, is intolerable and will lead to great difficulty, if not destruction."[19] At one Cabinet meeting, an

[17] *Congressional Record,* 75th Cong., 1st Sess., 2337.
[18] *Ibid.,* p. 2472.
[19] James A. Farley, *Jim Farley's Story* (New York, 1948), p. 85.

insider said, Garner was so angry at Roosevelt and Secretary of Labor Frances Perkins that he "rose and stood behind his chair and gave Perkins hell and she began to cry and Roosevelt abruptly terminated [the] cabinet meeting."[20] On another occasion, he and Roosevelt shouted so loudly at one another over the sitdowns that Robinson had to silence them. Garner himself said later that this meeting sparked "the only angry discussion we ever had."[21]

But it was Byrnes who destroyed the surface calm of the Senate. Late in the afternoon of April 1 the Senate was placidly concluding debate on the Guffey coal bill when Byrnes suddenly arose. Denouncing the sitdown strikers, he offered an amendment to the coal bill and frankly termed his amendment a "condemnation of the sitdown strike."[22] Byrnes's proposal would have outlawed any sitdown strikes in the coal industry (not then affected by sitdowns).

Byrnes's move, as usual, was calculated. As knowledgeable observers realized, Byrnes was concerned because John L. Lewis was beginning to turn his attention to South Carolina's textile mills.[23] Not so blunt or outspoken as Garner, Byrnes sought to stop sitdowns by indirection. If the amendment passed, the President, faced with a coal bill potentially harmful to the CIO or with no coal bill at all, might find it necessary to sign. Yet if he did so, he would be on record as agreeing that sitdowns were illegal. Whichever way Roosevelt turned, he would be on the spot; he could no longer avoid the issue.

The amendment aroused the Senate. Breaking the usual pattern of Republican silence, Vandenberg echoed Byrnes's sentiments. Garner, overjoyed, literally leaped from the

[20] Clapper Diary, Dec. 28, 1937, Clapper MSS. His source was Emil Hurja.

[21] Timmons, *Garner*, p. 216.

[22] *Congressional Record*, 75th Cong., 1st Sess., 3017.

[23] *Time*, April 12, 1937, p. 19; Joseph Alsop and Turner Catledge, *The 168 Days* (Garden City, N.Y., 1938), p. 237.

rostrum and embraced his Republican foe before the eyes of all. "I want to congratulate you," he exclaimed. "It was about time somebody said that."[24] Instead of adjourning for the weekend as planned (it was a Thursday), the Senate debated the plan that afternoon and the next day.

Robinson agreed with Byrnes, but as leader he was unwilling to permit the President to be embarrassed. Half-heartedly, and with sly grins instead of the usual fire, he took the floor to oppose Byrnes's motion.[25] It would mean, he said, turning miners "out into the storm." He then began meeting Byrnes and his opponents in search of possible compromise. Over the weekend, however, Byrnes refused to withdraw his amendment, consenting only to make it apply to all sitdowns so as not to reflect upon coal miners. On Monday, April 5, the Senate voted on this new amendment. Robinson and Roosevelt won, defeating the amendment 48-36, but only after promising to take up the question of sitdowns in a separate resolution later. The coal bill then passed easily. Soon afterward, Robinson and Pittman arranged for a compromise concurrent resolution declaring that sitdowns were "illegal and contrary to public policy." The resolution added that industrial spy systems, company unions, or refusal of an employer to permit collective bargaining were also contrary to public policy. Since a concurrent resolution was not binding, few senators objected to such a neutral statement; it passed 75-3.

The vote on the Byrnes amendment indicated the extent of Senate sentiment against the sitdown tactic. Republicans,

[24] Vandenberg Notes, April 2, 1937, Vandenberg MSS, Scrapbook 1937.

[25] *Time*, April 12, 1937, p. 19. In notes written at the time Vandenberg claimed to be surprised at the lack of Democratic opposition to his speeches against sitdowns. "Each moment," he wrote, "I expected to be assaulted from the Democratic side of the chamber. But each time I challenged the presidential responsibility, and looked over toward Senator Robinson . . . he was—to my amazement—nodding his head in approval." April 2, 1937, Vandenberg MSS, Scrapbook 1937.

continuing their opportunistic strategy of restraint, largely contented themselves with voting: twelve of sixteen sided with Byrnes. In addition, twenty-six of the seventy-six Democrats voted for or were paired for the Byrnes plan, including nine of the twenty-two southern Democrats. Others voting with Byrnes included not only the fourteen conservative Democrats of 1935, and new dissenters such as Clark and Connally, but a sizable group of moderates such as John H. Bankhead of Alabama, Richard B. Russell of Georgia, and Harry S. Truman of Missouri.[26] The conservative coalition on the amendment was unsuccessful, but it was much stronger than it had been since the utilities controversy.

This issue, though short-lived, was an ominous portent for the New Deal. Roosevelt had at no time conceived of himself as the patron of labor. Convinced that the working man was entitled to government aid against poverty or oppression, he viewed himself as President of all the people, not of a particular class. In 1935 Senator Robert F. Wagner of New York, not Roosevelt, had led the struggle for the Wagner Act guaranteeing fair collective bargaining. Similarly, the President favored no one (and satisfied no one) in the sitdown controversy, and he was later to remark concerning the "Little Steel"-CIO struggles, "a plague on both your houses."

But to Garner, Byrnes, and many citizens the CIO seemed to be a New Deal adjunct, begotten by it. Lewis had accompanied his successful organizing with the cry, "the President wants you to join a union." In 1936, the AF of L-CIO's so-called Non-Partisan League of Labor had been an important source of funds and votes for the New Deal. It was impossible to tell Byrnes and Garner that the new unionism, though protected by the New Deal, was largely inevitable. Thanks partly to Robinson's loyalty, the New Deal escaped serious embarrassment on the issue, but the

[26] See *Congressional Record*, 75th Cong., 1st Sess., 3136.

leadership ranks were restless. In this sense, not even the court plan had been so divisive.

Compared to the relief fight which followed, the sitdown struggle was a minor skirmish. Before it was over in June, all four leaders had openly opposed the President for the first time; indeed, they were on the verge of serious and lasting disagreement.

The President's budget address on April 20 touched off this controversy. Although it called for economies, it also requested a $1.5 billion appropriation to continue the Works Progress Administration (WPA) through fiscal 1938. This organization, headed by Harry Hopkins, had been created to distribute much of the funds passed in the relief bill of 1935. At the start of 1937 there were more than two million Americans on its payroll.

Roosevelt's request went first to the House, where it encountered well-organized opposition from a band of congressmen who kept the issue in doubt for more than a month. Finally, on June 2 the House passed a WPA bill in line with Roosevelt's request. By this time opposition to the appropriation was stronger than ever. Congressmen were already suspicious of administrators such as Hopkins. In itself this feeling was nothing new: executive-congressional clashes were ancient history in Washington. But the court proposal had compounded this problem, for senators felt that executive bureaucrats had been responsible for its presentation. They also resented the ever tighter circle of New Dealers who had the President's ear, few of whom were congressmen. As one observer put it, these advisers were "just Tommy Corcoran's friends one moment, and the next they were the group solidly allied, mutually helpful, constantly relying on one another."[27] Hopkins, who supped nightly at

[27] Joseph Alsop and Robert Kintner, *Men Around the President* (New York, 1939), pp. 114-15. See also Timmons, *Garner*, pp. 225-30, for Garner's reactions.

the White House table, was a particular target of this congressional hostility. Reputed to have said "people are too damned dumb," this former social worker was to hostile congressmen the epitome of the brash and irresponsible bureaucrat.[28] "The trouble with Harry," said one conservative observer, "as with so many others that Franklin Roosevelt gathered around him, was that he had never spent his own money."[29]

This kind of antagonism, though significant, was not primarily responsible for the aversion to large-scale relief spending that many senators felt in 1937. The main reasons were economic. To many congressmen it appeared that the crisis conditions of 1933-1934 were diminishing. Fewer people were on relief rolls; output at last exceeded that of 1928; unemployment, though heavy, was at a low ebb. Congressmen who had reluctantly consented to unbalanced budgets since the start of the Depression felt that 1937 was the time for more drastic economies than Roosevelt anticipated.[30] As Robinson complained at the time, "It is hard to make our people conscious of the necessity for retrenchment in public expenditures. Sometimes I get very much discouraged. Thousands of Arkansans come here during the year begging, begging, begging. . . . It is going to be very difficult to ever get away from this habit of giving out federal favors. You cannot imagine how persistent are the forces of plunder."[31] Garner echoed these sentiments. "As you well know," he wrote Farley, "I have believed for the last two

[28] Arthur M. Schlesinger, Jr., *The Politics of Upheaval* (Boston, 1960), p. 355. See also Searle F. Charles, *Minister of Relief: Harry Hopkins and the Depression* (Syracuse, 1963), pp. 23-25, for a physical description of Hopkins.

[29] George Creel, *Rebel at Large* (New York, 1947), p. 296.

[30] Robinson to John B. Moore, April 4, 1934, cited in Nevin E. Neal, "A Biography of Joseph T. Robinson," (unpublished Ph.D. dissertation, University of Oklahoma, 1957), p. 412, is an example that Robinson felt this way long before 1937.

[31] To W. T. Sitlington, cited in *ibid.*, p. 413 (dated 1937).

years that we should have been materially reducing our expenditures; that we could not go on indefinitely borrowing money to run the government."[32] And in the first week of May, Byrnes, believing that Roosevelt had broken an apparent promise to settle for less than $1.5 billion, spoke his mind emphatically: "As a member of the United States Senate I voted for every recovery measure. As a member of the Appropriations Committee I actively supported every relief appropriation. If today the same conditions existed I would vote for the same appropriations. *But the same conditions do not exist.* The recovery program of this administration has accomplished its purpose. *The emergency has passed.*"[33] No speech so well illustrated all the economic reasons behind conservative desires for a cut in relief.

Behind this talk of budget-balancing were other fears. Many moderate senators, Byrnes in particular, objected to the lack of plan behind the WPA. No comprehensive study had been made, they emphasized, of unemployment. What was causing it? Was it structural, technological, or seasonal? How many unemployed were unemployables? To Byrnes the WPA was a hit-or-miss proposition offering purely transitory benefits. It was "wasting" billions of dollars without in any way treating the fundamental causes of the malady. Conservatives also feared the establishment of a permanent Roosevelt relief "machine." Hopkins' later reputed remark, "spend and elect, spend and elect," already seemed to be one very plausible explanation of Roosevelt's phenomenal success. To Republicans this probability had long been obvious and frightening; in 1937 it was beginning to upset newly disaffected Democrats as well. As they pondered the possibilities of successfully defying the President over the court proposal, they asked themselves how the

[32] Farley, *Jim Farley's Story*, p. 85.

[33] New York *Times*, May 4, 1937, p. 13. Italics his. See also Byrnes to FDR, April 27, 1937, Roosevelt MSS, OF 79-Misc.

President would react. One answer was obvious: he might give control of relief money to hostile political factions in their home states. Before long, they feared, there would not be an anti-New Deal senator in Washington.[34]

Serious Senate maneuvering did not begin until the bill passed the House on June 2, at the same time that Roosevelt was finally beginning to consider compromise on the court issue. By this time the Capitol was sweltering, the Senate was already hopelessly divided over the court issue, labor unrest continued, and economy sentiment was stronger than ever. Norris wrote: "I thought at the beginning of the session a larger amount of relief was not only necessary but that it would not be difficult to secure. However, recent events have demonstrated that the plea for economy coming from all over the country has taken possession of Congress as well as everyone else. It looked for a moment as though the amount in the bill would be cut down very materially by the House, and there will, in my judgment, be a very stiff fight in the Senate on this subject."[35]

The situation was tailor-made for a Republican frontal assault as in earlier days. But most Republicans, realizing the effectiveness of silence on the court issue, decided to continue their policy of restraint. "There is compelling reason for silence right now," Landon advised. "We Republicans must let the storm blow by, praying as Americans that it will not be too late for free elections when it subsides."[36] Wisely, they decided to let Democrats widen the breach among themselves.

As chairman of an appropriations subcommittee on relief, Byrnes led the dissident Democratic forces. At first he tried to persuade his colleagues to cut $500 million from the President's request. Unsuccessful in this effort, he

---

[34] See Charles, *Hopkins*, pp. 167-68, 174-205, for a discussion of relief and politics.

[35] To Darwin J. Meserole, June 5, 1937, Norris MSS, Tray 33, Box 6.

[36] To Clapper, June 11, 1937, Clapper MSS, Container 48.

settled for a less obvious expedient requiring local relief agencies to contribute 40 percent of the total cost of WPA projects. Since many local agencies had no funds, this plan would have substantially curtailed relief spending. Another provision authorized the President to intervene where a local agency claimed inability to pay, but Byrnes's plan was still expected to result in sizable cuts.[37] And his proposal would have required many local agencies, honestly unable to pay, to take a pauper's oath to institute presidential intervention. One more feature of the Byrnes plan set a statutory limit of 3 percent administrative costs, a difficult if not impossible figure for the WPA to meet. The committee approved Byrnes's bill, 13-10. Nine of the thirteen were Democrats. From the start Roosevelt's relief program faced an organized revolt led by an erstwhile ally.

Six days later Robinson intervened with a "compromise" amendment. Changing the local share to 25 percent, Robinson's plan also authorized the President to approve projects without pauper's oaths and without the required amount from nonfederal funds. Ostensibly this amendment aimed to please the administration, but astute observers knew better. Robinson proposed the plan only after he and Byrnes had ascertained that the 40 percent plan had little chance of passage. At no time had he consulted the administration. "We have a condition of general prosperity," he proclaimed. "The time has come, if we are to safeguard the credit of the Treasury, to require those able to do so to contribute an equal amount."[38] Robinson was really proposing to give the administration half a loaf when it could have had the whole thing.

The events of the next few days fully exposed the rebellious temper of the Senate leaders. For the first time since 1933 Senate leadership shifted to the hands of Senator Alben

[37] See New York *Times*, June 11, 1937, p. 7.

[38] *Congressional Record*, 75th Cong., 1st Sess., 5866. See also "Robinson on Relief," *Nation*, CXLIV (June 26, 1937), 720.

W. Barkley of Kentucky and a band of New Dealers, as Robinson, Harrison, and Byrnes struggled for the new 25 percent plan. Garner also opposed Roosevelt's request. "You're wasting your time on this court matter," he told an opponent of court reorganization. "Don't you know that inside ten days there'll be a request for a blank check for $1.5 billion for relief? Don't you know you can't beat $1.5 billion?"[39]

Four days after Robinson's proposal Roosevelt's new leaders won. Robinson's "compromise" failed, 49-34, as did a last effort to substitute Byrnes's 40 percent plan, 58-25. But on the Robinson plan, the split already apparent on Byrnes's sitdown amendment recurred. Counting pairs, twenty-five Democrats joined the conservative bloc, including Pittman, Robinson, Harrison, and Byrnes. Garner, after naming Byrnes to head a special committee to study unemployment, disgustedly entrained for Uvalde, despite the urgent pleas of the President.[40] The $1.5 billion request passed the next day by voice vote.

The relief bill, even more than the sitdowns, had profoundly stirred many southerners. Twelve of the twenty-two southern senators voted or were paired for Robinson's compromise. Bailey's reasoning suggested why: "the further the government goes in these matters, the worse the situation will be. The Northern States are getting four dollars per capita to every dollar for any Southern State, and of course the Southern States are paying their full share per capita. The people in the North are twice as well off as the people in the South."[41] Because relief payments were usually

[39] Alsop and Catledge, The 168 Days, p. 132. See Robert S. Allen, "The New Deal Fights for Its Life," Nation, CXLV (July 10, 1937), 35-36, for a critique of the roles of these four leaders in several congressional battles of 1937.

[40] See New York Herald Tribune, June 20, 1937, p. 5.

[41] Josiah Bailey to Mayor J. B. Gray (Murphy, N.C.), May 26, 1937, Bailey MSS, Relief File.

heaviest in the cities, and because the South was so largely rural, many southerners believed that they were throwing money back over the Mason-Dixon Line. Actually, Bailey's statistics were only part of the story. Thanks to farm benefits and to low tax payments the South fared as well per tax dollar as the North, but, as so often happens, it was what people thought that mattered, and many southern conservatives thought the North was again bleeding the South of its hard-earned capital. As in the days of Reconstruction, they insisted that they were unwelcome guests at the "Great Barbecue."

Because Negroes were usually among the people most in need of welfare, many southerners also had racial objections to heavy relief payments. In the North, they claimed, continued relief spending increased New Deal reliance upon the Negro vote; in the South, they complained, it raised the Negro to the white man's economic level and created a shortage of cheap farm labor. Southern sentiments such as these began to account for the defection of the leaders at the same time that they remained loyal on the court plan. By no means all southern senators felt as they did. But the leaders had finally become concerned enough to break, and the sectional aspects of these issues were largely responsible.

If the sitdown and relief issues symbolized the growing distance between Roosevelt and his Senate leaders, the struggle to name Robinson's successor as leader dramatized it for all to see. Indeed, from Robinson's death on July 14 until the election of his replacement a week later, the Senate did little else except struggle to fill the vacancy.

The permanent assistant leader since 1936 had been Alben Barkley of Kentucky, a senator since 1927.[42] His party regularity was unquestioned: except for a vote to override Roosevelt's bonus veto in 1936, a vote in which almost all

[42] See also J. B. Shannon's study of Barkley, in J. T. Salter (ed.), *Public Men In and Out of Office* (Chapel Hill, N.C., 1946), pp. 240-56.

senators had joined, he had never deserted the President on important legislation. When Robinson left the Senate the day before his death, he had left the interim leadership to this dependable aide.

But Barkley had only the official post, and he held it because he was dependable and because other leaders, such as Harrison, had committee chairmanships which kept them busy.[43] In influence and seniority Harrison was a more logical leader. The only other prominently mentioned senator was Byrnes. Garner, for one, was known to favor him. Byrnes, however, quickly withdrew and announced for Harrison.[44] With no word from the White House, Harrison would have been the natural choice of his colleagues.

The next day, however, Roosevelt publicized a letter to Barkley. Known as the "Dear Alben" letter, it began by expressing a wish for a decent respect for Robinson's memory before talk of his successor arose. But since candidates were being mentioned, Roosevelt said, he felt "compelled" to write to Barkley, because "you are the acting majority leader of the Senate." He then concluded with the ostensible purpose of his letter: to insist that the effort for court reform continue.[45]

Although Roosevelt nowhere in the letter revealed his choice for leader, senators were quick to infer that he favored Barkley. Why not address it to Harrison, or Pittman in the chair, senators asked? Angry at what they deemed to be presidential interference, Byrnes and Harrison went to the White House the next morning. They emerged with Roosevelt's promise, however useless now that the letter was published, of neutrality.[46] Few senators were deceived.

[43] See Key Pittman to Byron Harrison, July 20, 1937, Pittman MSS, Box 13.

[44] James F. Byrnes, *All in One Lifetime* (New York, 1958), p. 101.

[45] Alben Barkley, *That Reminds Me* (Garden City, N.Y., 1954), p. 155, tells his side of the story. See also New York *Times*, July 16, 1937, p. 1.

[46] New York *Times*, July 17, 1937, p. 2.

As the vote approached it was apparent to both sides that it would be close. Harrison believed that the vote of Theodore G. Bilbo, his fellow Mississippian, would probably be the deciding ballot. The two men, however, were not on speaking terms because Bilbo, both a violent Negrophobe and a regular New Dealer, had campaigned to unseat Harrison in 1936. Byrnes went to Bilbo on Harrison's behalf and Bilbo told him that if Harrison would only speak to him he could have his support. Harrison's reply, according to one later account, was blunt. "Tell the son of a ——— I wouldn't speak to him if it meant the Presidency of the United States."[47]

Bilbo probably would not have backed Harrison under any circumstances, so Harrison's forces hardly counted him as a loss. Harrison received a more telling blow when Senator Dieterich of Illinois told him that pressure had forced him to change his vote.[48] This was the key shift. The next day in a tense gathering Barkley won by secret ballot, 38-37. "That last ballot," said Barkley, "looked like a bed quilt. I bit my pipe stem in two."[49]

Until their deaths both Roosevelt and Barkley insisted that it had been a free fight, without White House influence. This was not true. With his "Dear Alben" letter, Roosevelt had suggested his choice. More important, Dieterich's shift was no more than the best-known case of White House pressure. As Ickes put it, "Ostensibly, the President kept his hands off, but men like Corcoran were doing everything they could for Barkley, realizing that the election of Harrison would be disastrous to the President's program."[50] "Barkley must win," Roosevelt told Farley privately. "Har-

[47] George Allen, *Presidents Who Have Known Me* (New York, 1950), p. 71.

[48] New York *Herald Tribune*, July 22, 1937, p. 2.

[49] New York *Times*, July 22, 1937, p. 1.

[50] Ickes, *Secret Diary*, II, 166, July 21, 1937, and 170, July 25, 1937.

rison would repeal the capital gains tax. He would do it now if he could."[51]

It is easy to understand Roosevelt's feelings in the matter; trusting the more liberal Barkley, it was natural that he should want him as his chief senatorial aide. Moreover, he won the fight and in this sense it did his somewhat diminished prestige no harm. But it was not worth it. Senators resented what they considered meddling in a family concern. More important, in picking Barkley the President had made a fundamental change in the style of Senate leadership. Though popular enough, Barkley lacked lasting ties of personal affection and common experience with other senators —an advantage which the Robinson-Harrison-Garner-Byrnes team had enjoyed in plenty. Veterans such as Glass and Pittman owed no favors which Barkley could insist upon in narrow legislative situations. To these men, indeed, Barkley appeared an exalted White House errand boy. Henceforth Roosevelt would have to depend for Senate support more and more upon outside pressures, upon lobbyists, upon crisis situations; never again could he depend upon the subtle web of intimate personal relationships that Robinson and Harrison had spun so carefully. In the last analysis conservatives, not New Dealers, benefited from the struggle.

Finally, the contest marked the end of Harrison's feeling of loyalty to the President. As soon as the vote was over, there was a grand show of party harmony. Harrison and Barkley shook hands and exchanged compliments, and Roosevelt invited them to the White House for friendly talks. But Harrison was free. Already upset by the welfare legislation of the session, he also felt unfairly treated. Soon he would openly denounce a New Deal measure. Byrnes had already done so; Garner was angry; Robinson was dead; and Harrison completed the picture. The old leaders were on the outside looking in.

[51] Farley, *Jim Farley's Story*, p. 125.

Unfortunately for Democratic party harmony, the Senate had to contend with another divisive economic issue, the fair labor standards bill. Roosevelt had long wished to guarantee minimum wages, maximum hours, and child labor restrictions but had feared Supreme Court opposition. When the court reversed itself in March 1937, he saw his chance and submitted a proposal in a special message in late May. A bill incorporating the plan quickly followed, introduced in the Senate by Black of Alabama and in the House by William P. Connery, Jr., of Massachusetts. Subsequently the proposal became known as the Black-Connery bill.

Complex in scope, the bill's main objectives and methods were clear.[52] It empowered Congress to set minimum-wage scales and maximum-hours schedules; the most commonly mentioned base figures were forty cents per hour and forty hours per week. It also called for an independent five-man labor board to be appointed by the President. This board would have the authority to increase minimum standards after proper hearings, if collective bargaining had already been attempted and failed. The bill also proposed to outlaw child labor involved in interstate commerce.

While the court and relief issues were occurring in June, joint hearings on the labor bill began in committees headed by Black and Connery, and it quickly became obvious that the bill would face Senate opposition. As Bailey wrote in a sarcastic reaction typical of conservative sentiment, "I am meditating on the new Labor Bill and thinking about issuing a statement declaring for minimum wages and maximum hours and the millennium. I think we ought to add the millennium to the program. Otherwise it will not be complete."[53] Conservatives such as Bailey objected to the crea-

[52] Descriptions of the bill are given in James M. Burns, *Congress on Trial* (New York, 1949), pp. 68-82; and Paul H. Douglas and Joseph Hackman, "The Fair Labor Standards Act of 1938" (I), *Political Science Quarterly*, LIII (Dec. 1938), 491-515.

[53] To Ben B. Gossett, June 5, 1937, Bailey MSS, Personal File.

tion of another New Deal agency, and southern conservatives in particular feared the destruction of southern competitive advantages.

Such reactions were predictable. More surprising, and more damaging, was the lack of enthusiasm among labor groups. Testifying before the Senate committee, both John L. Lewis of the CIO and William Green of the AF of L expressed grave doubts about entrusting the labor board with discretionary power. These men feared that such governmental authority would undermine the chief union weapons of collective bargaining and the strike, eventually relegating unions to an insignificant role. They also did not know what to expect of a government board. Prolabor under one administration, it might reverse itself in the next. Green especially feared that another board such as the NLRB would be partial to the CIO. Finally, Lewis and Green were suspicious of statutory limits on wages: as union leaders had been saying for years, the "minimum will become the maximum." Their testimony was distinctly unenthusiastic.

Early in July the Senate committee unanimously reported a revised bill more in line with labor objectives. Retaining the proposed board, the new bill stripped it of the power to increase wages over forty cents per hour or to reduce hours below forty hours per week. The board might set minimum standards at these levels, but from there unions would carry on. Though the bill excluded large numbers of workers from its provisions, it was on the whole acceptable to administration forces.[54] In this guise it reached the Senate floor for action a week after Barkley's choice as leader.

The ensuing debate lasted the greater part of three days. Most Republicans, hewing to their strategy of restraint, said

[54] Some liberals did not think so. See Robert S. Allen, "Washington Sweatshop," *Nation*, CXLV (July 17, 1937), 63-64.

little and once again a Democratic split developed on the Senate floor. For the first time on a major issue not one of the old Senate leaders even pretended to be on the administration's side. Instead of Harrison's, Byrnes's, and Garner's standing against a stubborn group of outspoken Republicans and irreconcilable Democrats, it was Barkley, Black and the New Dealers against a Republican-southern and western Democratic bloc.[55]

For the first two days administration forces were generally but not always successful in defeating a series of amendments designed to exempt various classes of seasonal workers from the bill. Cannery workers, for instance, needed for long hours at certain seasons, were excluded from the hours provision. Rural state senators, accustomed to paying very low wages for farm labor, feared the wage portions of the bill; they also objected to limitations on the hours of farm labor. Southern senators also denounced the absence of guarantees for regional differentials on industrial wages. Nurtured for decades upon the idea of a prosperous, industrial "New South," many southerners considered the bill a threat to hard-won economic progress and a surrender to organized labor.[56] "In other words," shouted Cotton Ed Smith in a rhetorical question, "if South Carolina's living conditions are so kindly that it takes only fifty cents a day, for illustration, to enable one to live comfortably and reasonably, and in the New England states it takes a dollar and a half, then the wage in South Carolina should be raised to a dollar and half? Why . . . don't some of these people call in God and tell Him that He must stop this thing of making one section more advantageous than another?"[57]

[55] This was not so on every aspect of the bill. See New York *Times*, July 29, 1937, p. 12.

[56] See an excellent column by Catledge, New York *Times*, Aug. 8, 1937, IV, 3.

[57] *Congressional Record*, 75th Cong., 1st Sess., 7872.

Harrison expressed southern resentment most forcefully. Rising to speak against an important New Deal bill for the first time, he unleashed his pent-up wrath. He began by berating Secretary of Labor Frances Perkins in his sarcastic fashion of old. "If the measure is passed," he said, "that Ma—*Dame* is going to have a good deal of say in its administration. And to be perfectly frank, because I do not want to withhold anything from my colleagues, that is one of the many reasons why I am *not* for this legislation." Continuing, he described the bill's adverse effects on the South and concluded with a revealing statement of his personal pique. "If the administration is progressive I am progressive. If this administration is conservative, then I am to be classified as a conservative." But, he continued, he was like a hardworking ox that has been driven too much in the hot sun. "Perhaps I do not want to travel as fast as some people because I might get out of breath. . . . I like to get under the shade and rest a little."[58] Roosevelt's reaction was blunt; he said to Ickes, "Pat Harrison has gone off the deep end."[59]

Administration forces had the votes, and the next day Harrison and his bipartisan band went down to defeat. In a motion to recommit the bill they lost 48-36. On the final vote the tally for the bill was 56-28, as seven Democrats and one Republican for recommittal switched to Roosevelt's side.[60]

Many reasons accounted for Roosevelt's triumph. The final bill contained enough exemptions, especially on hours provisions, to pacify many hesitant senators, and Green had finally issued an unenthusiastic but nonetheless favorable verdict upon the bill shortly before passage. The opponents

[58] *Ibid.*, p. 7882.
[59] Ickes, *Secret Diary*, II, 182, July 31, 1937.
[60] Those who switched were Chavez (N.M.), Clark, Maloney (Conn.), McCarran, Overton (La.), Pittman, Radcliffe, and Tydings. Davis, a Republican from Pennsylvania, did likewise. Gillette (Iowa), oddly, opposed recommittal and the final bill.

also knew the bill faced a difficult struggle in the House; perhaps the final battle could be waged there. Finally, Democrats were eager to patch up some sort of truce and go home. As Wheeler said, "It is not easy, after glorifying a man for years, to debunk him overnight."[61] And even Bailey, who opposed the bill, wrote just before final passage: "Now that the struggle [over the court plan] is over and the outcome is so satisfactory, I suggest the policy of reconciliation to all concerned. I am perfectly willing to hold the hands of the President in every good cause. . . ."[62]

The recommittal vote again revealed a sectional split within the Democratic party. Of the thirty-six senators for recommittal, twenty-two were Democrats; three more paired themselves for recommittal. Of these twenty-five, eleven were southerners. Thus of the twenty-one southern Democratic senators (Robinson's seat was vacant) half opposed the bill, while two more did not vote; of the remaining fifty-four senators only fourteen dissented. As if to prove the sectional aspect of the bill, the two Republicans who voted for it were not western progressives such as Borah, Johnson, or Nye: after the court bill, these men were never again reliable New Deal supporters. Rather, the Republican supporters were James J. Davis of Pennsylvania, a former steel worker and secretary of labor under Harding, Coolidge, and Hoover; and Henry Cabot Lodge of Massachusetts. Davis was sensitive to labor pressure; Lodge, significantly, figured the bill would not affect highly paid Massachusetts workers but that it would help destroy the southern competitive

[61] Alva Johnson, "President Tamer," *Saturday Evening Post*, CCX (Nov. 13, 1937), 51.

[62] To Eugene Meyer, July 28, 1937, Bailey MSS, General File. Senator Francis Maloney of Connecticut also sought Democratic harmony after the court struggle. "I do not want to revive a discussion of the matter," he wrote. "I felt intensely about it, but it is now over and I should like to forget it as we face other governmental problems." Maloney to Eugene Meyer, July 26, 1937, Landon MSS, Political File, 1937, M-O.

advantage responsible for the flight of New England mills to the South.[63]

The votes of Davis and Lodge indicated that differences of opinion on the bill were not only sectional, but more broadly urban-rural. The proposed amendments—most of which sought to exempt various farm workers or farm related industries such as processing, canning, and warehousing—suggested a broad rural opposition to the bill. In the key recommittal vote only five of the twenty senators from the ten most urban states voted to recommit; of the remaining seventy-six senators, thirty-five voted for or were paired for recommittal.[64] This kind of opposition—partly partisan, partly sectional, and partly rural—would be repeated in many subsequent New Deal battles over economic issues.

Finally, the fair labor standards bill in the Senate witnessed the widening of the gulf between Roosevelt and his former leaders. Besides Harrison, Byrnes also voted against the bill, and Garner was equally adamant against it. Barkley passed his first test with relative ease but with no help from the hierarchy of old. From this time forth the old leaders would be amidst the conservative bloc as often as not.

Three controversies detained the Senate for three more grueling weeks and aggravated these sectional-economic alignments.[65] They were housing, antilynching, and the appointment of Senator Black to take Justice Van Devanter's place on the Supreme Court.

[63] For Lodge's views, see Joseph Alsop and Robert Kintner, "Republican with a Bite," *Saturday Evening Post*, CCXI (July 30, 1938), 8. For Davis, see James J. Davis to Joseph Pew, Oct. 14, 1937, Davis MSS, Box 28.

[64] The five were Democrats Maloney, Copeland, Bulkley, Donahey, and Republican Vandenberg. "Urban" is defined according to census statistics. See 1940 Census, Vol. II, *Characteristics of the Population*, Part I, 8. See also Appendix A.

[65] Many Republicans were in no hurry to go home. Clifford R. Hope wrote to say he was not in favor of adjournment because "every day that the Democrats stay here and fight among themselves is a fine day for the Republicans." To R. E. Stotts, July 26, 1937, Hope MSS, General Correspondence, 1936-1937, R-T.

Housing had long concerned northern urban Democrats such as Wagner but had received only lukewarm backing by Roosevelt. Undaunted, Wagner pressed ahead, urging a bill to loan municipalities $700 million for slum clearance and construction of low-cost housing. Reaching the floor soon after the vote on the labor bill, Wagner's proposal encountered determined opposition led by Byrd. This bloc, hostile to growing expenditures in urban areas, succeeded on a 44-39 vote in slashing maximum construction costs per family unit so low that the bill's proponents claimed the final bill would result in little if any construction at all.[66] Another successful amendment proposed by Tydings limited the amount spent in any one state to 20 percent—an obvious strike at urban state Democrats such as Guffey of Pennsylvania and Wagner of New York. On the key Byrd amendment twenty-nine Democrats joined thirteen Republicans and two Farmer-Laborites to win. Significantly, ten of the twenty-two southern Democrats, including Byrnes and Harrison, were among Byrd's backers, whereas only nine opposed. Ten of the twenty-one Plains and Rocky Mountain Democrats also joined the economy bloc, as did Farmer-Laborites Shipstead and Lundeen.[67] On the other hand, even Copeland and Walsh voted with Wagner for the bill. Like the labor standards bill, the housing proposal illustrated the combined sectional and urban-rural split into which the Senate was falling on this type of economic legislation. And, for the first time, the rural-conservative coalition had succeeded in winning an important voting test.[68]

[66] For this act, see Timothy L. McDonnell, "The New Deal Makes a Public Housing Law: A Case Study of the Wagner Housing Bill of 1937" (unpublished Ph.D. dissertation, St. Louis University, 1953). Also Robert S. Allen, "The New Deal Fights Back," Nation, CXLV (Aug. 28, 1937), 187-88.

[67] Congressional Record, 75th Cong., 1st Sess., 8196.

[68] After passing the Senate, it encountered delaying tactics in the House, and finally passed in late August. The final version largely reflected the views of conservatives.

The next issue, antilynching, immediately followed a grand Democratic senatorial "harmony" dinner honoring Barkley, at which a live pigeon flew about the dining room and where even the ice cream was dove-shaped in an effort to convince skeptics that all was peaceful on the Democratic side of the aisle.[69] The antilynching problem quickly destroyed this illusion. A few northern Democrats, urged by Negro constituents to stem the distressing frequency in lynchings before and during the Depression, had been pressing for federal action on the problem for many years.[70] Earlier in the 1937 session the House had finally succeeded in discharging an antilynching bill from Sumners' hostile Judiciary Committee and in passing it. The bill held local law enforcement authorities responsible for the lynching of prisoners "escaping" their custody. Southerners hotly resented this kind of federal interference and had waged successful Senate filibusters against it in past years.

Roosevelt recognized that the bill would snarl other legislation in a filibuster if it reached the Senate floor. Thus he had not pressed for the measure in the past and did not do so in 1937. As the bill's House sponsor later said, "I got very little active support from the White House in the first or second term."[71] Undeterred, Wagner arose the day after the "harmony dinner" to introduce it on his own.

The result was almost comical. Barkley knew that Wagner's recognition would spark a southern filibuster and had already handed Garner a list of Democrats whom he wished to receive prior recognition. But when Wagner leaped up, Barkley's supposed allies were slow on their feet. Garner, disgusted with the entire trend of events, recognized Wagner. Barkley then objected, a move which would have

[69] New York *Times*, Aug. 11, 1937, p. 4.

[70] See *Time*, April 26, 1937, pp. 16-17, for the story of a particularly sickening lynching in Mississippi that spring. A large crowd watched two Negroes blowtorched and then burned while tied to trees.

[71] Joseph Gavagan, Oral History Project, Columbia University, p. 46.

necessitated withdrawal of the motion if his objection received unanimous consent. But McNary, shrewdly foreseeing another Democratic rift, foiled this attempt by objecting to Barkley's objection. The expected filibuster then began, and it was only after considerable maneuvering that Barkley stopped it by promising Wagner the measure would be reconsidered at the start of the next congressional session. At that time it would provoke a six-week filibuster.

The episode was even more revealing of the tempers of many southern Democrats. In earlier days they would have moved bitterly to the attack, but this time they talked of offering only token opposition.[72] Viewing the bill as an insincere gambit by northern Democrats to win Negro votes, they rightly figured its passage would embarrass liberal southerners. If Black, for instance, refused to back the filibuster, he might be beaten in 1938. And whatever Roosevelt did, he would lose votes. To sign it might be to sign away much of the South; to veto it would alienate the Negro base of his liberal coalition. When Barkley finally succeeded in delaying the measure, their plans did not materialize. The talk, however, was symptomatic of the anger of southern conservatives at the trend the New Deal was taking.

As if to cement conservative hostility, Roosevelt the next day provided the Senate with its last controversial issue of the session; in a surprise move, he nominated Black for the vacant Supreme Court justiceship.[73] On the surface, Black was a logical enough choice, for he was intelligent, loyal, and liberal. But Roosevelt well knew how the Senate would

[72] New York *Times*, Aug. 12, 1937, p. 1.

[73] The surprise element surrounding Black's nomination was as great as that surrounding the announcement of the court plan. Roosevelt simply enclosed his nomination in a bundle of others taken by messenger to the Capitol.

Roosevelt continued to chortle at the thought of conservative discomfort. As he wrote at the time, "Just now I have a discombobulated Congress, running around in circles. . . ." FDR to Felix Frankfurter, Aug. 12, 1937, Roosevelt MSS, PPF 140.

react. Despite his ability, Black was not a popular senator.[74] Cutting in debate, aloof in manner, he irritated conservatives of both parties by his unabashed liberalism. Asked for his reaction to the nomination, an incensed Glass could only reply, "Don't start me off again."[75] The mark of Black's unpopularity was the Senate's refusal to waive hearings on the appointment, an unusual insult to a member of the Senate.

Roosevelt realized that the Senate would eventually have to confirm Black: it was hallowed senatorial practice to agree to appointments of its own members. "They'll have to take him," he gleefully told Farley.[76] And take him they did. Five days after the nomination appeared in the Senate, the same Judiciary Committee that had rejected the court plan, 10-8, approved the appointment, 13-4, though only after a fist fight had narrowly been averted. The next day, after a tumultuous six-hour debate, the Senate confirmed Black's appointment, 63-13. Six Democrats stubbornly joined seven conservative Republicans in opposing the nomination on the final vote.[77]

In this atmosphere the Senate moved to conclude its business. Two days after Black's confirmation Roosevelt further antagonized conservatives by referring to the "privileged minority" that was destroying American democracy, and three days after this remark, Guffey, the *bête noir* of conservative Democrats, sparked a furious debate by attempting to read his conservative colleagues out of the party, mentioning by name Holt, Wheeler, and O'Mahoney.[78]

[74] For Black, see Alsop and Catledge, *The 168 Days*, pp. 300-302.

[75] *Literary Digest*, CXXIV (Aug. 28, 1937), 6.

[76] Farley, *Jim Farley's Story*, p. 98.

[77] Ickes, *Secret Diary*, II, 196, Aug. 18, 1937, noted: "Even Cotton Ed Smith of South Carolina who 'God-damned' the nomination all over the place when it was first announced, didn't have the courage to stand up and vote against a fellow Senator from the Deep South." See Connally's reaction in Connally, *My Name Is Tom Connally*, pp. 192-93.

[78] For Guffey, see Joseph Alsop and Robert Kintner, "The Guffey Capture of Pennsylvania," *Saturday Evening Post*, CCX (April 16, 1938), 16.

"Guffey," wrote Bailey, "has committed a very grave offense and we should be satisfied with nothing less than war to the hilt. I am not up until 1942, but I intend to stand with the Senators who are up next year."[79] On this ominous note the Senate adjourned.

The Senate, Arthur Krock remarked in a post-mortem examination of the session, was remarkable for two developments in 1937. It reestablished its legislative power, and it did very little legislating.[80] He added that both developments emanated from a deep Democratic split for which Roosevelt was largely responsible.

The contrast to Roosevelt's earlier Congresses makes it clear that this assessment is indisputable. The Senate had reasserted itself. It had also accomplished relatively little, though passage of a fair labor standards plan, a modified housing bill, a farm tenancy bill, a new neutrality law, and extension of previous emergency powers by no means marked it as a "do nothing" Congress. Roosevelt's court plan had also revealed previously concealed flaws in his congressional relations. There had been, as Tugwell later admitted, "incredible ineptitude of the White House management."[81]

Voting statistics show what had happened. The four controversial votes of the session—sitdowns, the Robinson relief plan, labor bill recommittal, and the Byrd housing amendment—tallied, respectively, 36-48, 34-49, 36-48, and 44-39. On each bill, some twelve to fourteen quiet Republicans joined a vocal group of twenty-two to twenty-nine Democrats. The average opposition was thirty-eight, or nearly 40 percent of the Senate; the average Democratic

79 To Van Nuys, Aug. 24, 1937, Bailey MSS, Political File. Roosevelt congratulated Guffey: "It was a good speech. . . . You said vigorously many things that needed to be said." Roosevelt to Guffey, Aug. 21, 1937, Roosevelt MSS, PPF 451.

80 New York *Times*, Aug. 22, 1937, IV, 3.

81 Rexford G. Tugwell, *The Democratic Roosevelt* (Garden City, N.Y., 1957), p. 435.

opposition was twenty-four, or almost one-third of the party total of seventy-six.

On the seven key bills of the 1935 session, however, the average anti-New Deal bloc had been composed of twelve Republicans and but fourteen Democrats. Republican opposition had changed little numerically since 1935, but Democratic opposition had doubled. One of the many reasons for this change was the revolution in Senate leadership.[82] Of the ten votes cast by Robinson, Harrison, and Byrnes on the four measures, eight defied the administration. More important, their defections set an example for others to follow. The leadership revolution was both significant in itself and a sign of the friction that was grinding the Democratic party into two irreconcilable factions.

This revolution also symbolized an ominous sectional and urban-rural division based upon socio-economic legislation. Of the 98 conservative Democratic votes cast on the four key votes, 40, or 10 per issue, came from the twenty-two southern Democrats. Only 58 came from the remaining fifty-four Democrats. Looked at from another angle, these ten southerners formed 42 percent of the average Democratic opposition of twenty-four, though they composed but 29 percent of Democratic Senate membership. Compared to 1935 when only three southerners had opposed the Wagner Act, and only two the relief act, this was indeed a remarkable shift.

The chasm was not simply sectional. Some fourteen anti-New Deal Democrats, or more than one half of the twenty-four-man conservative core, came from sections other than the South. It must also be remembered that none of the twelve to fourteen conservative Republicans was a southerner: opposition to the New Deal was by no means restricted to the South. The conservative bloc on these issues

[82] O. R. Altman, "First Session of the 75th Congress," *American Political Science Review*, XXXI (Dec. 1937), 1083.

was as much a rural one as anything else. It came predominantly (though the votes of men such as Gerry and Copeland indicate not wholly) from the least urbanized states—the Deep South, upper New England, and the Rocky Mountains.[83] These men simply dared in 1937 to oppose what they had instinctively feared for some time: heavy relief and housing expenditure to cities; substantial benefits to labor at the expense of agriculture; heavier tax loads to support these projects. Given a chance to voice their opposition when Roosevelt's luster faded over the court bill, they did so.[84] As one expert phrased it later: "These coalition congressmen, whether Democrats or Republicans, represent the dominant social forces, that is to say, the most influential interests in their predominantly rural districts. By and large theirs is an anti-metropolitan ideology induced by a phobia of our American Babylons with their slums and laboring masses organized in unions that exert pressures at the polls through political action committees. . . . Their existence is deep-rooted in our economic, political, and social structure and their behavior was thus a part of the normal functioning of our constitutional system."[85]

From this perspective Roosevelt's tactical errors do not appear to have been so important as some observers thought. Even granting the careless way in which he handled the

[83] See J. Frederick Essary, "The Split in the Democratic Party," *Atlantic Monthly*, CLX (Dec. 1937), 651-58.

[84] See V. O. Key, Jr., *Southern Politics in State and Nation* (New York, 1949), pp. 345-68, for a complex statistical treatment of hundreds of roll-call votes during the New Deal years. Key's conclusions approximate those expressed here, though it must be remembered that Key's study deals only with a *southern* Democratic-GOP coalition.

For another roll-call survey (in the House only), see Julius Turner, *Party and Constituency: Pressures on Congress* (Baltimore, 1951), pp. 93-94. Turner shows that urban-rural voting became increasingly common in the years from 1920 to 1944. He emphasizes, however, that the pressures of party were by far the most meaningful pressures on House roll calls.

[85] Wilfred E. Binkley, *President and Congress* (3rd rev. ed.; New York, 1962), pp. 339-40.

court bill, two things are worth considering. First, Roosevelt received substantially what he wanted in the Senate on all but the court bill (he never conceived of the housing or antilynching measures as administration bills). And second, on the socio-economic issues, it was not so much tactics which accounted for the opposition but the urban nature of the measures themselves. Even without the catalytic effect of the court bill, sizable conservative opposition to measures of this sort would have developed.

Roosevelt's successes, not his failures, explained what was happening in the Senate. His political skill had helped to give him by 1937 a rampant liberal coalition of almost unmanageable size and determination, while his recovery program had seemed to lift the country from the trough of depression. Both politically and economically, Roosevelt enjoyed success such as few presidents had known. But though his supporters insisted upon more legislation, the improved economic situation led many cautious congressmen to feel that it was time for retrenchment. William Allen White wrote at the time, "That essential silence of his support in the proletariat, and the conspicuous thunder of middle class opinion, swung Congress away from the President. Any President is powerless before middle class opinion. And the sad ironic thing about the proletariat is that as wages rise, the boys in the proletariat join the middle class, become vocal through the middle class and so until we have one long catastrophic depression which will materially cut down the power of the middle class, no president can rely on mere majorities to back him up in any serious fight."[86]

Given this situation a split in Roosevelt's unwieldy coalition was just a matter of time. Even if he had really tried—and he did not—to grant the nation its "breathing spell" in 1937, he would have found it almost impossible to

[86] Walter Johnson (ed.), *Selected Letters of William Allen White* (New York, 1947), p. 379. Letter dated July 28, 1937.

restrain his supporters.[87] There was little Roosevelt could have done in 1937 to prevent the sitdown crisis: CIO workers saw it as a necessary tactic. There was no politically happy way to handle the relief issue, since to have requested a cut would have alienated more of his supporters than it would have mollified. He was committed to a labor standards bill and could hardly have reneged on his promise. And the demands for antilynching and housing legislation were especially troublesome; he sought neither yet discovered that both were unavoidable congressional issues. All these controversies were but political reflections of profound social changes quickened by the ravages of depression and the benevolence of the earlier New Deal. In this context it is a little surprising that the revolution in Senate leadership and the sectional-economic divisions took so long to occur.

By 1937 Roosevelt had a rampant new Democratic party by the tail. Neither its master nor its captive, he could only act, as one acute critic put it, as "arbiter between conflicting pressures."[88] He had either to risk alienating men such as Harrison who thought "the emergency is over" or to disavow his powerful coalition by halting the New Deal in its tracks: by 1937 he could no longer satisfy both. It was perhaps inevitable that a humanitarian and activist such as Roosevelt should have chosen the former. It was a fateful choice.

[87] The Farm Bureau increased in membership from 163,246 in 1933 to 409,766 in 1937. Union membership rose from 2,857,000 in 1933 to 7,218,000 in 1937. Figures quoted by Walter Johnson, *1600 Pennsylvania Avenue* (Boston, 1960), pp. 333-34.

[88] Altman, "First Session," p. 1083.

5

POLITICS OF INDEPENDENCE:
THE HOUSE

SINCE THE utilities controversy of 1935, the House of Representatives had lapsed again into relative acquiescence. Though it did not always rejoice at administration proposals, it continued to be the more reliable of the two houses through 1936, and conservative representatives did not make any serious efforts to coalesce against the administration.

Like the Senate, the House had bridled at Roosevelt's undistributed-profits tax proposal of 1936. But Doughton's Ways and Means Committee softened the plan, and it swept through with only token opposition, 267-93.[1] A small bipartisan band also demurred at Roosevelt's 1936 request for a $1.425 billion deficiency relief appropriation, but on the final vote only thirty-eight dared oppose it.[2] A somewhat different group sought to forestall the 1936 soil conservation bill, but only ninety-seven ended by voting against the final version.[3] On all three issues the great majority of opponents were Republicans: anti-administration Democrats numbered, respectively, eleven, eight, and twenty-five. In general, the 1936 session affected the House much as it had the Senate— very little. Those who had distrusted the President in 1935 continued to do so in 1936; those who had looked to him for more New Deal reform were generally satisfied. And the election of 1936, with 331 Democratic representatives chosen in the landslide, made the President's prospects in the House more auspicious than ever. The lower chamber promised not only to be more tractable than its forerunner, but it also appeared to be more liberal than the Senate.

Yet by the end of the 1937 session the House, though not as a body so conservatively inclined as the Senate, was perhaps more unpredictable, even without a court plan or leadership contest to intensify personal rancor. The chief reason for this shift was similar to that which had transformed the Senate: new demands for reform by elements of the rampant Roosevelt coalition at a time when many congressmen felt "the emergency was over." Yet the nature of the anti-administration opposition in the House was often different. Above all the session revealed the determination of the House to be an independent, assertive institution. Roosevelt would encounter this kind of trouble in the lower chamber for many years to come.

Thanks primarily to the opposition of Sumners, the court reorganization plan began in the Senate and never reached the House. The bill was certainly as unpopular in the lower chamber as it was in the Senate, yet since congressmen were

[1] See New York *Times*, April 29, 1936, p. 1.
[2] *Congressional Record*, 74th Cong., 2nd Sess., 7023.
[3] *Ibid.*, p. 2579.

spared from formally considering it, they also escaped some of the personal feuding that so disastrously divided the Senate. The chief effect of the court plan on the House was to provide conservatives with evidence that Roosevelt was vulnerable, encouraging them to assert themselves on other issues. These other issues—sitdowns, relief, and labor standards—witnessed the formation of an effective conservative bloc in the House as well.

As it had in the Senate, the sitdown crisis proved the occasion for conservative oratory and maneuvering. It also prompted the emergence of another colorful Democrat as an undependable of the future: Martin Dies, Jr., of Texas. His role in the 1937 session was to become as symbolic as Byrnes's was in the Senate.[4]

Dies was a lanky, somewhat sloppy six-footer who was fond of chomping on soggy cigars and lounging about in cloakrooms, his feet sprawled over chairs, telling back room stories.[5] A representative since 1931, he had held down the Texan slot on the important Rules Committee since 1935. Before 1937 he had generally supported the New Deal; indeed Dies later claimed that the President gave him special permission to slip in the side door of the White House at any time.[6] During the early New Deal years, however, Dies was best known for his penchant for making the headlines. The leader of the so-called Demagogues Club which promised to vote for all appropriations and no taxes, he was also fond of amusing his colleagues by stomping loudly down the aisles to record his votes on roll calls. As Marquis Childs said in a harsh passage, Dies "had the most complete and utter scorn for the whole institution of Congress. A protective rind of cynicism was what he showed to the world. I

---

[4] Allan A. Michie and Frank Rhylick, *Dixie Demagogues* (New York, 1939), pp. 55-67. Also *Current Biography*, 1940, p. 243.

[5] Fred R. Barkley, "Martin Dies of Texas," *Current History*, LI (Dec. 1939), 29-30.

[6] Martin Dies, *Martin Dies Story* (New York, 1963), pp. 138-41.

doubt whether I have ever encountered a more cynical man than this lank Texan with the sallow gray face."[7]

For all his cynicism, Dies was no fool. And he felt strongly about one subject: aliens. To Dies, whose father Martin Dies, Sr., had also expressed pronounced anti-alien views as a congressman, it was perhaps natural to curry favor with hard-pressed constituents by blaming foreigners (most of whom did not vote) for the social tensions of his district.[8] From his first days in the House Dies championed the view that the solution for the Depression lay in deporting as many foreigners as possible to open jobs for native-born Americans.

Allied with this xenophobia was a belief that aliens and radicals dominated the CIO.[9] By 1937 this feeling was not merely a political device to gain headlines: it was also a sincere belief. Gone was the cynical, story-telling clown. "The expression he wears now," added Childs, "is commonly a scowl. The man is hag-ridden."[10] This young and ambitious Texan saw in the sitdown issue a chance to strike a blow at the CIO and reap a bountiful harvest of publicity— all in one deft stroke.

At this point Garner, his friend and fellow Texan, entered the scene. Sharing Dies's views of the CIO, he encouraged Dies to offer a resolution for a full-scale investigation of the sitdown tactic.[11] Dies obliged with a ringing speech on March 23 which received "repeated outbursts of applause" from his House colleagues.[12] At first, the resolution seemed destined for death in the Rules Committee. For Dies, how-

[7] Marquis W. Childs, *I Write from Washington* (New York, 1942), p. 91.

[8] See William Gellermann, *Martin Dies* (New York, 1944), pp. 17-18, 28-29, 49-52, for the influence of his father and his views on aliens.

[9] See Dies, *Martin Dies*, pp. 41-51, for Dies's views on Communism and the sitdowns.

[10] Childs, *I Write*, p. 92.

[11] *Congressional Record*, 75th Cong., 1st Sess., 2637-38. His resolution preceded Byrnes's sitdown amendment by ten days.

[12] New York *Times*, March 24, 1937, p. 1.

ever colorful, was not popular with his colleagues, and his motion clearly sought to embarrass the administration. There was little reason to expect that Chairman O'Connor and the rest of the committee would pay much more attention to this move than they had to Dies's repeated thrusts in previous sessions. Then Byrnes offered his dramatic sitdown amendment to the coal bill in the Senate. Heartened by this show of defiance from an administration leader, the Rules Committee began to show an interest in Dies's motion and approved it the next day.

The committee vote was disturbing to administration supporters. To begin with, O'Connor again demonstrated his limited loyalty to the administration. At the start of the session Roosevelt had alienated him by refusing to help him contest Rayburn for the majority leadership. The day before the committee vote on the Dies resolution, O'Connor lunched with Roosevelt and emerged to proclaim that the President had said nothing at all about Dies's resolution; during committee deliberations he continued to maintain that the committee was free to act as it chose. Accordingly, not only O'Connor but normally pro-New Deal Democrats sided with Dies on the question. Afraid that an unfavorable vote on the resolution would appear to condone sitdown strikes, they found O'Connor's interpretation entirely congenial.[13]

The revolt was short-lived. Two days later Byrnes's motion went down to defeat in the Senate, and administration spokesmen passed the word that O'Connor had misinterpreted the President. By the time the resolution reached the House floor on April 8, New Dealers had restored a semblance of order. In an uproarious session the Dies motion finally lost eighteen days after it had been first offered in committee. The vote was 236-150.[14]

The count revealed a considerably broader sentiment

[13] *Ibid.*
[14] *Ibid.*, April 9, 1937, p. 1.

against the administration than had been expected at the start of the session. Counting pairs, a coalition of 155 congressmen sought to "expose" the CIO and its ties with the New Deal. More significant, 78 of these rebels were Democrats—some 50 more than on any other key vote since the utilities bill two years earlier. As one congressman phrased it accurately, "the Supreme Court is still occupying the headlines back here although it is having to share them now with the sit-down strike. A good many of the Democratic members of Congress are really concerned because it appears that the President is dodging the issue which has been raised by Mr. John L. Lewis. . . ."[15]

The vote exposed the same kind of sectional and urban-rural divisions which were then developing in the Senate. Of the 78 rebellious Democrats, 43 were southerners, and 64, or 82 percent, represented rural districts.[16] Such administration stalwarts as Marvin Jones of Texas, chairman of the Agriculture Committee, and Rayburn himself joined O'Connor, Dies, and the others in their efforts to discover the influences behind the sitdown "menace."

Roosevelt had again triumphed in the House. But when Dies could corral the backing of 155 representatives, it indicated that the House would approach future issues in a considerably more independent spirit than it had since 1933. As Dies said shortly thereafter, "I regard the period of emergency at an end, and regardless of what crackpots and theorists think about it, I am going to vote from now on my own convictions."[17] In this posture he was not alone.

The relief issue strengthened this kind of feeling. In prior sessions the lower chamber had offered only token conservative opposition to relief bills. The Depression had

---

[15] Clifford R. Hope to Mrs. Ray Heel, March 30, 1937, General Correspondence, Hope MSS, 1936-1937, C-H.

[16] *Congressional Record*, 75th Cong., 1st Sess., 3301. For the definition of "rural" district, see Appendix A.

[17] New York *Times*, April 22, 1937, p. 1.

affected every congressional district, and each representative had considered it his particular duty to tap the Treasury for as much money as possible. Consequently economy sentiment in the House before 1937 hardly approached that of the Senate, and the flood of appeals for more spending had usually submerged such sentiment altogether.

But jockeying over relief spending in 1937 began in the House almost immediately following the President's April 20 message asking for $1.5 billion for the WPA. Economizers had already demanded across-the-board cuts in future appropriations, and such administration aides as Lindsay Warren of North Carolina, chairman of the Accounts Committee, and John J. Cochran of Missouri, chairman of the Committee on Executive Expenditures, began passing the word that continued federal spending might produce another tax bill. Quoting Micawber's advice to David Copperfield, Warren warned, "Annual income, twenty pounds; annual expenditure nineteen pounds, nineteen, and six; result happiness. Annual income, twenty pounds; annual expenditure, twenty pounds, zero and six; result misery."[18]

At the same time these congressmen, though favoring economy in principle, were not eager to see it applied to cherished projects of their own. A few days after the relief message an Agriculture Department appropriations bill for $927 million reached the floor. Immediately, Republican John Taber of New York arose to propose an amendment to slice the amount by 10 percent. But powerful farm elements, less consistent economizers than Taber, stepped into the breach. Edward O'Neal, president of the influential Farm Bureau Federation, spoke for all pressure groups on the subject of economy. "We are for economy," he said, "but not for an economy which will paralyze agriculture."[19] The next day, Taber's motion quickly went down to defeat,

18 *Ibid.*
19 *Ibid.*, April 23, 1937, p. 1.

219-32. Strong though economy sentiment may have been, it was powerless against a well-organized lobby and hopeless when urged by a Republican.

The flurry, unimportant in itself, exposed both the appeal of spending in the House and the foolishness of House Republican tactics. Taber and other House Republicans were convinced that their refusal to compromise with the New Deal had helped reelect them in 1936. "A good deal of our trouble," Taber wrote, "has been a lack of courage and the lack of a definite policy. . . . In those districts where Republican leaders have pussyfooted or supported the Roosevelt administration we have done very poorly."[20] Failing to appreciate the shrewdness of the McNary strategy of silence, they antagonized moderate Democrats. One of the reasons the Senate was often the more effectively conservative of the two chambers before 1939 was this simple difference in Republican tactics.

At this point Roosevelt left for an extended fishing trip, and Congress, freed from the whip hand, began to display more spirit. House Republican leader Bertrand Snell of New York, as unwilling as Taber to let the Democrats do all the talking, took to the air on May 8 to attack the administration, especially its proclivity for spending. "Four years ago," he said, "we had an emergency. Now we have progressed—yes, we have progressed from an emergency to a crisis. That is the outcome of four years of New Deal effort."[21] With Roosevelt absent discipline sagged noticeably: for much of the time, the House adjourned in confusion. One freshman Republican complained: "it seems

[20] Wadsworth agreed. Republicans, he said, "will put up a better showing than during the last two Congresses. The men seem to be feeling more combative. A part of this feeling is due to the fact that a great many of them ran ahead of Landon in their respective congressional districts, and that, generally speaking, the so-called hard-boiled reactionaries ran best." To J. J. Wadsworth, Jan. 5, 1937, Wadsworth MSS, Box 33.

[21] New York *Times*, May 9, 1937, p. 1.

Congress has placed itself in a position of doing nothing except what the President seems to want; and that when he is away, we do nothing at all."[22]

Then the House rebelled. On May 11 an appropriations subcommittee headed by the conservative Clifton A. Woodrum of Virginia voted 5-4 to slash $500 million from the relief request. The leadership came from upstart Democrats. "It is time," Representative Joe Starnes of Alabama proclaimed, "for the House to assume our legislative functions."[23]

This show of independence was brief. The President, due to return in three days, passed the word that Woodrum's cut was intolerable, and Hopkins went to the Hill to educate individual congressmen. Two days later the full Appropriations Committee reversed Woodrum's stand, 23-14.[24] Still, Woodrum succeeded in retaining an amendment requiring the WPA to allocate the $1.5 billion month by month. This clause sought to obviate the necessity for a deficiency request in 1938.[25]

A week later the measure reached the floor. House conservatives offered the same arguments as those used in the Senate and added an overtone of resentment at being treated as the lesser of two chambers. But spending pressures were too great for Woodrum and his fellow economizers. Though the House retained his allocation amendment, it also approved the full $1.5 billion demanded by Roosevelt. The margin of victory was 210-123 on a preliminary teller vote. Another amendment to cut the appropriation to $1.2 billion also lost on a teller vote, 175-145.[26]

[22] Edward H. Rees (Kan.) to William Allen White, May 11, 1937, W. A. White MSS, Box 189.

[23] New York *Times*, May 12, 1937, p. 1.

[24] For Roosevelt's role, see Walter Heacock, "William B. Bankhead and the New Deal," *Journal of Southern History*, XXI (Aug. 1955), 357.

[25] Paul Mallon, in the Washington *Star*, May 14, 1937, A-11, discovered that one key secret vote was only 20-19 in favor of the administration.

[26] *Congressional Record*, 75th Cong., 1st Sess., 4898-4939.

Although Democratic opposition to heavy relief spending was more substantial than it had been in previous years, it was not yet strong enough to defeat the administration.

The next act indicated the growth of House independence. Just when it seemed that the relief plan would sweep through on a final roll call and proceed to the Senate, a hastily organized coalition of opportunistic Republicans, conservative Democrats, and pork-barrel advocates joined in an attempt to remove Roosevelt's discretionary powers to distribute funds. Hopkins had consistently and successfully countered such attempts in the past with the explanation that work projects could not be planned in advance and that executive discretion was necessary. In 1937, however, congressmen, including many who were not at all disturbed by deficit spending, again sought to earmark the funds for specific projects. Such a move would not only have reduced Roosevelt's potential political power but would have guaranteed certain sums of money to projects within their home districts. The relief controversy had quickly changed from a conservative-liberal struggle over economy to a move to keep the power of spending in congressional hands.[27]

The pork-barrel alliance succeeded. Disregarding Rayburn and other leaders, ignoring the pleas of economizers such as Woodrum, the bloc received aid from Republicans and earmarked $505 million for the relief fund. The coalition reserved $300 million for PWA projects, $150 million for road construction, and $55 million for flood control work. In each case the alliance neatly distributed the projects over enough congressional districts to win satisfactory majorities.[28] To add the last touch of independence, the rebels set a limit of $10,000 on all WPA salaries, a direct slap at Hopkins whose pay was to have been $12,000.

The suddenness and determination of the pork-barrel

[27] New York *Times*, May 29, 1937, p. 5.
[28] These were teller votes. See *ibid.*, May 26, 1937, p. 1. Also Arthur Krock, *ibid.*, May 28, 1937, p. 20.

group alarmed the administration. For almost a week Bankhead and Rayburn dallied, hoping to eliminate the amendments before a final vote occurred. Roosevelt even invited some of the rebels to the White House to discover if they would compromise. He also implied that he might refuse to spend the earmarked money, leaving rebellious representatives without a single piece of pork to show. Finally, he reminded them that they must all face reelection, and it was a rare congressman who denied Roosevelt's power at the polls.

Eventually, compromise satisfied both sides. In a session lasting until one in the morning, the earmarking amendments lost on an exhausting series of roll-call votes. Even Hopkins emerged unscathed when friends removed the $10,000 limit on salaries. The only damaging amendment that remained denied relief to those unskilled workers who refused private employment. Finally, the $1.5 billion request passed, 323-44, with southerners composing most of the Democratic opposition.[29]

Roosevelt had again demonstrated considerable strength in the House, but he had not won an unblemished victory. To satisfy the House he had to agree to release the PWA revolving fund for some of the projects demanded by the rebels, who emerged smiling at their success.[30] The administration had kept political control over WPA money, while the earmarkers obtained the funds elsewhere for their pet projects. The real losers, as so often in the House, were the economizers. The House struggle over relief had resulted in a sharp defeat for conservatives of both parties. Where

[29] The most revealing vote was on an amendment to cut the figure to $1 billion; the opponents included 49 Democrats, of whom 35 were southerners. The rest were scattered, though none was from the East. See *Congressional Record*, 75th Cong., 1st Sess., 5227.

[30] *Time*, June 14, 1937, p. 12. See also Wilburn Cartwright, "Sixteen Years in Congress" (unpublished MS, 1942), Cartwright MSS, Part II, 178-79. Cartwright was a leader of the earmarking bloc.

spending was concerned, conservative blocs were impossible to maintain.

The struggle left congressmen feeling much as they had felt during the utilities fight: sensitive and rebellious. During the final debate this resentment was particularly clear. Even Rayburn pronounced that "the country is going to start getting out of the relief business," while John L. McClellan, a young Arkansas representative, brought cheers when he shouted that he was "sick and tired" of being "told what to do."[31] A day later, Maury Maverick of Texas, one of the most liberal congressmen, demanded an investigation of the WPA's role in elections. The relief controversy revealed that Roosevelt was still in command of any issue with the political appeal of spending. But it also showed what damage shifting coalitions might do; it exposed growing reservations about the WPA; and, above all, it left the House a much more independently minded body.[32]

Perhaps no controversy of the session so well illustrated the new assertiveness of the House as the brief but heated flurry which arose following Roosevelt's request for a study of tax avoidance. In proposing the study the same day as the House was finally beating down the earmarking amendments, Roosevelt sought to expose "economic royalists" who used legal loopholes to avoid paying their full share of taxes.[33] Accordingly, he asked Congress to authorize a Treasury Department investigation of tax avoidance.

Senate conservatives, viewing the request as a way of increasing revenue, did not object to Roosevelt's idea. Even Byrd publicly praised the move. Though the Senate altered the President's request somewhat, it granted the Treasury

[31] *Congressional Record,* 75th Cong., 1st Sess., 5213.

[32] For a discussion of House sentiment, see Arthur Krock, New York *Times,* June 3, 1937, p. 24.

[33] Samuel Rosenman (ed.), *The Public Papers and Addresses of Franklin D. Roosevelt* (13 vols.; New York, 1938-1950), VI, 238-50.

Department wide powers of subpoena. With these powers the Treasury could determine the course the investigation would take.

The focus of interest then turned to the House, still smarting from the struggle of the night before. Again the House rebelled. When leaders requested unanimous consent to the measure, O'Connor demanded recognition and heatedly denounced the proposal. Pointing to the part of the bill that authorized Congress to grant subpoena powers to Treasury agents, O'Connor cried, "This section is probably the greatest surrender and delegation of Congressional power which has ever been suggested to the House of Representatives."[34]

Maverick, Roosevelt's erstwhile ally, was almost as perturbed. Protesting the unseemly haste involved, he added his complaints to O'Connor's. "We are constantly accused of being rubber stamps," he said. "I do not admit that, but I want to say that I do not believe that anything like this should be so suddenly considered."[35] Like many loyal Democrats, Maverick did not object to the purpose of the investigation; he merely resented what he regarded as White House disregard of congressional prerogative.

Denied unanimous consent, the bill went to O'Connor's Rules Committee, which unanimously endorsed his changes. The new bill authorized a joint congressional committee to conduct the investigation. Treasury agents might be used, but they would not be permitted to hold hearings, to subpoena witnesses, or to publicize income tax returns. A week later O'Connor introduced the new version. "This resolution," he cried, "crystallizes the sentiment of this body to preserve the independence of Congress. . . . I resent that interference from those employed in the executive branch just as much as I resent interference with what we do by the

---

[34] *Congressional Record*, 75th Cong., 1st Sess., 5244.
[35] *Ibid.*

executive branch."[36] Despite opposition from Republicans who opposed the very purpose of an investigation, the resolution swept through the House much as O'Connor wanted it. Soon thereafter, the Senate accepted his terms and the investigation began under congressional auspices.[37]

Brief though it was, the tax controversy illustrated the same kind of House resentment at executive domination that had characterized the utilities and relief battles. Again, the division was not so much that of conservatives versus New Dealers as of a general distrust of bureaucracy and of "blueprint" legislation. Whereas House rebels had not wholly achieved their aims in previous struggles, they did so on the tax question. Turner Catledge remarked of the congressional mood: "Q. Is there a perceptible feeling of revolt in Congress to many measures if not the general trend of the President's program? A. Yes unquestionably.

"Q. Has it yet done any serious damage to his plan? A. No.

"Q. What of the future? A. Assume nothing."[38]

The tax controversy subsided in the second week in June, and for the next six weeks the House managed to avoid divisive debates. Attention focused upon the Senate, then wrestling with the court bill, the majority leadership, and the labor standards bill. House tempers cooled as administration aides relaxed pressure on representatives for the time being. At a Democratic "harmony" weekend in late June

---

[36] *Ibid.*, p. 5444.

[37] Once again Republican extremism in the House did not help the cause of conservative bipartisanship. Knutson of Minnesota declared, "Last year you Democrats were going after the Huey Long crowd for tax dodging. And what happened? Why, Jim Farley went down there and got into bed with those fellows" (*ibid.*, p. 5448). And a few days later Hamilton Fish of New York created a minor sensation by insisting that Roosevelt himself be investigated for tax dodging. Calling Hyde Park a "palatial estate," Fish, whose district included Roosevelt's home, added, "If you are going to investigate tax dodging, let's begin with Mr. Roosevelt." New York *Times*, June 12, 1937, p. 1.

[38] New York *Times*, June 6, 1937, IV, 8.

Roosevelt even let Dies induct him into the Demagogues Club, and many other neglected Democrats had a chance to talk affably with the President. House Republicans, continuing to make strong anti-administration speeches, frustrated what sentiment there might have been among conservative Democrats to join a bipartisan conservative coalition.

But conservative congressmen in no sense had decided to embrace the administration. As the session dragged into the summer months, they became increasingly eager to go home. To all but the most loyal New Dealers it appeared that nothing was to be gained by prolonging the session. After all, wasn't the emergency over? "A lot of the boys want to go," said one congressman. "After all, they are quite right in saying most of these things can wait. If we pass the tax loophole bill next January it will affect the same income items it would now, and be a better bill. The same thing is true of farm relief, and wages and hours laws need study. If there's a row over what's left of the judicial reform bill, I don't see any sense in prolonging the session for that . . . we might as well adjourn."[39]

The same sectional antagonisms that were plaguing the Senate also divided the House. Already disturbed by the sitdowns, relief, and antilynching battles (an antilynching bill had passed the House thanks to a discharge petition in April), southern congressmen reacted angrily when bountiful harvests in late July threatened to depress cotton prices. They urged Roosevelt to renew commodity crop loans to guarantee cotton farmers twelve cents a pound.[40] Wheat and corn state congressmen joined the movement, demanding the same treatment for their constituents as southerners

[39] Quoted by Krock, *ibid.*, Aug. 1, 1937, IV, 3.

[40] For the House farm bloc, see Wesley McCune, *The Farm Bloc* (Garden City, N.Y., 1943), pp. 53-57. For other material relating to this problem, see FDR to Theodore Bilbo, Sept. 3, 1937, Roosevelt MSS, OF 258.

were seeking for theirs. Both houses quickly advanced legislation to deal with the problem, despite Roosevelt's expressed reluctance to grant their demands. The crop loans issue, still unresolved in early August, was but one more element in the brew which was upsetting rural politicians in both houses.

In the midst of this problem the fair labor standards bill finally emerged from the House Labor Committee. Though somewhat different from the bill that had so recently passed the Senate, it was acceptable to most congressmen.[41] Although organized labor remained unenthusiastic about the measure, most observers were certain that the bill would pass the House if voted upon. This was precisely the problem. To receive consideration before the end of the session, the bill had to obtain a special rule from the Rules Committee. And it was obvious from the start that such a rule would be difficult to secure.

To begin with, the committee included four Republicans, three of whom for partisan reasons were certain to vote against a special rule for the bill. Dies, still suspicious of organized labor and furious at Roosevelt's refusal to capitulate on cotton crop loans, also opposed the labor bill. From the start there was a core of four members who disliked the bill. But since there were fourteen on the committee, this bloc in itself was of little importance.

But the real powers on the committee besides O'Connor were not Dies or the Republicans, but two quite different southerners, Howard W. Smith of Virginia and Edward E. Cox of Georgia. They posed the largest obstacles to the administration. The younger of the two was Smith. Fifty-four years old at the time, he had been a congressman since 1931, a member of the Rules Committee since 1933. Grave

---

[41] See James M. Burns, *Congress on Trial* (New York, 1949), pp. 73-74; and Paul H. Douglas and Joseph Hackman, "The Fair Labor Standards Act of 1938" (I), *Political Science Quarterly*, LIII (Dec. 1938), 491-515.

and unobtrusive, Smith was a frail and courtly figure who wore wing collars and pince-nez and reminded one critic of a "slick small town lawyer of the 1880's."[42] This comment described his background. Educated at military school, he received a law degree at the University of Virginia. By 1937 "the judge," as he was called, was a bank president and pillar of the church in his home town.

No man was more stridently opposed to the New Deal. A member of the Glass-Byrd machine, he considered himself the true descendant of Thomas Jefferson in the House; indeed, Monticello was in his home district. Safe from defeat at the polls and opposed to almost all ventures of the national government into the social and economic life of the nation, he had long been recognized as one of the most conservative Democrats in the House. From 1933 to 1939 he opposed nearly half of all major New Deal measures.[43]

For labor bills he reserved a special dislike. In part his objection to unions stemmed from a fear that they would destroy southern industry. But his rural Virginia district contained relatively little manufacturing: essentially, he simply lacked sympathy for urban life, for labor officials, for immigrants, or for regimentation of any kind, be it political or economic. In 1941 he would submit an amendment to the Wagner Act "to restore the God-given right of every man to work without paying tribute to a labor union."[44] With Dies, he equated the CIO with radicalism and anarchy, and in years to come not even Dies could match Smith's fervent quests for antilabor and antiradical legislation. On the question of acceding to a special rule for the labor standards bill Smith had no difficulty in making up

[42] See *Current Biography*, 1941, pp. 798-99. Also *Time*, Aug. 15, 1938, pp. 11-12, and Kenneth G. Crawford, "Open Season on Reds," *Nation*, CXLVIII (May 6, 1939), 519-20.

[43] Figures based on thirty-one key House roll calls, 1933-1939. He opposed nearly 50 percent of these major measures. See Appendix A.

[44] *Current Biography*, 1941, p. 798.

his mind. He would join Dies and the Republicans in opposition.

Cox, a slightly older man, was fifty-seven in 1937 and had been a Georgia congressman since 1925. Handsome and thick-haired, he had been on the Rules Committee before the New Deal and by 1937 was its third-ranking member.[45] He was as fiery a man as sat in the House. On one occasion he pulled a colleague's hair in debate; on another he started a fist fight on the House floor. One observer described well the contrast that Cox made with Smith in committee meeting: "The volatile Cox of Georgia works up an emotional fervor of opposition to the New Deal, the rail-thin Smith of Virginia, with his inevitable gates-ajar collar, interpolates caustic comments. Amid the confusion Sabath [the committee chairman at the time] gently taps his block with the handle of his gavel, murmuring: 'gentlemen, gentlemen,' in mild reproof, and gives the impression of a man trying to hold back a steam roller."[46]

Cox had already been an unreliable Democrat before 1937. But his opposition had not been so steady, so inherently Jeffersonian as Smith's. During the utilities debate he had spoken for the "death sentence." No New Dealer, Cox had nonetheless been receptive to some aspects of the Roosevelt administration.

But the events of 1937 made him an open opponent of the New Deal. To begin with, the court plan profoundly disturbed him. It was, he proclaimed, "an open and bald assault upon the institution of liberty."[47] Then the growth of organized labor sent him forever off the New Deal reservation. Like his friend Garner, Cox believed instinc-

[45] *Ibid.*, 1943, pp. 150-51; also New York *Times* (obituary), Dec. 25, 1952, p. 29. Also Willson Whitman, "Georgia Bottleneck," *New Republic*, CIV (June 9, 1941), 784-86.

[46] See J. T. Salter (ed.), *Public Men In and Out of Office* (Chapel Hill, N.C., 1946), p. 207.

[47] New York *Times*, Feb. 16, 1937, p. 4.

tively in individual initiative and private property, and when
Roosevelt refused to halt the sitdowns, he was furious.
Furthermore, his Georgia constituency contained small
manufacturing and textile plants, and he was responsive to
their views. "I warn John L. Lewis and his Communistic
cohorts," he cried, "that no second-hand 'carpetbag expe-
dition' in the Southland, under the banner of Soviet Russia
. . . will be tolerated."[48] No member of the Rules Committee,
or indeed of the whole House, was so implacably opposed
to the labor standards bill.

Cox, Smith, and Dies, with three Republicans, made a
near majority of the fourteen-man committee. And thanks
in part to their determination, two other southern Democrats
on the committee quickly joined them. They were William
J. Driver of Arkansas and J. Bayard Clark of North Carolina.[49] These two men, relatively recent additions to the
committee, had previously gone along with the administration. But they agreed with Cox that this bill would hurt
the South.[50] "Where I could borrow votes before," O'Connor
complained, "nobody is lending anything these days."[51]
Within a very short time, O'Connor, who favored the bill,
found himself in a minority on his own committee. A conservative coalition had assumed command.

Faced with such implacable hostility, the administration
surrendered, and Rayburn quietly arranged to drop the labor
standards bill. In addition, Roosevelt finally promised he

[48] Quoted in *Time*, Aug. 23, 1937, p. 12.

[49] For Clark's views see Clark to O'Connor, Oct. 26, 1937, O'Connor MSS,
Hours and Wages Bill File.

[50] For Driver, see Travis M. Adams, "The Arkansas Congressional Delegation During the New Deal, 1933-1936" (unpublished M.A. thesis, Vanderbilt University, 1962), pp. 46-50. Significantly, Driver's district contained
no city with a population of more than 10,000.

[51] *Congressional Record*, 75th Cong., 1st Sess., 11664. O'Connor's relations with the southerners were not cordial anyway. For his view of Dies
see O'Connor to Kenneth M. Romney, Aug. 19, 1936, O'Connor MSS,
Leadership File. ". . . from long experience with him [Dies] you can take
anything he says in reverse."

would assure a twelve-cent cotton price for 1937. In return, the victorious Rules Committee agreed to a temporary suspension of the rules to speed noncontroversial measures through the House.[52] It was one of the administration's darkest days in the House.

Undaunted, a group of House liberals tried again to save the labor bill. Without a special rule, they possessed two alternatives. One was to consider the bill under suspension of the rules, a procedure which permitted only forty minutes of debate and required a two-thirds vote. Bankhead and other House leaders discouraged this effort, partly because many disgusted representatives had already left town, partly because Roosevelt himself wanted certain changes in the bill and did not want it passed as it was, and partly because Rayburn had promised the Rules Committee that he would not resort to this tactic.[53] Supporters of the bill then gave up trying to prod the cautious leadership and circulated a petition for a Democratic caucus to bind the party on the measure. But on caucus day only 157 Democrats attended, 8 short of the requisite majority. Some 25 to 30 Democrats, mostly southerners, skulked in cloakrooms or loitered in corridors.[54] It was a disappointing finale for proponents of the bill.

The remainder of the House session was brief. At the last moment the Wagner housing bill, by then pretty well emasculated by rural congressmen, passed the House.[55] On

[52] New York *Times,* Aug. 14, 1937, p. 1.

[53] For evidence why the bill failed to receive substantial support outside the Rules Committee, see Cong. Edward H. Rees (Rep.-Kans.) to William Allen White, Aug. 6, 1937, W. A. White MSS, Box 191. He said: "This wage-hour bill is a rather tough problem. I haven't had any labor group asking me to support it. I have had a good many other groups asking me not to support it."

[54] New York *Times,* Aug. 20, 1937, p. 9.

[55] On the housing vote the final tally was 275-86. Of the forty Democrats against or paired against the bill, thirty-one were southerners. No eastern Democrat opposed the final bill. See *Congressional Record,* 75th Cong., 1st Sess., 9294.

the final day, the House was a dreary, dull contrast to the singing and cheering chamber of prior years. One congressman fell asleep in his seat, and Rayburn, in the chair, nodded absently as he stared at a cartoon. Most of the others whiled away their time in the Capitol restaurant, where congressmen consumed fifteen cases of beer for relief from the 100-degree heat. Minutes after adjournment not a congressman was to be found in the chamber.[56]

The House session of 1937 witnessed most of the same phenomena that had afflicted the Senate. Though House leaders remained loyal, they could not extinguish the feeling among their colleagues that the emergency was over. Nor could they alleviate the urban-rural and sectional antagonisms reflected so ominously in the sitdown, relief, and labor bill controversies. In the 1937 session 153, or 46 percent of the House Democrats, represented urban districts —as opposed to 29 percent in 1931. Most of these city-oriented Democrats were enthusiastic supporters of the Roosevelt program; their rural colleagues were not. As in the Senate, the division within the party was often a rural-urban, sectional matter intensified by the political awakening of the urban elements in the Democratic party.[57] In this sense the problems faced by Roosevelt in the House, like those he encountered in the Senate, were not caused by lapses in strategy.

[56] New York *Times,* Aug. 22, 1937, p. 34.

[57] Some of the foregoing is taken from the excellent study by Julius Turner, *Party and Constituency: Pressures on Congress* (Baltimore, 1951), pp. 80-83. Turner noted that Democratic cohesion on House roll calls in 1937 was less than in other years sampled (1920-1921, 1930, 1944) for either party. He also discovered a "significant metropolitan-rural division" among House Democrats on 34.1 percent of roll calls during the 1937 session (pp. 27, 74-75). Similarly, he discovered that the party loyalty of rural southerners in 1937 was 78.2 percent as opposed to 87.6 percent for urban southerners (p. 89).

I have also examined the degree of urbanism of all representatives, 1933-1939, and my conclusions are similar. See Appendix A for definition of "urban."

Developments in the 1937 House session resembled those in the Senate in two other ways. Veteran Democrats, though chosen originally by pre-Depression constituencies, were as a group only slightly less partial to the New Deal than the younger men who first came to Congress under Roosevelt. The liberal-conservative division was not one of veterans versus "coat-tail" congressmen.[58] Second, few important conservative Democrats were House leaders. More often they were less senior men such as Cox, Woodrum, Pettengill, Huddleston, Clark, or Driver. As in the Senate, official leadership was a sobering responsibility, and except for Sumners and O'Connor, few first-line leaders deserted. For rank-and-file members deprived of the prestige and responsibility of leadership, it was easier to desert the administration.[59]

[58] It was true, however, that most so-called "100 per cent New Dealers" were newcomers. See Stanley High, "The Neo-New Dealers," *Saturday Evening Post*, CCIX (May 22, 1937), 10.

[59] Rexford G. Tugwell, in *The Democratic Roosevelt* (Garden City, N.Y., 1957), p. 401, commented on the tendency of conservative Democrats to vote with the administration owing to the "buttressing of official position."

In general, I feel Tugwell's point is well taken. Of the top House leaders, Rayburn, Bankhead, Byrns, Rainey, and John McCormack (Mass.) were usually responsive to Roosevelt's wishes. Ordinarily loyal committee chairmen included Marvin Jones of Texas (Agriculture), Edward Taylor of Colorado (Appropriations), Henry Steagall of Alabama (Banking and Currency), James McReynolds of Tennessee (Foreign Affairs through 1937), Sol Bloom of New York (Foreign Affairs thereafter), Samuel Dickstein of New York (Immigration), Mary Norton of New Jersey (Labor), Adolph Sabath of Illinois (Rules after 1938), and Doughton of Ways and Means.

Those chairmen not so reliable, besides Sumners and O'Connor, included Clarence Lea of California (Interstate Commerce), Andrew May of Kentucky (Military Affairs), Joseph Mansfield of Texas (Rivers and Harbors), and Wilburn Cartwright of Oklahoma (Roads).

Yet even these generalizations must be made cautiously. Steagall, for instance, often needed considerable prodding, as the 1937 housing fight revealed; and McCormack (see chap. 7) revolted on a tax issue in 1938. Conversely, though Cartwright could be cantankerous on matters dealing with roads, he was usually dependable otherwise; and McReynolds, though usually cooperative on foreign affairs questions, was one of the leading southern opponents of the fair labor standards bill.

In other respects the situation in the House was recognizably different. Enough New Dealers existed to pass key administration measures with room to spare, if the measure could get to a vote. But as the court and labor standards issues indicated, a full House vote was not always possible. Thus, conservative tactics in the House were, and would be, different. Whereas Senate conservatives had to rely upon filibusters (as in the court and antilynching fights) or upon debilitating amendments (as in the sitdown, relief, and housing controversies), House conservatives dared not let measures reach the floor. From this time on they relied heavily upon the few men in the Rules Committee. A bipartisan conservative coalition in the House, if it were to exist at all, could operate successfully only within this powerful group. And it was over the economic and sectional issues of the 1937 session that this coalition first became effective.

An additional psychological factor spurred the occasional intransigence of the House: it felt neglected. Whereas almost every senator, no matter how new and unimportant, had talked and lunched with the President, many House Democrats had never been consulted at all. With no personal bonds to tie them to the other end of Pennsylvania Avenue, they found it easier to express the combination of personal resentment and ideological suspicion which had first broken out in the utilities fight. This psychological factor helps explain why some newcomers chosen on New Deal platforms quickly kicked over the traces. Most veterans had not experienced the anonymity of their less-experienced colleagues, but they did resent what they considered to be White House favoritism of the Senate. In this desire for respect and recognition Maverick, Sumners, Dies, and O'Connor were able to agree.[60]

[60] As early as April 1936 O'Connor had written concerning the forthcoming Democratic National Convention, "the official program is so cluttered

The House session of 1937 revealed the politics of sectionalism.[61] But as much as anything else, it exposed the politics of independence.

with Senators that no members of the House can get on it. Of course, this is in accordance with the attitude of the 'Boss' to recognize only Senators, but when it comes to cases, his real 100 percent friends are in the House." To James Farley, April 23, 1936, O'Connor MSS, Farley File.

[61] For a good survey of the South and the New Deal, see J. B. Shannon, "Presidential Politics in the South," *Journal of Politics,* I (April and August, 1939), 146-70 and 278-300. Like Tugwell, Shannon noticed that many southerners were deeply concerned over the fate of the Democratic party during and immediately after the 1936 campaign.

6

GROPING FOR COALITION

FOR ALL the President's troubles, by August 1937 he was still able to make one irrefutable claim: prosperity was returning. Unemployment was reduced and industrial activity much increased. As congressmen fled Washington to mend their fences, they were careful to remember one thing: the New Deal, apparently, had worked.

Then came the decline. Industrial production fell off sharply; stock prices plunged precipitously; businesses failed. By the end of the year, some two million people had lost their jobs.[1] The downswing might not have been serious had business been ready or willing to take up the slack. But businessmen, still timid, were afraid to invest. Without sufficient stimulation from public or private sources, the unhealthy economy sagged dangerously. The recession of 1937 had arrived.

What might have occurred in Congress without this sharp

change in economic conditions is conjectural. Most likely, the existing divisions would have continued, neither more nor less severe than they had been. But the recession changed the situation considerably. Whereas the 1933 emergency had been the "Hoover Depression," the new crisis became the "Roosevelt Recession," and New Deal claims returned to haunt the President. The recession was a decisive event in the growth of congressional conservatism. It confused Roosevelt, making him indecisive and dilatory; it eroded more of the fabulous Roosevelt magic; it destroyed the unity and resolve of the New Deal coalition; and it caused some congressmen to grope toward a permanent bipartisan coalition.

The problem was Roosevelt's, for Congress was no longer in session. But the recession had caught him unprepared and inevitably, he felt, good times had to return. Furthermore, as he sought help on potential solutions, he found advisers divided. Some, such as Morgenthau, insisted it was time to balance the budget and renew business confidence in the soundness of government finance. The administration, Morgenthau said later, "had to take away the crutches to test whether the patient was able to walk by himself."[2] Others, the "100 per cent New Dealers" so cordially disliked by conservative congressmen, urged resumption of heavy government spending. Among this group were Hopkins, Ickes, and several other young economists and lawyers in executive departments.

Baffled, Roosevelt did nothing. Hoping for an upswing as a natural turn of events, he decided to bide his time. He also toured the West during the fall and returned with renewed confidence in his personal popularity. Convinced

[1] Kenneth Roose, "The Recession of 1937-1938," *Journal of Political Economy*, LVI (1948), 241. For causes and remedies, see also Randolph E. Paul, *Taxation in the United States* (Boston, 1954), pp. 220-34.

[2] John M. Blum, *From the Morgenthau Diaries: Years of Crisis, 1928-1938* (Boston, 1959), p. 388.

that the people would force Congress to act upon the unfinished business of the 1937 session, he called for a special session to begin in mid-November. His opening message asked for enactment of the fair labor standards bill, a farm program, reorganization of the executive branch, and regional planning along the lines of the TVA. All were requests he had made before.

In the meantime, conservative congressmen had been spending their brief vacations carefully. Aware that Roosevelt's prestige had suffered as a result of the court plan and sitdowns, they began to hope that he might adopt a more conservative posture. "Some of my friends," wrote Bailey in August, "think I am a fool for entertaining the hope that Mr. Roosevelt will become more conservative, but I do entertain this hope. I think I can see his situation. He is a man who likes innovation. He is extremely ardent to do well."[3] Other conservative Democrats agreed with Bailey. Unwilling to precipitate a party split themselves, they hoped that the President would pay attention to their conservative ideas. But they were acutely aware that only they could hold the President to a conservative track. Ever since the Supreme Court had reversed itself in the spring of 1937, they realized that the judiciary would no longer be a dependable bulwark against New Deal "radicalism." And with Black's addition, the court was certain to adopt a liberal path in the future. Congress would have to take the court's place in stopping the New Deal.

With these thoughts in mind, Bailey and his friends tried to secure congressional backing during the fall recess. Already, Gerry had emphasized to Bailey that the President's prestige had diminished.[4] Encouraged, Bailey determined to discover the reactions of his friends George and Byrd. George agreed with Gerry, and Byrd, after talking with

---

[3] To O. Max Gardner, July 1, 1937, Bailey MSS, Political File.
[4] Gerry to Bailey, Oct. 19, 1937, *ibid.*

people in Virginia's tobacco belt, wrote, "Roosevelt is still personally popular but the people are turning against all of his major policies."[5]

Bailey then decided to act. "What we have to do," he wrote Byrd in September, "is to preserve, if we can, the Democratic Party against his [Roosevelt's] efforts to make it the Roosevelt Party. But above this we must place the preservation of Constitutional Representative Government. We must frame a policy and maintain it—and this must be done in the next Congress. We must ascertain on whom we may rely—get them together and make our battle, win or lose. . . ."[6] Already, Bailey was thinking of a united and consistent conservative bloc to temper the New Deal.

By the time the special session opened on November 15, such conservative opinions were common. The recession had already become a serious and apparently permanent phenomenon. Furthermore, the President had taken a beating from the press. Publisher Roy Howard wrote his editors, "I think it should be our definite policy to print everything cogent and understandable that is calculated to impress the public with the fact that the government is demonstrating a drunken sailor's attitude toward the billions gathered from the taxpayers."[7] Finally, congressmen were not at all happy about being called back to Washington to enact bills for which there seemed to be no hurry and which seemed to them to have no bearing on the recession. "Many of the members came back in a bad humor," Doughton wrote, "resenting a special call for which the Committees of Congress were not ready."[8] O'Connor, angrier than ever, wrote a colleague, "Well, it happened! I know how you feel about

5 To Bailey, Sept. 9, 1937, *ibid.*

6 Sept. 25, 1937, *ibid.* For Bailey's role in the special session, see John R. Moore, "Senator Josiah W. Bailey and the 'Conservative Manifesto' of 1937," *Journal of Southern History,* XXXI (Feb. 1965), 21-39.

7 To Lee B. Wood, Aug. 26, 1937, Clapper MSS, Container 8.

8 To E. W. G. Huffman, Nov. 22, 1937, Doughton MSS, Folder 671.

being 'proclaimed' into a special session. . . . Me too!"[9] The congressional reaction to Roosevelt's 1933 message to Congress, a newspaper commented, had been one of "uproarious applause and frenzied activity." In November 1937 there was only a "polite and unenthusiastic reception."[10]

Moreover, some congressmen returned anxious to form conservative coalitions of one kind or another. Hope of Kansas, observing the continued hostility of many Democrats toward the administration, wrote, "I feel a coalition of this group of Democrats and of the few Republicans who are left in Congress can do much to restore representative government."[11] In the Senate others besides Bailey arrived with intentions of defying the President. Wheeler stopped in Chicago on his way to Washington to talk with Frank Knox, the Republican vice-presidential nominee in 1936. According to Knox, Wheeler emphasized that "the fight on Roosevelt's leadership is to be renewed with increased vigor in the special session just beginning."[12] Conservatives in both houses were eager at least to halt the New Deal, at most to do so with bipartisan coalitions.

In this mood, Congress proceeded to consider the President's program. After some delay, the administration presented a farm bill, and following considerable maneuvering both houses unenthusiastically passed revised versions.[13] A conference committee then struggled with the bills, reaching agreement in 1938.

[9] To Lyle Boren (Dem.–Okla.), Oct. 21, 1937, Boren MSS.

[10] New York *Times,* Nov. 16, 1937, p. 15.

[11] To George Abell, Nov. 29, 1937, Hope MSS, Official Correspondence, 1937-1938, A-CRH.

[12] Knox to Alfred Landon, Nov. 17, 1937, Landon MSS, Political File, 1937, H-K.

[13] See the reaction of Rep. Wilburn Cartwright (Dem.–Okla.). He wrote, "Looks as if the Farm bill is going to be the only bill passed this session and I don't know whether it is going to be worth passing or not." Letter to Mrs. Cartwright, Dec. 7, 1937, Cartwright MSS, Personal Correspondence, 1934-1936.

Otherwise, Congress was unresponsive. Realizing that both executive reorganization and regional planning were sensitive issues, congressional leaders failed to bring them to the floor. Meanwhile, the Senate, adhering to Barkley's promise in the summer of 1937, had to endure a southern filibuster against the antilynching bill. Many congressmen were also proposing to repeal the undistributed-profits tax. The record of legislation in the special session was essentially insignificant.

The House at first provided the drama of the session, for House leaders once again sought to pry the fair labor standards bill out of the Rules Committee.[14] At first signatures to a discharge petition came easily, and a week after the opening of the session, the petition had 153 of the requisite 218 names attached. But by November 30 there were only 193 signatures, and Cox, leading the opposition to the petition, claimed he had promises from at least ten to withdraw from the list if necessary.[15] Furthermore, with no powerful lobby such as was propelling the farm bill through both houses, a noticeable lack of urgency pervaded the entire procedure. "The Rules Committee," noted one reporter, "are not being hanged in effigy or seriously denounced anywhere. They move about floor and cloakroom on terms of affectionate friendship with colleagues who are trying to bring the legislation to a vote. They get few unkind letters, they say, and many favoring ones. Mostly there is a vast, indifferent silence."[16]

At this point House leaders renewed their efforts. Rep.

---

[14] The Democratic opposition within the Rules Committee by this time was not only southern. Rep. Lawrence Lewis, a Democrat from Denver, also opposed the bill. When it appeared that the House would discharge the bill from his committee, however, he believed it wise to grant it a rule; otherwise, committee prestige would be weakened and leadership in the House would go to "blocs." See Lewis Diary, Dec. 1 and Dec. 2, 1937.

[15] New York *Times,* Dec. 1, 1937, p. 19.

[16] *Ibid.,* p. 22.

Mary T. Norton of New Jersey, leading the labor bill proponents, offered an amendment to the plan then in the Rules
Committee. Her amendment, aimed at satisfying William
Green's objections, would have abolished the proposed five-
man board and vested power in a one-man administrator in
the Labor Department. Meanwhile, other leaders passed the
word that they would not support the farm bill—still to be
considered in the House—unless farm state representatives
helped sign the petition. Few situations illustrated so sharply
the way in which many congressmen identified themselves
with particular economic and sectional interests. The urban-
rural cleavages that had already been opened up by the
sitdown, relief, and housing battles of the previous session
were apparent for all to see.[17]

To opponents of the bill such as Dies this maneuvering
was outrageous. "They have swapped everything today but
the Capitol," the erstwhile cynic pontificated. "They have
traded and promised everything to get them on that petition. . . . They promised so much there won't be anything
left for the federal government."[18] Such complaints were to
no avail. The next day, December 2, Representative Joseph
J. Mansfield of Texas, crippled and confined to a wheelchair,
rolled to the well of the House and affixed the final signa-
ture.[19] It appeared as if the labor bill, at last, would sweep
through the House.

Confusion then shrouded the issue. Green, still dissatisfied with Mrs. Norton's proposed changes, began to frown
upon the whole procedure. Even a one-man administrator
within the Labor Department was unsatisfactory, he be-

[17] See *Time,* Dec. 13, 1937, pp. 14-15, for a colorful account of the
trading. See also Roosevelt MSS, OF 200-WW, for administration pressure
on Louisiana congressmen through the Louisiana machine.

[18] New York *Times,* Dec. 2, 1937, p. 13.

[19] *Ibid.,* Dec. 3, 1937, p. 1. Mansfield was not in favor of the bill
but felt it should be voted on. The 218 included 196 Democrats, 9 Republicans, 8 Progressives, and 5 Farmer-Laborites.

lieved, for one man, regardless of who he was, might set unsatisfactory wage standards. The bill, he insisted, should be entirely inflexible: it should set a flat forty-hour maximum week, forty cents an hour minimum wage, and should be enforced by the Department of Justice. Unions, he declared, should secure subsequent gains. Furthermore, he flatly opposed regional wage differentials, thus cementing southern and rural opposition to his new ideas.

For the next ten days this confusion continued. Representative Lawrence J. Connery, who had assumed his deceased brother's Massachusetts seat, devised a bill incorporating Green's new terms, but the Labor Committee approved Mrs. Norton's amendment incorporating administration of the bill in the Labor Department. Then the whole House, with many city representatives aiding the farm lobby, passed the farm bill. But urban support of the farm measure did not pacify opponents of the labor bill. Instead, Cox and Dies intensified the attack. "The passage of this measure," said Cox, "is the worst thing that could take place at this time. It would throw a million out of work."[20] Not to be outdone, Dies injected the racial issue. "There is a racial question involved here," he said amidst a chorus of rebel yells. "Under this measure what is prescribed for one race must be prescribed for the others, and you cannot prescribe the same wages for the black man as for the white man."[21]

Two days later, December 15, the voting began. First to be considered was Connery's plan embodying Green's inflexible bill. A combination of administration supporters holding out for the Norton bill and an almost solid phalanx of southern and rural conservatives defeated this plan 162-131. Green, still distrusting the Norton version, then urged recommittal of the entire bill. Two days later he succeeded. In the most

[20] *Congressional Record*, 75th Cong., 2nd Sess., Appendix, 441-42.
[21] *Ibid.*, pp. 1387-88.

smashing defeat Roosevelt had ever received in the House a coalition sent the labor standards bill back to committee. The vote was 216-198, as twenty-eight representatives who had signed the discharge petition turned against the bill. Fifteen of these were rural Democrats from the North and West; six were southerners; and three were Republicans.

This significant vote revealed the extent to which Roosevelt's coalition had disintegrated in the House. A total of 133 of the 216 opponents of the bill were Democrats, or more than one-third of the Democratic strength in the House. Except for the utilities vote, on which 166 Democrats had deserted the administration, and veterans' bonus bills, this was by far the strongest Democratic disaffection from the New Deal to that time. Revealingly, 74 Democratic opponents of the labor bill had also opposed the "death sentence": obviously, these men found much of the New Deal unacceptable.

The vote was the clearest indication of sectional divisions of any vote to that time. Of the 99 southern Democratic representatives, 81 voted for recommittal; of the 53 westerners, 20 also voted for recommittal. Of the remaining 177 Democrats, only 31 opposed the administration.[22] In all, 99—or 74 percent—of the bill's opponents represented predominantly rural districts. Since only 54 percent of the House Democrats were rural, this roll call brilliantly illuminated the urban-rural conflicts that were dividing the Roosevelt coalition.

As later events would make clear, the vote left a slightly misleading impression of conservative strength. The bill was an indication not only of conservative power but of

[22] The vote also indicated again that new Democratic representatives were only a little more reliable than veterans of pre-Roosevelt service. Of the 121 Democrats then in Congress whose service predated the New Deal, 55 opposed the administration here. Of the 210 "coat-tailers," 78 opposed the administration.

recession psychology. Almost all congressmen, regardless of political persuasion, were concerned with alleviating the recession before they faced their constituents in November. The labor bill, however, seemed to promise more, not less, economic stress. Raising wages at a time of falling prices seemed the best way to drive many marginal industries out of business altogether. "If this bill is recommitted," one debater insisted, "you will see a change for the better in two days."[23] Though few were honestly so sanguine, the fear that the bill would do little if anything to solve the recession was one of many concerns which caused recommittal of the bill.

Above all, the drama again revealed the dependence of the New Deal upon pressure groups, particularly in the more vulnerable House. In the simplest terms results of the special session suggested that when a powerful lobby supported a bill, it usually passed; such had been the case with the farm bill. But when a lobby was indecisive or unenthusiastic, as labor was in this case, congressmen were left to follow the next strongest pressures, whatever they might be. In the past the administration, buttressed by Roosevelt's great electoral strength, had been the pressure before which they had been forced to bow. But by December 1937, Roosevelt's prestige was diminished. Beaten on the court bill, trapped in the center on the sitdown and relief problems, and apparently unsuccessful in curing the Depression, the New Deal no longer seemed the potent electoral force it once had been. Moreover, the President, disturbed both by the recession and by a painful tooth, failed to exert the personal pressure upon congressmen that he had on past occasions. When his coalition united, it was still invincible. But when it did not—and it was on this kind of sectional-economic issue that it did not—congressmen were much more free to vote as they

[23] *Congressional Record*, 75th Cong., 2nd Sess., 1828.

pleased. Divisions among liberals, as much as alliances among conservatives, accounted for the startling defeat of the bill.

While the House struggled over the labor bill, Senate conservatives began to work for the coalition which Bailey had conceived of at the start of the session. "It seems to me," he wrote, "that we are now at the crossroads where it will be absolutely necessary either to turn further to the left and control practically all business and agriculture or some concession will have to be made so that the industries in the United States can look forward with some degree of certainty to an uninterrupted program."[24]

When Bailey talked with his colleagues during the special session, he found many in general agreement with this line of thought. They agreed that it would be a good idea to frame a general statement of policy, one which was conservative yet one to which the President could largely subscribe, and to persuade the administration to approve it. If they succeeded in doing so, the Senate would have the initiative and the President would be committed to a conservative platform.

Moreover, in Bailey's mind at least, such a plan would have a salutary effect in uniting conservative senators. Prior to this time conservatives had often voted together. But except for the court controversy, there had been little organization across or even inside party lines on issues as they arose. In the House such organization was both impossible and, paradoxically, unnecessary—impossible because of the size and confusion of the chamber, and unnecessary since the Rules Committee would often suffice. But in the Senate, Bailey thought, discipline might lend some stability to conservative strength. Whether he was thinking of a permanent bipartisan conservative coalition is uncertain, for he had to be careful of constituents who did not look kindly upon

24 To O. L. Moore, Nov. 6, 1937, Bailey MSS, Relief File.

alliances with Republicans. But clearly, he hoped that those senators who signed a proposed statement of principles would feel committed to stand together in the future on issues covered in the statement.

In retrospect such an ambitious venture seems a little ludicrous, for the chasm between men like Bailey and the administration was already deep. Conservatives also knew Roosevelt well enough to realize that he was temperamentally inimical to "statements of principle" or to commitments which prevented freedom of action. Yet their boldness showed their confidence, and it revealed that the recession had temporarily stymied the President: it was now left to others to pull rabbits out of the hat.

Bailey had more immediate strategic problems to face. Where should he look to find a conservative leader? There were at once too many and too few. As a hostile reporter had observed a few months earlier, the conservative group in the Senate had "an oversupply of leaders. It has more prima donnas than the Metropolitan Opera Co. Several, such as 'Kemal Pasha' Vandenberg and Bennett Clark, cher-' ish presidential ambitions. Burke of Nebraska is an incorrigible grandstander and Burt Wheeler has so far abandoned his one-time liberalism as to consort openly with Alice Longworth, Frank Kent, and other reactionary storm troopers. None of the group is personally liked in the Senate and their malice is so great that other Senators are wary of them."[25] This judgment, though harsh, did lay bare one weakness of Senate conservatives: they had no recognized leader and too many outspoken individuals. To unite so many individualists on any program would indeed be a remarkable achievement.

Bailey faced the opposite problem as well: how many of these individualists would be willing to endorse publicly

[25] Robert S. Allen, "Washington Sweatshop," *Nation*, CXLV (July 17, 1937), 63-64.

a program framed without administration sanction? All conservatives had already defied the President on more than one occasion, and Republicans would certainly be willing to do so again. But few Democrats, anti-New Deal or not, relished the prospect of an irrevocable split in the party. Defy the administration on given occasions, yes. But to commit themselves to a permanent program of action without administration approval was not an alluring prospect.

Finally, who should be included in the framing of a statement of principles? There Bailey encountered the most difficult problem of all. If he restricted his associates to Democrats, he thereby destroyed the loose coalition that had operated during the court controversy. Yet if he actively sought bipartisan coalition, what would constituents in the one-party South have to say? Would such blatant bipartisanship be a sign that conservative Democrats were renouncing their rights to any future consideration from the party? And what of Republicans? Would they be willing to submit to permanent domination by conservative Democrats?

Bailey was undaunted. Corresponding widely with business and financial leaders, he found them receptive to the idea of a conservative statement of principles. And within the Senate, Bailey counted upon the support of at least a few of his colleagues on the Democratic side of the aisle. Byrd, Glass, Copeland, and King made a minimum nucleus of four. The position of Republicans was uncertain. But at least one, Vandenberg, was expected to join in a bipartisan venture; in November he had issued a conservative statement of principles himself. Convinced that GOP support would not be the kiss of death—especially since the sponsorship would be Democratic—Bailey welcomed his comrade in arms to the fold.

The next step was to confer and devise some formal strategy, but meetings had to be conducted quietly, for the conservative group wanted above all to avoid premature publicity. As one of Bailey's correspondents insisted, "If the attempt upon the part of you and your associates to provide leadership and a definite program proves abortive, either because of premature announcement or inability to get a large number of signatures or for any other reason, the psychological effect will be disastrous. Such failure would give the impression that not even a few persons could be found in the Senate who are willing to offer themselves as leaders of such a program."[26] So the conservative leaders decided to hold quiet little gatherings. On December 2, a bipartisan supper was scheduled at a Washington hotel, and the next day ten conservative senators met in a private dining room at the Capitol for a kind of "round-table" discussion.[27] Sponsored by Byrd, the luncheon featured quail supplied by Republican Senator John G. Townsend of Delaware. Lewis Douglas, Roosevelt's former budget director who had resigned over spending policy in 1934, spoke to the guests. Besides Byrd, Townsend, and Douglas, the diners included Vandenberg and seven other Senate Democrats: Glass, King, Copeland, George, Smith, Bailey, and Van Nuys.[28]

Since the meeting was private, what happened there was not definitely known at the time. But the press was aware of the gathering and waylaid some of the participants after the feast was over. "There was agreement," said one anonymous guest, "that Congress must act, even if it has to take the initiative away from the President. There must be reassurance so that capital will get into action and come out of

[26] Hamilton Long to Bailey (also to Byrd), Dec. 16, 1937, Bailey MSS, Political File.

[27] See Styles Bridges to Bailey, Nov. 29, 1937, *ibid.*, Personal File. In this brief note, Bridges remarked that the dinner will be "just a small group and will be a strictly personal and confidential affair." The luncheon meeting was reported in the press. See New York *Herald Tribune*, Dec. 4, 1937, p. 1, and later accounts in New York *Times*, Dec. 19, 1937, IV, 1. Bridges seems to have remained completely out of sight thereafter.

[28] New York *Herald Tribune*, Dec. 4, 1937, p. 1.

hiding. There must be less heckling and harassing."[29] The conservative plan, said a press account, was first of all to compose a declaration of principles but was also "replete with the possibility of open coalition later upon the floor of the Senate."[30]

The press had guessed well. As Vandenberg noted privately at the time, Douglas confirmed the most gloomy predictions of conservative spokesmen. He was, Vandenberg said, "bluntly pessimistic about the outlook of the country unless early action should demonstrate the existence of a strong congressional feeling for a quick, stabilizing legislative program which would, in effect, 'take the ball away from the president' and give business a chance." As a result, Vandenberg continued, the group "informally resolved upon attempting a coalition statement to the country."[31]

The next task was to compose a statement of conservative principles and to corral as many signatures as possible. At first prospects appeared auspicious. Soon after the quail luncheon, Gerry, reliving the role he had played during the court fight, gave two dinners at his home. Attended by Bailey, Glass, Byrd, George, Copeland, King, Smith, Tydings, Van Nuys, Vandenberg, and Warren R. Austin of Vermont, these genial occasions served as strategy and drafting sessions. With Bailey as a kind of chief editor, Gerry as patron, and Vandenberg as author, the statement was soon ready for týping and distribution. Meanwhile, these determined conservatives toured the cloakrooms, hoping for as many as thirty signatures before releasing the statement for publication. They received some encouragement; besides the diners, Townsend, Walsh, Donahey, Clark, Holt, Maloney, and Moore were rumored to be sympathetic.[32]

[29] *Ibid.*
[30] *Ibid.*
[31] Vandenberg Notes, Dec. 1937, Vandenberg MSS, 1937 Scrapbook.
[32] New York *Times,* Dec. 19, 1937, IV, 1.

But the hazards were formidable. Bailey soon discovered that many conservatives were unwilling to commit themselves publicly. These men agreed that the Senate should begin to devise ways to relieve the Depression, but very few were willing to sign anything that had the earmarks of a "manifesto."[33] This kind of feeling was particularly strong among men such as Harrison and Byrnes. Though dissatisfied with the administration, these men were still unwilling to throw away all their influence by provoking an open break. Within two weeks of the luncheon, the conservative group thus had to give up the idea of getting a large number of signatures. But they continued to work on the document, hoping that when it was finished a hard core would subscribe to it, with others assenting to it in practice as subsequent issues developed. On December 15 the document began the rounds of the cloakrooms for final assent.

What might have come of the plan had the conservatives enjoyed more time to collect greater support is debatable. But they were not given the chance. On December 16 newspapers broke the story in large page-one headlines. Below the large type they printed the essence of the "manifesto," as reporters called it, and revealed the machinations which had been developing since the special session began.[34] To readers it seemed that these conservatives, for all their protestations of loyalty to the administration, were determined to defy the President. The press shattered the secrecy which the conservatives needed to solidify their strength and exposed what appeared to be a plot against the New Deal.

The sequel to this premature disclosure was amusing. Conservative senators, until then so hopeful of regaining the initiative, raced for cover. To appear as backers of a widely supported manifesto of general principles was one thing; to appear in the guise of bipartisan plotters was another. For

33 *Ibid.*, Dec. 16, 1937, p. 1.
34 New York *Herald Tribune*, Dec. 16, 1937, p. 1.

the next few days no senator would admit more than knowledge of it. Vandenberg and Gerry, believed to have been its authors, refused comment. Bailey admitted only to having been an "editor."[35] The conservatives presented a sorry picture. Flushed into the open before they were ready, they cowered in the shadows, hoping the spotlight would pass them by.

Liberal senators were delighted about the dilemma of their conservative colleagues and began to needle Bailey and his cohorts on the Senate floor. When Burke tried to have the manifesto read into the record, they descended upon him with joyful anticipation. Led by Sherman Minton of Indiana and Claude Pepper of Florida, Roosevelt's most enthusiastic supporters since the Senate revolution, New Dealers tried to pry information from Burke about the author of the statement. "Does not the Senator," Minton sneered, "know somebody who will be the father of this waif at this gladsome Christmas time?"[36]

At this point Bailey came out in the open. "I will father it," he proclaimed. "I will assume the responsibility just as far as one Senator can for anything. I endorse every word in it. Now let it stand on that."[37] Other conservatives followed. Vandenberg, Austin, and Copeland also arose to boast of their part in the manifesto. And when senators had filled the chamber in answer to a quorum call, Bailey again took the floor to read the manifesto and explain its purpose.

In Bailey's words the manifesto emerged as neither an original nor particularly controversial document. Only about a page long as reprinted in the *Congressional Record*, it consisted of a preface and ten main points, all of which said in effect that it was time to cease government interference with private enterprise.

---

[35] New York *Times*, Dec. 19, 1937, IV, 1.
[36] *Congressional Record*, 75th Cong., 2nd Sess., p. 1935.
[37] *Ibid.*

The manifesto began by expressing what obviously was the concern of the hour: the recession. "The time has come," the manifesto proclaimed, "when liberal investment of private savings in enterprise as a means of employment must be depended upon, and, without delay, heartily encouraged by the public policy and all Americans." Public spending, it continued, had been necessary before, but "a repetition of that policy would not serve again, and moreover, is out of the question. It ought to be borne in mind that private enterprise, properly fostered, carries the indispensible element of vigor." This was the same kind of thinking that had been so apparent earlier in the year in the controversy over relief spending: emergency measures had been tolerable in 1933, but it was time to return to fiscal orthodoxy.

Ten main points followed. Not surprisingly, the first called for thorough revision of the undistributed-profits and capital-gains taxes of 1936. Tax revision, the manifesto said, would "free funds for investment and promote the normal flow of savings into profitable and productive use." Second was a plea for a balanced budget. But this did not mean higher taxes. It meant "reduced public expenditures at every point practicable. . . . We intend that a consistent progress toward a balanced budget shall be made—so consistent that none may question the consummation in due season." This argument, like the preface, was but one more example of conservative faith in fiscal orthodoxy as a means of reviving business confidence.

The next point referred to the sitdowns. "We insist," said the statement, "upon the constitutional guaranties of the rights of person and of property—the right of the worker to work, of the owner to possession, and of every man to enjoy in peace the fruits of his labor." This section reflected a widespread conservative fear of the CIO and of union invasion of industries in their home states.

The next three arguments insisted that government in no

way compete with or harm private enterprise. Point seven urged, again, that "there ought to be a reduction in the tax burden"; point eight emphasized that "we favor the vigorous maintenance of States' rights, home rule and local self government"; point nine sought to reduce the political effect of New Deal relief bills—"The administration of relief ought to be nonpolitical and nonpartisan and temporary"; and the last point restated in emotional terms the fervent conservative belief in "the American system of private enterprise and initiative, and our American form of government. . . . They carry the priceless content of liberty and dignity of man. They carry spiritual values of infinite import, and which constitute the source of the American spirit."[38]

Bailey and his conservative allies were merely recording collectively what most of them had believed at least as early as 1935. In so doing they hoped for unity and stability in conservative ranks. As Bailey wrote at the time, "There must be a definite rallying ground. We must have an end of this business of one man denouncing regimentation, another denouncing Congress, another denouncing the President, another protesting against the tariff, and so on and so on. On the other hand, we must have a constructive policy upon which the American people may concentrate their support."[39]

In order to publicize the manifesto Bailey told friends that he sent out roughly a million and a half copies in the next few weeks.[40] But the administration contemptuously ignored the manifesto, and Congress adjourned shortly afterward with conservatives as individualistic and disorganized as ever. "Later on," Bailey admitted in February, "it may be possible to get a great number of senators to sign it. In the meantime, in view of the negotiations between the Presi-

[38] *Ibid.*, pp. 1937-40.

[39] To David Lawrence, Dec. 20, 1937, Bailey MSS, Political File.

[40] Bailey to Editor, Greensboro *Daily News*, March 24, 1938, *ibid.*, Economy File.

dent and business [Roosevelt appeared to be pursuing a conservative, conciliatory posture at that time] we have thought it best to be silent, lest we be accused of confusing matters unnecessarily."[41] The manifesto, evidence though it was of some conservative sentiment for a permanent bipartisan coalition, was soon a distant memory, even for most of the participants.

If Bailey's efforts revealed renewed conservative determination to temper the New Deal, they also exposed the formidable obstacles blocking efforts for a bipartisan conservative bloc in the Senate. One problem was the simple and persistent one of senatorial individualism. Senators, coming from different states with differing needs, refused to be shackled to any fixed statement of principles. As Vandenberg put it, "I frankly doubt whether the desirable number of signatures could have been obtained because many Democrats who expressed complete sympathy with our objectives were disinclined to put themselves down in black and white in what they said would be construed as a declaration of war on the President. A number of Republicans declined to sign, although agreeing with the statement itself, because they felt it was *politically* unwise for Republicans to encourage the coalition idea as a matter of *politics*."[42]

Vandenberg's plaintive remarks suggested an even more obvious and important coalition weakness: partisanship. Many Democrats were not happy at the prospect of public partnership with Republicans. Even Glass, safely entrenched within his machine, deprecated coalition arguments. "I am merely intent," he had said earlier, "upon preserving my party regularity which in Virginia is almost as desirable as preserving one's religious integrity."[43] Such men were will-

[41] To Hamilton A. Long, Feb. 8, 1938, *ibid.*, General File. Copy also to Byrd.

[42] Vandenberg Notes, Dec. 1937, Vandenberg MSS, 1937 Scrapbook.

[43] To Bainbridge Colby, Sept. 1, 1936, Glass MSS, Box 347.

ing to vote with the GOP on occasion, and on particularly controversial issues such as the court plan, they were even able to devise joint strategy with them. But even in the court fight, Democrats had insisted upon leading the coalition, such as it was. Bailey's cherished dream of bipartisan opposition to the New Deal could, and did, occur when there was a meeting of the minds among conservatives on both sides of the aisle. But many conservative Democrats were unwilling to go further than that.

Republicans were equally divided. Thanks primarily to McNary, Senate Republicans had taken second place to conservative Democrats during the controversies of the first 1937 session. But from the beginning a central element of this Republican strategy of silence had been to aggravate intraparty divisions among Democrats. It had been a distinctly partisan strategy. McNary and other party leaders never envisioned the permanent submergence of the GOP under a conservative Democratic label.

By late 1937 many Republicans had concluded that Roosevelt's appeal, at last, had declined enough to permit a Republican renaissance. Indeed, while Vandenberg and Austin were helping to compose the manifesto, McNary was conferring with Landon and Frank Knox, Landon's 1936 running mate, in the Capitol.[44] Already, these men were preparing their spring and summer offensive against Democrats. Coalition politics had looked somewhat appealing to the GOP when there was no alternative. But when a Republican resurgence began to seem possible, Republicans such as McNary quickly turned away from political associations with the conservative opposition.

[44] McNary's feelings about the conservative national hierarchy were amusing. "This morning," he wrote, "I had breakfast with Colonel Knox, Republican vice-presidential candidate. . . . Yesterday I had lunch with Governor Landon. I will be glad when these ginks get out of town." McNary to Mrs. W. T. Stolz, Dec. 11, 1937, McNary MSS.

Thus it was McNary who gave reporters the evidence they needed to publish their premature accounts. When the manifesto reached his hands in the cloakroom, he simply saw to it that the press received a copy. Bailey complained that "unfortunately the statement fell into the hands of the Republican leader who thought that the utterance of it would injure the Republican cause. He thought that it would steal away a Republican opportunity. His Party is preparing a policy and did not want any one else to prepare one. The premature publication, therefore, was brought about wholly because this man and some of his associates took a partisan view that the declaration of principles would help the Democratic cause and hurt the Republican cause."[45]

Vandenberg was even more furious. Realizing that McNary's copy of the manifesto was the only one not returned, he guessed that his colleague had given it to the press. "Premature publicity—*thanks to treachery*—ended the episode," he fumed. "The next time we want to plan a patriotically dramatic contribution to the welfare of the country, we shall let no one in who is not *tried and true*."[46]

But McNary, though motivated in part by partisan considerations, also was unsympathetic with the conservative cause. Like other old progressive Republicans, he wanted no part of a manifesto embracing only conservative ideas. The manifesto exposed the power not only of partisanship but of the divisions within the Republican party as well.

It was as many observers of the American political scene had noticed: political parties in the United States were, and are, low-grade organisms which somehow manage to survive no matter what the competitive struggle.[47] Certainly, the Republican party in 1937 was as moribund as at any time

[45] To Julian Miller, Dec. 20, 1937, Bailey MSS, Personal File.
[46] Vandenberg Notes, Dec. 1937, Vandenberg MSS. Italics his.
[47] See Walter Lippmann, *Interpretations, 1933-1935,* ed. Allan Nevins (New York, 1936), p. 300, Jan. 31, 1934.

since its founding. Yet even at low ebb it had the emotional appeal of its party label, a nationwide organization, and a host of party workers and political hopefuls on the state and local levels.[48] Professionals knew that they needed local organizational backing to stay in office. Their first allegiance was to party, not coalition.[49] In the months to come partisan warfare would negate coalition efforts time and again.

When the special session ended a few days after Bailey's abortive attempt, most experts agreed that the entire session was wasted effort. A "Coolidge Congress," Raymond Clapper branded it.[50] Republicans derisively called it a "Goose-Egg" session. But the session was really not so dull as that. In five weeks it had sent a farm bill to conference, and it had at least acted upon the labor standards bill. These were no mean accomplishments when compared to the pace of many Congresses before and since.[51]

But the session was remarkable less for its accomplishments than for its attitude. From the start Congress had shown that it would act independently. The session also exposed again the sectional-economic divisions in Roosevelt's coalition. Still popular, Roosevelt was impossible to ignore. But he could no longer dominate Congress unless his coalition coalesced on a program. Conservatives, disturbed earlier in the year at the continuation of the New Deal in "good" times, now showed that they were equally opposed in recession. Partisanship or not, conservatives would have to be reckoned with in the future.

[48] See William Allen White's comment in *Time*, Nov. 19, 1934, pp. 13-15. He noted that the Republican party had a "foothold in the courthouses of 1,000 counties. Parties do not die from the top but from the roots and the roots of the Republican Party in the East and Middle West are still full of courthouse sap. . . ."

[49] This point is excellently illustrated in Julius Turner, *Party and Constituency: Pressures in Congress* (Baltimore, 1951), *passim*.

[50] Montgomery (Ala.) *Advertiser*, Dec. 23, 1937, p. 4.

[51] For this more optimistic summation, see Lippmann, New York *Herald Tribune*, Dec. 23, 1937, p. 21.

7

RECESSION POLITICS, 1938

WHEN THE 1938 session opened in January, the recession showed no signs of disappearing and congressmen remained as divided as ever in their prescriptions for cure. Roosevelt continued to temporize. Greatly distressed by the severity of the slump, he persisted in the wishful thinking that business would save itself. Bailey and his friends began to hope that no "drastic" extension of the New Deal would occur.

Mutual suspicion between the liberal and conservative camps nevertheless continued. In December, Ickes and Assistant Attorney General Robert H. Jackson attacked the "Sixty Families" and the "Chiselling Ten Per Cent" of rich businessmen whom they blamed for the nation's economic sickness.[1] Their charges succeeded only in infuriating conservatives of both parties. "It is clear," chortled Ickes, "that the war is on fiercer than ever between the reactionaries and the liberals within the Democratic Party."[2]

Conservative congressmen also continued to consider themselves the bulwark against the New Deal. Publisher Frank Gannett, corresponding with George, Van Nuys, and others, expressed their sentiments: "Since the President now controls the Supreme Court," he wrote, "our only hope lies in influencing the members of Congress. This we are trying to do."[3] Bailey, Byrd, and their friends persisted in this kind of thinking.

Roosevelt's opening message to Congress failed to improve the situation. As he read it to the joint session, a hostile group of senators, carefully ensconced in first-row seats, glared sullenly at their chief; when he finished, they offered no applause.[4] As Roosevelt realized, his message evoked little enthusiasm. Calling for labor-management cooperation, reiterating his request for passage of the bills he had sought in the special session, and hinting that he would oppose any major changes in his tax program, Roosevelt was above all rather vague.[5] Though few objected to the message, fewer still were pleased. Edwin C. Johnson of Colorado, a moderate Democrat, went so far as to say, "I hope that Congress will go much further than the President advocated in balancing the budget and encouraging business. Enterprise and industry must be given every assurance of fair treatment on the part of the government."[6]

The President showed no signs of adopting such suggestions. A few days later he submitted his budget for fiscal

[1] New York *Times,* Jan. 1, 1938, IV, 3, described conservative reactions.

[2] Harold Ickes, *The Secret Diary of Harold Ickes* (3 vols.; New York, 1954), II, 287-88, Jan. 8, 1938.

[3] To E. A. Dodd, Feb. 5, 1938, Gannett MSS, Box 16.

[4] Ickes, *Secret Diary,* II, 288, Jan. 8, 1938.

[5] Samuel Rosenman (ed.), *The Public Papers and Addresses of Franklin D. Roosevelt* (New York, 1938), VI, 522-32.

[6] New York *Times,* Jan. 4, 1938, p. 17.

1939; though moderate, it envisioned a $950-million deficit and warned that a need for increased defense spending might upset the balance even further. Then on January 8 he gave a strong Jackson Day speech, adopting the Ickes-Jackson approach by accusing a minority of businessmen of selfishness in time of crisis. Reporters asked Bailey, seen entering his hotel (where the speech was just about to begin), why he was not going in to listen. "I like Jackson," he said. "But the Jackson I know is not named Bob."[7]

A restless Congress thus confronted the President in the opening weeks of the 1938 session. A movement for repeal of the undistributed-profits tax continued to grow; the farm program remained deadlocked in conference committee; Byrnes's special committee on unemployment began hearings on ways to revise or terminate the WPA; an isolationist bloc almost managed to discuss the Ludlow War Referendum plan;[8] and for the third time the antilynching measure, remaining first on the calendar, provoked a dispiriting southern filibuster. Roosevelt still made no move to end the recession. "The uncertainty of what he will do had made the businessmen timorous," wrote McNary. "I think it has much to do with the present recession."[9] Ickes added, "it looks as if all the courage has oozed out of the President. Except for a brief assertion of leadership . . . he has let things drift. . . . Ever since the court fight, he has acted to me like a beaten man."[10]

Though congressmen dawdled and Roosevelt wavered in

[7] *Ibid.*, Jan. 9, 1938, p. 17.

[8] *Ibid.*, Jan. 11, 1938, p. 1. The Ludlow plan proposed a constitutional amendment requiring a popular referendum before permitting the President to declare war. In the 1937 special session it had received enough support to be discharged from committee, and it took considerable presidential pressure in 1938 to defeat a motion to discuss it. Ludlow was a Democratic congressman from Indiana.

[9] To George Putnam, Jan. 28, 1938, McNary MSS.

[10] Ickes, *Secret Diary*, II, 326, March 2, 1938; 340, March 17, 1938.

these opening weeks of the session, not all the odds favored the conservatives. Indeed, serious problems which would confront conservatives throughout the session were already developing. One, partisanship, grew as election time approached. The result was a gradual but still damaging deterioration of bipartisan unity, loose though it had been. Gannett, urging a conservative coalition for the fall elections, was dismayed at this spirit as early as January. "What bothers me," he wrote, "is the growing opposition to men like Van Nuys by Republicans who think he is a New Dealer. They overlook the great benefit he has given the country by defeating the Court Bill."[11]

Another conservative problem was the recession. In late 1937 the recession had provided considerable ammunition for the conservative arsenal by exposing an apparent New Deal failure. But as the economic trough deepened, pressure from constituents increased. Taught by the New Deal that government could be a powerful agent in effecting economic recovery, many Americans began to demand that Congress do something. In an off year this pressure might have been ineffective, but in 1938, neither party dared categorically to oppose government intervention in the economy. Before the session ended this popular demand would wreak havoc with conservative economic theory.

Four major battles occupied much of the session. These were reorganization of the executive department, tax repeal, relief spending, and labor standards. Two, reorganization and tax repeal, resulted in substantial conservative triumphs; the others in essentially conservative defeats. Together they illustrated the strengths and weaknesses of congressional conservatives in 1938.

The first of these was reorganization of the executive department. This issue predated the New Deal and had been one of Roosevelt's chief concerns since 1936. At that time

[11] To W. A. Sheaffer, Jan. 3, 1938, Gannett MSS, Box 16.

he had commissioned a committee of political scientists to recommend ways to improve the efficiency of the executive branch.[12] After the 1936 election, the committee did so, submitting a five-point plan. It recommended presidential authority be granted to:

1. Consolidate all independent agencies and boards in twelve large cabinet rank departments, including two new ones of Social Welfare and Public Works.
2. Extend the merit system to include all non-policy-determining positions. One administrator would replace the existing three-man Civil Service Commission.
3. Abolish the office of Comptroller General and replace it with the office of Auditor General. The new official would have the responsibility of post-auditing federal accounts. Pre-audit functions previously held by the Comptroller General would move to the Treasury Department; quasi-judicial functions of regulatory agencies would be turned over to the Attorney General.
4. Strengthen the Budget Bureau and place it within the White House instead of the Treasury. Consolidate planning in a central National Resources Planning Board, also under the control of the White House.
5. Add six new administrative assistants to the President, men with a "passion for anonymity."

The administration bill, submitted to Congress in January 1937, authorized Roosevelt to issue executive orders for these purposes. These orders were to be effective immediately and were to remain in force unless disapproved within sixty days by both houses of Congress. If the President then vetoed Congress' disapproval, congressmen would need two-thirds margins in each house.

Roosevelt had little reason to expect much opposition. In the economy act of 1933 Congress had granted him powers, good for two years, to shift agencies about and to cut ex-

[12] See Louis Brownlow, *A Passion for Anonymity* (Chicago, 1958), pp. 343-86, for the account of the chairman of the presidential committee.

penditures as much as 25 percent.[13] And previous Presidents, including Hoover, had favored similar reorganization schemes. Few people questioned the need for overhaul of the executive branch, especially after its enormous growth during the early New Deal. Most men also admitted that executive reorganization was unlikely if left to congressional initiative; some such blanket authority as Roosevelt requested appeared to be the most fruitful approach.

But when Roosevelt first showed the plan to congressional leaders in January 1937, opposition developed quickly. Irreconcilables such as Glass regarded the plan as an unwarranted quest for power by the President. "Under the proposed reorganization scheme," he wrote later, "the President could have no use even for a rubber stamp; he could do his own rubber stamping."[14] Byrd was also annoyed, partly because Roosevelt's plan failed to stress a need for executive economy and partly because the President had ignored Byrd's own reorganization committee founded in 1936. More disturbing, leaders such as Rayburn reacted with "shocked silence" when told that the Interstate Commerce Commission would be affected by the proposal.[15] "It will mean," prophesied Catledge immediately, "a fight every inch of the way in Congress."[16]

Congressional opposition came from many directions. Republicans feared that extension of the civil service would give permanent status to Roosevelt appointees, creating a whole bureaucracy of "Farleyites."[17] Organization Demo-

---

[13] Even in 1933 Congress had occasionally balked at his use of these powers. See *Time*, June 19, 1933, p. 11, for an example.

[14] To Rev. J. Ernest Stack, Aug. 31, 1937, Glass MSS, Box 380.

[15] Brownlow, *Passion*, p. 391.

[16] New York *Times*, Jan. 11, 1937.

[17] Albert Shaw, *Review of Reviews*, XCV (Feb. 1937), 27. See the view of Clifford R. Hope of Kansas. "There has never been an administration," he wrote, "which went to the extent of this one in its handling of political patronage. Practically every New Deal job has been specifically exempted from the civil service and a tremendous number of deserving Democrats

crats, on the other hand, distrusted the civil service proposal for just the opposite reason: they were afraid it would dry up the wells of congressional patronage. Congressmen of all persuasions were suspicious of this aspect of the plan. The six proposed new assistants also aroused some opposition. A few, such as Byrd, opposed this recommendation on economy grounds. Others grumbled that there were already enough bureaucrats around the President. Later, a Republican representative would mock the proposal by offering an amendment providing that the six new men be relatives of the President: Elliott Roosevelt, Franklin D. Roosevelt, Jr., John Roosevelt, Anna Roosevelt Boettiger, and Sistie and Buzzie Dall.[18] And still others frowned upon the creation of a Department of Welfare. They insisted that it would permanently institutionalize agencies such as the WPA.

The most widespread opposition, however, stemmed from more general fears. Many congressmen wanted to shelter particular departments which had treated them well in the past or whose work they did not want to see placed under presidential scrutiny. Rayburn, for instance, had already expressed disapproval at the idea of tampering with the ICC; others wanted to protect Comptroller General J. Raymond McCarl, a friend of many veteran conservatives;[19] and most congressmen from states with national forests, including Pittman and McNary, disliked Ickes' ill-concealed ambition to transfer the Forestry Service from the Agriculture

taken care of. Now the proposal is to blanket all of these political appointees into the civil service so they will have lifetime jobs if the New Dealers happen to lose out." To Fred M. Beaty, July 29, 1937, Hope MSS, General Correspondence, 1936-1937, A-B.

[18] *Time*, Aug. 9, 1937, p. 9. Sistie and Buzzie Dall were FDR's grandchildren by his daughter Anna's first marriage to Curtis Dall. She later married John Boettiger.

[19] The comptroller general, appointed before Roosevelt's first inauguration, could and did create annoying delays in legislation through watchdog procedures. For McCarl's view of the WPA see Searle F. Charles, *Minister of Relief: Harry Hopkins and the Depression* (Syracuse, 1963), pp. 139-40.

Department to Interior. Few congressmen had not established smooth lines of communication with one or more government agencies of particular relevance to the problems of their districts; all these men opposed upsetting existing channels.

Many congressmen also viewed the plan as another demand for presidential power. This line of thinking was slow to crystallize, but when Roosevelt proposed his court plan a month later, conservatives insisted that the reorganization scheme reflected the same ambition for dictatorial powers. Actually, the two plans were dissimilar. The reorganization plan was merely an attempt to give the Chief Executive the authority necessary to achieve efficiency within his own domain, and it did not involve a fundamental alteration in the balance of powers. But to many it seemed that way. Give Roosevelt the power to abolish, transfer, and create new departments, they argued, and you discarded congressional checks on executive management: you were one more long step on the road to American fascism.

What might have happened had the bill been considered with no intervening court battle is uncertain. Though hostility was considerable, many congressmen undoubtedly would have supported the plan on a final vote. Roosevelt in January 1937 was fresh from his overwhelming election victory: if the court plan had not dispelled so much of his magic, it is entirely possible that reorganization would have passed without much difficulty. Indeed, the House approved two of the proposals that summer: the six new assistants, and the reorganizing of departments. The respective votes were 260-88 and 283-76, Republicans forming most of the opposition.[20]

But the plan never had a chance in 1937. As Byrnes, its

[20] For an excellent discussion of the course of the bill see Lindsay Rogers, "Reorganization: Post-Mortem Notes," *Political Science Quarterly*, LIII (June 1938), 161-72.

Senate manager, said later, "The President's attitude toward the Court and his failure to act on the sitdown strikes, to say nothing of the 'lump sum' relief funds so favored by Hopkins, did not make it easy for his reorganization policies. We therefore adjourned in August without taking action."[21] In the special session the antilynching and farm measures were higher on the agenda. Except for the two bills passed by the House, 1937 was a barren year for executive reorganization.

By 1938, Congress indicated it would not accept the bill as it was, and Byrnes, working carefully with the President, amended it. The new bill exempted from reorganization a few independent regulatory agencies with so-called quasi-judicial functions, such as the NLRB, Board of Tax Appeals, and Federal Trade Commission.[22] It also denied Roosevelt the power to create new departments or agencies whose functions had not already been authorized by Congress. Otherwise, the bill resembled the original report, and the President still found it adequate.

But just as the new bill satisfied Roosevelt, it continued to upset conservatives. Without exception, Republicans made it a partisan issue. Western progressives such as Borah and McNary, distrusting what they believed to be another move for centralized power, joined their conservative brethren against the plan; it was the first united Republican stand on a major issue since the court plan, and for similar reasons. The old irreconcilable Democrats of 1933 and 1935 were equally suspicious. For all practical purposes most of these Democrats by then were total outcasts from New Deal circles, for Roosevelt had broken personal relations with them over the court issue and had hinted on more than one occasion that he would seek political revenge. Some honestly feared what Roosevelt might do with his reorganization

---

[21] James F. Byrnes, *All in One Lifetime* (New York, 1958), p. 105.

[22] Ickes, because of his desire to put the Forestry Division within Interior, shed some light on feelings involved in the issue. See his *Secret Diary*, II, 314, Feb. 13, 1938; 318, Feb. 16, 1938; and 325, March 2, 1938.

powers, and all realized that the bill offered an excellent opportunity to damage his prestige.

Besides these men, many Democrats who had opposed the court plan also defected. Connally and Clark became leading opponents of the bill. Van Nuys, Lonergan, Maloney, Adams, and Donahey joined them. Still others, such as Charles O. Andrews of Florida, Johnson of Colorado, and Prentiss M. Brown of Michigan, last-minute opponents of the court bill, also inclined against the reorganization scheme. In the end they, too, would vote against the administration.

Significantly, the old Senate leadership of Byrnes, Harrison, and Garner did not join them. Indeed, Byrnes was the leader of administration forces for the bill. Congress, he realized, would never approve reorganization plans on its own, and the President must have authority to clean his own house. Harrison and Garner, though unenthusiastic about the plan, saw no compelling reason to oppose it. The Democratic division on this controversy was as good an example as any illustrating the fallacy of speaking of an inflexible conservative coalition voting as a bloc on every issue.

Irreconcilables again needed a leader. Republicans, though more partisan than in 1937, obviously had to be silent if moderate Democrats were to join the conservative fold. Irreconcilable Democrats realized their leadership would also dramatize the issue as another "reactionary" onslaught. Conservatives needed a liberal front such as they had enjoyed in the court fight.

In Wheeler they again found their man. No longer the eager liberal he had seemed in 1936, Wheeler continued to vote with the administration on some occasions. Since the court controversy, he had backed the labor bill and supported Roosevelt's requests for relief. His personal relations with conservatives, though warmer than they had been during the utilities fight, were still not particularly close. Yet his relations with the administration were even cooler.

Roosevelt had cut off his patronage and channeled Montana public works through political enemies. These reprisals infuriated Wheeler.[23] Equally important, to Wheeler the reorganization bill resembled the court plan. Both seemed to be unwarranted encroachments of the executive upon the other branches of the government. When Byrd proposed that Wheeler lead the conservatives, Wheeler was more than receptive. Once again, he was to direct a coalition of Republicans, conservative Democrats, and moderate Democrats fearful of excessive centralization of power.[24]

His plan of attack was similar to that employed in the court fight. Reaching Republicans by way of his continuing friendship with Borah, Wheeler soon established a bipartisan strategy. Republicans were to leave vocal opposition to the Democrats and content themselves with voting against the administration. Meanwhile, Democrats were to devise a bundle of damaging amendments, hoping at most to amend the bill to death, at least to gain time. By appealing to the special interests of each uncommitted senator, Wheeler hoped eventually to amend the bill beyond recognition.

When the bill reached the floor in late March, Wheeler's bloc lost on amendment after amendment. Byrnes, steadfastly refusing to grant ground, skillfully held his forces in line. The decisive test occurred on an amendment by Wheeler proposing to make each reorganization request subject to the expressed approval of both houses of Congress within sixty days. The amendment would have left the President at the mercy of congressional consent, always difficult

[23] See Burton K. Wheeler, *Yankee from the West* (Garden City, N. Y., 1962), pp. 342-52. Also Richard T. Ruetten, "Showdown in Montana, 1938: Burton Wheeler's Role in the Defeat of Jerry O'Connell," *Pacific Northwest Quarterly*, LIV (Jan. 1963), 19-29.

[24] Joseph Alsop and Robert Kintner, Washington *Star*, June 6, 1938, A-9, regarded Wheeler as the real leader of anti-administration forces in the Senate.

to obtain on anything in so short a time. Wheeler nearly succeeded. The vote was 43-39 against the amendment. Twenty-four Democrats, including such normally loyal administration men as Pittman, joined all fifteen Republicans against the administration, but powerful pressures by Byrnes and others succeeded in defeating the amendment. John H. Overton and Ellender of Louisiana, for instance, supported the bill partly because of administration persuasion by way of the powerful Louisiana machine.[25].

Other proposed amendments then followed, but administration forces stayed firm and, confident of success, agreed to adjourn for the weekend. But Frank Gannett's National Committee to Uphold Constitutional Government intensified a propaganda campaign against the bill; Green of the AF of L denounced the plan; and conservatives pointed to Roosevelt's summary removal of a TVA director a few days earlier as evidence of his dictatorial tendencies.[26] Hitler's recent *anschluss* in Austria added to these fears. And on that Sunday, Father Charles E. Coughlin, a Detroit priest whose radio addresses attracted millions of Americans, joined the propagandists opposed to the plan. The bill would "set up a financial dictatorship in the person of the President. . . . The immediacy of the danger insists that tomorrow before noon your telegram is in the hands of your Senator to stop the Reorganization Bill as Washington stopped George III. . . ."[27]

The response was remarkable. Estimates varied, but most agreed that the pleas of Coughlin and others over the weekend resulted in a flood of some 300,000 telegrams. Western Union customers in New York on Monday morning had

[25] Ickes, *Secret Diary*, 345, March 19, 1938. For the vote see New York *Times*, March 9, 1938, p. 1, and *Congressional Record*, 75th Cong., 3rd Sess., 3644.

[26] See Gannett to Chester J. Laroche, March 26, 1938, Gannett MSS, Box 16; to E. Ray Hardenbrook, April 4, 1938, Box 16.

[27] See *Time*, April 4, 1938, pp. 10-11.

to wait more than an hour in line. The deluge seemed to unnerve senators, and as the final vote approached, it looked for a moment as if the remarkable telegram campaign might sway enough senators to defeat the bill.

Nevertheless, most administration supporters remained loyal. Remembering the spontaneous popular opposition to the court plan, they realized that the campaign against reorganization smacked of pressure-group skill, and few deserted the President. Wagner, disturbed by the reactions of Catholics in New York, shifted to the opposition, but the ranks on both sides otherwise held firm. A motion to recommit lost, 48-43, and the bill finally passed, 49-42.[28] On the key recommittal vote, all fifteen Republicans, two Farmer-Laborites, and twenty-six Democrats, more than one-third of Roosevelt's party strength in the Senate, opposed the administration.

Though the conservatives had lost, they were not discouraged. Their coalition, though hastily and loosely organized, had held together well through two weeks of debate and amendments. Even Republicans had relegated themselves to a secondary role, putting aside partisan attacks for the common cause.[29] Bailey said:

We lost the fight in the Senate today but I do not feel at all downcast or disheartened. I am inclined to think in my heart that it was a good fight to lose. I consider that we have awakened the American people and that really the vote today transferred the battle to the House, in which we have some rather profound assurances of constructive resistance. . . . That we could

[28] *Congressional Record*, 75th Cong., 3rd Sess., 4204. Also New York *Times* analysis, March 29, 1938, p. 1.

[29] Republican silence goaded Byrnes. "The galleries must suppose," he cried, "you gentlemen [Republicans] have no minds at all, since you are entirely dumb on the question before the Senate. But I know that's wrong. I know you have minds, but your minds are entirely on the 1940 election." Hitler's Brown Shirts, he added, were "no more regimented." See Joseph Alsop and Robert Kintner, "Let Them Do the Talking," *Saturday Evening Post*, CCXIII (Sept. 28, 1940), 18.

hold forty-three votes ought to be quite satisfactory. A little analysis will show that Van Nuys was absent, and that Smith and Gillette, who ordinarily are with us, were not with us. These three would have made a tie.[30]

Bailey was right about the House.[31] By then its attitude toward the bill was radically different from what it had been a year earlier. To begin with, Roosevelt's jubilant remarks following Senate passage of the bill did not endear him to conservatives of either house. "It proves," he said, "that the Senate cannot be purchased by organized telegrams based on direct misrepresentation."[32] This statement, suggesting that those who opposed him were hirelings of reaction, antagonized conservatives. Sensitive to slurs upon legislative integrity, conservative congressmen shared the resentment felt by their Senate colleagues.

More important, telegrams and letters to congressmen continued to pour in; editorials denounced the plan; and orators assaulted the "fascism" and "communism" involved in the bill. Some 150 "Paul Reveres" rode into Washington from all directions, shouting warnings as they passed.[33] Since many congressmen already distrusted various aspects of the bill, the popular pressure encouraged them to consider open revolt. Because support of the bill promised to please few voters, it seemed safe to vote against it.

[30] To Julian Miller, March 29, 1938, Bailey MSS, Political File.

[31] Ironically, the bill could have gone directly to a conference committee, inasmuch as the House had already passed part of the plan in 1937. But Byrnes failed to present his bill in the form of an amendment to this House bill, and when he tried to send his bill directly to conference, it required unanimous consent. Clark prevented this. See O. R. Altman, "Second and Third Sessions of the 75th Congress," *American Political Science Review*, XXXII (Dec. 1938), 1099-1122.

[32] New York *Times*, March 30, 1938, p. 10. The remark was made at a press conference, and the President deliberately told reporters they could quote him directly, an unusual gesture on his part. He did so even though Marvin McIntyre, his secretary, leaned over to advise him against it.

[33] *Time*, April 18, 1938, p. 16. For a particularly irate letter see Ethel M. Watson to FDR, April 4, 1938, Roosevelt MSS, OF 285-C, Box 13.

The President was aware of these sentiments and sought to reassure the House. Two days after the Senate passed the bill he issued a statement from Warm Springs, Georgia, where he was spending a brief vacation. "I have no inclination to be a dictator," he said. "I have none of the qualifications which would make me a successful dictator. I have too much historical background and too much knowledge of existing dictatorships to make me desire any form of dictatorship for a democracy like the United States."[34] This remarkable statement, so unnecessary and so plaintive, revealed that the charges of dictatorship had not fallen upon deaf ears.

The statement was not enough. The next day the House produced the "wildest scene of this session, punctuated by boos, laughter, and sarcastic comment."[35] Bipartisan opposition, led by such implacable Democratic opponents of the administration as Samuel Pettengill of Indiana and John J. O'Connor, forced a reading of the entire 82-page bill and created innumerable other parliamentary tangles. Republicans for the most part wisely adopted a strategy of silence. As one Republican congressman observed, "I think the strategy which the opposition ought to follow here is exactly the same as in the Court fight, namely, let the Democrats who are courageous and patriotic enough to oppose their own leadership go ahead and take the lead."[36]

The Rules Committee also refused to grant any limitation on debate. The chief obstacle was again O'Connor. As jealous as ever of House prerogative and as distrustful as ever of Roosevelt, he opposed giving the bill a special rule. And two days after Roosevelt's reassuring message, he rose to assault the bill. "I am not afraid of a dictatorship in this country," he declaimed. "I believe our great President was

[34] New York *Times*, March 31, 1938, p. 1.

[35] *Ibid.*, April 1, 1938, p. 1.

[36] Hope (Kan.) to Barton P. Griffith, April 4, 1938, Hope MSS, Legislative Correspondence 1937-1938, R-U.

sincere when he stated last midnight that he had no desire to be a dictator. . . . The fact is, nevertheless, that our people are inflamed almost to the point of revolution and I use my words guardedly, at the thought of the possibilities of this bill. Some letters mention 'bloodshed,' others 'resort to arms.' . . . Rightly or wrongly, this is no time to further incense our people, who have gone through eight years of a depression and who since last fall suffered a relapse."[37] The reorganization plan, he proclaimed shrewdly, was disturbing business confidence and prolonging the recession. Spurred by such oratory, the House quickly quelled, 191-149, a move by administration leaders to limit debate.

Confronted with this kind of opposition, Roosevelt returned to the Capital and began to look for compromise. Within a few days he had agreed to exempt a number of agencies, including the Federal Office of Education and the Veterans Bureau. He also agreed to allow the orders to be negated by majority, rather than two-thirds votes of both houses. To no avail; O'Connor and many others maintained the attack, forcing more amendments upon the bill. Indeed, the measure soon became only a shadow of what it had been in 1937.[38] Then the blow fell. In a dramatic defeat for the administration the House recommitted the bill, despite its ameliorative amendments, 204-196. For all intents and purposes, it was dead.[39]

The vote was an especially clear indication of the kind of coalition that faced the President. The winning total of 204 included 88 Republicans, 108 Democrats, 6 Progressives, and 2 Farmer-Laborites. The near-unanimous GOP stand demonstrated the remarkable cohesion that Republicans had developed by this time under Snell's leadership. It also

[37] *Congressional Record*, 75th Cong., 3rd Sess., 4609-12.

[38] *Ibid.*, pp. 4991-5025, 5082-5122.

[39] The vote surprised many conservatives. Hope wrote, "It will be a miracle if we are able to beat it in the House." To E. E. Lake, March 31, 1938, Legislative Correspondence, 1937-1938, R-U.

revealed the extent to which the bill had become a partisan issue in both houses. "The bill," wrote James Wadsworth, Jr., of New York, "is a wretched thing . . . the President is vindictive. He hates and resents opposition and does not hesitate to try to punish his opponents."[40]

The Democratic vote was more interesting. As in the Senate, sectional and urban-rural factors were not important. Smith and Cox continued to oppose the administration, but Dies, Sumners, and many others did not. Those opposed to the bill included 20 (of 77) eastern Democrats, 13 (of 31) border staters, 33 (of 99) southerners, 27 (of 71) middle-westerners, and 15 (of 53) westerners.[41] Of the 108 Democratic opponents 47, or 43 percent, were urban representatives. This percentage was much higher than that which ordinarily voted against liberal labor or spending bills.

The Democratic vote was also considerably different from that which had recommitted the fair labor standards bill only four months earlier.[42] A total of 52 Democratic supporters of reorganization had opposed the labor bill, while only 56 of the 133 Democratic opponents of the labor bill also opposed reorganization. The conservative coalition in the House, such as it was, shifted a great deal from issue to issue.[43]

Perhaps the most revealing aspect of the vote was the eight-man Progressive-Farmer-Laborite group that deserted

[40] To Maj. Gen. John S. Thompson, April 5, 1938, Wadsworth MSS, Box 24.

[41] These sections, again, are divided as follows. South: eleven states of the Old Confederacy; East: New England, New York, Pa., Del., N. J.; Border: Md., W. Va., Ky., Mo.; Midwest: Old Northwest plus Minn., Iowa; West: the rest.

[42] The following table shows the number of Democrats opposed to each bill (of the total number of Democrats from that section).

	East	Border	South	M-West	West	Total
Labor	6 (of 77)	10 (of 31)	81 (of 99)	16 (of 71)	20 (of 53)	133
Reorg.	20 (of 77)	13 (of 31)	33 (of 99)	27 (of 71)	15 (of 53)	108

[43] David Lawrence, Washington *Star*, April 11, 1938, A-9, emphasized this lack of anti-administration solidarity.

the administration. Had five of these eight switched their votes, reorganization would have passed. Pressure groups had not influenced them. Rather, they were generally upset at Roosevelt's reluctance to do anything about the recession, piqued at Roosevelt's disregard of them, and fearful of centralized power.[44] Their stand was evidence that the reorganization plan was a political issue involving a clash between the legislative and executive branches. Like the utilities issue which it resembled in so many ways, it pitted a jealous lower house made courageous by intense lobbying against an administration seeking powers it did not seem to need.[45]

The President did not lose because of poor tactics. Though not blameless in this respect, he generally conducted himself in a reasonable fashion. In contrast to his blindness on the court bill, he presented a possible plan, and though he might have compromised earlier, he showed a willingness to bend under pressure. Nor was it quite fair to blame the plan itself. Its provisions did include many touchy issues, patronage being just one of them. But as most congressmen privately admitted, the bill was emphatically not a move toward dictatorship. Finally, it was not accurate to give all

[44] See Kent Keller (Dem.–Ill.) to FDR, April 18, 1938: "There is a group of aggressive progressive Democrats who have stuck by you through thick and thin, about seventy-five in number, as well as a number of other progressives not classed as Democrats, and I do not believe that you have ever called in a single one of this group in consultation as to administration policies. . . . I must insist that that group deserves to be consulted. . . . There are a lot of them who are able, educated, experienced, with national vision, courage, and loyalty to your ideals. It is out of this group and their followers that must ultimately come the leaders who are to carry on your ideas and ideals in the years to come." FDR penciled on this letter, "Mac [Secretary Marvin McIntyre]–Have him come in to see me." Roosevelt MSS, OF 119.

[45] Sen. Elbert Thomas of Utah explained the defeat. "It was not a question of letting the President reorganize," he said. "It was: 'Can we keep Roosevelt from reorganizing.'" To Frank Jones, April 26, 1938, Elbert Thomas MSS, Box 24.

the blame, or credit, to O'Connor and the Rules Committee. Though O'Connor's refusal to grant a special rule was obstructive, the entire House supported him in a vote on the floor. All these factors had bearings on the final outcome, but they were not fundamental causes.

The basic reason for defeat of the plan was simple: it offered nothing to the New Deal coalition. Unlike relief spending, farm aid, or labor standards, the plan attracted no strong pressure groups. The recession also worked against reorganization. Opponents could, and did, relate the "dictatorial" ambitions of the President to the failure in business confidence. The issue provided conservatives of both parties with an excellent club with which to batter presidential prestige. Considering the historic difficulties in obtaining congressional approval of any executive reorganization schemes and the absence of popular pressure for the bill, it was not too surprising that the administration went down to defeat.

Finally, the issue revealed the same kind of coalition strategy, and much the same conservative lineup, which had successfully stopped the court plan in the Senate. On both occasions a group of moderate and conservative Democrats, greatly encouraged by organized pressure groups, placed "liberal" men in charge and enlisted silent Republicans as additional voting strength. The somewhat shaky foundations of conservative bipartisanship thus remained intact.

While this struggle was evolving, the second key issue of the session was reaching a climax: the undistributed-profits tax. By 1938 the conservative drive to revise it was well underway.

Roosevelt had been willing in late 1937 to permit slight revisions to favor very small corporations but had otherwise shown great reluctance to accede to conservative demands. Cherishing the tax as one of the main weapons against economic royalists, he viewed major changes as a surrender. But he soon realized that congressional sentiment against the tax was irresistible; better to salvage what he could. Accordingly, he gave grudging support to a Treasury plan, then being discussed in a ways and means subcommittee headed by Fred Vinson of Kentucky. This version proposed to cut the tax to 16 to 20 percent for corporations with annual earnings of more than $25,000; those with less would pay between 12½ and 16 percent. To compensate for lost revenue, the subcommittee devised a so-called "third basket" tax. This levy would affect only those closely held corporations with net incomes of more than $50,000 which distributed 60 percent or less of their earnings. Treasury officials considered this a fair tax despite cries that it discriminated unfairly against family businesses.

In the Senate administration prospects were already dimmer than in the House. Whereas Democrats on the Ways and Means Committee approved retention of the undistributed-profits tax in principle, Harrison, in his powerful post as Finance Committee chairman, favored repeal. So did Byrnes, whose special unemployment committee was then holding hearings to discover, among other things, why the recession had struck with such force. In late February Byrnes called his old South Carolina friend, Bernard Baruch, to the stand. Baruch proceeded to add his voice to the demand for tax revision. He also recommended tax exemptions for small businesses.[46] This testimony, so artfully publicized and so carefully timed, left few experienced observers with any doubt that Harrison and Byrnes, two of Baruch's "Old Masters," were behind it.[47] It was a good example of the smooth way in which these Senate chieftains operated.

Baruch's testimony was not enough to stop Doughton's full committee from reporting the bill favorably the same

[46] New York *Times*, March 1, 1938, pp. 1, 15; March 2, 1938, p. 1.
[47] John M. Blum, *From the Morgenthau Diaries: Years of Crisis, 1928-1938* (Boston, 1959), pp. 443-44.

day. But Representative John W. McCormack of Massachusetts, a veteran close to the House leadership, joined in a supplementary minority report against the third basket tax. When the bill reached the House floor the day after Baruch's testimony, McCormack protested vigorously against the plan. The third basket tax, he proclaimed, was "absolutely unsound, unfair, and discriminatory."[48] Frankly addressing Republicans, he appealed for a bipartisan coalition against the administration. Republicans, naturally, were easy converts. Many moderate Democrats joined them, believing that the third basket tax would harm recovery and cost them votes in their home districts. With this help McCormack succeeded a few days later as the House on a teller vote deleted the third basket levy, 180-124. The vote, Morgenthau said, was "the worst slap the President had had to take during his entire administration."[49] The next day the House restored some of the revenue lost by the defeat of the third basket tax and passed the rest of the bill without difficulty; the vote was 293-97, with Republicans forming most of the opposition.[50]

The bill then shifted to the Senate, embroiled at the time in its two-week reorganization battle. After a few delays, Harrison had his way. In late March his committee deleted the undistributed-profits tax, 17-4. In its place it substituted a flat 18-percent tax on corporate income. It also weakened the progressive capital-gains tax and included special exemptions for small corporations.[51] The bill was practically a carbon copy of Baruch's recommendations a month earlier, though in repealing the profits tax entirely, Harrison's committee went one step further. To Roosevelt it was profoundly distasteful.

[48] *Congressional Record*, 75th Cong., 3rd Sess., 2855.

[49] Blum, *Morgenthau Diaries*, p. 444.

[50] *Congressional Record*, 75th Cong., 3rd Sess., 3269.

[51] Blum, *Morgenthau Diaries*, p. 444; New York *Times*, April 6, 1938, p. 1.

The next day (the day before the House defeated the reorganization bill) Senate sentiment for tax revision expressed itself. Garner, fully in accord with his friends Harrison and Byrnes, took the chair and began to race through the bill. Instructing the clerk to hop, skip, and jump through the complex bill, Garner snapped, "without objection, amendment's agreed to . . . without objection, amendment's agreed to." Barkley and his cohorts sat helplessly, aware of the futility of interfering. In twenty minutes Garner had disposed of most of the bill and, beaming, turned over the chair to Minton of Indiana. "We passed 224 pages of the tax bill in twenty minutes," he chuckled. Minton, ordinarily a "100 per cent New Dealer," finished the job. In forty-five minutes all but 4 of the bill's 902 sections had passed the Senate, with only one roll call to disturb the pace.[52] Two days later, before Roosevelt had had time to absorb his reorganization defeat, the Senate passed the bill much as Harrison had reported it. Final passage did not even require a roll call.

The Senate's action was a tribute to Harrison's stature among his colleagues. Over Roosevelt's objections he had not only led the way in destroying one of the President's cherished principles but had done so with great speed and near Senate unanimity. Moreover, it was no minor setback. Whereas Roosevelt's defeat on reorganization had indeed been a stunning blow to administration prestige, the defeat of the profits tax was an attack on an *established, existing* New Deal principle previously passed by these very same senators. No legislative battle so well illustrated the way in which the recession aided conservatives in the election year of 1938. And no issue so clearly demonstrated that the old leaders, Harrison, Byrnes, and Garner, though no longer close to the administration, retained at least as much influence as Barkley and the official leadership. For the change

[52] New York *Times*, April 8, 1938, p. 3.

in Senate sentiment since 1936, the tax controversy of 1938 was a revealing episode.[53]

By April 10 Roosevelt had suffered two setbacks. One, over reorganization, came at the hands of the House in a dramatic and hotly contested vote; the other, over taxes, came from the Senate through the more subtle but equally devastating fashion of committee emasculation. But the fundamental reason for conservative success in both cases was similar: the presidential position on both bills attracted little support from the elements of his liberal coalition.[54] Programs with appeal to these powerful elements were still all but irresistible to Congress. But these groups had little to gain either from reorganization or from the undistributed-profits tax. So congressmen received little pressure for the bills, a great deal against.[55] Feeling no compulsion to back the administration and afraid of provoking their constituents in an election year, they simply followed the path of least resistance. Even occasional partisan attacks by Republicans failed to drive moderate Democrats back into the New Deal fold. Neither recession nor partisanship cracked the conservative bloc on these two major issues. April 1938 was a low-water mark of the New Deal.

While Congress worked at destroying Roosevelt's tax and reorganization plans, the President was still seeking a remedy for the recession and still receiving conflicting advice from his aides. Morgenthau, holding out against a re-

[53] This Senate action did not end controversy over the bill, for Roosevelt refused to surrender, insisting that conferees retain the profits tax. Eventually it was retained in principle, only to be repealed completely in 1939.

[54] Even Mrs. Roosevelt, though opposing the congressional stand, was resigned to letting the conservatives have their way. She wrote Baruch: "I am anxious to see us let business have some of the reforms which they think will solve their problems, not because I agree *in toto*, but because I think there is much in psychological effect." Quoted in Margaret L. Coit, *Mr. Baruch* (Boston, 1957), pp. 450-51. Letter, June 20, 1938.

[55] Rexford G. Tugwell, *The Democratic Roosevelt* (Garden City, N. Y., 1957), p. 466, commented on the importance of pressure groups in this case.

newed spending program, had recommended in March an expansion of Reconstruction Finance Corporation (RFC) lending powers. This expansion would empower the RFC, a Hoover creation, to lend more money to business; it would require no new Treasury outlay, no inflation, no heavy relief spending; all the loans would be liquidated. Conservatives viewed the proposal as a way of forestalling more radical measures, and Glass quickly introduced it in the Senate.[56]

Roosevelt's less conservative advisers were unhappy. For them public spending was both politically attractive and, according to Keynesian economics (with which some, though not all, of these men were familiar), economically desirable. With the recession showing no signs of abating in early April, they finally converted Roosevelt to their view. Glad at last to have made the decision he had delayed so long, Roosevelt pushed ahead with renewed vigor and determination. On April 11, two days after Garner had banged Harrison's tax bill through the Senate, Roosevelt announced he would send to Congress a sweeping multibillion-dollar spending program to cure the recession.[57] Three days later, after working far into the morning, he did so.

The message, accompanied by a fireside chat, was broad in scope. It anticipated spending or releasing some $6.5 billion in federal funds. Of this amount, slightly more than $2 billion was to be circulated by desterilizing Treasury gold reserves and relaxing reserve requirements for member banks of the Federal Reserve system. This liberalization would not require legislation. An additional $1.5 billion, to be spent in RFC loans, had already been introduced by Glass, swept through Congress, and was signed by the President. The remaining $3 billion would require congressional approval.

[56] Raymond Moley, *After Seven Years* (New York, 1939), p. 148.

[57] New York *Times,* April 12, 1938, p. 1; *Time,* April 18, 1938, pp. 17-18. See also James M. Burns, *Roosevelt: The Lion and the Fox* (New York, 1956), pp. 320-36.

This sum included a request for $1.25 billion to see the WPA through February 1, 1939; $275 million for the Farm Security Administration (FSA), National Youth Administration (NYA), and Civilian Conservation Corps (CCC); and $1.5 billion to be distributed through grants and loans by the Public Works Administration.[58] These proposals upset economy-minded congressmen. "Priming the pump," O'Connor snorted, "won't do any good if there's no water in the well." McNary, echoing widespread doubts about the efficacy of public spending, added, "It has been tried before without success. I approach the plans with fear."[59]

From the start it was obvious that many Republicans would oppose the plan. Encouraged by their recent victories, they left their shelter behind conservative Democrats. Without waiting for a "liberal" leader like Wheeler, they assailed the plan from all quarters.[60] Republican arguments were not new, but their vehemence was, if possible, greater than ever. Some, such as Taber, had long regarded spending programs with unsurpassed hatred, and the pump-priming plan was no exception. "The wild spending orgy which is now proposed," he wrote, "is exceedingly dangerous."[61] Even George Norris (by then an Independent), though planning to vote for the bill, expressed his qualms about continued, long-term public spending; "this cannot go on forever," he wrote, "and there will come a time when even the federal government will have to cease."[62]

A few conservative Democrats joined the fray. Besides O'Connor, Glass muttered a few acid words, and Byrd, always economy-minded, denounced rumors of the plan before the President even announced it. Most of them agreed with the private objections of Bailey. "I do not have faith,"

[58] Rosenman, *Public Papers of FDR*, VI, 221-35.
[59] New York *Times*, April 15, 1938, p. 1.
[60] *Ibid.*, April 18, 1938, p. 8.
[61] To A. R. Thayer, April 13, 1938, Taber MSS, Box 74.
[62] To Henry P. Nielsen, April 18, 1938, Norris MSS, Tray 33, Box 6.

he wrote, "in this pump priming business. I will agree that it may do some good for a few months, but I must look forward to the ultimate consequences. I am not here to do good for a few days at a time."[63]

But most anti-New Deal Democrats said little; sensibly, they let Republicans lead the opposition. In part their silence reflected willingness to let Republicans carry the attack. And in part it revealed a belief that the plan was not so radical as it seemed. After all, of the approximately $3 billion which they would have to discuss, nearly $1 billion was slated for loans, and much of the rest (for the WPA, CCC, NYA, and FSA) would have been requested anyway to carry these operations through another fiscal year. The pump-priming plan promised to raise the national debt, but not a great deal more than normal appropriations would have done; in this respect, some conservative Democrats were able to find grounds for grudging support.

Above all, most conservative Democrats realized that all-out opposition would be suicidal. Election time was too near, spending too popular. "There are just millions of complaints . . . about the W.P.A. and other alphabetical activities," Bailey wrote. "Nevertheless large numbers of people are in love with them. By and by, we will reach the stage where something can be done, but at present any criticism is interpreted as being opposed to the Administration and as disloyalty to our great President."[64] Sullenly but realistically, conservative Democrats let Republicans take the offensive. Their attitude, one columnist reported, was, "Well, we tried it before and it hasn't worked, but if that's what he wants, let's let him have it."[65]

[63] To John P. Swain, May 19, 1938, Bailey MSS, Political File.

[64] To H. P. Whitehurst, April 26, 1938, *ibid.*, Relief File.

[65] Joseph Alsop and Robert Kintner, Washington *Star*, April 27, 1938, A-11. This was the view of Senator Theodore F. Green, a New Deal Democrat from Rhode Island. See Green to Mrs. Nathaniel P. Hill, May 23, 1938, Green MSS, Box 39.

The bill began in the House, where it ran into the economizing subcommittee directed by Clifton Woodrum of Virginia. By early May this group finished work on the measure, reporting a version retaining most of the funds sought by the President but parceling them out piecemeal in specified amounts to the various agencies. The President would not be able to do as he pleased with the money: he could influence each agency to spend the money in certain ways, but he could not shift money from one agency to another. The subcommittee also limited administrative costs.[66]

Minor as these harassments were, they did not last long. A few days later the full Appropriations Committee approved the substance of administration requests, and Edward T. Taylor of Colorado, chairman of the committee, made quick work of Woodrum's attempts to limit executive discretion. Going to the White House for a brief conference, Taylor returned with a scribbled presidential amendment to Woodrum's scheme: "subject to the approval of the President."[67] The only Woodrum amendments to remain intact were his old standbys: relief money had to be allocated on a month-by-month basis, and workers who turned down higher-paying private jobs were not eligible for WPA work. These amendments did not unduly worry administration forces.

Conservatives had even less luck on the floor a few days later. By then few Democrats opposed the plan, for they fully realized that it was too attractive to Roosevelt's electoral coalition. Open opposition passed to the Republicans, and not even all of them were willing to jeopardize their chances of reelection. "I am enclosing a copy of my remarks on the recovery bill," one Republican wrote. "I think I will have to vote for it. I don't want to be in the attitude of

66 New York *Times*, May 7, 1938, p. 1.

67 *Ibid.*, May 10, 1938, p. 1. The bill as reported did not include the RFC or CCC or flood control items. These were handled separately.

voting against relief. You can see that it puts a fellow in a rather tough position."[68]

The result was a quick administration victory. Only three days after it emerged from committee, the bill passed with ease, 329-70, with only eleven Democrats opposed and with twenty-three (of ninety) Republicans backing the administration.[69] The bill was entirely satisfactory to the President; indeed, it authorized slightly more than the $3 billion Roosevelt had requested and left him free to distribute it.[70] The conservative bloc in the House, recently so effective against the labor standards and reorganization bills, collapsed completely in the face of temptations for spending. "Congress," said one somewhat cynical report, "having got a taste for relief pork five years ago, was not prepared to go on a self-imposed diet."[71]

It had been obvious from the beginning that the Senate would offer greater opposition. Since only one-third of the chamber faced reelection in the fall, senators could afford to be a little less responsive to popular pressure. More important, the events of late April and early May had reawakened suspicions of the political power inherent in Roosevelt's control of relief. On May 2 Senator Claude Pepper, a New Dealer from Florida, beat his more conservative Democratic opponents in a Senate primary enlivened by charges that Pepper benefited from sinister use of WPA funds. At the same time Governor Olin T. Johnston of South Carolina proclaimed that he would seek Cotton Ed Smith's Senate seat that fall. Since his announcement came from the White House steps after a conference with Roose-

[68] Edward H. Rees to William Allen White, May 12, 1938, W. A. White MSS, Box 212.

[69] *Congressional Record*, 75th Cong., 3rd Sess., 6836.

[70] The measure directly appropriated $2.519 billion and authorized an additional $500 million for PWA grants and loans, for a total of $3.019 billion. Roosevelt had requested $3.012 billion.

[71] *Time*, May 23, 1938, p. 9.

velt, it seemed probable that the President was thinking of purging conservative Democrats from the party.[72] To potential victims of 1938 this prospect was frightening. These early indications of the purge of 1938 served to intensify conservative determination to keep relief funds out of Roosevelt's hands.

With these battle lines drawn, the measure began its Senate career in an appropriations subcommittee headed by Alva Adams of Colorado, an economy-minded banker. But Adams faced reelection that year. Though strong in his bailiwick, he did not relish a costly primary battle with a New Deal opponent, and he guided his subcommittee in the direction of compromise. On one hand, his subcommittee added $175 million to the WPA fund to make it last an additional month in 1939. But it also approved an amendment prohibiting future PWA projects from conflicting with private utilities operating under public regulation, and it limited the cost of WPA materials (except in emergency cases) to seven dollars per worker per month.[73] The next day the full committee, under Glass' furious leadership ("I'm not in favor of this damned bill," he sputtered),[74] approved these changes and added a few more. One added $212 million in farm parity payments to the bill; another sliced $100 million from the PWA section.

The committee's action showed that conservative strength in the Senate had become almost as ineffectual as that in the House. In the past the Appropriations Committee, dominated by Glass, Byrnes, and Adams, had often been a bedrock of economizing sentiment. Yet in this case it reported out a bill which (thanks primarily to the farm parity section) added nearly $300 million to administration

[72] New York *Times*, May 17, 1938, p. 1.

[73] *Ibid.*, May 21, 1938, p. 1. The utilities amendment, one estimate said, would have curtailed forty-nine proposed power projects worth $56 million.

[74] *Ibid.*, May 22, 1938, p. 1.

requests, and which failed in any way to earmark the relief money to reduce Roosevelt's political power.

Adams' dilemma helped explain this unexpected generosity. He was one of eleven Senate Democrats who were suspect in New Deal circles and who had to face elections in November.[75] Though most were relatively well entrenched in their home states, none were anxious to antagonize the President. While Roosevelt's renewed combativeness goaded Glass and Bailey to new heights of fury, it served to diminish the ardor of their more vulnerable conservative colleagues.

Once safely through the Appropriations Committee, the measure was assured of relatively quick action on the floor. And quick action it had. Conservative amendments received little support, and even the amendment barring PWA competition with private utilities failed on a voice vote. The Senate accepted Byrd's amendment limiting WPA administrative costs to 5 percent; it earmarked some $50 million of WPA funds; and it retained the $212 million farm parity increase.[76] Otherwise, administration forces triumphed. On the morning of June 4 the pump-priming bill passed with ease, 60-10.

The final bill was a stinging defeat for conservatives. Far from reducing spending, it actually added close to $100 million to the House bill, itself more than Roosevelt had requested.[77] The increased farm subsidy was chiefly responsi-

[75] The others were George, McCarran, Lonergan, Smith, Van Nuys, Gillette, Clark, Dieterich, Bulkley, and Tydings.

[76] New York *Times*, June 4, 1938, p. 1.

[77] Actually, the Senate version was $568 million more than passed by the House. But $212 million was for farm parity payments and $300 million for housing, then being considered separately by the House. The final bill, approved with little difficulty in conference, appropriated or authorized some $27.5 million more. The final bill thus appropriated or authorized some $3.750 billion—or roughly $700 million more than Roosevelt had requested. The farm parity item was retained despite Roosevelt's insistence that taxes be provided to cover the additional expenditure.

ble: once again the farm lobby had proved irresistible. The recession ordinarily worked against the administration, but on questions of spending it served to ride roughshod over the economizers.

The vote was an equally good indication of conservative caution. Counting pairs, the tally was 76-14, with 6 unrecorded. Of the fourteen opponents, eight (of fifteen in the Senate) were Republicans. McNary and Johnson were among them, but other western progressives such as Nye, Frazier, and Capper backed the bill.[78] Lodge and Davis, as responsive to labor pressure as they had been over the fair labor standards bill, also supported the measure. Republican divisions, temporarily healed in such political issues as the court plan and reorganization, reappeared over spending in an election year.

Only six of the seventy-seven Senate Democrats deserted the administration. They were Burke, Byrd, Bailey, Copeland, Glass, and George L. Berry, a 1937 appointee from Tennessee. All except Berry were safe from the electorate in 1938. But their conservative Democratic colleagues, in the past some eighteen to twenty strong, refused to join them. Three others, Tydings (who also had to run that fall), Donahey, and King, did not vote at all.

No issue so well illustrated the impermanence of the conservative bloc. Farmers, relief workers, union men, and Negroes were all quick to realize the potential benefits of increased federal spending and to exert pressure upon their congressmen. Since many of these constituents paid no income taxes, they had everything to gain and nothing to lose by passage of the bill. And as if this pressure was not enough to induce wavering congressmen, there was the additional temptation of forthcoming PWA projects within

[78] McNary wrote, "This morning about 12:30 the Senate passed the so-called pump-priming bill—it's a terrible mess in my opinion." To Mrs. W. T. Stolz, June 4, 1938, McNary MSS. Borah was not recorded.

their home states. No wonder the conservative coalition crumbled; as in the past, it was powerless when Roosevelt's liberal coalition united. Conservatives handed to the President considerably more power than they had withheld so recently in the reorganization controversy. The New Deal was not so dead as it had seemed.

As the pump-priming contest was developing, the fourth major issue of the session, labor standards, again began to create considerable controversy. After recommittal of the bill in special session, a new round of negotiations had begun. Robert C. Ramspeck, an urban congressman from Atlanta, introduced a compromise bill providing for regional differentials and an independent five-man commission. William Green of the AF of L., however, was still afraid that an independent commission would undermine union power and favor the rival CIO, and he opposed regional differentials in principle. Try as they would, Ramspeck and Green could not agree.

Mrs. Norton's Labor Committee, exhausted by these negotiations, finally sat down to vote on April 14, a few days after Roosevelt's defeat on reorganization and taxes, and the same day as his appeal for pump-priming. Ten of the eighteen committee members, convinced that no bill could pass without AF of L support, voted down Ramspeck's plan. The committee then approved Green's version, 14-4.[79] This bill failed to provide for regional differentials and set up a wage and hour scale beginning with a twenty-five cents an hour minimum and forty-four hour maximum and becoming forty cents-forty hours within three years. This was the bill which the full House had to consider.

From the start it was clear that the bill commanded little southern support. Even comparatively liberal southerners

[79] New York *Times*, April 15, 1938, p. 42. Also *Nation*, CXLVI (April 23, 1938), 454; and Paul Y. Anderson, "Republicans, Neutrality and Azaleas," *Nation*, CXLVI (April 30, 1938), 494-95.

Senators Arthur H. Vandenberg (R–Mich.) and Josiah W. Bailey (D–N.C.; *right*)

(Copyright United Press International)

SENATORS BURTON K. WHEELER (D–Mont.) AND PATRICK A. McCARRAN (D–Nev.; *right*)

(Copyright United Press International)

such as Bankhead and Ramspeck refused to work for it, and Walter Lippmann went so far as to brand the proposal a "sectional bill disguised as a humanitarian reform."[80] And the Rules Committee, for the third time, refused to allow the bill to reach the floor. The five southern members, led by Cox, Dies, and Smith, again formed the bulk of the opposition, and three of the four Republicans gave them a majority of 8-6. Significantly, Joseph W. Martin, Jr., of Massachusetts, aware that mill owners from his area favored the absence of regional differentials, voted against his Republican colleagues in the committee. The vote, occurring April 29, appeared to be the death knell of the bill.[81]

Four days later, however, Pepper, warmly advocating the bill to his Florida constituents, achieved his sweeping primary victory. Observers interpreted the outcome as evidence that the bill commanded considerable support even in the South. Furthermore, politicians realized that Roosevelt had favored Pepper. Would he not be able to designate other winners in the fall?

Even before this stunning triumph, liberal congressmen had talked of starting another petition to discharge the bill, and Pepper's victory gave enormous impetus to their cause. As one conservative congressman wrote glumly, "the Florida primary put the fear of God in the hearts of some of the Democrats. . . ."[82] One liberal spokesman even claimed to have 198 potential signatures two days after the primary.[83] None of their claims, however inflated, seemed absurd in light of what followed.

At noon on May 6 (three days after the primary), Mrs. Norton walked to the well of the House and placed a discharge petition on the speaker's desk. Signing it, she began

---

[80] New York *Herald Tribune,* May 21, 1938, p. 13.

[81] New York *Times,* April 30, 1938, p. 1.

[82] Hope (Rep.–Kans.) to Richard W. Robbins, May 17, 1938, Hope MSS, Official Correspondence, 1937-1938, P-R.

[83] New York *Times,* May 5, 1938, p. 4.

to corral support; after all, in the special session it had taken seventeen days to get the requisite 218 signatures.

She barely escaped the well of the House. As soon as she had signed, a horde of congressmen began pushing to be next in line. Quickly, she handed her fountain pen to those nearest her, but in a few minutes the scene had become chaotic. The sergeant at arms had to force would-be signers into a queue, and Bankhead, after calling repeatedly for order, had to suspend regular business. Cheers filled the chamber whenever a southerner or a Republican joined the line.[84] In an hour and a half 200 congressmen had signed. A lull followed, but then the Louisiana delegation, persuaded in part by administration negotiations with Louisiana boss Robert S. Maestri, swooped down the aisle.[85] In a few more minutes the petition had the magic number of 218. The whole process had taken two and one-half hours.

The names on the petition again showed the sectional-partisan cast to the issue. The 218 petitioners included 183 Democrats, 22 Republicans, 8 Progressives, and 5 Farmer-Laborites. Of the Republicans, 18 were from the more urban areas of the East Coast, and 4 more were Californians. Of the Democrats, only 22 were southerners, including Rayburn, Maverick, and young Lyndon B. Johnson of Texas.

For the next two weeks the pump-priming measure preoccupied both houses, with no appreciable changes in sentiment on the wage-hour measure. At last, the day arrived for a House vote. In a tumultuous session lasting far into the night administration Democrats beat down some fifty amendments, losing only on a few exempting certain agricultural and fishery workers and on the "Shirley Temple" amendment exempting child actors from child labor provi-

[84] For a colorful account, see *Time*, May 9, 1938, p. 11. See also New York *Times*, May 7, 1938, p. 1.

[85] For the Louisiana story see Alsop and Kintner, Washington *Star*, May 4, 1938, A-11.

sions.[86] Despite wild denunciations from Cox, the final bill passed with ease, 314–97.

This overwhelming roll call, even more than the pump-priming vote, showed cracks in the conservative bloc. Of the 97 opponents, 41 were Republicans. The remaining Republicans, many of whom were men such as Martin with labor constituencies to contend with, backed the bill. And of the 56 Democrats opposed, a far cry from the 133 in December, 52, including Cox, Dies, and Smith, were southerners. Only the hardiest rural Republicans and most intractable southern Democrats had dared to oppose the administration.

The bill then went to a conference committee, where prospects did not look bright, for the Senate bill passed in 1937 had provided for an independent five-man board and regional differentials, whereas the House bill provided for neither. Southern senators continued to talk about a filibuster should Senate conferees approve the House version. But strong as the southern threat seemed, congressmen, whatever their political beliefs, were anxious to close the session and go home, and all but the angriest of southern senators wanted to resolve the problem before the fall elections. House conferees, for their part, were willing to retreat somewhat if the labor lobby would let them.

A compromise resulted. Senators agreed to place administration of the bill under one man in the Labor Department. And House conferees surrendered on the divisive question of regional differentials on wages. The compromise version provided for advisory wage boards in most major interstate occupations. The boards were to take into account, among other things, "competitive conditions as affected by transportation, living, and production costs."[87] For the first year

[86] New York *Times*, May 25, 1938, p. 1.
[87] See text of bill, *ibid.*, June 13, 1938, p. 8.

the hourly minimum wage had to be at least twenty-five cents, for the second year thirty cents. Thereafter, the board might permit certain firms to maintain their wages at thirty cents for as long as five more years, at which time the minimum must climb to forty cents. Companies granted this privilege had a breathing spell of up to seven years. The labor lobby, aware that the bill would eventually satisfy most of their demands, reluctantly acceded to the compromise. Southerners, more reluctantly, did likewise. The fair labor standards bill, after more than a year of rugged congressional maneuvering, had finally become enacted into law.[88]

The act was far removed from the President's original request in May 1937. Thanks to southern and rural pressure, it exempted large numbers of agricultural workers and permitted many businesses to postpone paying what liberals deemed a living wage. And thanks to organized labor, the act allowed less discretion in actual administration. Once again an organized pressure group had demonstrated its power in Congress.

Yet the President could fairly claim a victory, especially in contrast to his two previous failures in 1937. Whatever the bill's shortcomings, it was a foundation upon which to build, and in later years this act was to be amended again and again until a reasonably solid floor under wages was in effect. Roosevelt more than held his own against the most determined bipartisan opposition and scored an impressive counterblow against a conservative group that had struggled relentlessly from beginning to end.

The remainder of the session, though turbulent, offered nothing to match the excitement of pump-priming or the labor bill. The Senate, continuing to fear political interfer-

[88] Votes on the conference version were by voice in the Senate and 290-89 in the House. Even Dies shouted "Aye" for this version. The hours sections remained unchanged.

ence by the WPA, commissioned a committee headed by
Morris Sheppard of Texas to investigate the 1938 primaries
and elections. Congress also finally agreed upon a joint
congressional-executive investigation of monopoly, to be
headed by O'Mahoney.[89] But even before the session ended
on June 16, many congressmen had started on the campaign
trail, and Cincinnati pitcher Johnny Vander Meer's two
consecutive no-hitters stole the spotlight from those who
remained.[90]

The session was one of the most revealing in many
years. It showed that conservative determination to stop
the New Deal was growing, and that on certain occasions
a combination of circumstances could deal the administration severe and humiliating defeats.[91] And although the
session in no sense exposed a well-organized, monolithic
conservative coalition, it did witness occasional bipartisan
conservative alliances along the same channels of communication established in 1937. Clearly, the Rules Committee
in the House and the Bailey-Byrd-Wheeler-Vandenberg net-
work in the Senate would continue to plague the administration in years to come.

But the New Deal was not dead. Partisanship had
helped to shatter the conservative alliance on more than one
occasion. Republicans, resuming the offensive after their
enforced silence of 1937, often forced moderate Democrats
to back the New Deal. Similarly, conservative Democrats,
especially southerners, had little use for Republicans at
election time. "I am not advocating a formal coalition,"
Bailey wrote in May. "I am trying to maintain a policy here

[89] For this story, see Joseph O'Mahoney, Oral History Project, Columbia
University, pp. 36-37; and Raymond Moley, "The Great Monopoly Mystery:
The Fascinating Story of TNEC's Neglected Record," *Saturday Evening
Post,* CCXII (June 25, 1938), 716.

[90] For the closing, see "The 75th," *Nation,* CXLVI (June 25, 1938), 713.

[91] See Appendix for statistical trends.

that will preserve the character of the Democratic Party."[92] His failure to get signatures for his manifesto in December had shown that coalition politics were difficult to launch: as the election approached, they became almost impossible.

Conservative congressmen also trapped themselves occasionally in contradictory positions on the economy issue. On one hand, they equated balanced budgets with the Millennium, deficit spending with the Devil himself. But as politicians and officeholders they could not dwell happily in the world of theory. Even Taber, one of the most economy-minded congressmen of the twentieth century, supported a constituent's demand for "pork" in this fashion: "There is no question in my mind but what if the government were not spending money the way it is, this particular situation could not be considered, but it [the demand for a local project] is certainly as meritorious as any of the others."[93] Bailey, equally attached to governmental economy, was just as aware of the problem. "It appears," he wrote Peter Gerry in late 1937, "that the farm legislation will make the balancing of the budget out of the question, but I shall not seriously oppose it. We are going to have inflation anyway and I do not know that it is worth our while to try to stop it now."[94] Aware of the wisdom of giving constituents what they wanted, many conservatives contradicted their economic theories in practice. These inconsistencies on the economy issue left conservatives divided among themselves and vulnerable to the charge of hypocrisy.

Finally, the 1938 session exposed the most fundamental

[92] To J. Sam White, May 9, 1938, Bailey MSS, Personal File. White was a Republican. See also the anonymous congressman whom Krock quotes in New York *Times*, June 17, 1938, p. 20. "We have to string along with the President for at least one more election. Except in certain districts, or where a man has a political following like Glass, there is no present alternative."

[93] To Horace W. Fitch, undated, Taber MSS, Box 113.

[94] Oct. 25, 1937, Bailey MSS, Political File.

conservative limitation of all: the New Deal was all but invincible on issues that awakened sizable elements of its coalition. Whenever conservatives faced no potent pressure groups, as on the reorganization and tax issues, they banded together and carried enough New Dealers with them to win. Otherwise, as in the cases of pump-priming and labor standards, they slid into factionalism almost from the start.

The New Deal still had some magic. The question was: how much? Did the rise of congressional conservatism reflect a nationwide trend, or was Pepper's triumph just one more example of Roosevelt's unparalleled electoral appeal? Until this question was answered the congressional box score would remain a stalemate. With this in mind, both sides turned to the crucial and imminent battles at the polls.

8

COALITIONS AND ELECTIONS:
THE PURGE

A S THE 1938 elections approached, political commentators were fond of observing that historic party realignments were underway. For some fifteen years prior to the New Deal, they insisted, the two major parties had been fundamentally alike. Democrats and Republicans had divided over the tariff question, and Governor Alfred E. Smith of New York, the 1928 Democratic presidential nominee, had symbolized an urban cast in the Democratic party that was absent in the GOP. But aside from these differences, the two parties had disagreed more over patronage than principle. "The aisles," commented Congressman Huddleston of Alabama before the New Deal, "don't mean anything except a good place to walk in and walk out."[1]

By 1935, however, it was obvious that the New Deal was working a major transformation within the Democratic party. As the administration drew closer to the CIO, Negroes, and other "forgotten men," conservative Democrats gradually discovered their philosophical kinship with conservative Republicans. And Republicans found the New Deal distressingly popular; if they were to stop it, conservative Democrats would be useful allies.

On the basis of this situation observers enjoyed predicting two major changes in the American party system. Anti-New Deal commentators foresaw the day when conservatives of both parties would unite under coalition tickets to fight the apostasy of the New Deal, while liberals speculated upon Roosevelt's reaction to such a challenge. Possibly he would try to purge conservative Democrats from the party. The result would be the great party realignment many had long desired: a clear-cut political system with a liberal and a conservative party. As coalition difficulties within Congress indicated, such a sharp departure from American practice would encounter serious obstacles. But these difficulties would not become obvious until 1938 and the events of 1934-1936 seemed to make realignment possible.

Conservatives began talking of electoral coalition as early as the spring and summer of 1934. In August Jouett Shouse, former executive chairman of the Democratic National Committee, announced the formation of the Liberty League, a nonpartisan organization supported by large financial interests in both parties.[2] Shortly thereafter, William R. Pattangall, Democratic chief justice of the Maine Supreme Court, sharply attacked the New Deal in an effort to induce

[1] Quoted in Julius Turner, *Party and Constituency: Pressures on Congress* (Baltimore, 1951), p. 36. The statement was made in 1931. For differences over tariff, see *ibid.*, pp. 69-70.

[2] See George Wolfskill, *The Revolt of the Conservatives: A History of the American Liberty League, 1934-1940* (Boston, 1962), pp. 21-36. Also Frederick Rudolph, "American Liberty League," *American Historical Review*, LVI (1950), 19-33.

conservatives of both parties to forget party labels. Other conservatives joined in promoting coalition talk, including columnist Mark Sullivan and Joseph B. Ely, former Democratic governor of Massachusetts. Perhaps the most avid voice for coalition was that of Bainbridge Colby, a New Yorker who had been Wilson's secretary of state. During the summer of 1934 Colby began urging Glass, Byrd, and others in Congress to work for coalition tickets across the country.

According to one report, Glass, Byrd, Gore, Bailey, and Clark were five Democratic senators who favored such proposals. But even their enthusiasm was distinctly limited. Few Republicans or conservative Democrats who had to run for reelection cared to become associated with Wall Street and the Liberty League. The League eventually took very little part in the 1934 elections, saving its broadsides for later days.

Colby's more "respectable" efforts also failed to produce more than a ripple of enthusiasm. Republicans were unimpressed, for Colby and his friends were Democrats who talked of coalition under Democratic leadership. Many Republicans also nursed forlorn hopes that they could beat the New Deal on their own. Even Glass wanted no part of the scheme, and in a letter to Colby the Virginian provided what would later prove to be one of the most serious objections to electoral coalitions. "You will understand," he said, "the impossibility of wrenching any considerable number of persons from their accustomed affiliation. . . . Furthermore, with nearly ten million mendicants on the Federal relief rolls and every State and nearly every community in every State indebted to the Federal Treasury, it seems to me a hopeless task to do anything more than to await with patience and fortitude the certain crash, now rapidly approaching."[3] It was safe for the Colbys, Elys, and

[3] To Bainbridge Colby, Aug. 10, 1934, Glass MSS, Box 320.

Pattangalls to call for coalition, but officeholders had to face reality. What party label would prevent "wrenching" politicians from their natural habitats? And how could such a movement be successful at the high tide of the New Deal? Coalition efforts in 1934 gained few influential adherents.

The remarkable success of liberals in the 1934 elections caused conservatives of both parties to think again. Far from adopting Glass's pessimistic attitude, they began to feel that only a coalition could stop the President in 1936. Vandenberg was so worried about "radical" influences in the Democratic party that he suggested a "virtual coalition government" in which Roosevelt would use "sane Republican assistance" as a "buffer" against the spenders in his own party.[4] Roosevelt naturally ignored Vandenberg's generous offer, and progressive Republicans such as Couzens and McNary almost choked at the absurdity of the proposal.[5]

Renewed attempts by Colby and others received more serious consideration. One magazine urged Republicans to nominate a Carter Glass–Lewis Douglas ticket which would call itself the Jeffersonian Democratic party.[6] Pattangall resigned his justiceship in May 1935 to take a more active part in coalition efforts, and Colby proposed a meeting of conservative Democrats to "consider some form of political action that is for country and above party."[7] And Sullivan in June urged that Republicans name Byrd, Glass, Douglas, or Alfred E. Smith as their presidential or vice-presidential

---

[4] New York *Times*, Nov. 16, 1934, p. 2, and Nov. 19, 1934, p. 5.

[5] James Couzens to Charles McNary, Nov. 19, 1934, McNary MSS. Couzens said "Senator Vandenberg is difficult in some ways. . . . I assume you saw Joe Robinson's reply to Arthur's suggestion that we have coalition government. I thought Joe's reply was pretty good. He said that evidently Vandenberg had made up his mind 'if he couldn't lick them, join them,' and that if Vandenberg was the Republican candidate in 1936, we would have vacuity, vaccilation, and Vandenberg. That was a rather disagreeable slam."

[6] Roger W. Babson, "Government by Coalition," *Review of Reviews*, XCI (Feb. 1935), 47-48.

[7] Washington *Post*, June 1, 1935, p. 2.

nominee. Such a move, he said, would guarantee the GOP its fifteen million votes of 1932, plus an additional seven million from disaffected Democrats. This total would be easily enough to win.[8]

The coalition movement progressed no further. Republicans continued to try to heal the conservative-progressive split which threatened to shear off the western wing of their party. In addition, their congressional campaign committees were embroiled in a struggle for funds with the national committee. In July 1935 the committees split entirely, making difficult any kind of coordinated national coalition.[9] Even Sullivan admitted later that the designation of a man such as Byrd at the head of the Republican ticket would generate great "confusion" on local tickets.[10]

More difficult to resolve than intraparty differences were the chasms of partisanship. Republicans looked to their own organizations to stop the New Deal, not to conservative Democrats. "If we show clear courage," James Wadsworth wrote at the time, "dissatisfied Democrats and Independents will flock to us by the thousands. Our party must show the way and thus convince the conservative Democrat and the conservative Independent that we can be trusted. We are their only hope!"[11]

If Republicans were unreceptive to coalition talk, Democrats were even more hostile than they had been in 1934. Nonofficeholding northern Democrats such as Ely and Colby were again enthusiastic, but southerners such as Glass and Bailey frowned on the idea. "I'm a Democrat, not a half-way Democrat," snorted Glass when asked for his reaction to Pattangall's suggestions.[12] "Since there is no candidate

[8] New York *Herald Tribune*, June 2, 1935, II, 1.
[9] New York *Times*, July 26, 1935, p. 3.
[10] New York *Herald Tribune*, June 16, 1935, II, 2.
[11] To John W. Kirby, Sept. 10, 1935, Wadsworth MSS, Box 24.
[12] Washington *Post*, June 1, 1935, p. 2.

against Mr. Roosevelt for the Democratic nomination," he wrote, "it would be senseless for me to be avowing opposition to his nomination, which is inevitable. . . . Moreover, as a practical fact, how do I know and how do you know that the Republicans are going to nominate anybody who would do any better than Mr. Roosevelt, or as well; hence how foolish it would be of me to now announce that I propose to support the next Republican nominee for President."[13] And Bailey gave a friend the classic southern argument against coalition. "President Roosevelt," he said,

is the head of our Party and also the President upon nomination of our Party. He will inevitably be renominated. Any course tending to prevent his renomination will divide the Party in our State and, if there were no other considerations, this would be sufficient. However, there are other considerations. A division in the party ranks would probably bring about the election of a Republican, and neither you nor I desire to be a party to any such consequences. . . . It is always the better course for a North Carolina Democrat to take a course calculated to maintain the unity of the Party.[14]

In the Democratic South the best chance for conservatism was within the Democratic party. Coalition there was unthinkable.

These partisan objections, strong enough in 1935, grew as the 1936 election approached, and the only serious coalition proposal came from the Republican New York *Herald Tribune* in June 1936. It urged the imminent Republican convention to name either Byrd or Ely as its vice-presidential nominee. Surprisingly, Landon privately favored a similar move.[15] But most Republicans saw no reason

[13] To R. H. Barksdale, Nov. 11, 1935, Glass MSS, Box 341.
[14] To C. L. Shuping, Aug. 31, 1935, Bailey MSS, General File.
[15] New York *Herald Tribune*, June 2, 1936, p. 1. For evidence of Landon's views, see Vandenberg Scrapbook, 1938, Vandenberg MSS. Here Vandenberg records a letter from Landon to Vandenberg dated Sept. 24,

to jeopardize local tickets by naming a Democrat as their number-two man, and, as Landon recalled later, the idea "never got to the point of serious discussion."[16] Byrd of course wasted no time removing himself from consideration. "Under no conditions," he said, "would I join any coalition party with the Republicans."[17]

Instead of forming bipartisan coalitions, both parties sought to bridge their internal divisions and thrash the opposition. In August a group of National Jeffersonian Democrats, including Ely, Colby, and a handful of others, announced they would not back Roosevelt.[18] None was an officeholder; none had anything to lose. Glass, running for reelection, continued to spurn the Republican party. "I am unable to see much difference between Roosevelt and Landon," he snapped, "except that the former is a first-class New Dealer and the latter a second-rate New Dealer; nor do I discover much difference between the Democratic and Republican platforms. Both are in favor of robbing the consumers of the country out of both pockets at the same time...."[19] Tydings agreed: "with all the evils of the present administration," he said, "it is vastly to be preferred to the nostrums to be presented with the advent of a Republican administration."[20]

Coalition movements in 1934-1936 never had a chance. Most professionals of both parties were aware of the dismal

---

1938. In this letter Landon told him to go ahead and quote the following if he wished to clear up rumors regarding a rift between the two men: "There is nothing to the story that I have any feeling toward Senator Vandenberg for his refusal to take the Vice-Presidency nomination at Cleveland. I really did not want him for Vice-President. I wanted to see a Democrat nominated."

[16] To author, June 26, 1964.
[17] New York *Herald Tribune*, June 3, 1936, p. 2.
[18] See material relating to this in Glass MSS, Box 347.
[19] To A. R. Strothers, Aug. 22, 1936, *ibid.*, Box 348.
[20] To Glass, Oct. 6, 1936, *ibid.*, Box 380.

fate of third parties in American history, and they sensibly refused to join one. These men had their places in local, state, and national party organizations and they considered it too perilous to change.

The events of 1937 again altered the situation. The election of 1936 marked the political awakening of a powerful New Deal coalition which even the administration was hard pressed to control. The component groups of this coalition, especially unions and Negroes, convinced many conservative Democrats that they had wretched bedfellows. Burke, Cox, and others resented Roosevelt's political alliance with John L. Lewis and the CIO, and conservative southern Democrats looked upon the New Deal-Negro alliance with unconcealed horror. "The catering by our National Party to the Negro vote . . . is not only extremely distasteful to me, but very alarming to me," Bailey wrote. "Southern people know what this means and you would have to be in Washington only about three weeks to realize what it is meaning to our Party in the Northern states. It is bringing it down to the lowest depths of degradation."[21] And Glass, ominously, was thinking of retaliation. "The South," he wrote later, "would better begin thinking whether it will continue to cast its 152 electoral votes according to the memories of the Reconstruction era of 1865 and thereafter, or will have spirit and courage enough to face the new Reconstruction era that northern so-called Democrats are menacing us with."[22]

As the events of the 1937 congressional session unfolded, these private complaints became more explicit, more insistent. Conservative Republicans in Congress, profoundly discouraged by the 1936 election, began to consider carrying their loose congressional alliance with conservative Democrats into the primaries and elections of 1938. The combination of conservative Democratic determination and conserva-

[21] To R. G. Cherry, March 1, 1938, Bailey MSS, Political File.
[22] To W. Gordon McCabe, Feb. 14, 1938, Glass MSS, Box 362.

tive Republican timorousness caused electoral coalition to seem a good deal more auspicious than it had ever been before.

While the court battle raged, congressmen had little time to think about the elections more than a year away; moreover, suggestions of coalition would have embarrassed conservative Democrats who were holding out against the plan. But as soon as the struggle was over, many people broached coalition openly, and others, such as the publisher, Frank Gannett, more quietly considered ways of perpetuating conservative strength in the Senate. Copeland, running that summer for the mayoralty of New York City, openly solicited Republican aid in his unsuccessful efforts to win the Democratic primary, and Republicans, in turn, gave him some encouragement.[23]

The most significant aspect of this new coalition talk was that it actually reached the stage of serious talk among high-ranking men in both parties. Vandenberg, anticipating his discussions with Bailey in December, told journalist Raymond Clapper in June that he favored some kind of coalition. "Republicans," he revealed, "are inclined to support anti-court plan Democrats." But, he continued, the efforts at coalition must be serious. Both sides must "guard against individuals trying to use the movement for their selfish purposes and also against allowing [a] row over [a] name to defeat it . . . a silly row over [the] name of [the] party might break it up."[24] In October he added, "I continue

[23] See Royal Copeland to William E. Borah, Aug. 26, 1937, Borah MSS, Box 413. He said, "Carter Glass and all the forward looking men on my side in the chamber, and those on your side who are not enamoured of the New Deal, are convinced that my success here would be the beginning of the end of this mad program of the President's." Borah was noncommittal.

[24] Clapper Diary, June 14, 1937, Clapper MSS. Clapper was close to many Republican figures, especially Landon and GOP National Chairman John D. M. Hamilton. He recorded their ideas regularly in his diary. His diary was in note form.

SENATORS (*from left*) BYRON ("PAT") HARRISON (D–Miss.), FREDERICK VAN NUYS (D–Ind.), EDWARD R. BURKE (D–Neb.), WILLIAM H. KING (D–Utah), AND JAMES F. BYRNES (D–S.C.)

(Copyright United Press International)

REPRESENTATIVES (*from left*) HOWARD W. SMITH (D–Va.),
JOHN J. O'CONNOR (D–N.Y.), LAWRENCE LEWIS (D–Colo.),
AND EDWARD E. COX (D–Ga.)
(Copyright United Press International)

to believe that some sort of a fusion or coalition or union ticket may be necessary. . . . It would not shock me at all to find myself in 1940 supporting the right kind of a Democrat at the head of such a union ticket."[25]

Vandenberg had talked this way before. Even more revealing were the views of Landon. In May 1937 he met secretly with Wheeler and promised to support Democrats who opposed the court plan, provided they decided to run as independents.[26] He also corresponded with Lewis Douglas, remarking that he knew of no one "in a better position to develop a coalition than you."[27] As late as November 1937 he wrote, "we will have to gather under one banner all the elements of opposition that disbelieve in the Roosevelt theories of government. . . . In fact as early as 1934 I said we would not whip Mr. Roosevelt until we combined, as the Liberals and Conservatives did in England in 1929 against the Labor-Socialist party."[28] As Clapper recorded in his diary in August, Landon was "itching to issue [a] statement urging coalition."[29] The hesitant but definite tendency of Vandenberg and Landon to coalesce with conservative Democrats was excellent testimony to Republican discouragement in 1937. Had these influential men joined in a public statement for coalition, at least part of their party might have listened.

Landon, however, encountered strong opposition from Republican National Chairman John D. M. Hamilton. As party chairman, Hamilton rejected any alliances, however tempting, which might upset local party organizations. Encouraged by Roosevelt's dwindling prestige, he had already begun to institute changes to revive the party, and he insisted

[25] To Landon, Oct. 19, 1937, Landon MSS, Political File, 1937, T-Z.
[26] To Henry P. Fletcher, June 10, 1938, *ibid.*, 1938, June-Sept.
[27] To Douglas, April 1, 1937, *ibid.*, 1937, D-F.
[28] To C. P. Dorsey, Nov. 29, 1937, *ibid.*
[29] Clapper Diary, Aug. 16, 1937, Clapper MSS.

upon testing conservative Democratic sentiment before letting Landon speak.[30] In so doing he discovered that Democrats such as Bailey were determined, if at all possible, to reform their party from within. Their main goal, they told Hamilton, was to name a conservative as the 1940 Democratic presidential nominee, a task in which the GOP could be of little help. If they failed, then—and only then— would they so much as consider bolting their party.[31] Combined with Republican grass-roots suspicions, this Democratic caution convinced Landon that the time was inopportune. Soon he was writing, "if there is a coalition of any kind it will be moved by forces far greater than any manipulation or promotion. It will be a natural trend based on an understanding laid on common ground. It cannot be promoted and it cannot be stopped if it is coming."[32]

One more Republican effort indicated the difficulties blocking coalition politics in 1937. The arch-conservative George H. Moses, a former Republican senator from New Hampshire, was one of the many politicians then out of office who dreamed of a coalition to upset the New Deal. And like many of them, he had not given up hope of regaining office himself. By late 1937 he was convinced that a Republican-southern Democratic coalition was possible. He wrote his old friend Glass in November: "You and I have often discussed realignment but you always raised the color question. This condition no longer exists. Jim Farley and the Roosevelt largess have made the colored vote in the North impregnably Democratic. 'Where thy treasure is, there thy heart is also.' Therefore, with the color line obliterated,

---

[30] For one of many accounts of Republican reorganization, see Ronald Bridges, "Republican Program Committee," *Public Opinion Quarterly*, III (April 1939), 299-306. See also C. A. H. Thompson, "Research and the Republican Party," *ibid.*, 306-14.

[31] Clapper Diary, Aug. 16, 1937, Clapper MSS.

[32] To George Coleman, Dec. 23, 1937, Landon MSS, Political File, 1937, B-C.

why cannot those of us who are free-white-and twenty-one get together and do a job as effective as Mussolini did when he made his march upon Rome?"[33]

Glass was noncommittal. "If we are to hope for a 'realignment of parties,' " he wrote, "the attempt must be made in more propitious circumstances than now exist, when the adversaries of such a movement have not an incredible campaign fund, picked from the pockets of taxpayers, and when the jobholders are not in authority in every community of the Nation, and when the Supreme Court itself is not frightened out of its wits by the ill-concealed menaces of an Administration at Washington."[34]

Conservative Republicans such as Hamilton were not alone in doubting the practicality of coalition in 1938; southerners such as Glass considered it bound to fail and desired above all to maintain Democratic seniority in Congress. As the primary season of 1938 began, chances for conservative electoral coalition were no more propitious than they had been in 1934 or 1936. Left to their own devices, conservatives were apparently unable to unite across party lines.[35]

At this point a new development threatened: the purge. Conservative Democrats wanted to avoid a clear break with the party, but it was becoming increasingly obvious that Roosevelt wanted to force them out. Furious at the "treachery" of men such as Bailey, George, and Van Nuys who accepted his support and then "deserted" him, the President became eager for revenge.[36] "He took no pains to hide his

[33] Nov. 1, 1937, Glass MSS, Box 380.

[34] To Moses, Nov. 8, 1937, *ibid.*

[35] Publisher Frank Gannett was one who remained optimistic for coalition. See Gannett MSS, Box 16, for several revealing letters on the subject.

[36] James M. Burns, *Roosevelt: The Lion and the Fox* (New York, 1956), pp. 197-202, 376-80, maintains that Roosevelt had an excellent opportunity to realign the parties but failed to take advantage of it. As this chapter will show, I am convinced that party realignment was all but impossible, except as a gradual development over time and from the bottom up.

anger," one reporter recalled. "Resentment crystallized into the desire to crush all who conspired against the throne."[37] "For weeks and months afterwards," Farley later remembered, "I found him smoldering against the members of his own party."[38] Roosevelt, as much as Bailey or Glass, was crossing the Rubicon.[39]

The President partially concealed his pique in 1937. But as soon as the session ended in August he traveled west to test his popularity. As usual, teeming crowds cheered him wherever he went; the trip refreshed him and restored much of his confidence. But his resentment was clear. In Montana he studiously avoided mentioning Wheeler's name, praising instead his Democratic Senate colleague, James E. Murray. In Nebraska he deliberately ignored Burke. In Wyoming he tried to snub O'Mahoney. Most important, patronage channels for Democrats who had opposed the court plan were mysteriously drying up. Roosevelt's attitude, one critic complained, was "high school girl revenge."[40] But it was unmistakable evidence that the President's anger was lasting. Conservative Democrats sensed that they might face trouble when primary season began.

By the end of 1937 commentators were almost unanimous in predicting a purge in the coming primaries. If conservative Democrats had to fight for their lives, would they cast aside partisanship to unite in the common cause? And would Republicans help? Or would the self-interest of each party make coalition as difficult as ever? On the answer to these questions hinged the fate of party realignment.

[37] George Creel, *Rebel at Large* (New York, 1947), p. 295.

[38] James A. Farley, *Jim Farley's Story* (New York, 1948), p. 95. Farley opposed the purge. Furthermore, he wrote his book many years after he had broken with the President, so his interpretation must be read cautiously. See his harsh description of Roosevelt's "petty attributes," p. 184.

[39] Stanley High, "Party Purge," *Saturday Evening Post*, CCX (Aug. 21, 1937), 16, expressed this view.

[40] Alva Johnston, "President Tamer," *Saturday Evening Post*, CCX (Nov. 13, 1937), 8.

The chief conservative objective was to pack the Senate. The House, though cantankerous, was also mercurial; it lacked the more durable conservative bloc which marked the Senate. Since conservative Senate strength in late 1937 numbered approximately thirty-five to forty, conservatives had to secure at least ten new members to be assured of a dependable bulwark against the New Deal. Roosevelt had to hold his own in order to make it appear that popular support (almost always diminished in off-year elections) remained behind his administration.

Though each election contest was to be different, it was still possible to generalize about the problems each side would face. Of the thirty-four senatorial races ahead, twenty-one involved seats of Democrats whom the President was willing to support.[41] These were the seats conservatives sought to win. Of the remaining thirteen seats, three belonged to Republicans and ten to conservative or unreliable Democrats. These ten Democrats were the ones with whom Roosevelt must be concerned in any attempt to purge.[42]

At the start of the primary season it was obvious that many of these senators were either sure of renomination or immune to interference from the enemy party. In this category fell nine administration Democrats and the three

[41] Ordinarily there would have been only thirty-two Senate contests (one-third of ninety-six). But the resignation of A. H. Moore of New Jersey necessitated a contest there, and Berry of Tennessee, appointed to fill a vacancy in 1937, also had to run.

[42] These divisions are necessarily arbitrary, as the names will indicate. Dieterich and Bulkley, for instance, really stood somewhere between both sides. The conservatives or unreliables were George, Smith, Tydings, Lonergan, McCarran, Adams, Berry, Clark, Van Nuys, and Gillette, and Republicans Gibson, Nye, and Davis. The others were Pepper, Barkley, Brown of New Hampshire, Caraway, Wagner, Duffy of Wisconsin, McAdoo, McGill of Kansas, Hitchcock of South Dakota, Pope of Idaho, Thomas of Oklahoma, Bone, Hayden of Arizona, Overton of Louisiana, Reynolds of North Carolina, Thomas of Utah, Bulkley, and Dieterich. Three others are counted here because though they were not running for reelection, their replacement with a conservative would have marked a change. These were Black, Reames of Oregon, and Milton of New Jersey.

Republicans.[43] Subtracting these twelve, twenty-two seats, all held by Democrats, still remained potential battlegrounds at nomination time. Twelve of these twenty-two seats were then occupied by administration men, ten by conservative or somewhat unreliable Democrats. These were the only areas in which purges or coalitions could develop.

One problem of conservative coalitionists was painfully apparent from the beginning. Conservative Democrats might seek Republican assistance in denying renomination to New Dealers, but Republicans in most cases knew that their aid would be futile or self-defeating. For instance, three administration Democrats, Barkley, Thomas of Oklahoma, and McAdoo of California, faced primary opponents who were anathema to Republicans. McAdoo's opponent was Sheridan Downey, whose pension plan of "$30 Every Thursday" made McAdoo look like a doddering reactionary. In these contests Republicans had little desire to exert themselves for men with whom they had little sympathy.

Four other contests for administration seats involved states where Republicans, bolstered by the decline in Roosevelt's prestige, hoped to win on their own in November. In Oregon the Democratic incumbent, Alfred E. Reames, was not a candidate for renomination. A similar situation existed in New Jersey. In both states untested Democrats would have to face rejuvenated Republicans in normally Republican states. In Ohio Robert A. Taft appeared a likely winner over Bulkley, and in South Dakota Republicans felt almost as confident with J. Chan Gurney, who had barely lost in 1936. In all these races Republicans were optimistic. Why help a Democrat, whatever his ideological persuasion?

[43] These were Democrats Reynolds, Hayden, Bone, Overton, Thomas of Utah, and Wagner, all of whom were also reelected. Brown of New Hampshire, Duffy of Wisconsin, and McGill were also renominated without undue hardship but lost to Republicans in November. Republicans Davis and Gibson also were renominated easily. Nye, the third Republican, had a difficult fight.

One other administration seat belonged to Dieterich of Illinois. But Republicans knew they were powerless to influence the Democratic nomination there. The Democratic machine would control the situation. Indeed, the machine eventually discarded Dieterich and named Scott W. Lucas, a congressman who ironically proved to be less tractable than Dieterich. Thus, of the twenty-one contests originally involving administration incumbents, nine were absolutely safe from coalition assaults at nomination time, and eight more offered little or no incentive for Republican coalition tactics. Only four of these twenty-one seats provided any kind of opportunity for effective conservative coalition. There is no more telling evidence of the almost insurmountable obstacles posed by the American party system against coalition politics.

As if the conservative cause was not difficult enough, the obstacles in three of the four remaining races involving administration seats were insurmountable. These contests were in southern states. In Alabama Congressman Lister Hill, an outspoken New Dealer, faced J. Thomas ("Tom Tom") Heflin, a veteran racist-demagogue. In Florida Senator Claude Pepper, an enthusiastic New Dealer who had been elected in 1936 to fill a vacancy for two years, faced four opponents, the most prominent of whom was Congressman J. Mark Wilcox, an opponent of both the fair labor standards and reorganization bills.[44] And in Arkansas quiet, black-clad Hattie W. Caraway, the only lady senator, placed her dependable New Deal record on the line against Congressman John L. McClellan, who had also opposed these two key bills. All three contests were clear tests featuring New Dealers against well-known politicians who enjoyed anti-

[44] See V. O. Key, Jr. (ed.), *Southern Politics in State and Nation* (New York, 1949), pp. 82-105. This is a chapter on Florida politics entitled, appropriately, "Every Man for Himself." For Pepper, see article by Francis P. Locke, in J. T. Salter, *Public Men In and Out of Office* (Chapel Hill, N. C., 1946), pp. 257-76.

administration support. Since all three involved primaries, it was conceivable that Republican money and Republican votes might be useful to the conservative side.

The outcome in Alabama in early January set the standard for the later Florida and Arkansas battles. Heflin, despite his demagogic past, received the support of many conservative financiers and industrialists. And Hill, though well educated and articulate, failed to generate great enthusiasm as the campaign began in the fall of 1937. Hill's strong support of the fair labor standards bill (at that time preoccupying the House in the special session) also threatened to cost him votes. In November 1937 most analysts predicted Hill would win, but not overwhelmingly.

At this point Hill's friends capitalized upon Heflin's past record. Heflin had bolted the party in 1928. In itself this was sinful enough to place him beyond the pale in the Democratic South. Then in late November Judge Leon McCord, a leader of Hill's campaign, capitalized on a speech by J. Will Taylor, a Republican congressman and national committeeman from Tennessee. Distributed from Birmingham under Taylor's congressional franking privileges, the speech attacked the fair labor standards bill and Hill's support of it.[45] It was a rather amateurish effort to damage Hill sponsored by Heflin's supporters, chiefly Birmingham industrialists fearful of the labor bill.

The result was amusing. McCord immediately lashed at the speech. It was, he said, an effort by the "Republican high command" to invade the sovereign state of Alabama.[46] Hill, shuttling back and forth from Washington, held up copies of the speech and denounced them as propaganda instigated by Birmingham Republicans. Democratic leaders quickly summoned emergency meetings throughout the state

45 Montgomery *Advertiser*, Nov. 26, 1937, p. 1.
46 *Ibid.*, Nov. 27, 1937.

to combat this Republican "threat."[47] Hill's supporters missed no opportunity to refer repeatedly to Heflin's Republican associates, both then and in 1928.[48]

Heflin was shocked and only two days after publication of Taylor's speech he tried to disavow it. It was, he said, "a miserable piece of propaganda put up to bolster the lost cause of Congressman Hill." Infuriated, he marched to a newspaper office that had printed the speech and delivered his rebuttal in person.[49] For the rest of the campaign Heflin and his friends continued to fight rear-guard actions against charges of Republican collusion. They had very little success in doing so.

Early in January Hill won the primary with 90,601 votes to Heflin's 50,189, receiving 61.8 percent of the vote compared to Heflin's 34.3.[50] By this time neither the result nor the margin of victory was surprising, for Heflin's campaign had faded perceptibly over the closing weeks, and he had spent the last week abed with pneumonia. Even without the charges of Republicanism hung around his neck, he certainly would have lost. But the way in which Hill's supporters had made Republicanism a key issue and the way in which even Heflin had scurried to refute Republican associations showed that effective conservative movements in the South had to be purely Democratic. Reconstruction, it appeared, was still very much a memory in the South.

The Pepper-Wilcox and Caraway-McClellan contests were similar. Pepper triumphed convincingly in May, and in the summer, Mrs. Caraway also won a victory for the

[47] *Ibid.*, Dec. 2, 1937, p. 1.

[48] See Max Lerner, "Mr. Roosevelt: Ringmaster," *Nation*, CXLVI (Jan. 15, 1938), 63-64, for an account of the primary.

[49] Montgomery *Advertiser,* Nov. 28, 1937, p. 1.

[50] See J. B. Shannon, "Presidential Politics in the South" *Journal of Politics*, I (Aug. 1939), 278-300, for an excellent survey of the 1938 primaries. A third candidate in this primary received 5,763 votes.

New Deal, beating McClellan in a much closer contest.[51] In both contests Republicans, painfully aware that their open participation would backfire, kept out of the picture. These three primaries proved that the New Deal was strong in the South. They also reiterated what had been true since Reconstruction days: Republicanism in the South was a political liability.

Only one of the twenty-one administration seats remained for conservative coalitionists to try to capture at primary time. This belonged to James P. Pope of Idaho, a fifty-four-year-old liberal who had been one of the chief architects of the 1938 farm bill. His Democratic primary opponent was D. Worth Clark, a congressman since 1935. Well-educated and articulate, Clark was a formidable opponent. He was also unenthusiastic about the New Deal and had voted against the utilities "death sentence," fair labor standards (in December 1937), and reorganization. Their views on foreign policy also contrasted sharply: Clark was an avowed isolationist, whereas Pope was one of the most fervent internationalists in the Democratic party.

Idaho law made the situation especially tempting for Republicans. Providing for Republican and Democratic primaries on the same day, the law permitted voters to participate in either one; Republicans could vote in large numbers for Clark if they wished. Republicans at last had a ready-made opportunity to back a conservative Democrat against an administration man, with no loss to themselves. If Republicans swept out Pope in the primary, it would not matter so much who won in November: either candidate, Clark or his Republican opponent, would be from the conservative end of the spectrum.

[51] For Arkansas politics see Key, *Southern Politics*, pp. 183-204. This excellent chapter emphasized the one-party factionalism within the state and the dishonesty of election officials. These factors probably made more difference than ideological questions. For Mrs. Caraway, see *Literary Digest*, Sept. 4, 1937, p. 7; for the primary, see *Time*, Aug. 22, 1938, p. 21.

Before the primary on August 10 rumors circulated that Republicans intended to do just that by deserting their own dull primary and supporting Clark against Pope.[52] Clark did not welcome such assistance; like almost all Democrats, he repeatedly sought to establish his kinship with Roosevelt. But he did make clear his admiration for Idaho's other senator, Borah, calling him "that great living statesman."[53] At the same time, Clark shrewdly appealed to Idaho's old people by proclaiming that the Townsend pension plan was worth a trial. On primary day he scored a stunning upset, beating Pope by nearly 4,000 votes in a total Democratic turnout of nearly 85,000. Pope was the only Democratic senator to lose a primary to a more conservative opponent.

The remarkable aspect of Clark's triumph was the voting turnout. Idaho had ordinarily been a Republican state before the New Deal. But in the 1938 primaries some 85,000 voted for Clark or Pope as opposed to some 30,000 voting in Republican primaries. Obviously, there was more to the extraordinary Democratic turnout (some 30,000 more than in a 1936 primary) than voter interest. Pope had lost because thousands of conservative, isolationist Republicans deserted their own contest to give the verdict to Clark.

Shortly thereafter the President denounced Republican tactics. The victorious Republican primary candidate, eager to find a way to explain his own low vote, agreed with Roosevelt's interpretation. Other Republicans vehemently disagreed. The GOP state chairman flatly contradicted Roosevelt's statement, pointing out that more people had voted in the Democratic gubernatorial contest than in the Senate race. He insisted that state GOP leaders had not pushed Republican voters into the Democratic primary.

Both Roosevelt and Idaho Republican leaders spoke some

[52] Idaho *Daily Statesman*, Aug. 7, 1938, p. 9.
[53] *Ibid.*, Aug. 1, 1938, p. 1.

truth. Republicans had certainly gone to the polls in large numbers to back Clark. But the GOP state leadership had made little effort to bring this about. As one reporter had observed before Roosevelt made his charges, "official Republican leaders strove hard to check the tidal wave of Republicans to the Democratic Party, but they found the temptation to cavort in the green fields of Democracy too strong."[54] GOP leaders opposed the intentions of their troops for partisan reasons. In an election involving a liberal internationalist Democrat and a conservative Republican, they reasoned, the Republican, aided by the decline in Roosevelt's prestige, might win. But Clark, they decided (correctly as it turned out), would not only receive Democratic votes in November, but those of large numbers of conservative Republicans as well.

The 1938 Idaho primaries offered the only example, in twenty-one chances, of successful conservative bipartisanship against an incumbent New Deal senator. But the result had required a congenial state law, isolationist sentiment, Townsendite votes, and rank-and-file participation. Republican leaders, there as everywhere, were unenthusiastic. To these leaders it made relatively little difference whether a conservative or a liberal won in November; their aim was to choose a Republican instead of a Democrat. Why build up Clark, or any Democrat, when it would hurt GOP chances three months later? The Idaho situation was an illustration of coalition politics, but they were largely unplanned, unwanted, and unexpected.

The real interest of the 1938 campaign season focused on the ten contests involving conservative Democratic incumbents. Roosevelt's anger at these men, fanned by the

[54] Ibid., Aug. 10, 1938, p. 1. Many observers felt that Clark's support of the Townsend Plan brought him some 10,000 votes and that Republican votes for Clark were mainly byproducts of Republican interest in the Democratic gubernatorial primary held the same day. See New York Times, Aug. 28, 1938, IV, 7.

congressional revolts on reorganization and taxes in early 1938, remained intense as the summer primary season approached. Indeed, he had tipped his hand somewhat in the Hill and Pepper contests. Though silent during the Alabama primary, he had permitted Hill to ride with him from Florida to Washington not long before. And a last-minute injection of WPA funds into the Florida primary had probably done Pepper no harm. Encouraged, Roosevelt began to consider intervention in the contests to come.

According to Farley, the President at one time considered moving against nine of the ten.[55] But political leaders quickly convinced him that some conservative Democrats could not be dislodged. Augustine Lonergan of Connecticut had the backing of his Democratic Senate colleague, Francis Maloney, and of Democratic Governor Wilbur Cross.[56] Alva Adams of Colorado not only enjoyed the support of local Democrats, but also of Edwin Johnson, his fellow Democratic senator. Clark of Missouri, a third unreliable, was also much too powerful to challenge, and Roosevelt hardly even considered meddling here.[57] A fourth, Patrick McCarran of Nevada, was almost as strong. A New Dealer would eventually oppose McCarran, but the President, recognizing McCarran's strength, wisely made no serious effort to interfere.[58] The early elimination of these four from discussions of purges left only five conservative or undependable Democrats in

[55] Farley, *Jim Farley's Story*, pp. 123-24. The tenth, Berry of Tennessee, did not need Roosevelt's enmity; Boss Edward Crump's was enough to defeat him.

[56] See Roosevelt MSS, OF 10, for FDR's view of Lonergan, and his insistence that Lonergan run on a New Deal banner.

[57] See Joseph Alsop and Robert Kintner, Indianapolis *Star*, June 19, 1938, p. 10, for Roosevelt-Adams relations. For FDR's hands-off attitude in Missouri see McIntyre to A. L. Meirr, Feb. 11, 1938, Roosevelt MSS, PPF 4658.

[58] For McCarran see *Current Biography*, 1947, p. 408. Also biographical sketch, Pittman MSS, Box 150. See *ibid.*, Box 14, for Pittman's distrust of his colleague. See Max Stern, "Senator McCarran: Wrench Thrower," *Today*, III (May 4, 1935), 11.

danger from the administration. They were Guy Gillette, Van Nuys, George, Tydings, and Cotton Ed Smith.

The first of the five to face a primary was Gillette of Iowa. A tall, handsome farmer, Gillette was fifty-nine in 1938 and known primarily as a leading spokesman for midwestern farm interests. He had been a congressman in the early New Deal and since 1936 had filled a two-year vacancy in the Senate. In many respects Gillette was hardly a conservative. During his congressional career he had supported most New Deal measures, including the utilities "death sentence" and executive reorganization. In 1937 he had backed neither the Robinson relief amendment nor the Byrd amendment to the housing bill.

But to Roosevelt the cardinal test of liberalism was the court plan, and Gillette had made the unfortunate error of opposing it. Hopkins, Corcoran, and other New Dealers insisted that Gillette could be beaten in a primary by Otha D. Wearin, a liberal congressman.[59] Roosevelt, encouraged by Pepper's recent victory, assented to mild intervention. Hopkins announced his preference for Wearin, and Jimmy Roosevelt, the President's son and private secretary, referred to Wearin as "my friend" in pointed remarks two days before the primary.[60]

But Gillette was a shrewd and hardy campaigner with many powerful friends. When Hopkins made his remarks, Wheeler rose to offer Gillette his support. Other conservative Democrats, including King, Bailey, and Van Nuys, talked about a "flying squadron" to Iowa in Gillette's behalf.[61] More important, Iowa's Democratic bosses, including Clyde L. Herring, Gillette's Senate colleague, backed Gillette.[62]

[59] Joseph Alsop and Robert Kintner, *Men Around the President* (New York, 1939), p. 183.

[60] Paul Y. Anderson, "Congressional Fadeout," *Nation,* CXLVI (June 18, 1938), 690-91. *Time,* June 13, 1938, p. 16.

[61] James F. Byrnes, *All in One Lifetime* (New York, 1958), p. 102.

[62] New York *Times,* June 4, 1938, p. 1.

Agriculture Secretary Henry A. Wallace refused to work for Wearin. Gillette carefully refrained from attacking Roosevelt but scored by denouncing "this gang of political termites boring from within . . . planning on taking over . . . the Democratic party." "I will not," he said, "be a rubber stamp member of Congress."[63]

Early in June Gillette won with ease, receiving more votes than his three opponents combined.[64] His victory was significant in that it suggested that New Deal candidates would not always be successful in subsequent primaries. Otherwise, the victory was not especially encouraging to conservative coalitionists. Iowa law, like Idaho's, provided for Democratic and Republican primaries on the same day. But Iowa voters were not allowed to cross over, and Republicans could do little to help Gillette. He beat a New Dealer but did so on his own.

Furthermore, top-ranking Republicans did not want to help Gillette. "Why support conservative Democrats?" National Chairman Hamilton asked at the time. "They help make up Democratic majorities in the Senate—sit on [the] Democratic side—vote to organize [the] Senate, . . . and never help Republicans who need it—like Jim Davis running in Pennsylvania now. [I] can't see why Republicans should abdicate for them."[65] Gillette would probably win the election, Hamilton later complained, simply because Iowa Republican newspapers gave him such favorable publicity during the primary.[66] Like their fellow professionals in Idaho, Republican politicians in Iowa hoped for victory in November, and they had little use for coalition politics so long as the GOP seemed to have a chance.[67]

[63] *Time,* June 13, 1938, p. 16; Indianapolis *Star,* June 6, 1938, p. 1.
[64] Alsop and Kintner, Washington *Star,* June 10, 1938, A-11.
[65] Clapper Diary, June 8, 1938, Clapper MSS.
[66] *Ibid.,* Aug. 23, 1938.
[67] An exception was Gannett. See Frank Gannett to Arthur B. Hyman, June 24, 1938, Gannett MSS, Box 16. "We used considerable influence out there in Iowa to get our supporters to vote in the Democratic primaries."

The next conservative "victim" was Frederick Van Nuys of Indiana. Independently minded, Van Nuys had been a target since 1937 not only of Roosevelt but of the powerful Indiana machine run by former Governor Paul V. McNutt, Governor M. Clifford Townsend, and Senator Sherman Minton. Indeed, Townsend had announced from the White House steps in 1937 that he "didn't think the organization could nominate Van Nuys again."[68] Van Nuys, a senator since 1933, had also been one of the ten signers of the majority report against the court bill.

Unlike Gillette, Van Nuys enjoyed little organization backing, and the machine could have disposed of him easily, especially since Indiana law provided for a state convention instead of a primary.[69] But Van Nuys had no intention of surrendering without a struggle. Long before the scheduled party conventions in late June and early July, rumors circulated that he would run as an Independent if denied the Democratic nomination.

Coalitionists then began to urge Republicans to support an Independent Van Nuys candidacy by endorsing him at their convention. Sullivan, true to form, supported such a course of action, as did Gannett.[70] Even Indiana Republican Chairman Arch N. Bobbitt appeared sympathetic to such a scheme.[71] Van Nuys' conservative Democratic Senate colleagues also promised him support. Walsh gave him a special dinner early in May attended by Wheeler, Copeland, Bailey,

[68] *Time,* July 20, 1937, p. 11.
[69] Mark Sullivan, New York *Herald Tribune,* May 26, 1938, p. 23, discussed the Indiana situation, again urging coalition.
[70] Gannett to W. C. Dennis, May 31, 1938, Gannett MSS, Box 16. "As you know," Gannett wrote, "I agree with you that Senator Van Nuys should be supported by the Republicans. I have done my best to get the Republican Party to endorse him if he runs as an independent. I fear, however, this is too late. It would be a tragedy to have Jim Watson nominated in the hope that through a split in the Democratic Party, the Republicans might return Watson to the Senate."
[71] Indianapolis *Star,* June 12, 1938, p. 17.

King, and Gerry. Burke, O'Mahoney, and Clark sent special messages to the dinner, and all promised their aid to Van Nuys if he should need it. Landon, hewing to his promise to support Democrats on Independent tickets, also tried to persuade Van Nuys to leave his party and to accept Republican endorsement.[72] With this sort of backing, Van Nuys' chances seemed excellent. Running as an Independent, he would also avoid the awkward problem of party labels. The prospects for conservative coalition had never looked more auspicious.

But other conditions worked against coalition. Hamilton once more offered his voice against it. Van Nuys, he said, had a 95 percent pro-New Deal record. "Republicans would look foolish supporting him."[73] "Anybody who . . . wants the party to endorse conservative Democrats," Clapper quoted him, "will have [a] fight on [his] hands and will be excluded from councils of [the] Republican Party if he can do it."[74] Moreover, the Republican convention was scheduled for late June, two weeks before the Democratic meeting. If Republicans endorsed Van Nuys at their convention, they ran the risk, unlikely though it seemed at the time, that Democrats would do the same. This turn of events would have left them without a candidate at all. Besides, Van Nuys emphasized his Democratic ties, declaring that he would not accept Republican endorsement.[75] Like Gillette, he stressed his support of the New Deal, not his occasional apostasy. The only Republican recourse was to recess until after the Democratic convention. If the machine then discarded Van Nuys and if Van Nuys then announced as an Independent, Republicans could thereupon meet to endorse

[72] Landon to Frank Gannett, June 17, 1938, Landon MSS, Political File, 1937, G-H.
[73] Clapper Diary, June 8, 1938, Clapper MSS.
[74] Ibid.; see also Indianapolis Star, June 12, 1938, p. 17.
[75] Indianapolis Star, June 29, 1938, p. 1.

him. With combined conservative Democratic and Republican votes he might win in November.

Sullivan and other coalitionists continued to urge some such recess strategy. They were ignored. Local Republican leaders, needing a recognized Republican at the head of their ticket to beat Democrats in local contests, refused to listen. Reflecting Hamilton's sentiments, many of them also asked why the GOP should support a New Dealer, and they insisted that a recessed convention would result in a divisive Republican fight. Better to nominate a good Republican and put an end to this talk of coalition politics. The partisans carried the day. Barely fighting off the political comeback of former Senator James Watson, the convention met on schedule and named Raymond E. Willis, a sixty-three-year-old conservative newspaper editor.

The epilogue was amusing. The Democratic machine soon talked of Van Nuys in more favorable terms. The day after the choice of Willis, Governor Townsend reversed his stand of a year before. Van Nuys, he said, might make a good nominee. A week later Van Nuys was renominated by acclamation, with even Minton sullenly acceding to the switch. Townsend and Van Nuys had not spoken to one another for a year: nonplussed, they fell into one another's arms, smiling broadly for the benefit of unbelieving photographers.[76]

The reconciliation was of course insincere. The Townsend-McNutt-Minton machine was simply unable to find another suitable candidate. If Van Nuys was dropped and ran as an Independent, he might steal enough Democratic votes to give Willis the victory. McNutt also nursed presidential aspirations: clearly, it would be foolish to divide the party in his own state. The only answer was to produce a show of party harmony and name Van Nuys. In November

[76] Ibid., July 8, 1938, p. 1.

it would be Democrats and Van Nuys versus Republicans and Willis. Coalition talk was forgotten.

The Indiana situation mercilessly exposed the problems of coalition politics. In no other state did Republicans and conservative Democrats have a more auspicious chance to unite. But partisanship destroyed the feeble overtures in this direction. Republican politicians, for local and personal reasons, wanted a Republican at the head of their ticket. And conservative Democrats, Van Nuys included, much preferred machine endorsement to that of conservative Republicans. Indiana voters, like those in Idaho and Iowa, were to have no clear choice between a liberal and a conservative in November. Party realignment, it appeared, was impossible.

Meanwhile, Roosevelt finally sounded the battle cry. As soon as the congressional session ended in late June, he used a fireside chat as the first salvo in his campaign to purge conservative Democrats from Congress. Referring to "copperheads" who tried to poison New Deal programs, he congratulated Congress as a whole for its constructive achievements. But, he added, "As head of the Democratic Party . . . charged with the responsibility of carrying out the definite liberal declaration of principles set forth in the 1936 Democratic platform, I feel that I have every right to speak in those few instances where there may be a clear issue between candidates for a Democratic nomination involving those principles or involving a clear misuse of my own name."[77] The drive for party realignment, though belated, was at last underway.

Having reached his decision, Roosevelt wasted no time. Soon after his talk he embarked on a cross-country trip, actively aiding his friend Barkley and guardedly endorsing Caraway, Bulkley, McAdoo, and Thomas of Oklahoma—all

[77] Samuel Rosenman (ed.), *The Public Papers and Addresses of Franklin D. Roosevelt*, VII (New York, 1941), 391-400.

facing primary opposition.[78] By contrast, he ignored Adams and McCarran. At the same time Roosevelt's political lieutenants began seeking popular candidates to oppose Smith of Virginia and O'Connor.[79] Congressional liberals began talking about packing the Rules Committee if conservatives were defeated.[80]

But his southern opponents in the Senate were Roosevelt's chief targets. As a group southern senators and representatives were ordinarily as reliable as Democrats from other sections, except upon economic issues particularly affecting their section. But it was just those issues—sitdowns, labor standards, antilynching, housing—which had been so important in the 1937 and 1938 congressional sessions.

In late March Roosevelt had already infuriated southern conservatives in a Georgia speech. Criticizing "selfish minorities," he talked of the "feudal" society of the South and added: "When you come right down to it, there is little difference between the feudal system and the fascist system. If you believe in one, you lean to the other."[81] Bailey,

[78] See Shannon, "Presidential Politics," for this trip. Farley, *Jim Farley's Story*, quotes Roosevelt's ideas on the Barkley primary: "I am anxious," he quoted Roosevelt, "to have Barkley re-elected. If Barkley loses the fight, Pat Harrison will become majority leader and I'm afraid Pat won't go along on liberal legislation" (pp. 124-25).

[79] Rayburn was leery about trying to purge O'Connor. "I have been wondering what kind of trouble he might create if the Administration takes an interest in opposing him and then he should be renominated and elected. Our trouble of last session with him would be a small affair compared to what we would have next session if he should lose the Democratic nomination and be nominated by the Republicans and his type of Democratic votes." Rayburn to Bankhead, Aug. 15, 1938. Quoted in Walter J. Heacock, "William Brockman Bankhead: A Biography" (unpublished Ph.D. dissertation, University of Wisconsin, 1952), p. 252.

[80] *Newsweek*, July 25, 1938, p. 5. There was also talk of removing Sumners as chairman of the Judiciary Committee.

[81] Rosenman, *Public Papers of FDR*, VII, 164-68. Roosevelt's speech, Bailey wrote, "was not only irritating, but, from any point of view, extremely unkind and unappreciative. . . . The South may not have done well, but it has done better than any other people ever did under conditions of the greatest adversity."

furious, expressed his reaction: "Our Party," he said, "is being taken away from us by John Lewis, Harold Ickes, Robert Vann [a Negro editor in Pittsburgh], White of the Society for the Advancement of Negroes, Madame Perkins, Harry Hopkins, Cothran [*sic*], and Cohen. None of them ever were Democrats. It is a singular thing that we have permitted men who were not Democrats to take our Party captive and that we have so many Democrats in the South who seem to be willing for those men to put men like Senator George, Senator Smith, Carter Glass, Harry Byrd and myself out."[82] The reactions of men such as Bailey failed to move the President, and early in July he referred to the South as the nation's "Number One economic problem—the nation's problem, not merely the South's."[83] Though this statement was hardly news, it did little to magnify southern pride.

By the spring and summer of 1938 both Roosevelt and his southern conservative opponents were more at odds than they had ever been, and the President saw little to lose by trying to purge them. Many southern conservatives—Bailey, Byrd, Glass, Connally, Harrison—did not face reelection in 1938, but two, George and Smith, looked vulnerable. And a third, Tydings, though not a southerner, shared their opposition to New Deal labor and housing policies. Anticipating his later course, Roosevelt in May had permitted Governor Olin Johnston to announce against "Cotton Ed" Smith from the White House steps, and in his "feudal" Georgia speech he had ignored George, who had introduced him, and praised a potential rival in the primary. In all three states he had encouraged liberal Democratic candidates to run.[84]

[82] To H. G. Gulley, May 25, 1938, Bailey MSS, Political File.

[83] Rosenman, *Public Papers of FDR*, VII, 421-26.

[84] Labor's Non-Partisan League released a statement in July grading various congressmen and senators "A," "B," "C," "D," on the basis of their labor voting record. Of senators, Thomas of Oklahoma and Barkley got "A"; McAdoo and Bulkley "B"; McCarran and Adams "C"; and George and

But he saved his heavy ammunition for the summer primary season. Stopping in Georgia at Warm Springs, he arranged to lunch on August 9 with Lawrence Camp, the hand-picked New Deal candidate against George. The next day before 50,000 people at Barnesville and with both George and Camp on the platform behind him, the President referred to George as a "gentleman and a scholar," and "my personal friend." But George could not, "in my judgment, be classified as belonging to the liberal school of thought. . . . I have no hesitation in saying that if I were able to vote in the September primaries in this state, I would most assuredly cast my vote for Lawrence Camp."[85] Gallantly, the courtly George walked up to the President after the speech, offered his hand, and said: "Mr. Roosevelt, I regret that you have taken this occasion to question my Democracy and to attack my record. I want you to know that I accept the challenge."[86]

That night the presidential train moved into South Carolina, where it stopped briefly in Greenville. There Roosevelt sniped indirectly at Smith.[87] A few days later, back in Washington, the President opened up on Tydings, who faced a primary battle against Representative David J.

Tydings "D." Others were not named. It also named forty representatives whom it wanted defeated. These included fourteen Republicans and twenty-six Democrats, including Rules Committee members Cox, Smith, Dies, Clark, and Driver; committee chairmen Sumners, McReynolds (Foreign Affairs—Tenn.), Steagall (Banking and Currency—Ala.), Mansfield (Rivers and Harbors—Texas), Lea (Interstate Commerce—Cal.), and Doughton. Seventeen of the twenty-six House Democrats named were southerners; none was an easterner. The survey is evidence of the feelings of organized labor against the South. See Augusta (Ga.) *Chronicle*, July 16, 1938, p. 8.

[85] Augusta *Chronicle*, Aug. 11, 1938, p. 1.

[86] *Ibid.*, Aug. 12, 1938, p. 1. See Roosevelt MSS, OF 300, Georgia, for miscellaneous material relating to Georgia politics.

[87] Shannon, "Presidential Politics," p. 287. The train had not been scheduled to stop in Greenville, but when it did, McIntyre, hearing FDR's remarks, quickly arranged to have it leave. See Roosevelt MSS, OF 200-CCC.

Lewis, a former coal miner who had helped to frame the Social Security Act. The Maryland senator, he said, had "betrayed the New Deal in the past and will again."[88]

Roosevelt helped select the three New Deal candidates— Camp, Johnston, and Lewis. He channeled federal patronage away from their conservative opponents. He sent political aides into the states with advice, speeches, and money. And he spoke directly for the liberal candidates. In the cases of George and Smith he interfered against the advice of Farley and most political advisers. Though his moves did not constitute a well-organized campaign, no American President since Andrew Johnson had taken a more active part in congressional elections. "Roosevelt," Glass prophesied correctly, "will do what he can to beat George and Smith and every other person who has crossed his path. . . ."[89]

The three campaigns were similar in many ways. None of the three conservative candidates dared attack the President directly; all emphasized and overemphasized their loyalty to the New Deal. "I have supported eighty per cent of New Deal measures," bragged Smith.[90] George added that he had backed "most of the major reform measures of the past six years."[91] Yet all three also pointed to their "independence," their dispassionate approach to issues, their freedom from "rubber stampism." Roosevelt, Tydings complained, wants a senator with a "detachable head, which he must leave with his hat in the cloakroom before going on the floor of the Senate. He must cease to think and then do what he is told—nothing else."[92] Above all, they attacked

[88] Baltimore *Sun*, Aug. 17, 1938, p. 1.

[89] To Harry Byrd, July 5, 1938, Glass MSS, Box 383.

[90] Charleston (S.C.) *News and Courier*, Aug. 16, 1938, p. 3.

[91] Richard L. Neuberger, "They Love Roosevelt," *Forum*, CL (Jan. 1939), 11-15, emphasized this preelection tendency of Democrats. George even referred to Roosevelt during his campaign as "that great and good man."

[92] Baltimore *Sun*, Aug. 25, 1938, p. 20.

Roosevelt's intervention in local politics. Terming the President's action a "second march through Georgia," George proudly added, "I am a Georgian, bred and born, a full time Georgian."[93] Smith, conducting his usual campaign of states' rights and white supremacy, closed his campaign by donning a flaming red shirt (in memory of Wade Hampton, a state hero of Reconstruction days), driving to the State Capitol, standing beside Hampton's statue, and making a rousing midnight speech against New Deal Reconstruction.[94] Conservative strategy avoided the liberal-conservative issue as much as possible, seeking to obscure ideology by appeals to state pride or racial prejudice.

The primaries also brought into focus the problems of coalition politics and party realignment. For the first time GOP Chairman Hamilton showed some interest in backing conservative Democrats. Early in July he made a plea in Mobile, Alabama, for Republicans and "Jeffersonian Democrats" to get together. Two days later in Virginia he placed a wreath on Thomas Jefferson's grave and renewed the request.[95] In Georgia James W. Arnold, the Georgia Republican national committeeman, publicly urged Republicans to back George in the primary.[96] In Maryland a few Republican spokesmen talked in a similar vein.[97] Republicans, for the first time outside of Idaho, appeared to be contributing to a unified, bipartisan stand.

Appearances were deceiving; Republican strategy, as usual, was self-seeking. In all cases those who urged coalition were those with nothing to lose. Hamilton knew that no Republican could win in the South and that it cost the party nothing to support men such as George. Republican

---

[93] Augusta *Chronicle*, Aug. 16, 1938, p. 1.
[94] *Time*, Sept. 12, 1938, p. 26.
[95] Augusta *Chronicle*, July 3, 1938, p. 1.
[96] *Ibid.*, Aug. 21, 1938, p. 1.
[97] Baltimore *Sun*, Aug. 18, 1938, p. 20.

leaders in Maryland officially disavowed coalition politics and entered a man of their own in the Republican primary. Conservative Democrats also went out of their way to disassociate themselves from these feeble Republican efforts in their behalf. Glass, furious at Republican refusal to endorse Van Nuys, signed an editorial denouncing Hamilton's visit to Jefferson's grave. Republicans, he said, "showed themselves more interested in Republican political advantage than in fighting, as well as speaking, for Jeffersonian principles."[98] Both George and Tydings refused to encourage those few Republicans who spoke openly for them. And perhaps the most revealing incident of all occurred in Walhalla, South Carolina, where Johnston supporters claimed that Republicans had displayed a banner for Smith outside a local furniture store. The store owner, informed of the charge, was irate. He was no Republican, he insisted; furthermore there were no Republican store owners in South Carolina. The name of the shop: "Nu-Deal Furniture Store."[99] This was fitting testimony to the value of Republican aid for southern political candidates in 1938.

The southern liberal reaction was even more revealing. Roosevelt had assumed that New Dealers and moderates in these states would line up solidly behind him. But they did not. In Georgia Roosevelt had relied upon the moderately liberal Governor Eurith D. Rivers and upon the usually dependable Senator Richard B. Russell. But Rivers maintained the traditional neutrality of Georgia governors and Russell remained aloof.[100] In South Carolina Byrnes refused to take part in the purge, and he contributed money to Tydings' campaign in Maryland.[101] Senator Radcliffe of

---

[98] Lynchburg News, July 6, 1938, p. 6.

[99] Charleston News and Courier, Aug. 29, 1938, p. 1.

[100] See Luther H. Ziegler, Jr., "Senator Walter George's 1938 Campaign," Georgia Historical Quarterly, XLIII (1959), 333-52.

[101] Byrnes, All in One Lifetime, p. 102.

Maryland, Roosevelt's former business associate, not only refused to help his chief but served as Tydings' campaign manager.[102] Like Johnson of Colorado, Herring of Iowa, and Maloney of Connecticut, Byrnes, Radcliffe, and Russell preferred to avoid the turbulent currents of party realignment.

The result was conservative triumph. George ran first in a three-man race, receiving 43.9 percent of the votes, while Camp, the New Deal choice, ran third with 23.9 percent behind the demagogic former Governor Eugene Talmadge. In South Carolina Smith received 55.4 percent of the vote to Johnston's 44.6. And in Maryland Tydings received 58.8 percent to Lewis' 38.5 percent.[103] In part New Deal failure stemmed from the absence of liberal support. In part it resulted from belated, haphazard, and disorganized strategy by the New Dealers.[104] Roosevelt's reliance upon half-measures rather than long-term planning (in New York City, he beat O'Connor partly because aides worked full-time at it) also was at fault.[105] The clever conservative campaigns also hurt the New Deal cause. Most of all, these failures revealed that Roosevelt, though personally popular, could not transfer his popularity to those he supported. In such cases local feelings and fears continued to be the dominant factors. Had he tried to purge in 1934 or 1936, at the height of his magic, it is possible he would have had greater success. But the nature of his failure in 1938 sug-

[102] Baltimore *Sun*, Aug. 29, 1938, p. 1. Also see Clapper Diary, June 12, 1938, Clapper MSS.

[103] Shannon, "Presidential Politics," p. 299.

[104] See Clapper MSS, Box 135, for letter from "R. S." (Ralph Smith) to Clapper. Smith, a friend and observer, wrote as follows: "Camp has no organization, no management, no money, no vision and—apparently no following. Never has a campaign been so bitched up." He added that every major Georgia daily newspaper was for George, that Camp read his speeches, that he discussed issues entirely unrelated to Georgia, and, the crowning blow, that rumors said Camp was part Negro.

[105] For the O'Connor fight, see Edward J. Flynn, *You're the Boss* (New York, 1947), pp. 149-50.

gests that the greatest care would have been insufficient. Party realignment faced too many impenetrable barriers.

The purge of 1938 had at least one noticeable result: it intensified the liberal-conservative split within the Democratic party. "The trend against Roosevelt," Byrd wrote, "is getting stronger every day. Great resentment (in conservative circles) was expressed against his efforts to defeat Democratic Senators and Congressmen who have not always supported the New Deal program. . . ."[106] Glass added, "the Southern people may wake up too late to find that the negrophiles who are running the Democratic Party now will soon precipitate another Reconstruction period for us."[107] Roosevelt and his liberal advisers maintained that the episode was a harmless defeat; after all, they reasoned, there was everything to gain and nothing to lose by trying. But as the 1939 congressional session would reveal, the attempted purge was costly not only in prestige but in legislation. Gillette, George, and Van Nuys would cast adverse votes against neutrality revision in July even though they were by no means isolationists at heart.

The failure of the purge gave heart to conservatives of both parties. Roosevelt-endorsed candidates did win a few contests. Pepper, Hill, Barkley, Caraway, Bulkley, and Thomas all triumphed. Most impressive, O'Connor lost in New York City. But Senators Van Nuys, Clark, McCarran, Adams, and Lonergan won renomination, and Clark defeated Pope in Idaho. Howard Smith won a primary with ease in Virginia, and the liberal Maury Maverick of Texas, whom the President had endorsed on his western swing, lost in a close battle.[108] Most telling, Roosevelt failed to defeat the

106 To Glass, Sept. 13, 1938, Glass MSS, Box 422.

107 To Jack Dionne, Oct. 17, 1938, ibid., Box 383.

108 "New Deal Round Up," Nation, CXLVII (Aug. 13, 1938), 139-40, gave a survey of primaries to that date. See ibid. (Aug. 20, 1938), 165, and (Sept. 17, 1938), 233, for later reports.

men he had tried hardest to unseat: Smith, Tydings, and George. Ten of the twenty-five Democratic Senate candidates with prior voting records on national legislation were from the conservative wing. The lesson to conservatives was obvious: it was possible to defy the President.

The primary season of 1938 was no more productive of party realignment than the campaigns of 1934 and 1936 had been. The roles of moderate Senate Democrats such as Herring, Russell, and Radcliffe painfully illustrated the unwillingness of officeholders to back schemes which might some day rebound on them. And local politicians often preferred to support state leaders rather than the more distant central government in Washington. Farley and other national leaders also viewed the plan with distaste; except for Tydings and O'Connor, Farley played no part in the purge. Only the "100 Per Cent New Dealers" in the executive department showed much enthusiasm for realignment. The lack of unity within the New Deal coalition was again revealed.

The absence of bipartisan cooperation among conservatives was equally striking. Conservative Democrats to a man were determined to work together to stop the purge. But they were loath to associate with Republicans, and even Van Nuys rejected Republican overtures at a time it appeared they might be necessary. Republicans were prepared to give nominal "aid" to conservative Democrats in the South, but there their help cost them nothing. Elsewhere, Republicans sensed possible GOP victory. Why help a conservative Democrat when a Republican might win? Even where Republican victory was unlikely on the state level, local GOP politicians rightly sensed that endorsement of a Democrat, however conservative, would undermine local tickets. On both sides party solidarity ruled the day, as indeed it has in almost every election under the American two-party system.

Roosevelt damaged his prestige with his rather impulsive attempt to purge. He ended by stiffening conservative Democratic resistance, and, as the elections would indicate, by further eroding his magic at the polls in November. But the interesting thing about the attempt was not only his failure but the potency of the two-party system. If the congressional battles of 1937 revealed the unreliability of the liberal coalition, the primaries of 1938 exposed the equally divisive chasms among conservatives. Party realignment failed to materialize.[109]

[109] James M. Burns, *Deadlock of Democracy: Four-Party Politics in America* (Englewood Cliffs, N. J., 1963), pp. 151-76, argues that Roosevelt had an excellent chance to realign parties during his first two terms but failed for lack of an ideological commitment for realignment. The President, he maintains, was a "broker" leader, relying upon charm and compromise to keep order in Congress rather than developing a strong liberal party. With this latter view I agree; Roosevelt did not seriously attempt to create a liberal party—the halfway aspect of the purge was the best example. Yet I strongly disagree that he would have succeeded had he tried. As the foregoing chapter indicates, the purely organizational side of politics was too strong for sudden change from the top. See also Arthur N. Holcombe, *The Middle Classes in American Politics* (Cambridge, Mass., 1940), p. 117, for a contemporary account pessimistic about chances for party realignment.

9

ZENITH OF COALITION, 1939

THE NOVEMBER elections proved what failure of the purge had already suggested: the electoral appeal of the administration had declined.[1] Republicans, apparently moribund in 1937, scored stunning gains throughout the nation. Roosevelt's personal popularity, according to all indications, remained strong, but voters did not have the same faith in his party.

The New Deal took its most painful beating in congressional elections.[2] Lonergan was the only conservative Democrat to lose; the others returned to plague Roosevelt, more hostile as a result of the campaign. The other Democratic irreconcilables also returned. "All political thinking up here," Bailey explained,

is addressed to the outcome in 1940. Probably the salvation of this country will depend upon the election in that year. If we can elect a sound, strong, and courageous President all will be well, but another Roosevelt would destroy us. He just does not know how to run the Presidency. His farm plans have utterly failed and his labor plans have had the dominion of bosses who are far more concerned to collect dues and to acquire political power than they are to help the working people. His general policy has been to create a universal dependence upon Washington and to extinguish State pride and State self-reliance.[3]

Roosevelt still had sixty-nine Democrats in the Senate. But at least twenty, and often as many as thirty, would be cool or downright hostile to any extensions of the New Deal.

A more significant shift in the Senate was the addition of eight new Republicans, six of whom replaced liberal or reliable administration Democrats. The President faced a Senate that included twenty-three Republicans and at least as many anti-New Deal Democrats.[4] The upper house promised to split down the middle on controversial legislation.

The situation in the House looked equally unpromising for the administration. Most of the seventy Democrats who had lost came from the industrial sections of the East and Midwest, and many of these men were liberals who had

[1] See Roosevelt MSS, OF 300, Boxes 104-106, for interpretations of the election expressed by Democratic state leaders to Farley.

[2] "The Republican Party; Up from the Grave," *Fortune*, XX (Aug. 1939), 33-36; Harry W. Morris, "The Republicans in a Minority Role, 1933-1938" (unpublished Ph.D. dissertation, State University of Iowa, 1960), pp. 281-82; and Milton Plesur, "The Republican Comeback of 1938," *Review of Politics*, XXIV (Oct. 1962), 525-62.

[3] To Carl Goerch, Jan. 23, 1939, Bailey MSS, Political File.

[4] Bailey gave his interpretation of the line-up to Walter Lippmann: "when the President lost out in the Purge and suffered further losses in the primaries and in the election, the balance of power in the Senate shifted to the moderate Democrats, and it appears to me that these moderates not only have the balance of power now but will have it in the first two years of the next Administration. If so, we shall go on as we have been going, that is, we will cooperate with the President whenever possible but we will resist radical measures. The Republicans have twenty-one votes and the moderates have twenty-eight, and there are at least ten who swing back and forth with the tendency to vote with the moderates." March 2, 1939, Bailey MSS, Political File.

assumed office during the 1934 and 1936 Democratic land-slides. In 1938 Republicans swept many of them into political oblivion, leaving conservative Democrats relatively untouched.[5] Of the 260 returning Democrats, at least 30 were largely or wholly disenchanted with the New Deal and 50 more were not at all enthusiastic.

The most important change was the huge Republican gain in the House. Republicans almost doubled their strength, increasing from 89 to 169. Except for Snell, who retired after the 1938 session, the hard core of eastern rural veterans such as Wadsworth and Taber returned more eager than ever to assault the New Deal. In the House Roosevelt's prospects were dim indeed: it would require only fifty Democratic rebels to defeat the administration, whereas discharge petitions, so useful to the administration in past sessions, would be all but unattainable. As one Republican congressman accurately predicted, "by working with conservative Democrats, the Republicans will be able to stop any of the more radical legislative bills."[6]

The Rules Committee was also largely unchanged. O'Connor did not return, nor did Driver of Arkansas, one of the five southern conservatives. But two New Deal committeemen also failed to return. Before the session even started, the fourteen-man committee was assured of a conservative majority: Cox, Smith, Dies, Clark of North Carolina, and four Republicans. Furthermore, the new chairman, Adolph J. Sabath of Illinois, would prove ineffectual in the session to come. Somewhat infirm, Sabath was a Jewish-Bohemian immigrant who spoke with a heavy accent. Though a valued spokesman for immigrant causes and a trustworthy New Dealer, he was often mimicked and easily ignored. His job

[5] Of the eighty new Republican seats, forty-five were gained in the Midwest, twenty-seven in the Northeast.

[6] Clifford Hope (Kan.) to Nettie Barrett, Dec. 14, 1938, Hope MSS, Legislative Correspondence, 1938-1939.

as chairman would be to preside but in no sense to rule. Cox, the ranking Democrat, would do that.[7]

Roosevelt's prospects were not bright. It was true that he could still point to impressive personal popularity documented by poll after poll and that many conservatives (including some new Republicans elected in 1938) had by then accepted the outlines of the New Deal. It was also true that as President he retained the initiative.[8] Moreover, as Roosevelt said at the time, "the idea is slowly sinking into the heads of people like Tydings and George and Bennett Clark that even if they control the 1940 convention, they cannot elect their own ticket without the support of this Administration—and I am sufficiently honest to decline to support any conservative Democrat."[9] Despite these balancing factors, his congressional margin was slim, his prospects dim. At a press conference following the election a reporter asked the President:

"Will you not encounter coalition opposition?"

"No, I don't think so."

"I do."—laughter.[10]

The key figure in the days before the new Congress was Garner. Abbreviating a vacation, he returned to Washington two weeks before the start of the session, and advised Roosevelt to accept the election as a popular mandate for moderation.[11] He also emphasized the need for legislation

[7] See the portrait of Sabath by John B. Reed, in J. T. Salter (ed.), *Public Men In and Out of Office* (Chapel Hill, N.C., 1946), pp. 196-209; and Marquis W. Childs, *I Write from Washington* (New York, 1942), p. 104.

[8] For an excellent study of Roosevelt's chances with the 1939 Congress see Ernest K. Lindley, "The New Congress," *Current History*, XLVIII (Feb. 1939), 15-17.

[9] To Josephus Daniels, quoted in Rexford G. Tugwell, *The Democratic Roosevelt* (Garden City, N.Y., 1957), p. 476.

[10] James M. Burns, *Roosevelt: The Lion and the Fox* (New York, 1956), p. 366.

[11] See Bascom N. Timmons, *Garner of Texas* (New York, 1948), pp. 240-42.

that would encourage the business community. "You've got to decide whether you're gonna get on or get off," he was reported as saying to his chief. "Have the baby or let it go."[12]

After this conference Garner, as always, said little for publication. But observers speculated accurately that Roosevelt had named him as an intermediary between congressmen and executive assistants, and for the next two weeks congressmen and high government officials paraded in and out of his office. Besides congressional leaders, his callers included Morgenthau, Wallace, Mayor Fiorello La Guardia of New York, and Hopkins—all eager for his help. One commentator considered Garner a modern-day Calhoun, a vice-president working openly with and covertly against his chief.[13] This was an exaggeration of Garner's role, but it nonetheless indicated the degree to which the conservative wing of the party assumed a key role before Congress even convened.

These conferences produced a rough agreement before the session started. Harrison withdrew his name from consideration as majority leader and the opening Democratic Senate caucus was "just like little birds in a love nest."[14] Roosevelt also made minor concessions. He would not, he intimated, insist upon executive draftsmanship. He would avoid the term "must" legislation. And he agreed to confer with his legislative leaders more often, reserving time each Monday morning for this purpose. It looked as if Roosevelt was anxious to develop harmonious relations with his Congress.[15]

[12] *Time,* March 20, 1939, p. 12.

[13] Joseph Alsop and Robert Kintner, Washington *Star,* Jan. 6, 1939, A-9.

[14] New York *Herald Tribune,* Jan. 1, 1939, p. 1. The statement was from Senator Robert R. Reynolds of North Carolina.

[15] Paul T. David has remarked that the practice of weekly meetings with top congressional aides began on Nov. 15, 1937. I have found no evidence, however, to suggest that these were either regular or important in 1938.

It was a short-lived and uneasy truce. On the first day of the session the Sheppard Committee, investigating WPA participation in the 1938 campaigns, reported evidence of "unjustifiable political activity in connection with the work of the WPA in several states." It also urged legislation prohibiting relief administrators from coercing voters.[16] Coming from Sheppard, a loyal administration man, this was an unwelcome report. Furthermore, the Dies Un-American Activities Committee the same day published a report containing sharp criticisms of Secretary of Labor Perkins and asking $150,000 to continue its work.[17]

For his part, Roosevelt had no intention of letting Congress assume the initiative. In his budget message he asked for a relief appropriation which infuriated conservatives of both parties. He also passed the word to legislative leaders to prune Dies's requested appropriation. And in a Jackson Day speech on January 7 he made a plea for party unity but then added that those who opposed him might do well to leave the party altogether.[18] As two columnists observed, Roosevelt during the purge had used "eye-gouging, toe-twisting, body-slamming" tactics; in 1939 he had simply shifted to the "more delicately murderous tactics of jiu-jitsu."[19] No other congressional session during the New Deal began in so ominous an atmosphere.

Events of the coming months justified this gloomy outlook. Groups and coalitions formed one day to combat the New Deal and realigned the next to help it. But the long

See David, "The Changing Political Parties," in Marian D. Irish (ed.), *Continuing Crisis in American Politics* (Englewood Cliffs, N. J., 1963), p. 55.

[16] New York *Times*, Jan. 4, 1939, p. 1. David I. Walsh of Mass., another committee member, wrote, "What a spectacle these reformers in the administration present in their alignment with the polution [sic] of the ballot box." To Father Talbot, Dec. 2, 1938, Walsh MSS.

[17] New York *Times*, Jan. 4, 1939, p. 10.

[18] *Ibid.*, Jan. 8, 1939, p. 1.

[19] Alsop and Kintner, Washington *Star*, Jan. 11, 1939, A-11.

session becomes intelligible if seen in four chronological periods:

1. January: Relief, the Initial Test.
2. February-June: A Period of Delay.
3. June Days: Shifting Coalitions.
4. July: The Conservative Revolt.

1

Conservative congressmen returned to Washington convinced that relief spending was excessive, and Roosevelt's budget message touched off the first battle. The total budget asked for some $9 billion, the second highest budget of the New Deal to date, and it frankly predicted a $3.9 billion deficit for the current fiscal year.[20] Because some $2 billion of the budget was destined for relatively noncontroversial defense measures, few congressmen were critical of the total figure. But Roosevelt also called for a deficiency appropriation of $875 million to help the WPA through the 1939 fiscal year. To some, notably the CIO and the Workers' Alliance, this was a conservative request. Moderate congressmen also realized that some money must be appropriated, since the relief fund approved as a part of the 1938 pump-priming plan provided money only through March 1. But for congressional economizers the additional $875 million was too much. Moreover, Roosevelt's message again asked for a lump sum to be distributed at WPA discretion.

Anti-administration forces began their assault in the House. Woodrum's subcommittee sliced $150 million from the request. It also added the usual Woodrum amendment allocating the money on a month-by-month basis. Before

[20] Samuel Rosenman (ed.), *The Public Papers and Addresses of Franklin D. Roosevelt,* VIII (New York, 1941), 36-53.

pressure groups could mobilize, the full House passed the bill for $725 million. The final vote had only 16 opposed, including Cox, Smith, and ten Republicans.[21] As Hope of Kansas commented at the time, "the atmosphere here in congress is certainly much different than it has been anytime since the present administration came into power. I don't know how far congress will go in cutting expenditures this year . . . but I do feel that if congress continues in its present mood that there will be some substantial cuts made."[22]

The bill then moved to Adams' Senate subcommittee. Adams, by then safely entrenched for six years, no longer exercised the restraint he had during the pump-priming controversy. Aided by Byrnes, he succeeded in having the subcommittee approve the House version, and he refused to change his mind even after Roosevelt called him to the White House, pointed to the snowy landscape, and asked how he could turn more than a million workers into the cold. Byrnes and Adams finally relented slightly by providing that no more than 5 percent of the cuts in relief rolls be made before April 1 and by approving another amendment specifically encouraging Roosevelt to ask for more funds if the need arose. Shortly thereafter the full committee approved the subcommittee version and on January 24, less than three weeks after Roosevelt's message, debate opened on the Senate floor.[23]

Frenetic maneuvering then began behind the scenes. Led by Garner, Harrison, and McNary, a bipartisan band of conservatives circulated cloakrooms promising rewards in return for support. Administration forces did likewise: Scott Lucas of Illinois, for instance, heard from the Chicago

[21] *Congressional Record*, 76th Cong., 1st Sess., 343.

[22] Hope to Warren Zimmerman, Jan. 20, 1939, Hope MSS, Legislative Correspondence, 1938-1939, Gen.

[23] Robert S. Allen, "WPA—or the Dole," *Nation*, CXLVIII (Jan. 28, 1939), 111-12, suggested Harrison originated this compromise.

machine, much as Dieterich had in the past.[24] Barkley, leading the administration forces, finally sanctioned a vote on January 27.

It was a shocker for Barkley and his men. In a dramatic roll-call vote, an amendment to restore the $150 million failed, 47-46. The anti-administration forces included the eight Democrats whom Roosevelt had thought of purging in 1938, all the other irreconcilable Democrats, Lucas of Illinois, Farmer-Laborite Shipstead, and twenty of the twenty-three Republicans. Many moderates joined the economy bloc partly because of the loopholes in the Byrnes-Adams version: if hardship resulted by April, they reasoned, Roosevelt could always ask for more.[25]

Shortly thereafter the Senate passed the committee version, and a conference committee did likewise. The final bill cut $150 million from the administration request and included both the provision against substantial reductions before April 1 and the amendment urging Roosevelt to ask for more if he believed it necessary. The struggle was over almost as quickly as it had begun, and Roosevelt's opponents exulted at their strength. "Things are looking a lot better around Washington for Republicans," Capper wrote. "I think we will be able to make some 'medicine' for the next campaign."[26]

In some ways the controversy, like many others of the decade, had little substance. The Senate amendments softened the effect of the cuts, and Roosevelt would ask for more before hardship resulted. Moreover, most opponents of the administration in both houses realized that a potential saving of $150 million was nothing compared to the national

[24] For McNary's role, see Walter K. Roberts, "The Political Career of Charles Linza McNary, 1924-1944" (unpublished Ph.D. dissertation, University of North Carolina, 1953), p. 257.

[25] For the vote, see *Congressional Record*, 76th Cong., 1st Sess., 887.

[26] To Alfred M. Landon, Jan. 25, 1939, Landon MSS, Washington, D. C. File, 1939.

debt. Finally, many senators were not so worried about the alleged political machinations of the WPA as they seemed. Byrnes took a poll of senators elected in 1938 and discovered that most of them considered the WPA a liability for office-seekers who supported it.

A more substantial argument, common to rural congress-men, was the view that heavy relief spending benefited urban areas at the expense of agricultural states and that the WPA swallowed up available cheap farm labor. Both argu-ments were of questionable validity. The amount of money received by most agricultural areas in federal farm benefits during the New Deal more than compensated for the low tax outlays which those areas expended, and many large farmers, far from needing a large labor force, were dis-charging laborers and tenants in favor of mechanized farm-ing. But valid or not, these feelings were important. Except for Republicans, the only senators from the most urban states who backed the reduction in relief were Lucas and Van Nuys. This urban-rural division was equally clear in the House. In both houses a rural coalition had developed.

Though it seemed that a monolithic conservative coali-tion had formed, appearances were a little misleading. It was true that McNary worked carefully with Democratic colleagues before the vote, and that Republicans and con-servative Democrats functioned as a team throughout the brief struggle. But like the conservative congressional align-ments of 1937-1938, this one was primarily a coalition of defensive convenience. It arose to meet a specific need and it vanished as soon as the need disappeared. Though its members included the usual hard core of irreconcilables, it was not the same as those of prior and subsequent battles. It lacked the backing of Maloney, Walsh, and Donahey, men who would join conservatives on many future occasions. But it included Truman and John Bankhead of Alabama. The issue revealed a substantial conservative trend in the Senate, and it exposed a working bipartisan bloc, but it no more marked the formation of a coherent or permanent conservative coalition than had the struggles over reorganization, labor standards, or taxes.

The relief controversy was nevertheless significant. It revealed widespread hostility to heavy relief spending, and it demonstrated the existence of a more determined economy bloc than ever before. It also showed the continuing rural-urban divisions in the nation, and it proved that a working bipartisan bloc could overcome the administration. All these factors were to recur later in the session. The rebels, by winning, served notice that the coming Congress could be obstreperous, independent, and largely impervious to administration pressure.

2

No single controversy emerged to give shape to the delaying period which followed and lasted until June. Rather, there occurred a series of minor skirmishes, shifting coalitions, and short-lived victories by conservatives as well as New Dealers. Despite the confusion, a few trends of importance developed during this time.

In the first place, neither Roosevelt nor congressional conservatives tried consistently to seek a truce. In the midst of the relief struggle Roosevelt continued to insist, over the objections of Byrd and Glass, upon the appointment of Floyd Roberts to a Virginia judgeship.[27] "I reserve the right," he had written Glass earlier, "to get the opinions of anybody else I may select—Governor Price [of Virginia] or Herbert Hoover, your old friend who makes moonshine in the Blue Ridge, or Father Coughlin, Nancy Astor, or the Duke of Windsor."[28] In retaliation Glass had worked diligently

[27] Rixey Smith and Norman Beasley, *Carter Glass: A Biography* (New York, 1939), pp. 396-99.

[28] March 21, 1938, Glass MSS, Box 6. This box and Box 268 give a fascinating picture of the episode.

throughout the summer of 1938 to obtain conservative support on the Judiciary Committee. Early in February the Virginia senators succeeded. Standing behind the tradition of senatorial courtesy, the Senate refused Roberts' appointment in an overwhelming 72-9 vote.[29]

This nomination was not the only appointment to arouse controversy. Indeed, the early months of 1939 witnessed a series of presidential nominations of New Dealers to high office. The President chose Hopkins as secretary of commerce, Frank Murphy as attorney general, Felix Frankfurter as a Supreme Court justice, Pope of Idaho as a TVA director, and Thomas R. Amlie, a former Progressive congressman from Wisconsin, for a position on the ICC.

None of these appointments pleased conservatives. "The President," Bailey wrote, "appointed Mr. Hopkins, Mr. Murphy and Mr. Frankfurter, each of them stamped with the radical stamp. This was depressing. Sometimes, I think this Administration is willing to do anything on earth except to encourage business and industry."[30] But they were willing to give the President a free hand in naming his own associates. Amlie's name later had to be withdrawn, but Murphy and Frankfurter sailed through with minor difficulty, as did Hopkins a little later. All except Amlie were confirmed by February. "Perhaps it is best not to beat the President's nominees," Bailey explained. "We must not waste our energy by fighting out issues on the smaller matters, nor should we do anything to take from the President the responsibility for the consequences of his six years. . . . So, if we appear to be yielding, just remember, we are 'stooping to conquer.' "[31]

A new struggle over executive reorganization was a more important source of executive-congressional hostility. After House recommittal of the bill in 1938, congressional leaders

[29] New York *Times*, Feb. 7, 1939, p. 1.
[30] To Carl Goerch, Jan. 23, 1939, Bailey MSS, Political File.
[31] To George Rountree, Jan. 23, 1939, *ibid*.

drafted a new plan which moved to the floor of both houses in March. Much milder than the original bill of January 1937, it exempted from reorganization almost all the independent regulatory agencies. It deleted the proposed changes in the Civil Service Commission and the comptroller general's office. And it sought to avoid the "dictator" issue by changing the method of putting plans into effect. The new bill simply empowered the President to propose specific plans, not executive orders. These plans would not go into effect until sixty days after their submission to Congress and could be vetoed by simple concurrent resolution of both houses within sixty days.[32]

This bill began its course in the House early in March. As in the past, House Republicans denounced it, refusing even to attend committee meetings.[33] But most House Democrats were anxious to avoid a clash over the matter.[34] A hostile amendment sponsored by Sumners lost, 209-193, and the administration version, largely unchanged, passed the full House, 246-153. It looked as if it would have little difficulty in the Senate.

Once again, however, the conservative forces which had combined in 1938 joined hands in battle. As he had done the year before, Wheeler proposed an amendment that would have required both houses to approve reorganization plans within sixty days, approval which a filibuster could

[32] Louis Brownlow, *A Passion for Anonymity* (Chicago, 1958), pp. 413-14. See Brownlow to FDR, Nov. 2, 1938, Roosevelt MSS, OF 285-C, Box 16, for Brownlow's suggestions along these lines.

[33] New York *Times*, March 3, 1939, p. 14.

[34] See memo by McIntyre to FDR, Jan. 11, 1939, concerning Senator Andrews of Florida, whom McIntyre quotes as saying, "as you know I was caught in a jam last time [on the 1938 vote]." See also letter from Knute Hill (Dem.–Wash.) to Pat Drewry (Dem.–Va.): "The Democratic members of the House should follow the leadership of the President in such vital matters as the reorganization bill. To continue to compromise with the Republican minority as some of you do will bring utter defeat to the Democratic Party in 1940." March 13, 1939. Both quotes in Roosevelt MSS, OF 285-C, Box 8.

presumably prevent. McNary kept his Republican band quiet but ready to deliver an almost solid bloc of votes. And Byrd and his conservative Democratic allies were prepared to join them.

Wheeler's coalition temporarily succeeded. On a dramatic vote on March 22 his amendment carried, 45-44, as twenty-one Democrats, twenty-two Republicans, and the two Farmer-Laborites opposed the administration. Except for Gillette, the Democrats whom Roosevelt had considered purging in 1938 were among the forty-five. So were Clark of Idaho and other unreliables such as Maloney and Donahey.[35]

Byrnes refused to accept defeat and rose immediately to offer a motion to reconsider. A parliamentary wrangle followed, but in a short time Byrnes's forces succeeded when Borah, as usual, opposed any move to stifle debate.[36] Byrnes thus had an additional day to round up support.

It was enough. That night Truman, who had been home in Missouri, flew to the Capital to join supporters of the bill. Dennis Chavez of New Mexico switched his position, explaining that he had voted with Wheeler the day before because he had not realized that an amendment protected the Forest Service from reorganization. Perhaps this was Chavez' reason, or perhaps it was administration promises: he was, sneered Ickes, "that kind of statesman."[37] Truman's addition and Chavez' conversion gave Byrnes's forces the margin, and they succeeded on a new vote, 46-44. The bill then passed 63-23, with only three Democrats—Tydings, Gerry and King—opposing it. Shortly thereafter Roosevelt proposed his first reorganization plan creating an Executive

[35] For vote, see *Congressional Record*, 76th Cong., 1st Sess., 3093.

[36] New York *Times*, March 22, 1939, p. 1. Borah's shift of course destroyed the one-vote conservative margin, thus permitting Byrnes's motion to carry. It was typical of Borah's devotion to "principle," regardless of results.

[37] Harold Ickes, *The Secret Diary of Harold Ickes* (3 vols.; New York, 1954), II, 603, March 25, 1939.

Department, moving the Budget Bureau to the White House, and combining a host of agencies under the general headings of loans, works, and security. A little later, he submitted a second plan. Neither scheme encountered effective congressional opposition. The reorganization issue, so emotional in 1938, faded quietly into the background.

The skirmish had been revealing. The Senate vote on the Wheeler amendment, like the alignment on the Sumners amendment in the House, indicated that reorganization was not a sectional controversy: aside from Bailey, Glass, Byrd, George, and Smith, all southern senators supported reorganization. It also indicated once again the shifting nature of the conservative bloc. Though Wheeler's proposal attracted forty-five senators, they were by no means the same as the forty-seven who had voted to cut relief funds two months earlier. Republicans opposed the administration on both issues. But eleven Democrats, including Byrnes and Harrison, who had opposed the administration over relief spending, backed it on reorganization. Seven who had backed the administration on relief deserted over reorganization. A conservative nucleus of twenty-one Republicans and fifteen Democrats opposed or were paired against the administration on both bills. The others showed they would shift in and out as they pleased.

A third source of executive-congressional hostility in this period was, once again, relief. Only two weeks after the Senate vote on relief in January, Roosevelt asked Congress to restore the $150 million it had so recently deleted. Unless Congress voted the amount, he said, there would be an emergency.[38] Neither house was disposed to relent. The President, one Republican sneered, had discovered "emergencies" or "crises" thirty-nine times in the past six years—

[38] New York *Times,* Feb. 8, 1939, p. 1. Roosevelt was angry at the cut. "Do you notice I'm whistling?" he told Ickes. "I always whistle when I'm mad." Ickes, *Secret Diary,* II, 570, Jan. 29, 1939.

or once every eight weeks. "Is it any wonder," he asked, "that the people are emotionally exhausted?"[39] Others went further. Led by Cox and Woodrum, a movement to investigate the WPA grew rapidly, and in mid-March Cox introduced a motion to do so.

House conservatives, still impressed with the need for economy, stalled, and Appropriations Committee Chairman Taylor finally had to assume leadership of the bill to keep it from Woodrum's hands. It was no use. On March 27 the House approved the WPA investigation by the overwhelming vote of 352-27; Woodrum became its chairman and soon publicized a series of disclosures harmful to the agency.[40] The next day urban Democrats helped defeat, 204-191, a farm subsidy dear to the hearts of rural congressmen.[41] The rural-dominated Appropriations Committee, enraged, then overrode Chairman Taylor and slashed Roosevelt's request to $100 million. On March 31 this amount passed the full House with ease, 290-110.[42] For the second time in two months the House had defied the President over relief spending.

Senate conservatives were equally determined. The Appropriations Committee, led again by Adams and Byrnes, unanimously endorsed the House bill a few days later. Sobered by this action, Barkley called a Democratic meeting

[39] *Time*, March 27, 1939, pp. 13-14.

[40] New York *Times*, March 28, 1939, p. 1.

[41] *Ibid.*, March 29, 1939, p. 1. The horse-trading on this occasion was similar to the urban-rural dealings in the 1937 special session over the farm and labor standards bills. Openly, Sabath proclaimed, "If men from the farm states want our help on parity payments they should help us get the $150 million for relief." Another urban Democrat added, "We don't even have so much as a flower pot in our district. We would like to go along with the farmers, but we would like to have some assurance that if we do we will get real consideration from the Appropriations Committee on the Relief Bill." Both quoted in *ibid.*, March 25, 1939, p. 1.

[42] *Ibid.*, April 1, 1939. For the bill were 218 Democrats and 68 Republicans; against it were 21 Democrats and 89 Republicans.

to advise his colleagues to accept the cut. But Barkley lacked Robinson's influence. The real power still lay with Byrnes, Harrison, and Adams, to whom Barkley seemed a White House sycophant. As a result, the meeting, like many he would call that session, was turbulent. Moderates and conservatives failed to appear at all, and the handful of liberals who arrived bridled at the idea of deserting the President.[43] The meeting dissolved in chaos, with Pepper, the most fiery New Dealer in the Senate, threatening to lead a floor fight for the full $150-million request.

Pepper made good his threat. Producing a letter from the President emphasizing the need for $150 million, he mobilized his troops in a revolt—in much the same way that Barkley himself had led administration forces against Robinson's relief plan two years earlier. Barkley, surprised by the letter and angry at Roosevelt's stubborn attitude, refused to budge. "My daily prayer," he said, "is not, 'Lord, show me a fight so I can get into it,' nor is it, 'Lord, show me a spot so I can put a Democrat on it.' "[44] It was a strange situation: Roosevelt and the New Dealers allied against regular Democrats such as Barkley, conservative Democrats, and silent, smiling Republicans.

Roosevelt lost decisively. Thirty-one Democrats, including such regulars as Barkley and Truman, joined eighteen Republicans to smash Pepper's forces, 49-28. Twenty-six Democrats and a lone Republican, John A. Danaher of Connecticut, backed Pepper.[45] The vote showed the change in the Senate since 1937. At that time Roosevelt had been able to defeat, 49-34, Robinson's amendment requiring local contributions of 25 percent. In 1939, his forces split down the middle. The relief issue in the Senate revealed again the

[43] "There was no one to crack the whip," La Follette complained about Barkley. Ickes, *Secret Diary*, II, 612, April 6, 1939.

[44] New York *Herald Tribune*, April 12, 1939, p. 1.

[45] New York *Times*, April 12, 1939, p. 1.

stubborn way in which Congress was coming to defy the President.

While these controversies over appointments, reorganization, and relief were evolving, both sides were making tentative gestures to institute better relations. Roosevelt began by changing his chief congressional aides. Instead of sending to the Hill men such as his son Jimmy ("Father would like it done this way"), Roosevelt gradually became dependent upon the easy-going Colonel Edwin M. ("Pa") Watson and Press Secretary Stephen Early.[46] Roosevelt and Hopkins also made vaguely reassuring remarks to businessmen, especially during February and March. Meanwhile, conservative Democratic congressmen sought to avoid needless quarrels. Bailey expressed this sentiment. Roosevelt, he said, "is at the end of his row and Congress is in control. It is important, of course, that the Congress shall not exercise this control in any arbitrary or willful way, but shall be reasonable and constructive."[47]

But these were just gestures. Conservatives talked of investigating not only the WPA but the NLRB, while others threatened to amend the Fair Labor Standards and the Social Security acts. And Roosevelt, for his part, still refused to scuttle his program, and by April he was again suggesting that conservative Democrats leave the party.[48] The period of delay witnessed growing hostility between Roosevelt and his Congress.

A second general trend of this period was Republican resurgence. In the Senate, McNary's band, though main-

[46] Alsop and Kintner, Washington *Star*, March 27, 1939, A-11.

[47] To Dr. J. M. Ruffin, Feb. 6, 1939, Bailey MSS, Personal File.

[48] This kind of talk really upset Bailey. "Am I to gather from the President's statements," he wrote Farley, "that he will not support the ticket if one whom he considers to be a conservative shall be nominated? . . . I am extremely loyal to the President's program of 1932, but he has taken certain courses since which I could not follow. Does this throw me out?" To Farley, May 1, 1939, *ibid.*, Political File.

taining a discreetly subdued posture, was as strong numerically as the bloc of conservative Democrats. Encouraged by
their return to life in the 1938 election, eager to carry their
comeback into 1940, Senate Republicans were more effective
than they had been any time since the New Deal began.

In the House the increase in Republican effectiveness
was truly remarkable, thanks in large part to the new Republican leader, Joseph W. Martin, Jr., of Massachusetts. Fifty-
four years old in 1939, Martin was a chunky, somewhat
homely bachelor who had been a representative since 1925
and Snell's assistant since 1933.[49] His Republican colleagues,
recognizing his talents, found no difficulty in choosing him
minority leader in 1939.

They could not have chosen a shrewder politician. Born
into a poor family, Martin had great respect for industry,
thrift, and hard work. "Never go in debt," he remembered
his mother saying. "I never had a charge account," he was
to brag at the age of seventy-five.[50] He held down a paper
delivery route as a boy, subsequently became a reporter, and
eventually saved enough to buy the paper. No liberal, he
ran Senator Henry Cabot Lodge's 1922 campaign, and in old
age was to say of the New Deal, "Many of the experiments
of the New Deal seemed to us to undermine and destroy
this society."[51]

This was the man who assumed the task of combating
the New Deal in the House in 1939. In earlier years it had
not been an enviable job, which in part explained Snell's
willingness to retire.[52] But Martin had three advantages over
Snell. First, he had 169 men behind him. Second, 80 of

[49] See *Current Biography*, 1940, pp. 563-65, and *ibid.*, 1948, p. 425.

[50] See Joseph Martin (as told to Robert J. Donovan), *My First Fifty Years
in Politics* (New York, 1960), p. 29.

[51] *Ibid.*, p. 66. For a sample of Martin's program in 1938 see New York
Times, June 17, 1938, p. 1.

[52] His main reason for retiring, he said, was because he was "tired,
worried about health and money." New York *Times*, July 11, 1938, p. 14.

these were freshmen: by and large, they would do what they were told. And third, the election had cheered his men. For the first time, it seemed not only forthright to oppose the New Deal, but safe as well.

To these ready-made advantages Martin added some of his own. He tried to accommodate those colleagues who desired a chance to speak, at the same time urging them not to hurl epithets that would alienate conservative Democrats. Congresswoman Edith N. Rogers of Massachusetts, for instance, was detailed to restrain the bellicose Hamilton Fish of New York.[53] Martin made it Republican practice to enter debate only after research into certain selected issues, rather than pitching headlong into every bill on the floor. In this research effort Hamilton and the National Committee were helpful, sponsoring a series of weekend seminars in and around the Capital. Martin also established an efficient whip system to make sure that Republicans would be on the floor for important roll calls; early in the session this system was so effective that Republicans won a series of roll-call votes.

Martin's most remarkable feat was in helping persuade his colleagues to follow McNary's strategy of silence on key issues. "The best way to combat the New Dealers," he wrote later, "was to put willing Democrats up to making the moves and delivering the speeches while we waited in silence to hand them our 169 votes on the roll call. We won a number of victories by this device, proving that wavering Democrats would often support a measure by one of their own party whereas they would balk if it was sponsored by a Republican." Getting Democrats to talk was easy. Martin used his old associates on the Rules Committee, Smith and above all Cox, whom he called the "real leader of southerners in the House." "He and I," Martin admitted later, "were the principal points of contact between the Northern Republicans

[53] *Ibid.*, Feb. 12, 1939, p. 1.

and the Southern Democratic conservatives."[54] Blatant Republican partisanship, the chief obstacle to House coalition, was reduced to a manageable level. Of all the developments of the 1939 session, the Republican resurgence and the Martin-Cox alliance were perhaps the most significant, and it was during this period of delay that they began to operate with telling effect.

Both of these trends of the period, congressional-executive hostility and Republican resurgence, contributed to a generally favorable score card for conservatives at the time. But a third general trend again exposed the inconsistency and partisanship that had plagued congressional conservatives since the beginning of the New Deal.

The conservative tendency to sacrifice consistency for political advantage was especially apparent in maneuvering over the farm bill. As part of his budget Roosevelt had requested an $840-million outlay to provide for farm program expenses in fiscal 1940. The House in late March finally passed a bill incorporating this request, but the Senate was less dependable. The Appropriations Committee which included Glass, Byrnes, and Adams overwhelmingly approved a bill calling for a total of $1.218 billion, or nearly $400 million more than the version passed by the House. Most of this increase involved an extra $225 million in parity payments and $113 million to allow the secretary of agriculture to purchase surplus commodities. To this time Senate economizers had succeeded in slicing some $70 million from budget figures; if passed, this bill would have demolished these savings five times over.

And so it did. "It is impossible to resist," admitted Bailey, "as we approach political campaigns, demands for great sums to be given to the farmers. The Republicans consider that if they get in the way of these appropriations, they may lose the farm vote. The Democrats know that their party will

54 Martin, *My First Fifty Years,* pp. 84-85.

lose it. Very probably the only way out is for the country
to have a very bad experience."[55] Bailey was not the only
one to succumb. A few days later the measure passed the
Senate, 61-14, in a form providing the full $1.218 billion
asked by the committee, and in June representatives switched
to back the Senate version.[56] The final bill appropriated a
total of $1.194 billion, $350 million more than the administration request.

As Bailey had remarked, the farm lobby was simply too
great to withstand.[57] Significantly, only four Senate Democrats voted or paired against the increase, Burke, Holt,
Gerry, and Walsh, the latter three from states where the
farm subsidy had little appeal. Where farm appropriations
were concerned, fiscal conservatism in Congress disappeared.

A second example of the stresses within the conservative
congressional bloc occurred a few weeks later. In the 1938
campaign many Republicans had made reckless promises,
arguing for the old-age pension scheme of Dr. Francis E.
Townsend, a genial, elderly Californian who had first attracted wide support in 1934 for a federal program promising
to pay those over sixty years of age $200 per month. Most

[55] To Samuel B. Pettengill, May 27, 1939, Bailey MSS, Political File.

[56] Hope of Kansas, a knowledgeable congressman on farm issues, indicated why moderates and conservatives found farm subsidies hard to resist
at this time. "Whatever may be said for or against farm subsidies," he
wrote, "my judgment is that as long as we follow the present policy of
spending for everything that comes along and passing legislation to enable
labor and industry to increase the price of things the farmer has to buy, we
are going to have to continue farm subsidies, probably in an increased
amount." To Don F. Berry, May 16, 1939, Hope MSS, Official Correspondence, 1939, A-B.

[57] For the role of the Farm Bureau Federation in this battle, see
Christiana McF. Campbell, *The Farm Bureau and the New Deal: A Study
in the Making of National Farm Policy, 1933-1940* (Urbana, Ill., 1962),
pp. 116-19. See also Edward O'Neal (President of the Farm Bureau), Oral
History Project, Columbia University, pp. 101-102. "Now what we'd do," he
said, "is get in a room—it sort of breaks the barrier to take a drink. We'd
just throw the cards out on the table. And oh, my heavens! That was the
birth of many a farm bill and legislation in parties like that." P. 102.

contemporary observers doubted the feasibility of the plan (it was to be financed through a transactions tax which experts agreed could not provide the huge sums the plan would have entailed), but their criticisms did not stop the movement from spreading, especially in California and other western states where increasing numbers of older people had retired.[58] It was to court the votes of such people that these Republicans, forsaking conservative theories, embraced the plan in the 1938 campaign. Though estimates varied, most columnists agreed that at least 40 of the 169 Republican congressmen in 1939 owed their elections partly to the backing they had received from the older generation.[59] Few circumstances of the New Deal period offered more telling commentary on the inconsistency of conservative congressional thought.

Doughton and his Ways and Means Committee determined to expose this Republican problem by submitting the Townsend Plan to the floor of the House. To make the Republican position doubly ticklish, he received a special rule for the plan from the Rules Committee Democrats, who were for once in agreement. The rule provided for a minimum of debate and promised to trap Townsend Plan Republicans in a corner: if they backed the plan, they would violate party principle and (in most cases) conviction; if they opposed it, they would forsake campaign promises.

The result in the last days of May was amusing to all but Townsend and the trapped Republicans. Desperately, Republicans sought to recommit the bill by proclaiming that the plan needed further study. To add still further irony to the situation, Republicans had just issued a barrage of economy speeches as part of what they called "National

58 See Arthur M. Schlesinger, Jr., *The Politics of Upheaval* (Boston, 1960), pp. 29-37; for a description of Townsend and his plan.

59 See "The Republican Party: Up From the Grave," pp. 33-36, 104; Kenneth Crawford, "Washington Big Show," *Nation*, CXLVII (Dec. 31, 1938), 6-7; and *Newsweek*, Dec. 19, 1938, p. 14.

Debt Week." But the GOP was powerless. Relentlessly, the rules called an end to the debate, and on June 1 with Townsend himself looking sadly on from the gallery the bill lost decisively, 302-97. Fifty-five Republicans voted in the minority. The next day Doughton did what he had planned all along: his committee approved mild social security amendments which passed both houses later in the session.

The issue was minor and has deserved the historical oblivion into which it has fallen. But it exposed conservative inconsistency, and it showed that conservative bipartisanship was, as always, subject to the severe strains of partisan politics. The Martin-Cox axis, for all its effectiveness on many occasions, by no means encompassed all issues. On problems such as these the bipartisan coalition failed to function at all.

The period of delay settled little. It merely postponed important issues until the end of the session. But it foreshadowed the later period, for it revealed the continuing hostility between the President and Congress; it witnessed the extremely important Republican resurgence, especially in the House; and it exposed, once again, the inconsistencies and partisan problems that beset congressional conservatives of both houses.

3

In contrast to the period of delay the month of June in Congress was frantic. Congressmen became embroiled over neutrality revision. They clashed over a bill to widen the lending authority of the TVA, over rivers and harbors legislation, and for brief periods over social security revision. Conservatives also succeeded in abolishing the undistributed-profits tax and in toning down Roosevelt's requests for relief money for 1940. The most revealing battle, however, occurred over devaluation.

By the Thomas Amendment to the AAA of 1933, the President had received authority to devalue the dollar by as much as one-half, and in 1934 he had used this power to set the dollar value at fifty-nine cents. Because Congress had renewed these powers the President was still authorized in 1939 to devalue the dollar by nine more cents. But like so many other emergency powers granted in 1933, the authority to devalue had to be renewed at two-year intervals, and it was to expire again on June 30. In the past renewal had been easy. In 1939, Congress would not be so obliging.

The House had offered little resistance when it considered the problem in April. Republicans, continuing their remarkable solidarity, almost unanimously endorsed a special report advising against extending the devaluation power. Dies joined them. "I am not willing to admit that the emergency continues to exist," he said. "If we are going to admit it, we ought to admit that the measures put into effect to end it have not ended it."[60] But few Democrats joined him, and many congressmen were anxious to go to the baseball park for opening day. The devaluation bill passed unobtrusively in late April on a partisan vote of 225-158.[61]

In the Senate the bill moved slowly, and it was not until mid-June that it finally emerged with a favorable report from the Banking and Currency Committee. Even so, few expected controversy to ensue. Administration forces appeared to have enough votes to approve it with little difficulty.

The full price of the period of delay then became apparent. Soon after the bill emerged from committee, rumors spread that a silver bloc would filibuster against extension of the devaluation authority unless Roosevelt agreed to raise

[60] New York *Times*, April 17, 1939, p. 1.

[61] *Ibid.*, April 22, 1939, p. 1. For a discussion of the battle, see Allen Seymour Everest, *Morgenthau, The New Deal, and Silver* (New York, 1950), pp. 69-75. See also Fred L. Israel, *Nevada's Key Pittman* (Lincoln, Neb., 1963), pp. 118-20.

the price paid by the Treasury for domestic silver, to end purchases of foreign silver, and to issue some $2 billion in new currency. Nearly twenty strong, this group was wholly western and reflected the great influence of the silver lobby in the Senate: even Adams and King, self-proclaimed budget balancers, were among them. Republicans and conservative Democrats were behind the scenes ready to help. It was an implausible but formidable coalition. As Pittman told the President, "we have got eighteen votes—and what are you going to do about it?"[62]

Roosevelt refused to surrender. The price paid for domestic silver was then 64.64 cents an ounce, some 21 cents above the world market price of 43 cents, and acted as a grand subsidy to silver producers whose influence in Congress was irresistible. Furthermore, the State Department argued that the buying of foreign silver was useful in relations with such nations as Mexico. To Roosevelt as well as to most other observers the silver bloc seemed to be a greedy influence group interested in lining the pockets of powerful constituents.

But the silver bloc was in control and after a few days of filibustering it decided to risk a vote. The result on June 26 was a strange voting pattern. On the first vote the devaluation bill went down to defeat, 47-31, with silverites joining conservatives to form the margin of victory. To reward the silverites for their aid conservatives then helped raise the silver price to 77.57 cents an ounce. The vote this time was 48-30, with only two of the twenty-three Republicans voting against the subsidy. In the process an amendment to bar foreign silver buying swept through on a voice vote.[63]

The episode exposed again the inconsistency of conservative congressmen when tempted by political considera-

[62] Everest, *New Deal and Silver*, p. 72.

[63] *Newsweek*, July 10, 1939, p. 13; Kenneth Crawford, "Happy Fiscal Year," *Nation*, CXLIX (July 8, 1939), 35.

tions. Most conservatives had long opposed foreign silver purchasing and welcomed the opportunity to abolish it. "There seems to be no justification," Bailey remarked, "for buying $880,000,000 worth of foreign silver for which we have no use."[64] Unabashed, they claimed that the abolition of foreign buying would easily compensate for expenditures incurred by the higher domestic subsidy. This is all that can be said in defense of their claim to be economizers. "It was a deal," bragged Republican Senator Clyde M. Reed of Kansas. "Nobody has ever denied that, much less myself, for in fact I was the most active man in making the arrangements."[65]

Roosevelt was not yet defeated, for House liberals stood firm, and a conference committee met to seek agreement. To exert more pressure the President returned to Washington from Hyde Park. He also let it be known that he would accept a silver price of 71 cents in return for the renewal of his devaluation power. On this basis the conferees, working feverishly to beat the June 30 deadline, reported out a new version. It restored the devaluation authority, set a 71-cent domestic silver price, and deleted the ban on foreign buying.[66] This bill reached the Senate floor June 30.

With this bait, the awkward Senate coalition began to crumble. Republicans, outraged at the restoration of the devaluation powers, carried on a filibuster past the midnight deadline. Not surprisingly, Tydings joined them. The House, however, quickly accepted the compromise, and most Senate silverites said that they would support it when conservatives stopped talking. Though Republicans continued to obstruct the compromise in the next few days, it was obvious that their erstwhile allies had deserted. "Pittman wriggled out on us in the midst of the fight,"

[64] To H. M. Ratcliff, July 7, 1939, Bailey MSS, Foreign Policy File.
[65] To William Allen White, July 7, 1939, W. A. White MSS, Box 222.
[66] New York Times, June 30, 1939, p. 1.

Reed complained. "McCarran, Ashurst and Adams and a couple more silver Democrats kept their word and went clear through with us."[67]

Reed's analysis was accurate. After the July 4 holidays the Senate finally voted, and the compromise slipped through, 43-39. Republicans again stood firm, all except Borah voting or paired against the bill.[68] With them were Adams, McCarran, Ashurst, sixteen Democratic irreconcilables, and the two Farmer-Laborites. But Pittman, Hatch, Wheeler, and the other western silverites left the anti-administration coalition. The bill renewed the devaluation power after a harmless five-day recess. It also wrote into law a 71-cent domestic silver price, in effect remonetizing silver at a legally fixed price for the first time since the "Crime of 1873." For all their efforts, conservatives lost on both counts. The only real victors were the silver miners of the American West.

4

When the devaluation bill finally passed after the July 4 break, several issues remained unresolved. One, neutrality revision, eventually resulted for a time in another presidential defeat. Others, including a brief controversy over a TVA bill, offered some drama. A southern Democratic-Republican alliance also succeeded in passing the Hatch Act aimed at "pernicious political activities" arising from the use of relief funds in politics. And southern Democrats led by Cox forced the House leadership to drop consideration of a bill to extend coverage under the Fair Labor Standards Act—even though John L. Lewis denounced Garner at the time as a "labor-baiting, poker-playing, whiskey-drinking evil old man." But these were unimportant in contrast to two larger issues which occupied center stage,

[67] To White, July 7, 1939, W. A. White MSS, Box 222.
[68] Congressional Record, 76th Cong., 1st Sess., 8567.

and which left a shambles of Roosevelt's congressional strength by the time the session closed in early August. These issues involved proposed amendments to the National Labor Relations Act and the recession.

The conflict over the National Labor Relations Board had a considerable history. The Wagner Act establishing the NLRB had passed with remarkably restrained opposition in 1935. But very soon afterward conservatives of both parties, especially those from rural areas, began to regret their acquiescence.[69] As Bailey complained, "Of course we all know that the Wagner Act . . . passed at the instance of agitators in organized labor. . . . We are either going to have a free government under a Constitution or we are going to have something else. It is quite clear to me what that something else will be. It will be a labor government based on National Socialism. It is reaching out for the farmers and the workers. Men like you and me must resist this and whatever price must be paid, we ought to be willing to pay it."[70] Even Doughton by 1938 agreed that an investigation of the NLRB would have a "wholesome and salutary effect."[71]

Not until after the 1938 elections did conservatives intensify their offensive. "I think the National Labor Relations Act the worst law ever put on the federal statute books," Glass wrote, "and would gladly vote for its repeal or its modification in any respect."[72] Even the AF of L was urging changes. Angry at what it considered the NLRB's partiality to the CIO, it proposed sweeping amendments giving more power to craft unions and changing the composition of the board.[73] Most conservatives were not so extreme as Glass.

[69] See Roper Memo to FDR, May 22, 1935, Roosevelt MSS, OF-3, for their reasons.

[70] To R. A. McIntyre, Nov. 8, 1937, Bailey MSS, General File.

[71] Doughton MSS, March 9, 1938, Folder 698.

[72] To E. D. Bransome, Feb. 25, 1939, Glass MSS, Box 362. See also boxes 364-65.

[73] Kenneth Crawford, "A. F. of L. into GOP," Nation, CXLVIII (March 11, 1939), 283-84.

They realized that they did not stand a chance of repealing the act. But they did hope that they might soften its effects in one of two ways: by inserting debilitating amendments, and by investigating the NLRB much as Woodrum was then investigating the WPA.

Conservatives particularly cherished the idea of investigation, but until June the administration astutely prevented efforts in this direction by intimating it would make changes on its own. The Senate Education and Labor Committee held sporadic hearings throughout the session, ostensibly to determine acceptable changes in the NLRB. The House Labor Committee met to determine similar alterations in the Wage and Hour Division of the Labor Department.

By mid-June Cox had waited long enough. Furious at Wage and Hour Division invasions of hosiery mills in his district, he asked Smith, his Rules Committee colleague, to introduce a resolution calling for investigations of both the NLRB and the Wage and Hour Division. With satisfaction Smith did so, and on July 18 the southern Democratic-Republican alliance in the Rules Committee favorably reported out the NLRB resolution to the House floor.

Two days later debate on the measure began, with Martin's Republicans again wisely letting the Democrats do the talking. Criticizing administration delay, Cox proclaimed, "If we wait for the House Labor Committee to take any action regarding the labor board, we will be here until Gabriel blows his horn." Smith gravely and bitterly added, "I voted against the National Labor Relations Board [in 1935] and I did so on the grounds that it was unconstitutional. I think it was palpably unconstitutional at that time. . . . But time has changed the Supreme Court and the Supreme Court has changed the Constitution."[74]

The conservative bloc had its way: the resolution calling

[74] "Who's Tampering with the Court Now?" *Nation,* CXLIX (July 29, 1939), 117.

for an investigation passed, 254-134. In the majority were 104 of the 260 Democrats and 150 of the 169 Republicans. Of the 104 Democrats, 72 were southerners, and 79—or 78 percent—represented rural districts.[75] It was the same kind of Republican-southern Democratic alliance which passed the Hatch Act on the same day. The House was approaching open rebellion.

In the future, the investigation would prove politically significant. Smith, named chairman of the committee, received wide press coverage throughout the remainder of 1939 and on through 1940, and the NLRB absorbed a constant fusillade of criticism for the next two years.[76] Equally important, the Smith Committee solidified personal contacts between the GOP and southern conservatives. In this committee Charles A. Halleck of Indiana, a future GOP House leader, first worked closely with Smith, a proud chairman of the Rules Committee in many subsequent Congresses.[77]

Meanwhile, a conflict developed over means to alleviate the lingering effects of recession. In a surprise message in late June Roosevelt recommended a $3.86-billion program of self-liquidating projects to be started with an $870-million outlay in the 1940 fiscal year.[78] This total included a request (already passed by the Senate) for $800 million to increase the lending powers of the United States Housing Authority. All the projects, he emphasized, would be financed by loans. Indeed, the proposal reflected Roosevelt's fiscal moderation and was considerably more conservative than the pump-priming scheme of the year before.

Reactions to the plan were mixed. New Dealers by and large were unenthusiastic. Blaming Morgenthau's budget-

[75] *Congressional Record*, 76th Cong., 1st Sess., 9593.

[76] For instance, see Kenneth Crawford, "Assault on the NLRB," *Nation*, CXLIX (Dec. 30, 1939), 726-27.

[77] Halleck interview, June, 1963, Washington, D. C.

[78] Louis Wehle, *Hidden Threads of History: Wilson Through Roosevelt* (New York, 1953), p. 215; New York *Times*, June 23, 1939, p. 1.

balancing influence, they derisively called it "splending."[79]
The RFC, they observed, already had the authority to make
this kind of self-liquidating loan. These liberals were convinced that the plan would have little effect either politically
or economically. Their distinct lack of enthusiasm was
evidence of the essential conservatism of the approach.

Conservatives, however, were unappeased. Byrd as usual
objected to the proposed expenditure, insisting that the
plan set up a "double budget and a double debt system
which are most dangerous."[80] To a friend Bailey wrote, "Mr.
Roosevelt's new lending policy is mainly a plan to make
all businesses dependent upon the lending policy of the
government. We will abandon the system of banking we
have had and establish a system of borrowing money from
the funds borrowed by the government. If we go too far,
we may count upon it that there will be no retreat after
a short time."[81]

Republicans, remaining united, were equally critical. "I
have nothing in common with Carter Glass, Bailey of North
Carolina, and George of Georgia," Reed of Kansas wrote in
a revealing letter, "except this one thing—that I am voting
with them to check a mad career—extravagant and economically lacking in comprehension that will ruin the country
and destroy our form of government if it is not checked.
Once it is checked and we can get back to something like a
normal basis for consideration of normal legislation, I will
not be voting with Glass, *et al* crowd. Under the present
circumstances, there is nothing else for me to do most of
the time. I am not happy about it, and I am just as unhappy
about the Norris-Roosevelt extreme as I am about the
Glass-Byrd extreme."[82] Reed, a moderate friendly with

[79] Alsop and Kintner, Washington *Star*, June 30, 1939, A-11; July 11,
1939, A-9.

[80] For reactions, see *Newsweek*, July 3, 1939, pp. 9-11.

[81] To Mrs. Louis Sutton, June 26, 1939, Bailey MSS, Political File.

[82] To William Allen White, July 15, 1939, W. A. White MSS, Box 222.

William Allen White, found the bill as objectionable from an economy standpoint as liberals did from the opposite approach.

The program also failed to excite the public. To many people, Mark Sullivan explained, it appeared to be "just another outpouring of money. All the arguments had been made for previous campaigns. That 'first fine careless rapture' which had attended New Deal projects when the New Deal was pristine had gone and could not be recaptured."[83] Aware of popular apathy, conservative congressmen determined to make an issue of it. "At a Republican conference Thursday," McNary wrote privately at the time, "the Republicans stated I could not go home until I managed that bill, as they are all opposed to it. It is important to the party from political angles and we think to the country for business reasons."[84]

Because of the complexity of the bill, it did not reach congressional committees until mid-July. By then it had been changed slightly. Criticism had caused the administration to slice the total amount (including the separate housing bill) from $3.86 to $3.6 billion. Beginning in the Senate Banking and Currency Committee, it met a bipartisan group which succeeded in deleting another $310 million. The committee's labors left the total at just under $3.3 billion.

More intensive controversy began on the Senate floor. Starting on July 25, four days after the House had passed the NLRB investigation, a conservative bloc led by Byrd began to chip away at the bill. It was a "gigantic pork barrel" and "state socialism by stealth," said a Republican manifesto. George called it a "palpable fraud," and Glass left the Senate for home in utter disgust, making sure to pair himself against the measure.[85] When the bloc finished with

[83] New York *Herald Tribune*, Aug. 2, 1939, p. 18.
[84] To Mrs. W. T. Stolz, July 22, 1939, McNary MSS.
[85] For the GOP manifesto, see New York *Times*, July 26, 1939, p. 1; for George, see *ibid.*, July 28, 1939, p. 3; for Glass, *ibid.*, July 26, 1939, p. 2.

the bill, it had carefully left alone the provisions for rural electrification and farm security; indeed, the bill looked suspiciously like another farm bill. Otherwise, the Senate cut an additional $850 million, leaving only $2.4 billion. The final Senate vote on July 31 was 52-28, with eleven irreconcilable Democrats and seventeen Republicans still unhappy with the bill.[86] Many others supported the measure because they felt the House would destroy it completely.

They were right. By this time the volatile House was almost completely out of control. Encouraged by Senate resistance, the House Banking and Currency Committee followed the lead of the upper chamber in slashing $850 million from the bill. Conservatives complained openly about the remains. Believing the plan was not so self-liquidating as it seemed, they insisted localities would be unable to redeem the loans, thus increasing the national debt. Opposition was so widespread that the Rules Committee even decided it was safe to give the bill a chance. Flushed with its recent victories, the House was eager to crown its newly acquired independence with a flourish.[87]

The next day, August 1, it did so. After but one hour's discussion on a motion to consider the bill, a conservative coalition swept to victory, 193-166. A 146-man Republican phalanx joined 47 rebellious Democrats to defeat the motion; another 63 Democrats, more than enough to have changed the outcome, failed to vote at all. Still others, Cox included, voted for the motion, planning to save their opposition for the final vote.[88] The self-liquidating projects bill died even before it had been formally debated, and conservatives rejoiced at its defeat. "It is my opinion," one Republican exclaimed, "that future historians may possibly take the view that this vote marked the end of an era. . . . it was

[86] *Congressional Record*, 76th Cong., 1st Sess., 10512.

[87] New York *Times*, Aug. 1, 1939, p. 10.

[88] *Congressional Record*, 76th Cong., 1st Sess., 10717; New York *Times*, Aug. 2, 1939, pp. 1, 18.

the first definite clear-cut repudiation by Congress of the theory that we can spend ourselves into prosperity."[89]

Still one more humiliation awaited the President, the housing bill. It came quickly. Two days later, anti-administration forces defeated a motion to consider the bill, this time by 191-170. On this vote 137 Republicans and 54 conservative Democrats were more than enough to carry the day. Large numbers of Democrats again failed to appear.[90]

This vote marked the third time within two weeks that House conservatives had dared to allow an important record vote and defeated the administration. Coalitions had succeeded on the NLRB investigation, 254-134; self-liquidating projects, 193-167; and housing, 191-170. There was no doubt about it: the House had definitely asserted its independence. Moreover, the coalitions continued to operate along the Martin-Cox axis established during the period of delay. Republicans opposed to the administration numbered 150, 146, and 137 respectively. And Democrats totaled 104, 47, and 54, of whom southerners accounted for 72, 21, and 36. The anti-administration coalition on these issues in the House was heavily Republican, with enough Democrats to swing the balance.[91]

It is easy to oversimplify the southern role in this

[89] Hope to Perry White, Aug. 3, 1939, Hope MSS, Legislative Correspondence, Farm-G.

[90] *Congressional Record*, 76th Cong., 1st Sess., 10958; New York *Times*, Aug. 4, 1939, p. 1. Many people agreed with Bailey that the bill was really not self-liquidating. "The recent Housing Bill," he wrote, "claimed to be an eight hundred million dollar bill, but an easy calculation will show that it called upon the Treasury for in excess of two billion dollars." To H. M. Wade, Aug. 9, 1939, Bailey MSS, Housing File.

[91] Once again the urban-rural conflict which had previously occurred on roll calls on this kind of legislation was evident. The percentage of Democrats who represented rural districts in 1939 was 57. Yet 69 percent of the Democratic opponents to the spending bill consisted of rural Democrats, and 83 percent opposed to housing were rural Democrats.

conservative bloc. Southerners clearly composed the largest group of conservative Democrats on all three issues; indeed, they formed an actual majority of Democratic dissidents on two of them. It was also true that the percentage of southerners opposed to the administration was greater than that of Democrats from other areas. But other factors dispel some of the clarity. All three issues had considerable sectional significance: the anti-administration vote on reorganization had revealed no such southern lineup. Moreover, because there were ninety-nine southern Democrats in all, it was obvious that a large percentage of them had supported the administration on spending and housing, the two most hotly contested issues of the three. Finally, by regarding the House according to sections without regard to party, it becomes clear that the percentage of southern congressmen who supported the administration on these (and other) issues was higher than that of congressmen from the East or the Midwest, sections with large numbers of Republicans. Southern Democrats often helped provide the backing needed by Martin's Republicans. But many were consistently loyal to the administration, and even conservatives ordinarily backed the New Deal in noneconomic issues.[92]

The coalition was also not so solid as it appeared. Though Republicans were remarkably cohesive, Democrats were more inconsistent. Of the 54 Democrats who opposed the housing bill, only 33 had opposed the similar spending bill two days earlier. And of the 104 who voted to investigate the NLRB, only 35 also opposed spending, 46 opposed housing, and but 28 opposed both. Only 12 Democrats voted against the administration on all three occasions, 9 of them southerners.

[92] For critiques of the myth of the "Solid South," see Dewey W. Grantham, Jr., *The Democratic South* (Athens, Ga., 1963); also see E. David Cronon, "A Southern Progressive Looks at the New Deal," *Journal of Southern History*, XXIV (May 1958), 151-76.

This lack of solidarity was neither surprising nor particularly unusual, for no two issues were identical. The housing bill, for all its apparent similarity to the spending controversy of two days before, disenchanted additional Democrats because on the intervening day an urban bloc cut crop loans from a deficiency appropriation bill. The significant point was not that anti-administration Democrats often voted apart, but that there was so considerable a difference on such similar issues within such a short period of time.

Despite all the cracks and divisions within the conservative bloc in both houses, Roosevelt's opponents could look back on the 1939 session with pleasure. Moreover, they could anticipate continued conservative strength in 1940. If the 1937 session marked the beginning of effective conservative power, the 1939 session marked its zenith to that time. To liberals and reactionaries alike it was obvious that nothing short of a marked change in congressional membership—or a renewal of economic crisis—could destroy the conservative blocs in both houses.

10

COALITION IN RETROSPECT

CLAUDE Pepper was angry beyond measure. Two days after the housing measure crashed to defeat in the House, and with Congress ready to adjourn, he rose to speak. At first the normal hubbub drowned his words, but Pepper had informed the press of his intention to speak, and many senators, expecting excitement, were eager to listen. They received a bitter earful.

"I am unwilling to let this session of Congress end," he began,

without lifting my voice to decry the unrighteous partnership of those who have been willing to scuttle the American government and the American people and jeopardize the peace of the world because they hate Roosevelt and what Roosevelt stands for. . . . I accuse that designing alliance of a deliberate attempt to sabotage the first real effort ever made in this nation to secure for the workers of America industrial democracy and economic emancipation. I accuse them of having prostituted their power to serve the U. S. Chamber of Commerce, the Manufacturer's Association, and the beneficiaries of special privilege, who hate in their hearts the man who has tried to lighten the burden of toil on the back of labor.

By this time the chamber was in an uproar. Barkley, afraid of a long and unpleasant debate, peered anxiously for a messenger to appear with news of House agreement to adjourn. But conservatives were not ready to leave. After several attempts, Burke finally succeeded in making a motion to cut off Pepper's tirade. Most senators, however, wanted to hear him through, and Pepper was soon allowed to resume. "This Machiavellian alliance," he continued, was "fostering and encouraging unhappy division in the ranks of labor." It served a "handful of Wall Street speculators and the little conniving clique of international money changers who have no flag and no cause but money." Concluding amid shouts and taunts, he expressed his undying aim to fight the group so as to "revive [the nation's] faltering faith to the high and unselfish patriotism of our forefathers."[1]

Downey of California then took the floor to try to pacify the conservatives, and as soon as he finished the Senate adjourned; Burke never had a chance to answer. But Pepper's speech was a fitting climax to a stormy session, and a liberal dose of acid on the already frayed bonds tying together the Democratic party. Pepper, Bailey explained to Gerry, "was a coward and a liar, and I hope yet to have the privilege of telling him so to his face. He might whip me on the spot, but that wouldn't be the last of it." Roosevelt, Bailey said, "figures on hard times and does not wish for recovery. He would perish like a rattlesnake in the sun under conditions of prosperity. Pardon the illustration. Mr. Roosevelt is not a rattlesnake. He rattles a great deal, but

[1] *Congressional Record*, 76th Cong., 1st Sess., 11165-68.

that is all I am willing to say. Perhaps you know the rattle-snake must stay in the swamp for the reason that he does not have any means of sweating or panting. His heat accumulates. Mr. Roosevelt belongs to that type of man who lives on hard times and discontent."[2]

Pepper's speech revealed more than the animosity within Democratic ranks. It also reflected one liberal interpretation of the 1939 congressional session. This view held, first of all, that Congress had hamstrung the President, and second, that a well-organized conspiratorial coalition was responsible.[3]

The first assumption was largely accurate. It was true that conservatives left untouched most of the routine appropriation bills, that with the exception of Amlie and Roberts they did not interfere with presidential appointments, and that they were generous with regard to defense. They also approved reorganization bills and failed in both houses to amend either the Wagner or Fair Labor Standards acts.

But the list of administration defeats and congressional omissions was much more impressive. Roosevelt lost three successive battles over relief; he barely retrieved his devaluation powers; and he witnessed the final destruction of his undistributed-profits tax. He had to suffer the discomforts of unfriendly House investigations by Woodrum, Dies, and Smith, and he was denied so much as a shadow of his spending and housing programs. Though his requests had been modest, his success was minimal. Pepper was right about conservative success. Unquestionably, conservative congressmen had developed sufficient strength to stymie the President.

If this was a conspiracy, however, it was not so well

[2] To Peter Gerry, Aug. 12, 1939, Bailey MSS, Political File. Also on Pepper, see Bailey to Frank Hawkins, Aug. 10, 1939, *ibid.*

[3] For a similar interpretation, see "Saved by the Bell," *Nation*, CXLIX (Aug. 12, 1939), 163-64. But see also "What Congress Really Did," *New Republic*, XCIX (Aug. 16, 1939), 32-33.

organized as it seemed. To begin with, conservatives lacked a consistent ideology. Professing states' rights, they were willing to pass the Hatch Act, a national law regulating state primaries. Decrying deficit spending, they persisted in pouring money into farm areas, in raising the price of silver, and in toying with extravagant pension schemes. Some conservatives opposed deficit spending yet opposed raising income taxes; others were willing to lower income-tax exemptions on middle-income groups. There was a recognizable ideological difference between conservatives and liberals of the era: indeed, the 1930's revealed a split perhaps deeper than in any comparable period of American history since the 1890's. But philosophies of government were sometimes less important than the problem of which side was to grab the brass ring.

The conservative bloc also cracked along partisan lines. This problem had been obvious long before the 1939 session and would become more so as election time drew near. Conservative Democrats were already having second thoughts about defying their popular President. The percentage of Democratic opposition to the administration on major bills in 1939 was little greater in both houses than it had been in 1937-1938—despite the heady results of the 1938 elections. Partisanship, like ideological problems, prevented sustained conservative cohesion.

If these generalizations suggested the lack of conservative unity, roll-call votes proved it. Excepting the remarkable Republican solidarity, it was not easy to predict the men who would take the conservative side of any issue. On the most controversial bills in 1939 a 40- to 50-man anti-administration bloc existed in the Senate, and a more amorphous group of between 190 and 250 in the House. But the only men who consistently opposed the President were most of the Republicans and the old irreconcilable Democrats. Together, these numbered around 35 in the Senate and 180 in the House on those rare occasions when they all voted. This was certainly a more consistent core than in past congressional sessions; moreover, it would continue to operate in the future. But it was neither solid nor monolithic. As Joseph Alsop put it, "in both houses, when a pro- and anti-New Deal issue is squarely presented, a shifting population of conservative Democrats can be counted upon to join the Republicans to vote against the President. The arrangement is not formal. There is nothing calculated about it, except the Republican strategy originated by . . . McNary of refraining from arousing the Democrats' partisan feelings by inflammatory oratory."[4]

Who were the conservatives? To begin with, they were not necessarily veterans who had outlived their era. In every session from 1933 through 1939 the percentage of veteran (pre-1933) Democrats who opposed the administration on major bills was only slightly larger than the percentage of those who rode in with the New Deal. Contrary to what might have been expected, Democratic congressmen who first served in 1933 or thereafter were not much more liberal than their predecessors. Moreover, these conservative Democrats were not all old men. Their average age in both houses was almost exactly that of their liberal colleagues.[5]

Sectional factors were more obvious. In the Senate nearly half of the twenty-two southerners often voted against the administration on nonagricultural economic issues. Byrd, Glass, Bailey, Smith and George were among these men on most occasions, as were Harrison, Byrnes, and Connally on more than one other crucial test. In the House numbers varied, but the percentage of southerners who voted conservatively on such issues was ordinarily greater than the

[4] Washington *Star*, Aug. 3, 1939, A-11.
[5] See Appendix.

percentage of Democrats from other sections. This factor should not be overemphasized. Except on race legislation, the South was not "solid" in Congress. Yet on many socio-economic issues in 1937-1939 southern Democrats were inclined to be slightly more conservative than the rest of the party.[6]

It was also true that most congressional conservatives rose from middle or upper middle class stock, that they were well educated, and that they reflected the views of conservative farmers and businessmen in their districts. Burke, for instance, often echoed the antilabor position of the National Association of Manufacturers, and in 1942 he would become president of a coal producers association. Glass was friendly with several Wall Street bankers, and George was frank to admit his partiality for private power interests in Georgia. Others, such as Tydings and Gerry, cherished friendships with prominent conservative businessmen in their home states. Many rural conservatives had few contacts with large corporate interests but more often than not were friendly with small-town bankers, businessmen, and manufacturers. Howard Smith was one of these, and Taber, Cox, and Snell three others. These congressmen possessed little feeling of identification with organized labor, Negroes, tenant farmers, or other deprived groups pressing for social welfare.[7]

Those few conservatives whose youth had been poor or who had once belonged to the ranks of organized labor had long since cast off such influences and had adopted an ethic of rugged individualism typical of many self-made men. Martin, for instance, recalled his youthful adversities fondly, congratulating himself upon his diligence and thrift. Donahey of Ohio, a one-time journeyman printer, believed equally staunchly in self-help and frugality. So did Gore,

[6] See Appendix. The most careful study along this line is V. O. Key, Jr., *Southern Politics in State and Nation* (New York, 1949), pp. 345-68.
[7] *Ibid.* See Appendix.

Vandenberg, and others whose backgrounds might otherwise have conditioned them to look more favorably on the desires of the underprivileged. These congressmen tended to share the views of conservative businessmen, especially on relief spending, labor bills, and tax policy.

Perhaps the most distinguishing characteristic of the congressional conservative of the period was the nature of his district. Those who represented predominantly urban districts usually sided with the administration on economic and social issues, whereas those from heavily rural districts often defied the administration after 1936. Rural southerners, for instance, were more consistently conservative than urban southerners. And eastern urban Democrats were usually the most dependable. In this sense it should not be surprising that there was a conservative upsurge after 1936, for it was then that the heavily northern-urban character of the New Deal became most obvious, and most ominous, to conservatives.

If these characteristics distinguished the congressional conservatives, what was responsible for increased conservative success after 1936? Part of the reason was the shrewdness and power of a few strategically placed individuals: McNary's overall strategy, Martin's organization in the House, Garner's pervasive influence in both houses. Another reason was the normal lack of leverage belonging to administrations completing their second terms. Personal animosities certainly contributed; the Democrats whom Roosevelt tried to purge delighted in evening the score. Many moderates, seeking a breathing spell in 1935, merely awaited an occasion to proclaim their independence. Finally, Roosevelt's continued aggressiveness made him few friends. Far from conceding ground to advance his foreign policy, as has sometimes been asserted, he persisted in his feeling that "the people are with me." Roosevelt by no means "caused" the conservative coalition, but with measures such as the court plan he hastened its development, and with actions such as the purge he helped to steel its resolve.[8]

Nothing so simple as a "conspiracy" or "failure of presidential leadership" accounted for the conservative renaissance. The main reasons were at once partisan, psychological, institutional, issue-based, and constituent-based. The biggest difference between the 1939 session and its predecessors was, after all, the presence in 1939 of so many Republicans. In the Senate they formed, for the first time since 1934, at least half the conservative bloc. In the more rebellious House Republicans formed some three-fourths of anti-administration strength on every close issue. The administration was in trouble from the first day of the session.

A change in congressional psychology was perhaps more significant. The events of 1937-1938 not only gave renewed confidence to conservative congressmen, but they intensified long-submerged feelings of congressional independence, particularly in the House, which was more responsive to the most recent election. In this sense the period from 1933 to 1936 was a Great Aberration: it was the only peacetime period in twentieth-century American history when a Chief Executive was so generally successful in dominating his Congress. Thus, although the sessions of 1937-1939 witnessed the emergence of a new kind of conservative bloc, they were also more simply a return to the normality of presidential-congressional hostility.[9] Had external events given congressmen confidence earlier, they probably would

[8] Alsop and Kintner, Washington *Star*, Aug. 3, 1939, A-11, gave Roosevelt much of the blame. "Democrats would not be found in coalition with Republicans," they said, "if he [Roosevelt] had not been obstinate in the court fight, determined to have Alben W. Barkley for Senate majority leader, and grimly set on the purge. These incidents, convincing Democratic conservatives that only 100 percenters were welcome on the New Deal side, are the real foundation of the coalition."

[9] James M. Burns, *Deadlock of Democracy: Four-Party Politics in America* (Englewood Cliffs, N. J., 1963), is a recent interpretation of American history in this vein. See his chapter on Roosevelt, pp. 151-76.

have kicked over the traces before 1937. That they did when presidential prestige declined should occasion no surprise.

The institutional nature of Congress reinforced this return to normality. The system of congressional representation in the 1930's was distinctly favorable to the rural areas of America, many of which were one-party areas as well. This situation was most obvious in the Senate, where southern, Plains, and Rocky Mountain senators filled half the chamber. Inequitable representation also existed in the House.[10] Before 1937 the nationwide emergency had obscured rural-urban divisions by forcing even rural conservatives to support emergency legislation. But after 1937 few rural areas faced a crisis comparable to that of 1933-1935. Most rural congressmen remained anxious to support special-interest legislation beneficial to their districts but not to assist measures for the relief of urban problems. To rural members such measures deprived their districts of funds which they might otherwise have received themselves. Urban congressmen, clamoring loudly after 1937 for help, too often found the simple problem of rural overrepresentation too great an obstacle.

The nature of the major congressional issues after 1936 was especially conducive to this kind of urban-rural division. Whether there were two New Deals prior to 1936 is a debatable point. In retrospect, however, it seems that a different kind of New Deal developed after 1936. From the largely southern-western party of 1933 the Democratic party

[10] See Arthur Holcombe, *The Middle Classes in American Politics* (Cambridge, Mass., 1940), pp. 99-103, for statistical computation of this rural domination. Writing at the time, he estimated that some 54 of the 96 senators and roughly 225 of 435 representatives represented predominantly rural districts or states. Of the 93 southern seats (not including Tennessee), Holcombe found 76 in the rural category. My own calculations place the divisions as follows: Senate—56 urban, 40 rural; House—199 urban, 236 rural. See Appendix. For a breezy account of southern power in Congress, see William S. White, *Citadel: The Story of the United States Senate* (New York, 1957), pp. 67-79.

had become a coalition in which northern urban elements dominated. Issues dear to these northern urbanites—relief spending, housing, pro-labor bills—accordingly formed major points of congressional controversy, whether Roosevelt desired them or not. Thus it was not surprising that Roosevelt faced greater opposition from the rural members of both Houses. Most of these rural congressmen had acceded to measures such as social security and even the Wagner Act in 1935. But when urban Democrats demanded more aid after 1936, they balked.[11] It was this "new" and unplanned New Deal, the frankly urban liberalism of men such as Wagner, that many formerly reliable rural congressmen determined to oppose after 1936.

The rise of congressional conservatism also reflected changing constituent attitudes. In many ways the state of America's economic health in 1939 was little better than it had been in 1934, and it might have been expected that economic impulses behind reform would have increased—or at least have remained steady. Yet after 1936 conservative congressmen were able to defy the New Deal without fear of reprisal from their constituents. Why was it that hard-pressed voters did not demand stronger measures after 1936?[12]

The answer, it seems in retrospect, was complex. Many constituents did continue to demand federal action to relieve their problems, but their demands were parochial and essentially selfish. Beset with their own economic needs, they were often apathetic otherwise. Farmers excitedly demanded

[11] For one example, see Jack B. Key, "Henry B. Steagall: The Conservative as a Reformer," *Alabama Review*, XVII (July 1964), 198-209.

[12] This trend of lower middle and middle class people who had been hurt by the Depression to act and vote in more conservative fashion after 1936 has been noted by many authorities. See, for instance, Samuel Lubell, *The Future of American Politics* (2nd rev. ed.; New York, 1956), pp. 61-85, 120-25, 165-209; and Robert and Helen Lynd, *Middletown in Transition* (New York, 1937), *passim*.

more money for agriculture; union leaders insisted upon legislation beneficial to organized labor; city machines requested higher relief and public works expenditures; and spokesmen for slum dwellers demanded a cluster of bills to relieve urban misery. These varied groups were able to unite successfully in presidential elections. They were even strong enough to influence congressional voting—farm bills and pump-priming were cases in point. But they never formed a unified working coalition in Congress, and because their orientation was distinctly local instead of national they failed to reach a consensus on many broad social welfare programs. To liberals it is a distressing thought, but the voting behavior of nonconservatives in Congress from 1937 through 1939 exhibited little more breadth of vision—and a good deal less unity of purpose—than the behavior of conservatives. The conservative coalition was less than monolithic, but liberals, more disparate as a group and faced with the more difficult problem of agreeing upon a positive program, were hardly a coalition at all.

Moreover, the economic situation of 1933-1934 was considerably different from that in 1937 or in 1938-1939. As early as 1937 many moderates believed that the emergency was over and that the New Deal should adhere to the breathing spell promised them in 1935. The relationship between economic conditions and periods of social reform remains a debatable historical point, but in 1937 improved times helped to diminish the ardor of many congressmen for relief and reform.

The recession which followed also differed considerably from the depression period of 1933-1934. Though economic hardship persisted, attitudes changed. In 1933 most business and community leaders were discredited, and congressmen, reacting to the strongest pressures, responded to the administration, not to the silent and confused power groups in their constituencies. But in 1935 many businessmen began to turn against the New Deal, and by 1937, no longer afraid of chaos, they freely castigated it. These conservative community leaders never recovered the status that they had enjoyed in 1929, but they did reassert their voices in public policy. Many moderate congressmen, dissatisfied with the New Deal for a variety of reasons—patronage, bureaucracy, spending—listened more carefully to such influential men than they had in 1933-1935. This renewed constituent determination helped account for the opposition of urban as well as rural congressmen to such measures as the undistributed-profits tax.

Congressmen had also become impatient by 1938. By then the New Deal was no longer new, and to many it had had ample time to prove itself as an agent of recovery. Its failure to end the Depression and its inability to avoid a recession damned it in conservative eyes. More important —and less obvious—the recession convinced many nonconservatives of the administration's economic naïveté. To these congressmen it appeared that an administration that could not solve the economic problem was also unqualified to speak authoritatively on such measures as regional development, executive reorganization, taxes, or labor policy. This lack of certainty among nonconservatives facilitated the conservative task after 1936.

Political factors also contributed to the strength of congressional conservatism. For all his power and prestige, the President was unable to dominate state political parties, and nominations of Democrats on the state level continued to be matters for state bosses to determine. Because even the disastrous Depression was slow to destroy American attitudes toward such matters as balanced budgets, federal power, and labor unions, state and local machines, reflecting this attitudinal inertia, continued to nominate and elect congressmen whose views were either moderate or business-oriented. Or they nominated men whose liberalism extended only to tapping the Treasury for purely local gains. The result was the election of many congressmen whose sense of loyalty to the New Deal was limited and who depended for reelection upon the powerful groups in their constituencies. Against this kind of situation presidential resources were of limited value.

Problems of foreign policy would occupy much of the time of succeeding congressional sessions. These dilemmas would create congressional alignments somewhat different from those which had operated on domestic questions since 1937. Most conservative Democrats, for instance, supported the President's moves to aid the Allies from 1939 to 1941, whereas a few progressives such as La Follette deserted the administration to vote with the majority of Republicans and with mavericks such as Bennett Clark, McCarran, and Walsh. On most questions of foreign policy through 1941 the conservative coalition failed to function.

But foreign policy considerations, strange though it may now seem, had not been divisive congressional issues before 1939, mainly because the President, concentrating upon meeting the domestic emergency, declined to defy congressional sentiment for neutrality legislation. The conservative bloc which developed in both houses by 1939 was founded primarily upon domestic issues, and the foreign policy controversies which ensued failed either to weaken or to strengthen the conservative outlook toward the domestic New Deal. For the rest of his presidency Roosevelt would continue to encounter strong opposition from the conservative coalition in Congress.[13]

[13] For the war years, for instance, see the remarkable picture painted by Allen Drury, *A Senate Journal, 1943-1945* (New York, 1963). See also Roland Young, *Congressional Politics in the Second World War* (New York, 1956).

APPENDIX

*A Statistical Analysis of Conservative
Democrats in Congress, 1933–1939*

THE FOLLOWING analysis makes no claim to being defini-
tive, but it may interest those who desire statistical evidence for generalizations made in the text. I hope it will
stimulate others to make the comprehensive study of roll-call
voting and of congressmen which will be necessary before
solid judgments can be made.

A   THE HOUSE OF REPRESENTATIVES

The "most conservative Democrats" in the House of Representatives are those who served in at least three sessions
between 1933 and 1939 and who opposed the administration
on 25 percent or more of the key roll calls on which they
were recorded. A total of 77 Democrats, or approximately
one-fifth of the 365 Democrats who served at least three
sessions during the period, fall into this category. Repre-

sentatives in this group will be referred to as "conservative Democrats" or "conservatives" throughout; all other congressmen will be referred to as "liberal Democrats" or "liberals."

The key roll calls used to establish degree of opposition to the administration were: 1933: Economy bill, FERA, AAA, TVA (Conference), NRA Recommittal, and Gold Payments; 1934: Reciprocal Trade, Gold Pegging, and SEC; 1935: WPA, Social Security, Public Utilities ("death sentence"), Wealth Tax, and Guffey Coal bill; 1936: Soil Conservation, $1.425 billion Deficiency Appropriation, and Undistributed Profits Tax; 1937: Dies Sitdown Resolution, WPA, Housing, and Labor Standards (Recommittal); 1938: AAA (Conference), Naval Expansion, Reorganization Recommittal, and Pump Priming; and 1939: Reorganization, Gold Devaluation, Neutrality (Nov.), Investigate NLRB, Spending bill, and Housing. Unless otherwise noted, votes were on final passage; pairs were included.

Unquestionably, a selection of different roll calls would have created a somewhat different list, but the votes were selected carefully. They include legislation of every type; they include at least three roll calls per session; and they represent votes on which there existed a clear division between administration and anti-administration congressmen.

Most Conservative House Democrats: Basic Data

Name	State	Tenure	Anti-admin. votes (%)	Section[1]	Urban or Rural[2]
Elliott	Cal.	1937——	60–65	W	R
Robertson	Va.	1933——	60–65	S	R
Coffee	Neb.	1935——	55–59	W	R
Lamneck	Ohio	1931–1939 (L)[3]	55–59	MW	U
Peterson	Ga.	1935——	55–59	S	R

Name	State	Tenure	Anti-admin. votes (%)	Section[1]	Urban or Rural[2]
Burch	Va.	1931—	45–49	S	R
Kleberg	Tex.	1932—	45–49	S	R
Smith	Va.	1931—	45–49	S	R
Allen	Pa.	1937—	40–44	E	R
Anderson	Mo.	1937—	40–44	B	U
Cox	Ga.	1925—	40–44	S	R
Lanham	Tex.	1919—	40–44	S	U
McGroarty	Cal.	1935–1939	40–44	W	U
Satterfield	Va.	1937—	40–44	S	R
Tarver	Ga.	1927—	40–44	S	R
Taylor	S.C.	1933–1939 (L)	40–44	S	R
Ashbrook	Ohio	1935—	35–39	MW	R
Bland	Va.	1918—	35–39	S	R
Boren	Okla.	1937—	35–39	W	R
Claiborne	Mo.	1933–1937 (L)	35–39	B	U
Darden	Va.	1933–1937; 1939	35–39	S	U
Drewry	Va.	1920—	35–39	S	R
Faddis	Pa.	1933—	35–39	E	R
Ford	Miss.	1935—	35–39	S	R
Garrett	Tex.	1937—	35–39	S	R
Granfield	Mass.	1930–1937	35–39	E	U
Harrington	Iowa	1937—	35–39	MW	R
Hoeppel	Cal.	1933–1937 (L)	35–39	W	U
Huddleston	Ala.	1915–1937 (L)	35–39	S	U
Lewis	Colo.	1933–	35–39	W	U
McLaughlin	Neb.	1935—	35–39	W	U
Moser	Pa.	1937—	35–39	E	U
O'Neal	Ky.	1935—	35–39	B	U
Poage	Tex.	1937—	35–39	S	R
Polk	Ohio	1931—	35–39	MW	R
Bell	Mo.	1935—	30–34	B	U
Chapman	Ky.	1925–1929; 1931—	30–34	B	R
Collins	Miss.	1921–1925; 1937—	30–34	S	R
Costello	Cal.	1935—	30–34	W	U

Name	State	Tenure	Anti-admin. votes (%)	Section[1]	Urban or Rural[2]
Gasque	S.C.	1923–1938 (June)	30–34	S	R
Luckey	Neb.	1935–1939 (L)	30–34	W	R
Patton	Tex.	1935–—	30–34	S	R
Pearson	Tenn.	1935–—	30–34	S	R
Pettengill	Ind.	1931–1939	30–34	MW	U
Ryan	Minn.	1935–—	30–34	MW	R
South	Tex.	1935–—	30–34	S	R
Whittington	Miss.	1925–—	30–34	S	R
Biermann	Iowa	1933–1939 (L)	25–29	MW	R
Boehne	Ind.	1931–—	25–29	MW	U
Clark	Idaho	1935–1939	25–29	W	R
Clark	N.C.	1929–—	25–29	S	R
Corning	N.Y.	1923–1937	25–29	E	U
Disney	Okla.	1931–—	25–29	W	U
Doxey	Miss.	1929–—	25–29	S	R
Edmiston	W.Va.	1934–—	25–29	B	R
Gavagan	N.Y.	1929–—	25–29	E	U
Gray	Pa.	1933–1939 (L)	25–29	E	R
Greever	Wyo.	1935–1939 (L)	25–29	W	R
Hobbs	Ala.	1935–—	25–29	S	R
Hunter	Ohio	1937–—	25–29	MW	U
Jarman	Ala.	1937–—	25–29	S	R
Johnson	Tex.	1923–—	25–29	S	R
Kitchens	Ark.	1937–—	25–29	S	R
May	Ky.	1931–—	25–29	B	R
McGehee	Miss.	1935–—	25–29	S	R
McMillan	S.C.	1925–1939 (Oct.)	25–29	S	R
Nichols	Okla.	1935–—	25–29	W	R
O'Malley	Wis.	1933–1939	25–29	MW	U
Pace	Ga.	1937–—	25–29	S	R
Rankin	Miss.	1921–—	25–29	S	R
Sanders	Tex.	1921–1939 (L)	25–29	S	R
Sheppard	Cal.	1937–—	25–29	W	U
Starnes	Ala.	1935–—	25–29	S	R

Name	State	Tenure	Anti- admin. votes (%)	Section[1]	Urban or Rural[2]
Sutphin	N.J.	1931——	25–29	E	U
West	Tex.	1933——	25–29	S	R
Welchel	Ga.	1935——	25–29	S	R
Woodrum	Va.	1923——	25–29	S	R

[1] Sections defined as follows: East (E): New England, N.Y., N.J., Pa., Del.; Border (B): Md., W. Va., Mo., Ky.; South (S): Old Confederacy; Midwest (MW): Old Northwest, Minn., Iowa; and West (W): the rest.

[2] "Rural" and "urban" here and in other tables refer to the predominant character of the congressional district represented by these congressmen. The urban character of a district was established as follows: The number and location of the congressional district from the *Congressional Directory* (1933-1939) was determined and the counties included in this district were noted. The 1940 census (*16th Census of the U.S.*, 1940, Vol. I, Population, pp. 8-10) definition of an urban area was adopted. Using this same census volume, the statistics which give the percentage of urbanism within each county in the state in which the congressional district is located were consulted. The percentage of urbanism in the district as a whole could thus be computed. If this percentage was more than 50, the district was called urban.

This method is admittedly limited. It does not distinguish between different kinds of urban (or rural) districts. Democrats representing New York City had different concerns than Democrats from Columbus or Indianapolis (who often opposed the administration). It also does not take into account the personal background of the congressmen; some congressmen representing urban districts were rurally born and bred and retained attitudes toward problems which were not shared by their constituents.

[3] (L) means lost election or failed to be renominated.

Sectional Factor

	S	W	E	MW	B	Total
No. of Conservative Democrats	38	14	8	10	7	77
Total No. of Democrats, 1933–1939	120	61	76	71	37	365
Percentage Conservative	32	23	11	14	19	13

Numerically, southern Democrats composed the chief Democratic opposition to the New Deal in the House. The percentage of southern Democrats who were conservative was also greater than that of Democrats from other sections.

Experience Factor

	"Veterans" (arrived pre-1930)	"Coattailers" (arrived 1933-1937)	Total
No. of Conservative Democrats	29	48	77
Total No. of Democrats, 1933–1939	145	220	365
Percentage Conservative	20	22	....

The percentage of veterans and of newcomers who were among the most conservative, 1933–1939, was roughly equal. Roosevelt was unable to handpick the candidates for office during his tenure.

State Politics

Most Conservative States	Number of Conservatives
Texas	9
Virginia	8
Mississippi	6
Georgia	5
California	5
Alabama	4
Ohio	4
Pennsylvania	4
South Carolina	3
Oklahoma	3
Nebraska	3
Total	54

These eleven states (six of them southern) over this period filled only about one-third of the Democratic seats in the House, yet they furnished fifty-four of the seventy-seven most conservative Democrats, or 70 percent of House Democratic conservative strength.

This table not only suggests the important role played by state political organizations in the selection of candidates, but it also shows the strength of Democratic conservatism in *parts* of the South and its weakness in the Northeast and urban Midwest. Virginia contributed eight conservatives, though she had only nine men in the House at one time. New York, with an average Democratic delegation of twenty-eight, contributed but two men to the list of conservatives.

Occupational Factor[4]

Principal Occupation	Number of Conservatives
Lawyer	46
Businessman	11
Farmer/Rancher	5
Teacher/Educator	5
Publisher	4
Laborer	2
Miscellaneous	4
Total	77

In addition to their primary occupation, five conservative Democrats also practiced some law, seven were involved in agricultural pursuits of one kind or another, six were bankers, and eight had taught at one time in their lives.

Since most congressmen of all political persuasions were lawyers, these statistics reveal little. The key questions are, of course, what *kind* of lawyer or businessman was the con-

[4] Occupations determined from secondary sources, manuscript collections, newspapers, and (in all too many cases) the brief biographical data available in *Biographical Directory of American Congress, 1774–1949* (Washington, D.C., 1950).

servative congressman? Was he a corporate or union lawyer; was he a merchant, a large manufacturer, or a salesman for a small firm? The available evidence is too scanty to allow firm conclusions, and it is clear only that very few conservatives had ever held jobs which brought them into close association with organized labor, tenant farmers, or other underprivileged groups.

Rural-Urban Factor

Fifty-three of the seventy-seven conservative Democrats, or 69 percent, represented rural areas, whereas only 54 percent (236 out of 435) of the entire House of Representatives was rural. It is therefore clear that conservatism among House Democrats was more prevalent among rural members.

Age Factor

The average age of the seventy-seven conservative Democrats in 1937 was fifty; the average age of all representatives that same year was fifty-two. The conservatives were not necessarily doddering old men. The age of a congressman had little to do (in most cases) with his voting behavior.

Educational Factor

Level of Education	Number of Conservatives
Failed to Finish High School	1
Completed High School	3
Completed Some College Training	6
Graduated from College	19
Completed Some Postgraduate Work[5]	48
Total	77

[5] The great majority of these men attended law school.

Because congressmen of all persuasions were generally well educated, this table in one sense reveals little. Yet the remarkably high number of conservative Democrats who received college or postgraduate training suggests that the majority of congressional conservatives came from families that were affluent enough to help their children through college and beyond. Together with the scanty evidence on occupational backgrounds, these figures suggest that conservative congressmen came from middle- to upper-class backgrounds.

Geographical Mobility of Conservatives

Of the seventy-seven conservatives, seventy-two were raised in the same state they eventually represented in Congress and five were raised in one state and represented another.

Of the seventy-seven, only eleven represented districts which differed in rural-urban character from the environment in which they had been born and raised; the remaining sixty-six represented districts having approximately the same character as the area in which they had grown up.

Although these figures often represent educated guesses as to the nature of a congressman's upbringing, they suggest that the large majority of conservative congressmen may have had a distinctly local outlook on legislative problems. This applies to many liberal congressmen as well; nevertheless, it may help to explain the parochial viewpoint of some conservatives of the 1930's.

B THE SENATE

The "most conservative Democrats" in the Senate are the thirty-five who served in at least three sessions between 1933 and 1939 and who opposed the administration on at least 12 percent of the key roll calls on which they were recorded. Senators in this group will be referred to throughout as "conservative Democrats" or "conservatives"; all other senators will be referred to as "liberal Democrats" or "liberals."

The key roll calls used to establish the degree of opposition to the administration are the same as those used in Appendix A, with the following exceptions: Added here are Black 30-Hour Work Week bill (1933), World Court (1935), Confirmation of Hugo Black (1937), Wagner Act (1935), Reciprocal Trade Extension (1937), Byrd Housing Amendment (1937), and Robinson Relief Amendment (1937). These were revealing Senate roll calls which either did not occur in the House or occurred with amendments clouding the issue. Not included here (because there was no Senate vote involved) is Investigate NLRB (1939). As in Appendix A, the votes are on final passage, with the exception of those noted above and the following: Dieterich Amendment to Utilities Regulation (1935); Labor Standards—Recommittal (1937); and Executive Reorganization (Wheeler Amendment, 1939).

These figures do not—and cannot—reveal the inherent conservatism of men such as Robinson or the practice perfected by men such as Harrison of watering down administration bills in committee.

Most Conservative Senate Democrats: Basic Data

Name	State	Tenure	Anti-admin. votes (%)	Age in 1937	Section[6]	Urban or Rural[7]
Glass	Va.	1920––	81	79	S	R
Tydings	Md.	1927––	77	47	B	U
Burke	Neb.	1935––	74	57	W	R
Gerry	R.I.	1917–1929; 1935––	68	58	E	U
Byrd	Va.	1933––	65	50	S	R

Name	State	Tenure	Anti-admin. votes (%)	Age in 1937	Sec-tion[6]	Urban or Rural[7]
Gore	Okla.	1907–1921; 1931–1937	58	67	W	R
Bailey	N.C.	1931——	58	64	S	R
Holt	W.Va.	1935——	57	32	B	R
Johnson	Colo.	1937——	56	53	W	U
Copeland	N.Y.	1923–1938	50	69	E	U
Smith	S.C.	1909——	44	71	S	R
Clark	Mo.	1933——	42	47	B	U
Maloney	Conn.	1935——	37	43	E	U
Adams	Colo.	1933——	36	62	W	U
Donahey	Ohio	1935——	36	64	MW	U
McCarran	Nev.	1933——	35	61	W	R
George	Ga.	1922——	33	59	S	R
Bulkley	Ohio	1930——	32	57	MW	U
Walsh	Mass.	1919–1925; 1927——	29	65	E	U
Coolidge	Mass.	1931–1937	29	72	E	U
Bulow	S.D.	1931——	28	68	W	R
Van Nuys	Ind.	1933——	26	63	MW	U
King	Utah	1917——	25	74	W	U
Gillette	Iowa	1937——	25	58	MW	R
Russell	Ga.	1933——	25	40	S	R
Connally	Tex.	1929——	24	60	S	R
Radcliffe	Md.	1935——	24	58	B	U
Lonergan	Conn.	1933–1939	21	61	E	U
Pittman	Nev.	1913——	19	65	W	R
Wheeler	Mont.	1923——	15	55	W	R
Byrnes	S.C.	1931——	14	58	S	R
Reynolds	N.C.	1933——	14	53	S	R
Duffy	Wis.	1933–1939	13	49	MW	U
Harrison	Miss.	1919——	12	56	S	R
O'Mahoney	Wyo.	1934——	12	53	W	R

[6] See footnote 1, above.
[7] See footnote 2, above.

Sectional Factor

	S	W	E	MW	B	Total
No. of Conservative Democrats	10	10	6	5	4	35
Total No. of Democratic Senators per Session, 1933–1939	22	24	12	10	8	76
Percentage Conservative	46	41	50	50	50	46

Although most Senate Democratic conservatives came from the South and West, the percentage of Democrats from each section who were conservative was remarkably similar.

Age Factor

The average age of conservative Democrats in 1937 was fifty-eight; the average age of the entire Senate was fifty-nine in 1937. Age in individual cases (Smith and Glass) was of some importance, but on the whole it appears to have had little to do with voting records.

Experience Factor

There were thirty-two Democrats in the Senate between 1933 and 1939 with continuous service in the Senate before 1933 who also served in at least three sessions after 1933. Of these veterans, seventeen, or 53 percent, were conservative. There were forty-four Democrats in the Senate between 1933 and 1939 whose tenure had begun between 1933 and 1937 who served in three sessions or more. Of these newcomers, eighteen, or 41 percent, were conservative.

Newcomers, in terms of percentages, were slightly more dependable in their support of the administration than veterans. (But note also that twenty of the thirty-five conservatives first reached the Senate in 1933 or later.) Senate veterans were also less dependable than House Democratic veterans (see Appendix A).

It is also worth reiterating that some of the most conservative—Gerry, Burke, and Holt—assumed office in 1935, a year of New Deal landslide. Once again, state organizations proved to be the important factors in the selection of candidates.

Urban-Rural Factor

A look at the backgrounds of conservative senators reveals that during childhood and early manhood twenty-three lived in areas which were predominantly rural or small town, whereas only twelve conservatives came from predominantly urban backgrounds. (This is a rough estimate based on sometimes skimpy information.)

An analysis of the rural or urban nature of the state represented by each senator yields the following:

	Conservative Senators	Liberal Senators	Total
Rural States	19	21	40
Urban States	16	40	56
Total	35	61	96

These statistics again leave little room for generalizations. Though most conservative senators came from rural backgrounds, so too did most liberal senators—the nation at the time of their childhoods (ca. 1890–1900) was largely rural.

Similarly, though the majority of conservative Democrats represented rural states, the connection between ruralism and conservatism among Senate Democrats was not so clear as it was in the House.

CONCLUSIONS

First, there was no "typical" congressional conservative in the 1930's. In terms of age, experience, and background, he resembled his liberal colleagues. Nevertheless, some tentative generalizations may be made.

The conservative was ordinarily very well educated; his occupational background, reflecting this high level of education, was usually professionally or business oriented; and his range of experience—to the degree to which it may be judged by his geographical mobility—was not wide. He was more likely to have been raised in—and to have represented—rural areas than his liberal colleague. More often than not, the conservative was a product of the farm or small town, and he brought with him to Congress the beliefs and prejudices of these areas. When the New Deal came to wear an increasingly urban hue after 1936, this kind of man was unprepared for—or unwilling to accept—the legislation which the new urban liberals demanded.

BIBLIOGRAPHICAL NOTE

THE SOURCES for a study of this kind are varied and enormous, and another author might profitably discuss the same subject from a very different approach. This treatment relies heavily upon manuscript sources, newspapers and magazines, and the *Congressional Record*. The method pursued was to read the Washington *Star*, New York *Times*, and Washington *Post* day by day while Congress was in session and to scan other newspapers, especially the New York *Herald Tribune*, for commentary by leading news analysts close to the scene. From these sources I gained knowledge of the most meaningful and divisive issues, a sense of their interrelationship, and a touch of the behind-the-scenes maneuvering which the debates do not reveal. *Time, Newsweek, Nation, Current History, Colliers, New Republic*, and *Saturday Evening Post* filled in many gaps. A reading of the debates in the *Congressional Record* provided a more complete picture of attitudes and helped to clarify many of the votes on amendments to important legislation. *Current Biography* was also helpful in providing sketches of congressmen.

Though useful, these sources were incomplete without manuscript evidence, and in this respect I was fortunate to find some very revealing collections of personal papers. By

far the most important were the papers of Carter Glass
and Josiah Bailey, located at the University of Virginia and
Duke University libraries, respectively. Also most useful in
spots were the papers of Arthur Vandenberg (Clements
Library, University of Michigan); Raymond Clapper (Library of Congress); William Allen White (Library of Congress); Frank Gannett (Cornell University Library); Clifford
Hope (Kansas Historical Society); Alfred M. Landon (Kansas Historical Society); Key Pittman (Library of Congress);
James W. Wadsworth, Jr. (Library of Congress); George
Norris (Library of Congress); Henry Hyde (University of
Virginia Library); Charles McNary (Library of Congress);
and Franklin D. Roosevelt (Hyde Park, N.Y.)

The following manuscript collections were also helpful:
Lyle Boren, Wilburn Cartwright, Percy Lee Gassaway,
Thomas P. Gore, Jack Nichols, and Elmer Thomas (all
University of Oklahoma Library); Arthur Capper and George
McGill (Kansas Historical Society); Royal Copeland, Ralph
L. Smith, and Norris Family Papers (Michigan Historical
Collections, Ann Arbor); Robert Doughton and John H. Kerr
(North Carolina University Library); Louis Ludlow and
John J. O'Connor (Lilly Library, Indiana University); Law-
rence Lewis (Colorado State Historical Society); Harry
Hopkins and Elbert Thomas (Roosevelt Library, Hyde
Park); John Taber (Cornell University Library); and David
I. Walsh (Holy Cross University Library). Also consulted at
the Library of Congress were the papers of Frederick Lewis
Allen, William Borah, Thomas Connally, Bronson Cutting,
James J. Davis, Theodore F. Green, Frank Knox, William
McAdoo, Gifford Pinchot, and Wallace White.

Footnotes tell the story of the most useful secondary
works and scholarly articles. Among these are the following:
Joseph Alsop and Turner Catledge, *The 168 Days* (the court
plan); Wilfred Binkley, *President and Congress;* Arthur Holcombe, *The Middle Classes in American Politics* (emphasizes
social bases of politics); Harold Ickes, *Secret Diary* (not

always reliable but always interesting first-hand account); V. O. Key, Jr., *Southern Politics in State and Nation* (indispensable in understanding southern politics); William Leuchtenburg, *Franklin D. Roosevelt and the New Deal* (a brilliant survey of the era); Samuel Lubell, *The Future of American Politics* (a provocative account of voting habits); Allan Michie and Frank Rhylick, *Dixie Demagogues* (a collection of generally hostile sketches of southern congressmen); Arthur Schlesinger, Jr., *The Age of Roosevelt* (three fascinating volumes carrying the New Deal through 1936); and Julius Turner, *Party and Constituency: Pressures on Congress* (a careful study emphasizing the effects of party on congressional voting). This study would have been much more difficult without the help of the *Political Science Quarterly* and *American Political Science Review*.

This study also made extensive use of newspapers, oral history interviews, and personal interviews. Besides the newspapers mentioned above, the following were consulted in spots: Augusta (Ga.) *Chronicle*, Baltimore *Sun*, Charleston (S.C.) *News and Courier*, Des Moines *Register*, Idaho *Daily Statesman*, Indianapolis *Star*, Lynchburg *News*, and Montgomery (Ala.) *Advertiser*. Oral accounts consulted, all at the Columbia University Oral History Center, were those of Sevellon Brown, Samuel Dickstein, Edward T. Flynn, Joseph Gavagan, Florence J. Harriman, John B. Hutson, Arthur Krock, Joseph O'Mahoney, Edward A. O'Neal, and James J. Wadsworth, Jr. I am grateful also to the following persons who granted me personal interviews: Joseph Alsop, Harry F. Byrd, Charles Halleck, Arthur Krock, Alfred M. Landon, Joseph W. Martin, Jr., and Burton K. Wheeler. And I thank the following who answered correspondence: Rep. Joseph W. Martin, Jr., former Sen. Edwin Johnson, former Sen. John Danaher, Bernard Baruch, Alfred M. Landon, former GOP Chairman John D. M. Hamilton, Rep. Claude Pepper, former Rep. John Taber, and former Sen. George Radcliffe.

The following theses were also helpful: Travis M. Adams, "The Arkansas Congressional Delegation During the New Deal, 1933-1936," M.A. thesis, Vanderbilt University, 1962; James J. Anderson, "The President's Supreme Court Proposal: A Study in Presidential Leadership and Public Opinion," Ph.D. thesis, Cornell University, 1940; Monroe L. Billington, "Thomas P. Gore: Oklahoma's Blind Senator," Ph.D. thesis, University of Kentucky, 1955; Joseph Boskin, "Politics of an Opposition Party: The Republican Party in the New Deal Period, 1936-1940," Ph.D. thesis, University of Minnesota, 1960; Escal Duke, "Political Career of Morris Sheppard, 1875-1941," Ph.D. thesis, University of Texas, 1958; Henry O. Evjen, "The Republican Strategy in the Presidential Campaigns of 1936 and 1940," Ph.D. thesis, Western Reserve University, 1950; Jefferson Frazier, "The Southerner as American: A Political Biography of James Francis Byrnes," Honors thesis, Harvard University, 1964; William J. Grattan, "David I. Walsh and His Associates: A Study in Political Theory," Ph.D. thesis, Harvard University, 1957; C. O'Neal Gregory, "Pat Harrison and the New Deal," M.A. thesis, University of Mississippi, 1960; Walter J. Heacock, "William Brockman Bankhead: A Biography," Ph.D. thesis, University of Wisconsin, 1952; E. Kimbark MacColl, "The Supreme Court and Public Opinion: A Study of the Court Fight of 1937," Ph.D. thesis, University of California, Los Angeles, 1953; Timothy L. McDonnell, "The New Deal Makes a Public Housing Law: A Case Study of the Wagner Housing Bill of 1937," Ph.D. thesis, St. Louis University, 1953; Harry W. Morris, "The Republicans in a Minority Role, 1933-1938," Ph.D. thesis, State University of Iowa, 1960; Nevin E. Neal, "A Biography of Joseph T. Robinson," Ph.D. thesis, University of Oklahoma, 1958; and Walter K. Roberts, "The Political Career of Senator Charles L. McNary, 1924-1944," Ph.D. thesis, University of North Carolina, 1954.

INDEX

Adams, Alva B.: backs utility bill, 40-41; view of New Deal, 1935, 50; view of court plan, 120; opposes executive reorganization, 220; and pump priming, 1938, 239-40; and 1938 renomination, 271, 278, 285; cuts relief bill, 1939, 295, 303; approves farm subsidy, 1939, 308; joins silver bloc, 313; opposes devaluation powers, 315

Agricultural Adjustment Administration: Thomas amendment to, 3; opposed by Byrd, 29-30; aids large farmers, 37; criticized by Gerry, 50; invalidated by court, 77

Alabama politics, 265-67

Allen, Frederick Lewis, 8

Alsop, Joseph, 329

American Federation of Labor. *See* Green, William

Amlie, Thomas R., 299

Andrews, Charles O., 220

Antilynching bill, 156-57, 193, 213

Arkansas politics, 265, 267-68

Arnold, James W., 282

Ashurst, William F.: opposes utilities bill, 39; views on court reform, 90, 91, 92, 95, 110; opposes devaluation powers, 315

Austin, Warren R.: partial to conservative bloc, 202, 204, 208

Bailey, Josiah W.: praises President, 1933, 12; states duty of senator, 15-16; early career, 26-27; votes in 1933-1934, 27n; hostile to New Deal, 1933-1934, 27-29; seen as fence-sitter, 28n; 1936 campaign, 50; seeks conservative bloc, 1936, 82-83; opposes court plan, 96-97, 117, 123; denounces New Deal race policy, 98-99; describes Connally, 111; and relief spending, 1937, 144; criticizes labor standards bill, 150-51, 153; denounces Guffey, 159; seeks conservative bloc, 190-91, 198-99; seeks conservative course, 1938, 212; criticizes Jackson, 213; opposes executive reorganization, 223-24; and pump priming, 1938, 235-36, 240; pivot of conservative bloc, 1938, 247; inconsistency on spending, 248; and electoral coalitions, 252, 255, 257; and Negroes, 257; disliked by Roosevelt, 261; backs Gillette, 1938, 272; backs Van Nuys, 1938, 274; denounces New Dealers, 278-79, 329; views 1939 Congress, 288-89, 289n; upset by appointments, 1939, 299; sees conservative strength, 1939, 305; comments on farm bill, 1939, 308-309;

White, William Allen: comments on 1934 election, 32; seeks GOP unity, 101; suggests GOP tactics, 1936, 109; views on court battle, 117; predicts sentiment for moderation, 162; mentioned, 319

Wilcox, J. Mark, 265, 267

Willis, Raymond E., 276

Willkie, Wendell L., 39

Woodrum, Clifton A.: slashes relief

Woodrum, C. A. (*continued*):
request, 1937, 172; cuts spending bill, 1938, 237; cuts relief, 1939, 294; seeks WPA investigation, 303; investigates WPA, 327; mentioned, 185

Works Progress Administration, 175, 213, 303. *See also* Relief and Spending

World Court, 35